Social Reconstruction
of the Feminine Character

DATE DUE

Social Reconstruction of the Feminine Character

SONDRA FARGANIS
Vassar College

ROWMAN & LITTLEFIELD
PUBLISHERS

ROWMAN & LITTLEFIELD

Published in the United States of America in 1986
by Rowman & Littlefield, Publishers
(a division of Littlefield, Adams & Company)
81 Adams Drive, Totowa, New Jersey 07512

Copyright © 1986 by Rowman & Littlefield

Library of Congress Cataloging-in-Publication Data

Farganis, Sondra.
    Social reconstruction of the feminine character.

    Bibliography: p. 225
    Includes index.
    1. Feminism—Philosophy.   2. Sociology.   I. Title.
HQ1154.F28   1986   305.4'2   86-17670
ISBN 0-8476-7325-1
ISBN 0-8476-7326-X (pbk.)

88   87   86
5   4   3   2   1

Printed in the United States of America

To Jim, Daphne,
and Dion

*

Contents

*

Preface

This book is an interpretive essay on a way to read contemporary feminist theory using the sociological approach suggested by the writings of Karl Mannheim on the sociology of knowledge. While neither a work *of* feminist theory nor a part of the multifarious, rich, and exciting literature that has emerged out of the concerns of the Women's Movement, it is indeed a book *on* feminist theory and can serve as an introduction *to* feminist theory. It is best read as a commentary on that literature and as an exposition using a perspective particular to a field of sociology.

The book has grown out of my interest in both explicating and unraveling feminist theory with my students and in grounding social theory, for their understanding, in an intellectual landscape that, in its Enlightenment and post-Enlightenment roots, encompasses the paradoxes of modernity in a specifically Western capitalist context. One purpose of my classes has been to demonstrate that one's sense of self is put on the line through issues raised by the contemporary Women's Movement: to argue that neither man nor woman can retreat from the issues of the day and that, furthermore, one ought to continue the dialogue with the classical and modern writers encountered in class even after the formalities of the academic year are completed. I hope that this book, which is intended for an intelligent, although not necessarily well read in feminist theory, audience, will interest the reader in the original sources from which these explicatory interpretations are derived, and that he or she will progress even further into the reading of feminist literature.

My evaluation of the sociological enterprise was inherited from my teachers at the Graduate Faculty of the New School for Social Research when its scholars represented the European tradition of social theory, which asked magnanimous questions about the conditions of humanity and the ways in which social structures interfaced with character and personality. The works of Karl Marx, Emile Durkheim, Georg Simmel, Max Weber, and Karl Mannheim, as well as the writings of C. Wright Mills and the Frankfurt School of Critical Theory and even some of the textual commentaries of Peter Berger, were a liberatory influence because they invested sociology with an attitude that made it a critic of power, a starting point toward creating a more humane society through the ability to penetrate the blinder of ideology that the social order had adopted to achieve systems integration.

Through my involvement in Vassar College's introductory sociology course, I have experienced the value of redirecting the initial concerns of students toward social theory. I am indebted to James Farganis and the National Endowment for the Humanities for their willingness to reinvest the sociological discipline with both meaning and intellectual standing by starting sociological inquiry off on a proper base, a base in theory. I have found that, after a grounding in theory, students confront feminist issues with alacrity, interest, concern, and a willingness to discuss, with both genders, issues of moral as well as social import.

All three influences — the New School, a humanistic perspective in sociology, the Vassar introductory course — place this book in a sociological tradition that can be extended and enriched through an intellectual dialogue with feminism. If I am correct in seeing the origins of sociology in a critique of individulism, a concern for what Robert Nisbet has called, following Durkheim, the social bonds integral to an emerging industrial order,[1] sociology shares with feminism a concern for the sociality of personhood — the ways in which persons are shaped by and involved with others in social contexts.

I wish to express my personal appreciation to the persons who have supported me through the writing of this effort: to Jim, who has given concrete meaning to the intellectual abstractions of concern, encouragement, criticism, and collegiality, and who has kept this project from stillbirth; to Daphne, who has given me spirit, and to Dion, who has given me substance, both of whom comprise a moral purpose in my life in return for the start I helped to give them; to my mother, Goldie Silverman, to my late father, Hyman, parents who were unrestrained in the love and affection they gave a daughter who expressed an interest in the world of ideas that, while alien to them, they intuitively understood had meaning for her. My friend Rhoda Sirlin read the manuscript in its entirety; I am grateful for the literary skills she brought to bear on my work. In a more traditional way, I wish to express my gratitude to the following: to the National Endowment for the Humanities for a Fellowship for College Teachers in Women's Studies at Duke University, and to the participants in that seminar who made succinct suggestions to help this book on its way; to Alison Jaggar for the two seminars I participated in under her tutelage at Douglass College, and to my fellow participants in both "Feminist Reconstruction of Self and Society" and "Feminist Ways of Knowing," who let me share my thoughts with them in an open and honest way and who generously shared their ideas; to the staff at the Hastings Center (the Institute of Society, Ethics and the Life Sciences), who invited me to be a Visiting Scholar and engage them in discussions on the emerging technological order; and to Vassar College for both a Mellon and a Sloan Foundation Grant to underwrite my participation at both Douglass and Hastings while I was on sabbatical leave to complete this manuscript.

Social Reconstruction
of the Feminine Character

* 1 *

Introduction

This book intends a sociological analysis of what has been thought of as the "feminine" by theorists influenced by and, in turn, influencing the changing economic and political status of women in contemporary American society. It uses the perspective of the sociology of knowledge to critique selected writings about women, to unravel the interests expressed in specific writings of various authors who view the feminine through a variety of intellectual prisms. It examines the structures in which feminist ideas are embedded. It is not an essay about the Women's Movement in the United States per se, although it suggests that the Movement, a collective effort toward change, forms part of the background for the formulations of social theories. Although I have been as much shaped and affected by the Movement as has anyone of my age, class, occupation, ethnicity, race and gender, this is not a Movement book nor a work of ideology, that is, a work *of* feminist social theory; rather, it is a work about that theory. The writers examined are interpretors of the feminine, who offer a way of looking at how a particular society comes to regard women. They do not provide a model for *testing,* in any precise scientific sense, the validity of their assertions; rather, they are commentators upon an essential aspect of the human condition. They are to be read in the manner in which one reads social theory rather than sociology, or political theory rather than political science.

First I will clarify what I mean by "feminine," a term used as both a noun and an adjective, which refers to the characteristics of women. It may well be that there are no traits particular to a single sex, yet this significant contention is not what is at issue in this book. Rather, I am concerned with the way in which writers have *perceived* women and, in this more limiting sense, have understood gendered characteristics. What constitutes the feminine and what are held to be the feminine traits are the questions I deal with in this book.

Feminism is an ideology in a descriptive, but not an evaluative or pejorative, sense. An extraordinary controversy surrounds the use of the term "ideology," especially as it evolves from a Marxist tradition that has sought to distinguish it from rational thought that is free of social prejudice.[1] For the social analyst, however, ideology is a complex of ideas about the taken-for-granted world, a Lippmanian picture in the head,[2] a set of ideas ranking values, norms of social interaction, and rules of behavior. A certain form of thought is considered to be ideological in the sense that it is a socially constructed way of looking at the world, a social set of beliefs, a grounding of ideas in human activity. I do not interpret ideology as "false consciousness" in the way that Marx does;[3] nor do I intend the distinction, provided by Mannheim's "ideology" and "utopia",[4] of legitimating and oppositional views of the world. To Mannheim, as well as to Marx, ideology is the worldview of the ruling group; it could be argued that, in the present instance, it is the view of patriarchy. Utopian thought is the view of the oppressed group and, it could be argued, is the view of feminism. Although Mannheim recognized how difficult it is in practice to distinguish between ideological and utopian thought, and how to do so one must take into account the *intent* of those who hold the views they do,[5] both forms of thought are views of the world that shape shape perception: one requires legitimation and the other, oppositional activity. In both instances, "certain aspects of social reality" are blocked out,[6] and only that which gives credence to the selected worldview is seen, at the necessary price of distorting reality. All political thought is "inherently ideological."[7] It is not that Mannheim regarded such thought as a summation of ideas, for this presumes the intent to deceive, or viewed such thought as being based on errors of perception, which presumes the lack of intent. Thought occupies a mid-point between accident and intent: it is a distortion based on the psychological need to block out certain parts of reality and to see things in a certain light, and a recognition that one's interests affect what one sees. It is a kind of reconstituted illusion. Modernity, characterized by the rapidity with which ideas and values change, alerts the social analyst to recognize how diverse is the universe of interests, and how varied and pluralistic is thought.[8] Mannheim wrote: "We must realize once and for all that the meanings which make up our world are simply an historically determined and continuously developing structure in which man develops, and are in no sense absolute."[9] If one retains antiquated views of the world or views that do not accord with social arrangements, one's thought processes are governed by a "false consciousness."[10]

Mannheim said—and I am aware of the varied ways in which Mannheim has been read[11]—that one comes to know a reality through one's interests; when these interests permit ony a partial vision, the ensuing "false consciousness" is either supportive of or in opposition to the power constellations of the society, themselves constituted on a partial view of the social world. Interests guarantee a plurality of perspectives; the totality accounts for these diverse perspectives.

Were one to take Mannheim's lead, one could develop the case for feminism as a thought-constellation of provocation and challenge to what feminists, among others, would call the predominant ideology, either understood as sexism or patriarchy. In the case of either ideological or utopian thought, the social analyst is dealing with ideas that structure beliefs, however different these beliefs might be in political and/or moral terms.

One can treat ideology as Sigmund Freud treated religion and religious sentiments: as illusions, as ways of resolving internal conflicts, as needs-gratification.[12] For ideology gives one purpose, roots one in psychological certainty, makes one feel protected and secure. Ideology, in a structural sense, fills the void created by uncertainty; it counters the malaise of mental uneasiness. Ideology stabilizes the reality of the individual; it is the outward expression of ego development. What Harold Lasswell has said of opinions holds true for ideology as well: "The significance of political opinions is not to be grasped apart from the private motives which they symbolize."[13] Private needs are answered by political ideologies; by displacing these needs onto a public object and rationalizing this displacement in terms of a public interest, the political ideology publicly soothes the private world. Ideology explains reality: it orients behavior and makes an order out of chaos. Without ideology, one experiences anxiety; with it, one resolves one's conflicts.

Chalmers Johnson equated values or beliefs with "definition of the situation," those "which legitimate the inequalities of social organization and cause people to accept them as morally justified."[14] These "definitions" are similar to Talcott Parsons's "common value patterns."[15] I find myself using the term "ideology" in the way that George Sorel spoke of "myths,"[16] which included a more general understanding of the idea of beliefs or objectives and the commitment to realize these and a preparedness to see such "myths" as historical in nature or rooted in concrete interests.[17]

In undertaking a sociological analysis, I have attempted, in this sense and only in this sense, to be objective in my discussion of such theory. I do not claim to be above the fray of ideological battle; all writers are individuals who are socially constituted, that is, are persons with social characteristics. Nor do I wish to become detached from a social reality that affects all whose lives are in the process of the construction, deconstruction, and reconstruction that is at the core of being-in-the-world.

*   *   *

To undertake the sociological analysis of feminism, I have chosen to extend the work of Viola Klein, and specifically her book *The Feminine Character,* past the point where her study of the feminine ends, explicating and commenting upon the perspective on women held by certain social theorists in the past two decades. Klein, an English sociologist influenced by Mannheim, uses "feminine" to refer to traits *held* to be particular to women.[18] How unchanging or eternal these traits are regarded to be, or how subject to historical transformation they may be, is the investigation upon which her study enters. Klein's subtitle, the "history of an ideology," in effect says that theories of the feminine cannot be divorced from the social conditions of their formulation. Hers is not a book of what the feminine is, but *what the feminine is thought to be;* and while the question of feminism's essential qualities may be of greater import than its historical contours, a sociology of knowledge perspective concerns itself with the sociality of sexuality and tries to avoid the entanglement of any discussion on essences.

The feminine, according to Klein, is a constellation of cultural roles, attitudes, and abilities related to, but not necessarily growing out of, the biological traits held to constitute being a woman, that is, grounded in chromosomes, anatomy, and hormones. "Feminine" includes cultural influences in a way that "female" does not. Insofar as "feminine" incorporates the social, it is similar to "gender," with its emphasis on roles as regularized conduct oriented toward the behavior of others; hence, gender roles reflect socially ascribed and socially oriented ways to act. Feminine is equivalent to Simone de Beauvoir's formulation of "woman" in that, by distinguishing "woman" from both "male" and "female," de Beauvoir emphasizes not only the social creation of a category of Other but also the dialectical relationship between persons and the natural world and between the needs of nature and the socially conditioned but no less important wants of culture. De Beauvoir writes: "one is not born, but rather becomes a woman."[19] In allowing for the importance of human intervention, action, and transcendence in becoming a person, one counters the determinism of simple biological or cultural explanations. The biological within a cultural context rooted in time is at the core of the social and the sociological, and it moves beyond the simplistic as well as specious dichotimization of nature/nurture, biology/culture, genes/environment.

One need also be aware of the abstraction involved in setting up any kind of categories. One assumes sex to be a grouping by distinction, which demarcates people into classification systems that reflect the reality. Sex as a category or, in Weberian terms, as a status group, is held to unify people, structuring their perception and defining and distinguishing them as an interest group. It is a category of prestige through which the society regards or values individuals. In this sense, de Beauvoir's "second sex" is a status: "man defines woman not in herself but as relative to him . . . .She is define and differentiated with reference to man and not he with reference to her; she is the incidental, the inessential as opposed to the essential. He is the Subject, he is the Absolute — she is the Other."[20]

The analyst must be aware of the objective or external attribution of unity through status as well as the particular member's subjective awareness of that status. Particularly relevant are Marx's writings on class and on the role that consciousness plays in the formation of one's particular place in society. How one acts is a factor not only of one's objective characteristics and how these are socially prescribed but also of one's own sense of these characteristics; to wit, of one's being considered woman by others and of the import that this attribution plays in one's life. Sex is only one of numerous possible classification systems applicable to persons. One need only think of factors of class, race, religion, and age to realize the possible varieties of feminine character as well as the way in which these factors shape interpretors' lives.

Females/males, women/men, feminine/masculine may, in fact, be arbitrary distinctions that preclude or hinder one's thinking in dialectical terms. Alison Jaggar has warned of the dangers of thinking in dualistic or dichotomous terms, which, according to her, act as graven images to fix categories so firmly in one's mind that one reads the reality as a category rather than allowing the category to be a mere heuristic device for beginning to understand the flesh and blood of concrete human existence. It is as if categorization became reification, the turning of a flesh-and-blood person into a "thing." Jaggar's "Feminism Against Dualism" is a recurrent theme in contemporary feminist writings,[21] although, paradoxically, feminine/masculine is itself open to the charge of being but another dualistic classification system. Moreover, those who write the classificatory systems are themselves persons in and of a culture, despite protestations of detachment and objectivity. Observers of the natural or of the social sciences are themselves rooted in time and place; what distinguishes them from history's ordinary actors is their preparedness to engage in the radical stance of distancing, of consciously standing back and reflecting upon the world and its objects that they are seeking to explain and/or understand. These are problems endemic to social inquiry and intellectual discourse: the same kind of problem occurs when one demarcates species of being and posits human versus other forms of nature.

I interpret Klein's use of "character" to mean that complex of ideas and ideals, rationally arrived at or socially constructed or imposed, which color one's being-in-the-world in the broad sense or predict one's behavior in the more narrow sense. I mean to include not only how one behaves but also how one feels — one's actions, emotions, behavior, and psyche. The term "character" is particularly sociological in that it emphasizes the integration of biological and psychological properties within the specifics of a social time and place.[22] Character is used as an ideal-typical construct, and in this methodological sense one speaks of the "feminine character" or the "technological character."

Klein, using Mannheim's framework for the sociology of knowledge, chose to discuss the ways in which certain writers had viewed the character of women. Her argument, stemming from Mannheim, was that the views one holds on women (as well as, for that matter, on any subject) are shaped by the social milieu in which one lives: ideas are formed within a specific social context, such that the knowledge, beliefs, and values of theories and of theorists are influenced by the factor of historical time. While it may be that no *single* view is held at any particular moment, since the cross-currents and conflicts of reality act to soften the monolithic hold that the approved ideas of the age might have, certain predominant ideas are shaped by events in the social world.

For Klein, the most significant components in shaping the respective theorists' views were the changing position of women, primarily their movement into the labor force, and the growing influence of scientific theory on how one viewed the world and persons in that world. Hers is also not a book *on* the feminine character, for as a sociologist she assumes that definitions of self are not external, but rather are shaped by the contours of politics and history and reflect the transformation of values experienced by societies over time, often as a consequence of the material ability to realize new forms of behavior.

I wish to suggest a corollary to this impact of the outside world on a writer's thoughts: sociological abstractions (for example, ideal-types in the Weberian sense such as "liberated woman," "autonomous female personality," or "total woman") influence the worldview of social persons who structure their own lives to accord with the logic and/or morality of the abstraction. I also am interested in how theory, even when addressed to a professional peer group, permeates a more generalized arena of discourse. If, indeed, a part of the public reorders its view of the world or an aspect of that world on the basis of a reconstituted model of human behavior, then the social analyst must inquire not only of the academic refinements of an argument but also of the practical ways in which the theory might come to be realized. Academic intent and consequences of intent do not go hand in hand, for the abstractions of philosophic discourse can affect the individuals to whom they appeal in ways other than expected, and ideas may be used in ways that were not intended by those who penned them. Whether the abstraction ought to be realized is not the social theorist's sole concern; also at issue are the costs and consequences of reconstructing social reality, since the delineation of the possible consequences that follow from ideas is at the very heart of sociological inquiry. I am trying to capture here that dialectic between ideological and material factors particular to the sociology of knowledge, the interaction of institutions and social consciousness that informs sociological theorizing and a good deal of feminist theory.[23]

Femininity, or what it means to be female in a specific culture, is not set at birth. While one could argue that gender demarcations never are as rigid as a model of total social control would suggest, in contemporary society sexual identity is more likely to be in a state of deconstruction and reconstruction than were the sexual ideas and ideals of earlier, more traditional societies. Modern society, especially as it is realized in the United States, is characterized by rapid social change, allowing some commentators to speak of the permanence of change, "of temporary systems, nonpermanent relationships, turbulence, uprootedness, unconnectedness, mobility."[24] The parameters of social and sexual identity are enlarged as technological developments and devices increase the possibilities for a variety of life styles. I do not mean to suggest that diversity is to be equated with an ethical "ought" or that it automatically assumes freedom of choice by individuals engaged in rational discourse with their selves or with other selves. "Diversity" is used descriptively to delineate the options made possible by modernity, and I would prefer to convey a double-bind of the burden of choice rather than the tranquility of tradition, paralleling Simmel's brilliant paradox of freedom made possible by the city which gives autonomy and individuality, with one hand, and fragmentation, reserve, and indifference, with the other.[25] One may also read out of the Frankfurt School this prophetic view of modernity, of a world filled with the amenities of consumerism amid the demise of genuine human freedom. I have specifically in mind the paradoxes retailed by Herbert Marcuse and Jurgen Habermas.[26]

I assume here certain strains of modernization, as one moves from *Gemeinschaft* to *Gesellschaft* where the bonds of tradition are replaced by ties that are, at one and the same time, more negotiable and less rigid. The burdens of freedom, to choose from among an array of alternatives, may be heavy: choices whether to have or not have children; to have a traditional family or a communal family; to have children through the services of a surrogate mother or to adopt them; to elect heterosexual or homosexual preferences; to embrace celibacy or sexual permissiveness — all are options rarely encountered at an earlier time but which, once they can be realistically — to wit, politically and technologically — posed, require not only redefinitions of morality but also individual choice and not the received solutions respecting those redefinitions.[27]

Issues broadly classified as reproductive, which include such practices as abortion, contraception, artificial insemination, in vitro fertilization, genetic and pre-natal screening, have been shaped by technology in a way previously unknown. While philosophic discourse on nature, or the natural, has always been carried on, in the last half of the twentieth century the machinery or techniques made possible by industrialization have qualitatively altered the contours of that discussion. Any discussion of self, of females, of males, must now take into account the role played by scientific inventiveness in reconstituting identity.

When Klein wrote about science, she allowed for the cultural context out of which science as an enterprise developed. She did not speak of science as being neutral or as occuring outside an historically constituted social order but, at the same time, as having an attitude particular to her own historical moment (just as mine is particular to mine), of science as a methodological orientation for determining the varieties of female existence. Science was, for her, a demystifier, a tool for stripping away the layers of socialized and socially constructed perceptions. She was right as far as she went, but she had not yet come to face what others have come to see as a consequence of demystification: the paradox of the possibility of autonomy, if one were free to construct one's own sense of self in a fully liberated society, and the possibility of social coercion and social control, as the demystifiers were able to establish models for behavior along lines they would conclude were in accord with scientific possibilities and, hence, with moral or ethical possibilities. The conflation of the technically possible and the morally desirable brings together that which one might not wish to fuse. Science is now chided in a way that it was not when Klein wrote; it is seen as obstructing freedom, and many writers will be adamant in their refusal to read a liberatory potential in the conquest or control of natural forces.

The objective of the social analyst is not to discredit science nor to be hostile to the technological achievements the abstract models have made possible. Rather, it is to inquire precisely what post-Enlightenment science *can* understand of the life-world, critiquing both its epistemology and its technical achievements by placing before the reader the possible outcomes that a given understanding of social reality might entail.[28]

Thus, my primary intent in this book is to extend Klein's analysis of the "feminine" character to cover the contemporary period, going beyond the first half of the twentieth century with which she was concerned. I also wish to underscore the value of a sociology of knowledge approach that situates ideas within an historical context. As a way of elucidating the ideas on women advanced by certain contemporary social theorists, I, like Klein, will use Mannheim's contributions to the sociology of knowledge, even while recognizing their apparent strengths and consequential weaknesses. I have selected a group of theorists whom I regard as making a significant contribution to the understanding of the feminine. I will argue not only that their ideas interact with, shape, and are shaped by the contemporary Women's Movement but also that each — the theories and the Movement — is involved in an often unforeseen dialectical relationship with an emerging technocratic order and that each reflects the modern social processes that are attempting to answer a seemingly ageless inquiry into the nature of sex differences.

An Early Theory of Feminine Character: The Work of Viola Klein

It has been suggested that in order to understand what a particular theory, perspective, or ideology means, one must understand it contextually through its specific social frame. This "social ecology of sociological ideas"[1] examines the climate out of which ideas emerge. One is not concerned with the specifics of personal biographies, however fascinating, as a way of determining the colors of the lenses through which data is filtered; rather, one is concerned with the intellectual milieu out of which ideas come and through which they are shaped, reshaped, and passed on.

Viola Klein's *The Feminine Character* is, in many ways, an unappreciated or ignored classic of sociological inquiry. In addition to being one of the few full-scale attempts to apply Mannheim's ideas on the sociology of knowledge to a particular subject matter, it antedates contemporary feminist efforts to explain how one comes to hold the ideas on women that one does. If one agrees that writers — whether sociologists or biologists, literary persons or persons of science — are influenced by their historical circumstances, then it will be of interest to see how those writing in the same time frame define the distinctive characteristics and the appropriate behavior, if any, of women, and to ask how the writers have come to this particular perspective rather than some other.

This chapter will summarize the thesis of *The Feminine Character*, highlighting Klein's substantive argument regarding how and why views of and toward women change. First published in 1946, the book is concerned with the relationship between writings about women and the social conditions out of which these writings are fashioned and within which they are placed. Perception, determined by the times in which one lives, changes as reality is reordered, which reordering is itself a consequence of the acceptance of new ideas. It is a dialectical paradox that only change and an apparently unalterable desire of the analyst to understand and critique the times in which he or she exists will remain constant.

Klein's treatise is concerned, as Mannheim was, with a rigorous and critical understanding of the social world, of the ways in which thought is both socially constructed and economically rooted and the ways in which individuals give meaning to their ongoing reality, but within a context that is structured by specific institutions. The sociologist, to make intelligible what people take to be their social world, looks for the shared meaning structures within the specifics of a given historical period. The individual is born into a society already "there" and already complete with patterns of behavior that are either maintained or changed. Mannheim asked that the sociologist unmask and become aware of the "concealed dependence of thought on group existence."[2] Following Mannheim, one would situate sexual roles and sexual attitudes historically and culturally, coming to see them in relationship to a larger social order or specific society. Roles are not to be accepted by the sociologist as static, fixed, and given but, rather, are to be understood, to use Mannheim's terminology, as manifestations of social behavior with a specific social origin: sociology "seeks to comprehend thought in the concrete setting of an historical-social situation out of which individually differentiated thought only very gradually emerges."[3]

Klein's thesis, as a contribution to the sociology of knowledge, allows one to see the consequences of adopting this particular sociological approach. Her exercise, after which I have patterned my own, is not simply to ask what a particular writer is saying — to seek the immanent meaning of that writer's work — but also to ask how the ideas expressed reflect the social processes of thought out of which that writer has come. It is to ask that one sees and understands the world as the writer does, and then to ask why he or she sees it that way. Ideas are socially constructed to reveal a certain perspective on the truth, and the construction occurs within a specific historical time frame. In this sense, while ideas are not culturally determined, they are culturally affected. Social persons may hold the ideas to be objectively true, but the sociologist will question or critique them, situating them and asking what historical function or purpose they serve. In following Mannheim, then, one assumes that both facts and values of femininity are socially conditioned: the facts of what constitutes womanhood are socially derived; sexual roles and sexual attitudes are to be understood not as given but as historical and cultural; and one is to come to see these roles in relationship to a larger social order or specific society.

For the moment, judgment may be reserved on the logical considerations that come into play were one to consider the sociology of knowledge as itself subject to the charge of being a specific cultural method of looking at society and the theorist as being no less immune from cultural influence than anyone else. This theory about theories presumes significant ontological considerations, which will be discussed in the next chapter.

Mannheim, in his forward to Klein's book, raises an important sociological question: Can social theorists talk about the "traits of the feminine character" without reference to the historical conditions that underlie their presumed eternality?[4] Klein, accepting the Mannheimian presumption that the views one holds are culturally circumscribed or socially constructed, analyzes the specific views of women held by a wide range of theorists — Havelock Ellis, Otto Weininger, Sigmund Freud, Helen B. Thompson, Lewis Terman and Catherine Miles, Mathias and Mathilde Vaerting, Margaret Mead and W. I. Thomas — in the period from the 1890s through the 1940s. Subtitling her book a "history of an ideology," she traces how a "feminine character" reflective of the times came to be described by select writers who took "women" as the object of their study. As ideology, the "feminine character" is a distorted or skewered view of the world that allows for the dominant constellations of power and that bears a functional relationship to the particularities of an individual's social background. It is not simply that a particular social thinker, given his or her particular psychological proclivities, will see the world in a certain way, but rather that a more generalized way of seeing the world particular to the historical moment colors the way in which all social actors take what they do to be true. Beyond the way in which one is psychologically put together, there are social values that structure perception, that legitimate certain ways of viewing the world, that give moral credence to particular patterns of relationships. Thus, one might speak of historical views of femininity as historical archetypes or prototypes or, in contemporary language, as paradigms — operative models of thought through which the data concerning women are filtered.

Klein saw her task, as a sociologist, to "unpack" the writings of social theory to show how historical circumstances shape views on women. For if "human thought . . . rooted in the cultural soil which has nourished it,"[5] one seeks to understand not the abstraction of a woman's psyche, but rather how circumstances affect the perception of that psyche — that is, how social categories structure perception of women. Her book is not a book about women, but about the *knowledge* one has of women that reflects "(a) the status of women in a given society; (b) the prevailing ideologies concerning women in a certain historical period; and (c) the author's personal attitudes towards women."[6]

The import of this, for Klein, is that what is held to be feminine — what sociologists now call female gender — shapes human expectation, and women are encouraged to become the role model that historical circumstance has defined as legitimate: "These views, transmitted by custom, social attitudes, public opinion, and in many other ways, are the framework within which personalities develop and to which, in one way or another, they have to adjust to themselves."[7] Even scientific knowledge of women cannot escape the trends and tremors of history, for the findings of science are also filtered through the lenses of observers shaped by and within a given cultural milieu: science is also "part of a coherent cultural system," a social product, a language, not "a completely detached and autonomous mental act."[8] What one chooses to study and how it is to be studied are as much effected by socio-historical factors as is the social analyst making or, more precisely, accepting the choices. Theory goes into the construction of reality; as circumstances change, roles change. The feminine is, then, a symbolic construction, a set of expectations socially constructed and subject to social change.

The particular *Weltanschauung* that shaped and colored the time period about which Klein is writing was affected by a confluence of factors that included: (a) the rise of science and its affinity with optimism, progress, and the ability to apply its methodological orientation to the resolution of social problems; (b) the changing economic and political status of women; and (c) an interaction between this scientific view of the world and this newly emerging group of women who wanted to be released from the grip of tradition and custom. Starting with the 1890s, science, as a set of methodological principles, turned its gaze on women, using forms of inquiry different from those used previously by poets or philsophers. Klein argues that until that time, "theories . . . were in the nature of personal opinion, of prejudice, religious taboo, or superstition";[9] they were based on emotion and did not aim to be reasoned or rational explications of the world or exercises in bracketing personal feelings and distancing selves from the prevailing cultural milieu.

Science, as a method, implied a commitment to the search for truth, a critiquing of myths and prejudices; moreover, social science was held to be not only the method for understanding social phenomena but also a practicum for alleviating the social problems and social conflict that occurred in the wake of massive social change. Klein regards science as a set of attitudes appropriate to the time, coming at that moment when the status of women was itself undergoing changes unleashed by the Industrial Revolution, which included, in particular, urbanization. Women were moving out of the household and into (or, to be historically more precise, back into) the labor force; and while there were still inequities in job opportunities and remuneration and it was still considered appropriate for women to marry and carry on traditional roles, there were increased opportunities for women to participate in public life.

Klein writes:

> There is a peculiar affinity between the fate of women and the origin of social science, and it is no mere coincidence that the emancipation of women should have started at the same time as the birth of sociology. Both are the result of a break in the established social order and of radical changes in the structure of society.[10]

One is reminded of Alexis de Toqueville's recognition of the rapport between science and democracy, between optimism and egalitarian sentiments, especially as these are worked out within a social context that is becoming increasingly more secular.[11] Not found in Klein's work is the turn against science that is to color contemporary discussions of looking at women "scientifically"; the role of science in not only constructing sexuality but also in controlling it is a more recent theoretical development that will be held up to critical analysis later in this book.[12]

It is within the context of these overarching ideas of science and democracy that Klein initiates discussion of specific social theorists. I will briefly recapitulate the import of her interpretive essays, which I have accepted without question as being fair in their reading of her selected authors.

The significance of Havelock Ellis was in his use of biology, with its roots in a model of natural science, to look at sexual diversity. Ellis postulated the difficulty of defining natural sexual characteristics in any precise and definitive sense. That there are sexual differences is apparent, but these differences do not imply that one sex is superior to the other. Natural science, as a method, became for Ellis a means to demystification, a set of techniques for sorting out where biology begins, ends, and interfaces with custom and convention. "His main purpose," Klein argues, "was to study the physical facts on which some of our strongest beliefs and idiosyncracies are based, and thus by the light of reason to illumine the dark complexity of ideologies."[13]

Influenced by Darwinian theories of evolution, perhaps even impressed with Comtian stages of social development, Ellis's writings reflected the notion of the dynamism of change: what constituted social woman was not a static rendering of physical and historical traits, but rather a constantly changing set of categories. While Ellis adhered to the idea that the two distinct biologically constituted sexes are intensely bipolar and while he saw differences in reproductive capacities leading to different psychic traits, Klein is correct in tracing his reading of biology to certain philosophical and religious attitudes toward nature prevalent at the time. Thus, he saw a "union of opposites,"[14] a harmonious synthesis neither part of which was supreme over the other, each of which was complementary toward the other. Since Ellis was a man to whom "the essence of life is tension between opposing principles,"[15] it is neither difficult to understand his interpreting female diversity as a consequence of different reproductive capacities nor to appreciate his seeing different psychic traits developing out of these reproductive capacities. In the context of the historical period in which Ellis was writing, the turn of the twentieth century, his views were at odds with more traditional ideas on male superiority; and while differences — mental and physical stability, mental and physical exhaustion, analytic powers of reasoning — that he ascribes to organic factors were later to be interpreted to be subject to sociological and cultural explanation, his debunking of ideas on female inferiority was radical.

Klein contrasts the way in which Ellis dealt with the scientific data on male-female differences with Otto Weininger's defense of male superiority. Weininger, writing at approximately the same time as Ellis, also intended to "unmask" the mechanisms through which persons make of their lives what they do,[16] but in contrast to Ellis and the trend among social theorists to look for empirical (historical and statistical) data to confirm their theoretical hypotheses, Weininger sought to construct an ideal-type Man and Woman by which to measure, compare, and evaluate actual persons. Transcendental in construction and designed to delineate what is permanent amid the diversity of historical instances, Weininger's models were not only distinct in their manner of formulation but also were peculiarly conservative or, at least, can be read this way in their specifics, for they spoke of being female as a philosophical problem that requires definition and understanding outside an historical framework. The Mother and the Courtesan are the ideal-typical female constructs, each having a different set of attitudes toward the goal and purpose of sexual intercourse—for procreation or for pleasure—and each existing to complement males. As is the case with ideal types, they are hypothetical constructs and not mirror images of reality; some of each type may be embodied in one flesh and blood individual.

Klein's critique of Weininger is that he was unable to see the role that culture plays in shaping persons, and that in looking for the essential and transcendent categories of human existence, he underestimated the historical choices, including factors of class, that affect gender roles. She writes that "the development of a personality depends to a large extent on the opportunities and the experiences available, and that the relation between man and woman . . . is the result of attitudes which a cultural tradition has produced."[17]

Klein reads Freud as writing within a Victorian setting whose specific set of attitudes toward women found resonance within his theories; nonetheless, Freud's preparedness to discuss sexuality as he did was at odds with the silence toward sex that was also a part of that Victorian heritage. Like Weininger, Freud's social alienation enabled him to discuss topics that were taboo for those intellectuals more rooted in the cultural mainstream.

The sociologist, prepared to critique all prevailing systems of thought, seeks to understand the social forces that give rise to the Freudian theses. Like Ellis, Freud was influenced, Klein argues, by the Darwinian perspective that had shaped the biological sciences. One could argue that Freud's "anatomy is destiny" is not only part of his rejection of irrational responses to notions concerning women—one cannot ask people, he might say, to be something other than they can be—but also his attempt to ground future discussions of masculine and feminine characteristics in the body's presentation of itself in the social world. Taking the female body as given, Freud wanted to explain the diversity of sexual development in terms of the real and apparent differences as they are perceived by the individual. His concern with the unconscious was to add another layer of truth to the question of one's being, to see how one's social personality is a consequence of one's biology. Freud's views on penis-envy, on the Oedipus complex, on castration, on vaginal and clitoral sexuality, and on narcissism have to be understood within this framework of grounding an understanding of character and personality in the interplay of biological and psychic factors. Klein's reading of Freud as saying that all females see their anatomical differences as "defects"[18] is of lesser import than that Freud saw social personality as a consequence of the biological. Klein implies that it behooves the reader to see past Freud's use of myths as a literary device, and to examine Freud's arguments within their intended framework. Here, again, one sees his preparedness to turn to science and away from abstract, philosophic discourse, for answers on the being-ness of female. Klein contrasts what she interprets as Freud's a- or trans-historicity with subsequent developments out of Freudian theory, suggesting that Karen Horney, Alfred Adler, and Erich Fromm, among others, provide a contrast to Freud's ideas on the effect that social and cultural factors play in determining how men and women come to regard themselves and their bodies.

Klein alerts us to the shifting sands of paradigmatic interpretation:

> It is interesting to note how, in the theoretical discussions of the problem of woman, the terms of reference have changed. Both parties, those advocating male superiority as well as those championing equality of the sexes or even feminine superiority, had for centuries looked to theology to supply them with arguments [rather than to] Natural Science [or to] biological tendencies and evolutionary trends. . . . More recently, the emphasis has again been shifted, and the main attention been directly toward the modifiability of human nature under the impact of personal experience and cultural milieu. This new attitude toward human nature arose at a certain stage in historical development when the quiet flow of tradition was disturbed and changes became drastic and obvious enough to make themselves felt in all walks of life.[19]

This emphasis on complexity and interaction, with its concomitant emphasis on the relationship of phenomena to the particularities of the moment, this linkage between sex and social factors, affected the natural sciences as well as the social sciences. What Klein calls the "adoption of a relativistic outlook"[20] occurred within the context of transformed economic and social conditions: rapid industrialization, that broadened the base of the labor force and created new kinds of jobs; advances in medicine that affected ideas of natural proclivities; and the development of birth control practices that could separate sexual participation from sexual procreation. These changes, which affected the status of women — the kinds of jobs they could hold and the divorce between sex and birth —

raised questions of women's inclinations not only for commentators on women but also for women reflecting on their own situation.

Sex, which, if discussed at all, had been discussed in theological and literary terms, now became a fit subject for scientific discourse. Within a *Weltanschauung* whose secularization was affected by Darwinian theories of evolution and natural selection and the challenge these made to theology and creationism, sexual practices as well as sexual attitudes were made the subject of intricate description and explanation. Helen Thompson researched relationships between sexual and mental differences. Lewis Terman and Catherine Miles, using psychometric tests, delineated masculine and feminine personality types and catalogued correlations between socio-environmental factors and sexuality. Mathilde and Mathias Vaerting researched ancient cultures to demonstrate the variability of codes of sexual dominance among different kinds of societies with different social stratification systems.

These developments were supports for the relativistic outlook, which found its classic statement in the writings of Margaret Mead. Stressing the need to allow for masculine and feminine diversity, Mead argued that the anthropologist must view each culture on its own terms: "Each culture creates distinctively the social fabric in which the human spirit can wrap itself safely and intelligibly. . . . . Each people makes this fabric differently, selects some clues and ignores others, emphasizes a different sector of the whole arc of human potentialities."[21]

Klein sees in Mead in specific, and in cultural anthropology in general, an emphasis on cultural diversity, on an infinite number of possible structural patterns through which "organic nature" can play itself out. While Mead's work differed from the historical writings of the Vaertings in her emphasis not class but on sex, she shared with them this emphasis on character being socially reproduced. Because her ideological framework was not Marxist in the way that the Vaertings was, her liberal lens was congratulatory toward cultural diversity both between and within cultures. I share Klein's assessment of Mead that the latter wanted "freedom from standardization [as] a necessary condition for the self-fulfillment of individuals,"[22] seeing in the plurality of diversity an iridescence of changing colors that provide the means to realize oneself.

Klein is correct in her reading of the nature-nurture controversy as one between the older biological sciences and the newer sociological ones. In the work of W. I. Thomas, one finds an affinity with Mead's cultural anthropology. Thomas was to see the techniques and imperatives of economic productivity as a key factor in the development of gender roles. By habit and by history, the sexes become suited to the jobs which need to be performed. While in the past there was a predisposition in males toward the dispersal of energy and toward patterns of energetic motion, and there was an alternative predisposition in women toward the

conserving of energy and toward reproduction, changed social conditions allow for a reconsideration of these models laid down in primitive
times. Klein interprets Thomas as arguing that personality "is the out-
come of a long process of interaction between social factors and a highly
plastic original nature";[23] change the "definitions of the situation" and social "attitudes" will automatically change.[24]

Klein is correct in arguing that the social sciences, in modeling themselves after a model of the natural sciences that is descriptive and intends
to be value-free, as well as in their use of a functionalism that explains
personality in terms of adaptability to social context, offer a new and radically different way of looking at human nature. This modern way of
looking at a woman as an object to be studied reveals, to Klein, a diverse
set of definitions and expectations of the feminine character, with some
agreement on femininity being a psychological trait variable as to historical time and changes in social and cultural roles.[25] With the exception of
Weininger and Freud, who attempted to discern something of an essential human nature, the theorists she examines tend to discuss sexual characteristics within the particularities of a given culture; their data, their
emphasis on the empirically verifiable, substantiated their theory of role
diversity.

Klein's work is of value on several counts. First, by drawing together a
variety of social thinkers who write at the beginning of this century, she
allows one to see how a certain attitude toward science and scientific data
colored their work, how their views were varied, and how certain troublesome problems which one would classify as essentialist or constructionist views of the phenomena "woman" affected their work no less than is
the case today. While Klein does not isolate a *single* way of thinking
as being characteristic of the time, she is able to delineate certain *general* patterns of thought particular to that age, most especially the uses of
scientific data to validate theories of sexual behavior. As has been mentioned, science is the language that replaces poetry, religion, and philosophy as the mode of discourse on women. The critique of science and scientists found in contemporary feminist theory is indicative of the changes
between Klein's period and the one of which I write. In this post-
Holocaust, post-Hiroshima period, the practices and personnel of science have been held up to scrutiny by political traditions that have come
to see the scientific enterprise as operating as a legitimator of established
ideology,[26] as well as by a reading os science—I have in mind the
Kuhnian influence[27]—that shows the degree to which values and politics
affect theory formation.

Second, what is crucial in Klein's work is that she provides a view of a
view: by adopting a Mannheimian perspective, she chronicles a modern
way of looking at the feminine. She suggests that not only is the modern

way distinct, in its emphasis on the ways in which cultural and environmental factors shape perception, but it is also at odds with other views that incorporate essentialist or trans-historical notions of person into their paradigm or models. More recently, Robert Paul Wolff has sought to capture the schism in philosophic thought respecting conceptualizing about persons: one view holds to persons as rational, as entitled to a certain kind of treatment regardless of time or historical moment, as morally free and equal irrespective of culture; another view holds to people as being bound by the specifics of time, space, and social characteristics and conditioned by biology and nature.[28] While he suggests a tension between the two that is at least characteristic of his own dilemma on how to regard persons — equal treatment, on the one hand, or preferential treatment that takes into account the specific conditions of a particular group of persons, on the other — Klein tends toward a reading of the modern view as of the second kind, viewing persons not in terms of abstract essences but rather as concrete social actors, detailing not universal psychological traits but cultural variants. And, because this is the way in which sociology, a modern discipline, would have one "read" people, there are certain sociological values imbedded in Klein's work as well: she is critical of theories of male superiority in a way that she is not of sexual equality; she is critical of views that attribute differences to biology in a way that she is not to views that attribute differences to culture; she is critical of talking about Man and Woman, but not about talking about particular men and women, or talking about persons in history but not about them at a particular historical moment.

The interpretive essays taken as a whole lay open the meanings and intentions of various social theorists writing on the subject of women. They also take account of what Hans-Georg Gadamer calls "historicality."[29] Klein, as a sociologist in the Mannheimian tradition, offers a method of interpretation that allows for an understanding of what a particular work intends to say and, moreover, why this may be the case. In his *Invitation to Sociology,* Peter Berger argues that the sociologist cannot bring eternal meanings to social situations, but can show the social groundings of all meanings.[30] This is the intention of Klein that I wish to take forward, from the 1960s to the 1980s, by asking of contemporary feminist theory: What does the argument of the theorist mean; that is, what do we take to be the author's intention? How do the ideas in the work relate to each other? Where does the argument fit historically; that is, out of what milieu does it arise and what seems to give it shape?

I wish to make a third and final point about Klein's work, and implicity about my own. In her explication of writings about women, Klein demonstrates the claim that the sociology of knowledge — the relating of ideas to concrete historical interests — is useful in critiquing what social theorists take to be true while at the same time indicating that the price of impeccable logic and fine analysis is that it may bring one no closer to the question of what *essentially* it means to be a woman. In fact, Klein's study reveals assumptions to be found in Mannheim, as well, that are integral to the sociology of knowledge, assumptions which differentiate this approach from that of the more overtly political perspective of other social theory. In his way, Theodor Adorno, writing from the perspective of Critical Theory, is on target in accusing the Mannheimian sociology of knowledge of being ridden with "innocuous skepticism [that] calls everything into question and criticizes nothing."[31]

Adorno is concerned with the social constructionism of the sociology of knowledge, which finds no way of critiquing that which is a consequence of historical conditions. For the Frankfurt School, it is not liberatory merely to describe historical entities; rather it is constraining, debilitating, and dangerous to have no moral or, in Habermas's terms "emancipatory,"[32] position from which to criticize the historical givens. One could argue that explication does not mean legitimation; one could still hold to some moral or political principle, such as the equality of persons, which is not shattered by the descriptive component of the sociology of knowledge. By showing the social location of ideas, one does not necessarily devalue all ideas; one does, however, shift legitimation to the social and political arena, which could, on the one hand, mean that politics creates truth or, on the other hand, that might makes right. What I am suggesting is that there are consequences to the exclusivity of the position that the self is a social construct and that ideas are historical creations. The consequences are the political ones engendered by the loss of an authentic self.

The Sociology of Knowledge

When one speaks of the sociology of knowledge *(Wissenssoziologie)*, one makes reference to an intellectual perspective or tradition that argues that there exists an essentially profound relationship between knowledge — broadly understood to mean ideas, values, and norms — and the social and historical conditions under which that knowledge exists. The sociology of knowledge is concerned with how different patterns of thought, or ideas, develop and how they relate to the concrete, empirical world around them. This sociological approach differs from a philosophical inquiry into knowledge, which is *about* knowledge — that is, about the ontological status of knowledge. In assuming or taking for granted the sociality of knowledge, that is, in starting with the given-ness of knowledge, the sociologist is speaking *on* knowledge, on specific knowledge systems, on the factors that make for one way of looking at the world rather than another. The sociological is not a discussion of how knowledge is possible, but why certain knowledge systems are prevalent when they are; it starts with the world as given.

It is, of course, correct to point out that certain philosophical assumptions are embedded within the sociology of knowledge. In relating ideas to the social world, one is assuming relationships between categories of being, "general propositions concerning the nature of social reality, history, man and reason."[1] Certain philosophical perspectives — for example, the recent work on Rom Harré on language as the definer of how one sees the world,[2] or Michel Foucault's genealogy of ideas with its emphasis on the variety of ways in which one could formulate most problems, especially most ethical issues, and with its appreciation of the nexus of language and power[3] — share with the sociology of knowledge an emphasis on the world as *constructed,* that is, on an understanding of the world based on social actors being able to choose what the world means from what is, in reality, *there* or what they have been conditioned or allowed to perceive of as being there.

This is not to suggest that persons have unlimited freedom to see the world in any way they choose, although some might argue that this is indeed the case; rather, the notion of "choice" is meant to suggest that the mind plays an active role in structuring perception. While knowledge is socially constructed, it as, as Peter Berger and Thomas Luckmann argue,[4] the individual who gives it meaning, who understands or misunderstands it, who acts on that perception, who gives subjective meaning to the world "out there." For its part, sociology is interested in the social factors that affect the choice of how one sees what one does; and its concern is not with abstract, but rather with concrete, thought, the thought of a person born into an already-given society, thought that is dependent upon history.

Social theorists have made integral to the sociological enterprise analyses of how historical occurrences affect the thought patterns out of which come the specific articulations of ideas and their reception by particular segments of the society. Mannheim, the modern synthesizer of this tradition within sociology, speaks for this approach when he says that the sociology of knowledge is concerned with "the ways in which social relationships . . . influence thought."[5] He speaks of how an individual's life is affected by the structure of group life, how the individual's actions occur contextually, how other persons—what sociologists call primary groups, significant or generalized others, role models and/or reference groups—and social institutions—schools, religious organizations, the media—mold and shape the individual. The "thereness" of the society into which a person is born provides the social ideology in which they are acculturated and the particular perspective of and on the world that they learn from the groups and institutions. Thinking is, in one sense, each individual's own concern, but the process occurs on and in a terrain that is effected by the group into which he or she finds himself or herself. The sociology of knowledge seeks to gain access to—that is, seeks to understand—that terrain, marked by "thought in its concrete setting of an historical-social situation of which individually differentiated thought only very gradually emerges."[6]

Before Mannheim, Auguste Comte, in his "law of three stages," had suggested that certain views of the world parallel certain social situations.[7] Durkheim, in his concern with the Kantian notion that the mind orders the world, understood the sociality of ideas—their determination and variation. One can extrapolate from his writings on the "collective conscience" an awareness of the interplay between the individual and his or her society: "There exists a social consciousness of which individual consciousness are, at least in part, only an emanation. How many ideas or sentiments are there which we obtain completely on our own? Very few. Each of us speaks a language which he has not himself created: we find it ready-made."[8] For Durkheim, the social sets limits to the abstract notion of an "individual" constituted outside society. More recently, Peter Berger has elaborated upon that duality of the individual in society and society in the individual "The individual *realizes* himself in society—that is, he recognizes his identity in socially defined terms and these definitions *become reality* as he lives in society."[9] And, with Luckmann, he has argued that:

the process of becoming man takes place in an interrelationship with an environment [that] is both a natural and a human one. . . . Humanness is socio-culturally variable . . . . there is no human nature in the sense of a biologically fixed substance determining the variability of socio-cultural formations. . . . While it is possible to say that man has a nature, it is more significant to say that man constructs his own nature, or more simply, that man produces himself.[10]

Since the historical legacy of the sociology of knowledge has been chronicled in great detail elsewhere,[11] my remarks here are to explicate the value of using this framework for analyzing contemporary writings on the feminine character. Toward this end, I will present not only a statement, albeit somewhat condensed, of what the sociology of knowledge is but also indicate some of the consequences that would follow were one to adopt a Mannheimian mode for social understanding. The criticisms of the Mannheimian rendering of a sociology of knowledge bespeak a series of problems that one must recognize even if one chooses, as I have, to utilize his insights to critique both the succinct and the nebulous aspects of contemporary feminist thought.

Marx, in speaking of the relationship between class and ideas — that is, in seeing ideas as interest-bound and in moving to bring ideas, which he regarded as political forces for various social interests, out of the realm of philosophical essentialism or idealism and into the social and political realm of concrete existence — initiated the basis for a certain kind of sociological inquiry. This elevation of the social to importance, heightening the need to consider real, empirical, historical persons and not idealized abstractions, and tying ideas to the person, lay behind Marx's oft-quoted: "The mode of production of material life determines the general character of the social, political and spiritual processes of life. It is not the consciousness of men that determines their being, but, on the contrary, their social being determines their consciousness."[12] Marxian theory is integral to one's understanding of how a society is constructed, maintained, and legitimated, for here one begins to see the import of material conditions for perception.

The kind of economic production in which a society engages affects the ways in which people relate to each other and has a significant bearing on the ideas people come to consider their own. Rather than starting with the ideas that persons hold and moving to see how these are realized, one starts with the reality of peoples' existence and analyzes how ideas evolve out of social relationships: "we do not set out from what men say, imagine, or conceive, nor from what has been said, thought, imagine, or conceived of men, in order to arrive at men in the flesh. We begin with real, active men, and from their real life-process show the development of the ideological reflexes and echoes of this life process."[13] Certainly, one cannot take at face value the reasons a person gives for holding the ideas that he or she holds; the individual might not be aware of the reasons for his or her action. One might distinguish between a "false" and a "true" consciousness, the latter being the rational awareness of what is in the individual's interest if he or she is to realize his or her personhood; that is, what he or she would wish for were he or she in a position to choose wisely. Even a false consciousness or alienated thought has, for Marx, a social dimension; that is, it is explicable in terms of the constitution or construction of one's social being at a precise and particular moment in time. While false consciousness is a denial of one's real interests (those not socially manipulated for someone else's benefit), how one falsely thinks is as much socially rooted, for Marx, as is thought that allows one to understand the reasons for one's particular historical conditions.

Marx is establishing a dialectical model, a dialectical relationship between being and thinking, out of which emerges the social action which then affects further being and thinking. In speaking of interests being governed or constituted by ideologies, of life experiences affecting perception, Marx places the social and historical dimension in the centrality of understanding human behavior. If one argues that Marx's concern is with the ways in which social factors shape thought, then one need read no simplistic determinism here. Rather, Marx attempts, initially philosophically and then overtly politically, to relate ideas to the concreteness of one's being, to see how persons act on both their physical and social conditions and how, by their actions, they produce a human culture of continuity and change.

Mannheim, building upon Marx's emphasis upon the historical, writes of the effect that group identity — how one is placed and places oneself in society — has on one's thinking. Sociology, he argues, is to refine one's understanding of the way in which people think. Its task is the revelation of the particularities and linkages between social thought, social action, and social actors; factors of class, age, sex, and ethnicity are to be considered in the sociological explanation of the functionality of specific ideas.

This attitude of regarding knowledge or ideas as being related to one's social placement is itself explicable in terms of a post-Enlightenment questioning of, or even disillusionment with, notions of absolute reason or absolute truth, accessible to the individual in his or her ordinary existence or even to the social analyst using the canons of scientific inquiry. If the Englightenment is characterized by the philosophical replacing the spiritual as the defining paradigm, there is a subsequent redefinition in terms of Marx's arguments for the relationship of thought to concrete historical factors of one's being and ideas to interests. For, given this emphasis on contextual meaning and the suggestion that truth, if it exists at all in any idealized form, is elusive once it enters the social world and becomes enmeshed with interests and ideas often in conflict with each other, those who value a sociology of knowledge must raise, as part of their analysis, a critique of notions of objective truth or all-encompassing truth systems. Mannheim suggests that truth must be approached from a variety of perspectives; if an absolute truth exists, that is, a truth that is regarded as being a trans-historical or trans-cultural idea, it must be accessible to the individual through some approach other than or in addition to sociological analysis or insight. Mannheim departs from Marx for whom there is a way, perhaps through proletarian consciousness that evolves out of a praxis or fusion of thought and action, of attaining knowledge of political and moral wisdom. For Mannheim, the sociologist must, in effect, *bracket* the eternality of thought and describe what is observed in its particularity. He warns that one cannot assume that there exists a "sphere of truth in itself" or talk as if there is truth "as such."[14] Such talk is epistemologically indefensible and politically dangerous: "those persons who claim to have discovered an absolute are usually the same persons who also pretend to be superior to the rest."[15] Access to the truth is a badge worn by political persons who seek to control others and stifle inquiry; it is, therefore, safer to be unsettled by uncertainty and "to look life in the face" than to buy comfort at the price of control.[16]

One can do no better than to refer to Arnold Brecht's delineation of kinds of truths. Factual truths, truths that accord to an empirical reality that can be obtained by adhering to the canons of the scientific method, those that are proved true "by observation," those that "correspond to reality,"[17] are evaluated differently by various philosophical traditions. For some people they are equivalent to, and for others radically different from, what Brecht calls metaphysical truths, which may exist but which have not and may never become visible and apparent. This latter category he labels "Truth,"[18] and whatever standing it has is outside the perspective of science and the scientific method, broadly understood to include a range of approaches such as positivism, behaviorism, empiricism, and phenomenology. Truths depend upon criteria of proof of a certain agreed-upon order, and in this sense one can speak of scientific truths and moral truths, a plurality of truths. Here one can see an affinity with pragmatism, with the way in which William James speaks of truths in terms of their usefulness and utility, their successfulness and workability.[19] More recently, Steven Lukes has summarized the controversey surrounding the thesis that truth is socially determined. Fearful of the logical conclusion that all truths are to be found in the eyes of the beholders, he argues that "there are no good reasons for supposing that all criteria of truth and validity are . . . context-dependent and variable . . . there are good reasons for maintaining that some are not, that these are universal and fundamental, and that those criteria which *are* context-dependent are parasitic upon them."[20]

The Mannheimian argument, which predates Thomas Kuhn's widely revered thesis in *The Structure of Scientific Revolutions* by twenty-five years, is that ideas develop and change not only because new facts are unearthed but also because old facts are reordered and looked at in a different way. In other words, theories, not facts or raw data, shape perception and determine how one "reads" the reality. It is as if theory comes between reality and perceptions of reality, between what is "there" and how one relates to what is "there." If, following Kant, "thereness" is accessible *only* through theory and the formulation of abstractions, then the "thereness" is always subjectively perceived, and social agreement about the "thereness" — what Kuhn means by the authority of science resting on the authority of the scientific community[21] — rather than a simple, objective awareness is at issue. Berger and Luckmann ask not only how a social reality is constructed but also ask what is considered to be knowledge in any given society. Knowledge, or what is taken to be true, "programs the channels on which externalization produces an objective world";[22] it says what is and is externalized and internalized as such. Contemporary discussions in the philosophy of science, often generated by the work of Kuhn,[23] despite their differences have an affinity with Mannheim, and even with Berger-Luckmann and Habermas, in their recognition that facts bear a relationship to interests; and yet, as with the latter, there is a search for a way of grounding values on universal principles comprehensible and agreeable to all.

While, I emphasize again, there are significant disagreements among these writers, Kuhn's thesis on the ways in which external factors affect the diversity of ordering and reordering data appeals to the sociologist writing on the sociality of knowledge. For, on one level, the *Structure of Scientific Revolutions* is a sociological analysis of changing conceptions of science. Paradigms, shared definitions that determine how facts are to be assessed, are similar to ideologies, providing assumptions that structure one's perception of the world, organizing material with which they are concerned, asking certain questions but not others, and using certain tools of analysis and not others. The normal scientists — "normal" here understood as ordinary or traditional — proceed without questioning the assumptions under which they work until a crisis, created by an anomaly that cannot be answered by the prevailing paradigm, arises and blurs the old patterns of perception and makes way for the new; often the shift occurs with no conscious awareness of what is transpiring and often when persons undergo the "gestalt switch" Kuhn so brilliantly describes.[24] What intrigues the sociologist is why a particular ordering scheme is used at a particular time; that is, which ideas seem to structure thought at the time and in the way that they do. Why, the sociologist asks, does one see the world in the way that one does; and what factors contribute to one's seeing it differently at another moment in time? Why are certain views incommensurate with one another? "Legitimation," Berger and Luckmann argue, is the "process of 'explaining' and justifying": it is the device by which society is made real and correct to the participants. They continue: "Legitimation not only tells the individual why he *should* perform one action and not another; it also tells him why things *are* what they are."[25]

Mannheim is aware that even the perspective of the sociology of knowledge has an historical moment. It appears and becomes prominent at those times when persons are questioning the received truths, when there is widespread disagreement about contemporary events, when the society is in crisis, when there is considerable social mobility of both a vertical and horizontal kind, and when intellectuals who traffic in ideas are freed from previous constraints.[26] Sociology is of value because it offers a "detached perspective" from the confusion and chaos.[27] Where there are grave doubts as to the validity of conflicting interpretations of reality, the social moment is ripe for, and in this sense appropriate for, the use of this kind of approach. Mannheim says that the "sociology of knowledge is . . . the *systemization* of the doubt which is to be found in social life as a vague insecurity and uncertainty."[28] By explicating the relationship between the thought of the individual and his or her society, the sociology of knowledge unmasks the once-hidden bond between the two as a way of unbinding the unrecognizable bond. It asks of any statement a question of authority: Who says something is the case?[29] It allows one to understand the rationale and logic of respective positions, and it allows one to see what functions are served by specific ideas. It requires the interpretation of the ideas of friends and foes alike, the relating of *all* ideas to their social roots.[30]

When Durkheim speaks of sociology's going below the surface and probing the whys and wherefores of social events and social ideologies, he is very close to Mannheim's charge that the sociology of knowledge is concerned with unmasking ideology and explicating utopian thought, the former understood as a picture of the world, of how the world operates, and how the social and political constellations are and ought to be. This unmasking is part of the Kantian "Copernican revolution," the placing of mind at the center of perception, such that not only errors and falsehoods but also factual truths and scientific models are conditioned by factors of a social and historical nature. With a person now held to be at the center, one can make the argument that knowledge is arrived at through the active creation of the human mind: the self is the central starting point, ordering the reality — the sense perceptions — around himself or herself through a synthetic act of mind. It is significant that what is shared is this attribute of mind, its ability to order and impose a meaning structure on raw or objective sense data. Those who follow the Kantian trajectory can argue that what is shared, in other words, is the mind's ability to reason and communicate, and that through this shared quality understandings may be possible and agreements on what is being observed may be reached.

This use of the sociology of knowledge *on* the sociology of knowledge explains ideas in conflict by alerting one to what Kuhn refers to as persons using different gestalts and what Mannheim refers to as persons "talking past one another," which occurs when for "each of the participants the 'object' has a more or less different meaning because it grows out of the whole of their respective frames of reference."[31] The sociology of knowledge helps one understand the rationale and logic of each respective position or paradigm; it allows one to see what functions are served by each paradigm and, thus, to suggest how each side can see the issues differently.

It has been argued that the sociology of knowledge has not only a method but also an accompanying attitude, that a certain morality and/ or politics follows closely from adopting a stance that refuses to call into question the honesty of one's adversaries, but instead suggests the mutuality of different ideologies. To the question whether any method is in accord with the sociology of knowledge, I answer that if the latter is trying to *understand* how one comes to know what one knows, then it shares this interpretive stance with phenemenology. Furthermore, if one were to argue that out of behaviorism flows a politics of social control, of a knower superior to the knowee, then out of a hermeneutic or phenomenological perspective, integral to the sociology of knowledge, flows a different kind of politics, more democratic and more tolerant. In speaking of the sociology of knowledge as a hermeneutic method, some commentators have seen it as having a moral dimension that inculcates the tolerance of diversity: "not the least valuable service which the sociology of knowledge has to render [is] that it can teach all men humility and charity, both of which are not only virtues of the heart, but potentially also virtues of the intellect."[32]

Not all writers see the sociology of knowledge as part and parcel of an interpretive or hermeneutic tradition. If what is integral to the sociology of knowledge is its "debunking" of ideological thought, then it shares with Marxism an intent to strip away falsehoods and clear the air of oppresive patterns of thought that assist in allowing some to dominate others. Jaggar points out that Marxism stresses the social, the historical, and the dialectical; truth and knowledge emerge out of human action set in a particular moment and in a specific stage of economic production. Knowledge is shaped by social actors and, at any given moment, dominance rests with a specific class. The sociology of knowledge, she argues, fits very well in the Marxist schema of ideas reflecting interests,[33] but Marxism has within it an action or practical dimension, an attitude toward knowledge that demands that it be used to change the order of domination and liberate persons from their oppression. For a Marxist, then, the sociology of knowledge must be used politically. If it is not—that is, if it used academically as a mode of interpretation—it could become a conservative legitimator of political forces: in choosing to explicate, it might stop short of deprecating the social forces that, from a more political perspective, demand disapproval.

I will elaborate somewhat on this point of whether there is an affinity between the sociology of knowledge and a certain epistemology, because there is a renewed interest in phenomenological sociology by both members of the traditional disciplines and those writing in the field of feminist studies, as well as an emerging literature on both the philosophical standing and/or political value of a phenomenological or hermeneutic approach.[34] If one argues that the sociology of knowledge requires that analyses proceed from the assumption that ideas are socially rooted and that ideas held by individuals, like identities of self, are constructed socially, one can understand the need to adopt a reflective, as opposed to a natural, attitude on the ideas held by oneself and other selves within a given, historical society. The sociologist wants to understand what an idea or an event means for a specifically constituted social actor; that is, he or she wants an understanding of an understanding. The idea or the event itself are not at issue, but what they are taken to mean by historical individuals. In this sense, the sociologist who assumes that reality is subjectively experienced is, at the same time, interested in an objective—to wit, detached or reflective—reading of that reality. At the least, the sociologist must take nothing for granted and must *bracket* the eternality of thought and describe what is observed in its particularity. What is observed is taken to be historically variable and, if there is a constant, it is the "seeing" itself, the reflective act.[35]

The handmaiden to this approach would, then, be the phenomenological perspective, as revealed in the writings of Max Weber and Alfred Schutz,[36] with their emphasis on *Verstehen,* with understanding social ideas and social actors by getting inside a phenomena and grasping how and why it functions as it does and by seeing the world through the eyes of the social actor being observed. Mannheim has an affinity with this reading of phenomenology, for he repeatedly emphasizes that the sociologist must *understand* what the world of the individual means to that individual.[37] This attribution of meaning from within, similar to Charles Horton Cooley's sympathetic introspection,[38] is a way of understanding not only what and how persons do what they do but also what they intend or mean by their action. It is a contextual analysis of particular social action.

Understanding from the point of view of the actor entails refraining from imposing one's own views on the other, views that he or she may not hold. It entails undertanding the intent of the other — Habermas's hermeneutic interest — either for its own sake or, as invested with an emancipatory interest by Habermas,[39] in order to communicate with *and* emancipate the unreflective actor from the hold of irrationality and unreason or sheer ignorance. The philosophical assumption of such an undertaking, which Schutz has also discussed,[40] is that if one can understand the other, one must be like him or her in some essential way; therefore, even a distinct, unique, or alternative way of looking at the world is accessible to another through the shared quality of human-ness.

In this connection, also, the interrelationship of subjective consciousness and objects in the empirical world, the sociology of knowledge can be likened to a phenomenological or a hermeneutic perspective, for if what one is conscious of is always an object (whether oneself, another person, an inanimate object, or an idea), that category is always located in an historical world.[41] The parallel can also be drawn between the sociology of knowledge and a Meadian reading of symbolic interactionism, with its emphasis on the mind's interaction with social matter and of individuals and societies being bound together.[42] Peter Berger speaks of the sociology of knowledge as being concerned with the dialectic "between social structure and the 'worlds' in which individuals live." He argues: "*Identity, with its appropriate attachments of psychological reality, is always identity within a specific, socially constructed world. Or, as seen from the viewpoint of the individual: One identifies oneself, as one is identified by others, by being located in a common world.*"[43]

One must not make too rigid a comparison between the sociology of knowledge and phenomenology, however, because the latter contains a tradition within its more general outlines that speaks of understanding, grasping, or intuiting the *essential* aspects of human-ness. Given this kind of a-historicity, one can understand Mannheim's choosing to disassociate himself from Max Scheler's reading of phenomenology. Mannheim argues that while the sociology of knowledge, as it comes out of a Marxist tradition, is a radical debunking of existing political and economic arrangements, in Scheler's hands this approach becomes a functional and/or conservative way of not only understanding but also legitimating social arrangements.[44] Phenomenology, when what is emphasized is the intuiting of essences and essential truths, moves from " 'unmasking' . . . to an impartial Sociology," from persons in particular historical situations to "a theory of the drives and of the mind of *man* in general," from the importance of history to "timelessness."[45] Phenomenology becomes conservative when it looks for the essence of man, rather than the historical facts of man's existence. Mannheim reminds his reader that persons live in and are surrounded by historical facts and that one must understand the self and others in this way. The social analyst cannot talk outside of history; moreover, he or she can understand and talk only from where he or she is, where he or she stands historically. Mannheim is unremitting in emphasizing that the analyst must be painstaking in placing ideas in a social context, assiduously relating ideas to their social position.

What, precisely, might an analysis of social thought and social action entail were one to use the approach of a sociology of knowledge? Werner Stark makes a valid distinction between two kinds of sociology of knowledge: "the macrosociology of knowledge . . . fixes its attention on the inclusive society and its influence, the social macrocosm," while "the microsociology of knowledge [is] concerned with the narrower world of scholarship and art, with the domestic world . . . of the man of scholarship and artistic creation."[46] Kurt Wolff has interpreted Mannheim as having set his nets widely, aiming to "grasp" what he calls "the spirit of a time";[47] for example, how can that which precedes science and theory, their "spirit" or *Weltanschauung,* be looked at or investigated with scientific precision?[48] Mannheim himself suggests two ways of understanding this sociological investigation: (a) to look at ideas from within and without, from the point of view that examines what ideas mean and from the point of view that examines their intent; and (b) to look at things using two different attitudes, one attitude on and of ideas, the second an attitude on and of ideologies. Thus, one would ask: Where is such thought to be located? What class, or occupations, or ages, or ethnic groups think in such ways? What kind of culture, with what kinds of worldviews, holds these ideas?

In brief, the assumption behind such inquiry is that thought has an existential and not an immanent or trans-historical base. The analyst, accepting this assumption, may find that not all similarly situated persons necessarily hold the same ideas: not all workers think favorably toward unions; not all women favor abortion. While one may still assume the historicity of ideas, it may also be the case that there is not always, or even necessarily, a *single* dominant idea, since knowledge, or ideas, is directed toward different audiences, which may account in part for the diversity of, and perhaps even the conflict between, social ideas.[49]

Scheler suggests that impulses — for example, sexual passion — might conflict with cultural ideas. Certainly, Freud's thesis of id-ego conflict suggests that reason, here understood as rational and logical discourse, might affect the ideas one holds to be true; that is, one might know that what one wants to be the case is not, indeed, the case. Nonetheless, again following Scheler, certain ideas as well as certain impulses might be more pronounced at one point in time than another. His views on the driving action of money in late-capitalist societies,[50] Erich Fromm's discussion of the acquisitive personality in capitalist societies,[51] and Marcuse's fusion of Marx and Freud so as to root character in systems demands[52] — all are interpretive understandings of the interplay between biology and culture and the ways in which character is socially and historically produced and conditioned.

All these considerations are intended to suggest that the assumption that thought arises historically does not mean that, at any given point in time, the social analyst can necessarily isolate a *single way of thinking* even though he or she might be able to characterize certain general patterns of thought, some or all of which may even be particular to that age or era. Marx himself allows that some individuals may think other than their class interest suggests they might: his remarks on a bourgeois component in the revolutionary, proletariat class and a revolutionary component in the bourgeois class are cases in point.[53] More recently, in her critique of the way science is, in general, practiced and the way it is invested with certain male values, Evelyn Fox Keller writes:

> Of course, not all scientists have embraced the conception of science as one of "putting nature on the rack and torturing the answers out of her." Nor have all men embraced a conception of masculinity that demands cool detachment and domination. Nor even have all scientists been men. But most have. And however variable the attitudes of individual male scientists toward science and toward masculinity, the metaphor of a marriage between mind and nature necessarily does not look the same to them as it does to women. And this is the point.[54]

As has already been suggested, one of the consequences of using a sociology of knowledge approach is that in one sense it handles or appraises all thoughts as being the same in that they all relate to the specifics of social conditions. The analyst must be precise in specifying what thought or thoughts are being discussed; that is, whether they are moral, political, or scientific ideas. Brecht, as well as Mannheim, has allowed for the possibility that not all thoughts are existentially or historically grounded, suggesting that there are differences between certain physical and social phenomena.[55] Here one goes back to the earlier discussion of kinds of truths. As argued previously, social inquiry can deal with all kinds of thoughts but only in the sense of understanding how that thought is perceived and acted upon by specifically located social actors. One can just as readily describe and understand a moral belief system as a scientific theorem; but the epistemological standing of a scientific fact and a moral belief may not be the same. One can just as readily discuss the functions — manifest and latent — that will be met by the prevalence of certain ideas in religion as well as in science; but, on one level, interpretations of Kuhn notwithstanding, gravity and sexual equality, velocity and altruism, are not qualitatively the same kind of thoughts. One can, with respect to diverse kinds of ideas, speak in terms of consequences and benefits. Seeing how an idea functions involves considering it sociologically, that is, treating it as an intellectual phenomena: one can see how scientific ideas affect the social order of things, as well as how political ideas advance one set of interests over another.

There is a well-established tradition in sociology that distinguishes between natural and social forms of knowledge. Charles Horton Cooley acknowledges that all knowledge is both constructed and filtered through a human lens, and that all knowledge has a grounding in a biological and psychological base. But he suggests that interpreting knowledge of things social is different, more interpretive — to wit, more "dramatic" or "sympathetic."[56] It is capable of being understood and, in that sense, known, and, provided it is subjected to a critical eye, the knowing questions what both the analyst and the social actor see. Cooley argues that the act of introspection, of genuinely understanding a person or event, is in some sense more objective than reporting behavior or events without an awareness of how structured one's own perception is in fact. Moreover, while an imaginative reconstruction is both creative and critical, the skill of doing this kind of sociology lies in the recognition of the rootedness of both observer and observed in a given social milieu and the possibility of utilizing the techniques for meaningful inquiry. As in other arts or sciences what is at issue is "competence."[57] Some ideas may be more cryptic than others; some theorems more puzzling than others. Yet each is in principle accessible to the human mind. If one were to argue that the ideals (in an ideal-typical sense) of science are rigorousness, empirical proof, accuracy of measurement, universality, and a systematic connectedness and completeness and that through these ideals one arrives at intersubjectively transmissible knowledge, then one could distinguish sociological interpretation from intuition (or private knowledge based on unverifiable observation) or, from religious revelation, all of which may exist but not be subject to communication in the same way.

Cooley further examines "competence" or the ability to understand the mind of another. The arguments suggesting the value of like-mindedness in affecting interpretation tend to disagree as to whether like-mindedness — women understanding women, for example, or blacks interpreting blacks — enhances, detracts from, or does not in any significant way affect interpretation. If like-mindedness does affect interpretation, the intellectual value of that effect is still open to question; that is, might too much empathy hinder the ability to distance oneself from the subject being observed? It can be argued that the ability to free oneself from dogma and presupposition, the grounding in an analytic discipline which trains one to question and unmask, and the familiarity with factual and statistical findings, allows one to speak with as much critical detachment as is possible in any form of empirical or hermeneutic method. In other words, the intellectual perspective rather than the class, race or sex of the interpretor may be of paramount importance.

Moreover, it is in this connection that one might read the call for a feminist sociology which would be a descriptive phenomenology of the female life-world[58] as a recognition of the political import of preferring one methodological perspective in the study of historical figures. It is the perspective that takes the observer to the world of women, to the concrete places wherein they are situated and live out their lives. This is the world made accessible to the reader by the interpretor, and there is no consistently logical reason why its deconstruction need rest in the hands of one who shares qualities with the subjects of the inquiry. The vicarious participation in another's experience, relished in both sociology and literature, needs a talented eye and a sympathetic mind, which may be independent of one's sexual characteristics or proclivities. It is not gender but the ability to be empathetic which is at issue, although I am well aware that much of the contemporary debate in feminist theory over the question of a feminist epistemology is concerned with precisely this issue of the conditions, social or otherwise, which may encourage this empathetic advantage.[59]

Certainly competence, or competent minds, have a social basis; that is, there are social conditions which encourage their formation. I do not equate competence with any statistical measure such as an I.Q.; rather, I define it as a quality of empathy. There may even be a cultural context out of which competence develops; that is, in the ideal-typical sense, one might construct a place where knowledge of the varied worlds of others is widespread, where information is fully available about social and political conditions in the society, and where there are appropriate epistemological preconditions for understanding.[60] Marcuse, in warning of the obliteration of political and social arenas wherein one could communicate and discuss questions of meaningful import and the creating of a one-dimensionality of discourse through the degeneration of both politics and philosophy with their mechanistic approaches to inquiry and their concern with giving support to the legitimators of the social order, speaks of the need to create a critical dimension to education by establishing a mode of discourse that is philosophical and an arena of discourse that encourages discussions which call into question the prevailing ideological supports of the system.[61] Habermas's call for a communicative ethos, based on a reinterpretation of how (epistemologically) and with whom (politically) one ought to be able to speak, is similarly concerned with creating the social conditions which will allow for undistorted speech.[62]

Mannheim has spoken of the sociology of knowledge as a form of communication that contributes to understanding. It is within this context of the social preconditions for genuine dialogue that one could place Mannheim's "socially unattached intelligentsia,"[63] those whose position of critical detachment — Weber's scientific "calling"[64] — affords them, potentially but not automatically, in principle but not in practice, insights into the prevailing social arrangements.

The sociology of knowledge, in its Mannheimian roots, does leave one in a quandary as to how the interpretors of the culture are any less removed from historical influence than the persons whose ideas they are interpreting. Certainly, Mannheim is aware that intellectuals writing about intellectuals are in a logical quagmire, for if all are historical actors, how is one able to stand on some Olympian height, or find some Archimedian point, from which to look down and take in all that is happening in the *polis* called the social world? Nonetheless, as a sociologist, Mannheim is interested in who the intellectuals are, where they come from, how they are regarded or esteemed in the society, what role they play and how these factors find expression in their products, that is, their ideas. These concerns are historical and analytical, and it is really an ideal-typical intellectual who Mannheim has in mind when he finds that he or she is trained to look at issues from a variety of angles, that he or she is *"equipped* to envisage the problems of his time in more than a single perspective, although from case to case he may act as a partisan and align himself with a class."[65] Bound by a similar education which itself provides for exposure to different kinds of people and diverse viewpoints, modern-day intellectuals are socialized into a situation that could generate toleration, but one must see them, at all times, as real persons, themselves historically constituted and acting in and within the same kind of cultural constraints that affect all other persons. Mannheim suggests that the intentions of intellectuals are open to analysis; that is, whether they intend their ideas to be partisan or neutral and, further, whether their ideas are read in the ways they had expected and/or hoped.

Mannheim argues that the unmasking of ideology which Marx initiated requires, as has already been said, the interpretation of the ideas of friends and foes alike, the relating of *all* ideas to their social roots. This transition involves moving from a political debunking of ideology to a more generalized sociology of knowledge:

> The sociology of knowledge seeks to overcome the "talking past one another" of the various antagonists by taking as its explicit theme of investigation the uncovering of the sources of the partial disagreements which would never come to the attention of the disputants because of their preoccupation with the subject-matter that is the immediate issue of the debate.[66]

Concerned with the consequences of this tradition, with that linkage between ideological debunking and the relativization of thought, Mannheim tries to find some way out. For if one argues that all knowledge stems from the social background of individuals, that all observers of knowledge are also historically situated and see things through their own lenses, that all values are a function of time and place, that all forms and structures are bounded by *a* time and *a* place, then how is one to decide what to value?

Mannheim suggests that his is not relativism but a relationist perspective,[67] by which he means a transcendence of individual standpoints and a calling into question of all positions, going with risking all of everything.[68] Many critics have called Mannheim to task for this distinction, which they find unsatisfactory[69] if for no reason than the possibility that relativism is relativistic itself. Leaving that aside, Mannheim's efforts to find a position that is neither judgmental nor naively value-free attempts to attain that which may be unattainable since the distinction between relativism and relationism may ultimately be a rhetorical one.

Is there not any way out of relativism, out of the chaos of appraising and perhaps even legitimating all alternative lifestyles because of a set of epistemological concerns that preclude the interpretor from passing judgment on the ideas and actions of social actors? Can one explain how and why social ideas occur without falling into the relativist trap? Is Mannheim's approach similar to Kuhn's, that is, an explanation of socially accepted truths but not an explanation of "truth" or "reality" itself? Is its logical conclusion that there is no "truth," just what is constructed to be the case, no "reality" but what one takes to be real, no science but what the scientific community regards as science? This problem is not of recent vintage, having been around since the beginning of philosophic reflection and social analysis, coming to its most telling moment with Weber's writings on value plurality and ethical neutrality. Philosophers have spoken of the paradoxes, of the relativism of absolutism and the absolutism of relativism, of whether ideas are of a time and place or whether they transcend a time and place.[70] Mannheim certainly makes the effort to open a door from one to the other position, and the effort bears analysis. Here, I can only make reference to the problem; it would take another effort to rework the Mannheimian debate, and the literture is already replete with instances of that being done.[71]

Hannah Arendt was prescient in her recognition of the dangers of Mannheim's grounding of thought in the here-and-now of the social world and in regarding all thought, be it ideological or utopian, as being in the service of political action. For her, Mannheim's rejection of the possibility of transcendent thought was, in many ways, the rejection of philosophy itself[72] and its replacement with sociological analysis. She sees Mannheim as rejecting the possibility of a contemplative life, a life of pure thought, freed from outside influence. In this context, she is troubled by his emphasis on the social constitution of the world in which persons live and his concern not with truth but the cultural circumstances which surround specific ways of seeing what is taken to be true. Others[73] will suggest that Mannheim has not distinguished philosophical from rhetorical thought and has, as a consequence, not allowed for thought that is above political and social influences. For his part, Mannheim had found it understandable that persons would cherish anodynes soothing to their feelings and want a way out of the morass of value choices. But if the journey to absolute knowledge and absolute morality had a bias in religion in the past, such a single truth system now, even if dressed in social scientific garb, could become a weapon whereby some could control others by their seeming hold on an access line to truth.

While ideas are relative to the person holding them, a sociology of knowledge, insofar as it seeks to unlock the text and to interpret intentions of meanings, relates ideas to their social background and allows for communication between persons. This intersubjectively communicable form of knowledge brings it into the realm of what we can know and talk about, and out of the realm of mysticism (what we may "know" but cannot communicate in the same, intersubjectively satisfactory way). It is Mannheim's hope that the sociology of knowledge, by bringing into the arena of discourse diverse ways of seeing the world and by relating those ways to concrete interests, lays the foundation for the agreement on values, for the laying out of differing perspectives is for him a first step in communication.

Read this way, one can understand Mannheim's early involvement with the Frankfurt School, although one can also understand their rejection of his sociological approach.[74] Certain issues were of concern to them both: a shared recognition that there was a distinct way of understanding the social world, and a recognition that knowledge of the social is even more dependent upon the vantage point of the observer than is knowledge of the natural. They both realized that one's human-ness was always enclosed within a given historical time-frame and that this human-ness was always subject to change. They also agreed that it might be the case that some category of persons see and understand social reality more fully than others.

These concerns raised a series of questions to which members of the Frankfurt School sought and still continue to seek answers.[75] Like Mannheim, they have had to wrestle with the logical consequences of the political activism of a Marxist heritage: How could a sociology of knowledge distinguish between true or false consciousness as these are understood by Marx? How could it avoid the scourge of relativism; for was a sociology of knowledge not more compatible with relativism than with theories which sought to ground human action in some kind of transcendental set of values? If the sociology of knowledge is valuable for its analytic canons and if it rejects value assessment by its practioners, is it not un-critical and, hence, does it not lend itself to becoming a conservative or legitimating agent of present power arrangements? If it is the case that one's social situation affects what one sees, how can it be said that some see more correctly than others, or occupy a privileged place which reveals more than others? Is this not a form of elitism?

If relativism means the obliteration of the distinction between ideas of right and wrong, relationism means situating the rightness and wrongness in a given context.[76] Mannheim is attempting to speak of truths for a specific historical moment. Explication does not mean legitimation to him, so one may read the sociology of knowledge as relativistic only in its descriptive component. Were it to evaluate the described particularities according to certain universal ideas, it could break out of this relativism, but one would have to ask the costs to truth which this breaking away would incur. What notion of truth is at issue? One is back in the circle of justification of epistemological concerns, the contested language of philosophy. Is one still not left with what is really right and wrong?

It has been suggested that Mannheim's relationism is his turning Weber "upside down." The following argument is made:

> While in Weber's methodology the valuations are subjective and the validity of knowledge objective, Mannheim arrives at a historical-social relativism concerning the validity of knowledge . . . and confers a sort of objectivity upon the forces which are assumed to determine valuation.[77]

Weber sees ultimate values—democracy, for example—as subjective ("democracy is good") but a discussion of democracy—what an ideal-typical democracy is, how it is arrived at, what functions are integral to it, what consequences follow from it—as objectively, that is, scientifically, possible. Mannheim, the argument goes, sees democracy as an objective ideal, but how one views it is a condition of who and where one is. Both Weber and Mannheim were concerned with ultimate values and the limitations of a methodology which allowed one to understand but not act on the relationship between ideas and the actions and motives of historical groups and individuals. At best, Mannheim had a faith in sociological inquiry as a first step towards the rational investigation of values out of which could come a shared consensus. His critics have carped at his fence-sitting, while his supporters have invested his particular writings with a general intent which is beyond relativism, subjectivism, and sociological determinism. Kurt Wolff writes that Mannheim offers one the chance to find the universal, or transcendental, self through an analysis of cultural selves. Like Schutz, Wolff sees that a presumed human nature that is common to all persons allows one to understand other persons, in different cultures, as well as other persons in different historical places and times.[78]

To the charge that the intellectual debunking of ideology effects the latter's function or validity, that is, by unraveling all mysteries one becomes "disenchanted" with the world, as Weber suggests, Mannheim counters that the sociology of knowledge, by devaluing the exclusivity of ideas and freeing one to see behavior and ideas as situational, acts to define and critique ideas and occupies a position somewhere between the dismissal and the destruction of belief systems.[79] He wants to steer a course through the Scylla of particularizing ideas and the Charybdis that discounts as sterile and futile all social analysis. Influenced by developments in science, most expressly in physics, he speaks of "situational determination" as a clearer way of thinking than the more mechanistic or deterministic approach of an earlier time.[80] At the core is the more traditional question of how what we know affects how we act.

One could take issue with Mannheim's equating the ideal-typical conditions for the creation of critical intellectuals and the existence of such conditions in the universities of his day. I am influenced by the Frankfurt School critique of the hold of positivism on intellectual life and Habermas's call for the creation of social places where undistorted communication could take place and lead to the development of a liberatory social science that in turn would inform social policy. One could entertain the possibility, succinctly stated by Werner Stark, that while intellectuals potentially could be able to see all perspectives, there is a logic to intellectualism, in many if not all modern societies, which predisposes it to a particular perspective, be it "super-rationalism" which encourages a radicalism untempered by social reality and a devaluation of "tradition, of religion, and even of art"[81] and which makes not for an unattached, free, open mind but just the opposite.

Peter Berger, writing with Hansfried Kellner, argues persuasively that one cannot escape the relativistic bind which the sociology of knowledge seems to impose by offering a privileged position to the social analyst; one cannot turn the "socially unattached intelligentsia" into an "epistemological elite." There may be political and scientific truths which one has a "reasonable chance"[82] of speaking about, if one brackets or distances oneself and one's values and feelings; that is, if one engages in what constitutes the sociological enterprise. But if all social reality is constructed and all understanding of that construction is a factor of one's own sociality and the social actor's own sociality, there is no escape hatch to ultimate knowledge: "What *is* the Archimedian point in which a true consciousness can be said to be grounded?"[83]

The sociology of knowledge, in its emphasis on "understanding," opens up and leaves unresolved conflicts and conflicting interpretations; it challenges any privileged standpoint and, in its offering of a series of partial views, confronts the difficulty of synthesizing these into a single, compatible, general view with discrete, harmonious parts. This reading of the sociology of knowledge may encourage some to see an affinity with classical liberalism and its emphasis on the toleration of diversity. An

alternative, Marxist reading suggests not so much toleration as the explication of diversity and the rooting of this in the inequitable distribution
of property and the class relations which ensue. The Liberalism and Marxism
have historically locked horns over the question of diversity and toleration, over whether such toleration is not in the interests of some groups
and a cover for concrete power constellations. The Mannheimian controversy can be situated within this intellectual context.

Knowledge about matters in the natural sciences may be effected differently by social conditions than might be the case with social, ideological
or religious knowledge.[84] What one wishes to avoid here is any lengthy
debate about the use of the words "determine" or "causes," while at the
same time recognizing that there may be differences between constraints
and strictures on different forms of knowledge, that there may be reasons
why certain kinds of knowledge (for example, biological datum) change
less than other kinds of knowledge (for example, fashions and gender
costumes).

Certainly one must be cognizant of the historical debate over the
methodological consequences which follow from the assumptions one
makes over the kinds of data with which the social and the natural sciences deal. One need only refer to the discussions on nomothetic and ide-
ographic science as these come out of the neo-Kantians and, especially,
Weber.[85] The Kuhnian reassessment of the ways in which science
changes is part of a larger attack on the foundations of modern science
and its roots in Cartesian philosophy, where the ideal of an objective observer capable of reporting what is occuring in the natural and social
world is being attacked by those theorists who seek to integrate the notion
of human agency with the giveness of a natural, social and political set of
realities.[86] Questions of the canons of science, the prescriptions of a scientific method, objectivity, detachment, and rationality are the obverse
side of the concern with the "specter of relativism" of which Richard
Bernstein writes. Certainly, in the discussion of Mannheim's sociology of
knowledge, one came to appreciate the role that historical conditions and
matters of personal judgment play in questions of understanding; and
there is a sense in which these polarities of objectivity and subjectivity,
"objectivism and relativism,"[87] provide a way of assessing the import of
Mannheim's work.

The present work is not concerned with the biology of females but,
rather, with the social conditions which define the feminine character.
While it assumes the "thereness" of society, of social facts and situations,
it regards the element of social construction to differ in social, as distinct
from physical, matters. By "thereness" one means what Berger and
Luckmann call "reality," phenomena which have an existence of their

own outside of social actors.[88] Gaining access to those phenomena is this book's general concern; gaining access to the socially constituted feminine character is its particular concern.

On one level, nature is there in a way that society is not. Science, however, as a practice, is affected by society and is also communicated to one through socially constructed paradigms. The social constraints of birth may be as powerful as those of mortality and the environment. In the writings of Mannheim, Kuhn, and Mills, descriptions are given of the ways in which ideas develop and change as new facts are unearthed, new generalizations are made, old facts are ordered and reordered in diverse ways. Science and social theory are both recorded by social actors who occupy a moment in historical space, who have distinct biographies. Feminist theory has raised serious questions about the presumed objectivity of all forms of science, not only with respect to the ways in which values influence research, or the ways in which science is a socially constituted activity, or the androcentric bias of scientific reporting, but also in terms of a presumed masculine mode that governs science, one that emphasizes manipulation, control, and detachment.[89]

It is still the case that society is more readily constructed, deconstructed and reconstructed — not everyday and not without pain and cost — than is nature. Nature appears to have certain incontrovertible truths, although even these may be historically transformed by the intervention of humans using the resources of technology — witness the new age ushered in by atomic research and the cracking of the DNA code. Yet one would not say that the idea of the earth's being flat was true at a certain point of time but not another; it seems more appropriate to say that the flat earth theory was a miscreance, a wrong belief, held to be true by most people.

The tradition originating with Durkheim, taken up by Peter Berger, reminds one of how everyday life is ordered, and that its order and being-there is the case without the individuals even being conscious of it. It is ordered by institutions, by habits and by expectations, all of which inform traditional or customary ways of behaving and which the social actor takes, over time, to be natural ways of doing things even though these are person-constructed. In this sense, social order is a human product, the result of a biological awareness of the need to relate to one's surroundings through set responses — "typification of habitualized action by types of actors."[90]

It has been pointed out by others[91] that not only may it be erroneous but it may also be politically dangerous to emphasize the sociality of self-construction, for in eliminating the self behind the socially constructed self, one places inordinate power in the hands of social forces. In giving to others the construction of one's social personality, one assumes that there is no authentic self, no human-ness or biological groundings which may structure behavior, no pre-social ways of being-in-the-world. There is a totalitarian consequence to Berger's argument that: "Society not only determines what we do but also what we are . . . " and that "identity is socially bestowed, socially sustained and socially transformed."[92]

The sociology of knowledge, in summation, while it may have its problems, its inconsistencies, its varied interpretations, does alert one to the historical specificity of thought. This specificity is presupposed by the Mannheimian position, and while I have chosen to follow it, I can appreciate those who oppose the kind of emphasis that Mannheim gives to "subjective"[93] knowledge. In its critique of Enlightenment principles, that is, of ideas of a transcendental reason, it is a most modern perspective, as is revealed by this kind of passage out of Mannheim:

> As long as we do not believe in some kind of supra-historical standpoint that suddenly descends upon us, and instead keep firmly in mind that we are trying to understand the historical from a standpoint which is itself historical we shall not only be incapable of overcoming our point of departure: we shall not want to overcome it.[94]

Lest it be argued that the sociology of knowledge is an old-fashioned perspective which arises out of a tradition of social theory that has little to offer in this sophisticated age, I conclude this chapter with reference to Mills's essay on "The Classic Tradition" in the *Images of Man*. Classical social theory, he argues, offers ideas of value because they are commentaries on the shape and state of modernity; they are rooted in a certain perspective that emphasizes the concreteness of the social, alerting us to what is important in piecing together the social puzzle. They are interpretive of their time, and insofar as we live in similar times, they are ways of understanding ourselves. Classical social theory does not offer identical views of modernity, but it does alert one to ways in which a particular model is used at one time but not another. Mills suggests that sociology must discern these differences and must suggest why a particular view prevails when it does; that is, the analytic task is to see ideas as particular to their times and, as such, reflective of the changes and crises of a moment in the social order.[95]

The Women's Movement as
a Social Movement:
The Historical Background

In following Mannheim, it has been argued that social ideas reflect the changes which are occurring in the economic, social and political realm; that is, ideas come out of material conditions, and social movements, generating either ideological or utopian thought, are to be understood contextually. There is a specific set of circumstances which affect the way in which ideas are shaped, reshaped and passed on to general or specific audiences. Feminisim must be understood within the context of the contemporary Women's Movement which arose in the United States in the 1960's and is a product of American history.

American feminism, used interchangeably with the term the Women's Movement, arises within the context of a society that has an ideology of equality and a "cult of true womanhood."[1] The latter draws its support from gender dichotomies held to be either biological and/or historical, but which, in either case, are too deeply entrenched in the culture to validate either their naturalness or their historicity. One can view the Women's Movement as the focal point of the debate concerning the ideology of equality and the cultural mazes of distinctiveness: between a regard for people as being equal in all of the significant ways and, therefore, subject to the same treatment, or having significantly distinct characteristics affording them different, if not necessarily discriminatory, treatment.[2]

In describing how the nineteenth century moved from viewing woman as "inferior" to "different," Nancy Cott suggests that how the differences were perceived varied with historical interpretation. The idea of "different spheres" of woman moving in different areas and using different talents and resources was at times seen as limiting women in so far as they were imposed by men to protect male power. "Different spheres" were used tactically at times by some women to gain power and influence, to move to positions of importance without having to overcome the restraints and barriers imposed by men who controlled the arenas — schools, for example — where women were to operate. "Different spheres" were seen at other times as a space, a place or locale, where women could establish a sub-culture of sisterhood. The interpretation of feminine difference varied, in part, according to the sources historians used for recording these differences. Cott notes that as the historians turned more to primary sources and used women's own letters and documents, the third assessment came to be regarded as the most correct.[3]

Cott also suggests that views of the feminine may also vary according to one's social location: do some women view being feminine as a disability and see arguments on distinctive traits as retarding their being treated equally with men? Are there other women who view differences as simply instrumental towards helping them achieve power? Are there other women who regard their differences as essential, either to the continuation of the traditional gender roles or as signs of uniqueness, worth and integrity? In other words, one's class and status, not only in terms of how these affect matters of income and power but also how they are subjectively assessed, may affect one's worldview on issues such as work, marriage, family, or abortion.[4]

In any event, what Cott makes clear is the need to be specific about where and when and by whom views of women are being expressed. This is certainly in line with a Mannheimian sociology of knowledge approach, which would: (a) explicate the ideological thought of feminism; (b) trace the historical forebears of the specifics of the ideology; (c) unpack the claims of the ideology; and (d) analyze the relationship between the ideology and different groups within the society.[5]

To elaborate upon major themes in the contemporary Women's Movement, it is necessary to ground the discussion in historical events. Debates over equality and differences have been affected by the changing status of women, which has been the consequence of a continuing movement for women's rights, at times more quiescent than at other times, affected by economic changes and technological innovations.

The status of women has been transformed since the 1940's when Klein wrote *The Feminine Character* which reflects: first, economic and technological changes; and, second, the presence of persons — perspicacious women — who understood the import of an advanced industrial society and who saw those changes as instrumental for a reassessment of women's social and political roles. In short, the ideas on equality and differences are shaped, and, in turn, shape the emergence and success of a movement which has as its backdrop changing patterns of economic relationships.[6] As social conditions, themselves affected by technological innovation in childbearing and childrearing patterns, began to allow for increased female participation in the labor force, and as this participation came to mean long-range, full-time employment, a movement was able to raise demands which were assessed differently than might have been the case at an earlier historical moment. New relationships between women and men, women and women, and women and the larger social order became possible given the kinds of jobs women could now fill and the redefinition of traditional roles as a consequence of technological innovation. Women live longer than they previously did and could, therefore, work for more years; even if they return to work after they raise their children, they have many years to contribute to the labor force. Contraception allows for family planning, and changing ideas on sex, the rise of sexology and sex experts, extraordinarily affect patterns of relatedness. The family, which had transferred productive functions to outside agencies during the Industrial Revolution would, in the twentieth century, be dramatically affected by changes in reproductive patterns, in childrearing and in housewifery, all of which brought into sharp relief the discrepancy between the ideology of motherhood and the economic preconditions for its obliteration or alteration.[7] The stage would be set for debating both how revolutionary as well as how valuable these changes were.

This chapter will chronicle the emergence and trajectory of the Women's Movement. I wish to assess what is qualitatively different about the contemporary phase of the Movement, focusing on who may identify with and even belong to the major reformist and radical segments of the Movement as well as on the key issues generated by Movement spokespersons and organizations. In addition, I wish to validate an interpretation of the changing status of women by looking at: changes in the work force; changes in women's legal rights; and changes in marriage and family patterns. If, as has been previously argued, identity is socially constructed (if not in its entirety at least in part), then what is being suggested is that the Women's Movement as a social movement has questioned the taken-for-grantedness of that construction and has argued for the replacement of old patterns of typification with new ones.

A social movement is a group of persons organized around an ideology; it is a form of collective behavior mobilized to bring about a set of changes on the basis of a belief system.[8] Alain Touraine intends the same definition: "By social movements I understand, in essence, *the conflict action of agents of the social classes struggling for control of the system of historical action*".[9] Even where the limits of a class analysis are presented,[10] contemporary social movements are seen to consist of a loosely or tightly organized group of persons who are questioning the perceived values of the presently constituted social and/or political order. A social movement, to be understood and appreciated, must be studied in context; its cast of characters must be historically and socially situated. The analyst must depict the conditions that generated the changes initiated by or articulated by the voices of unrest. It must be asked why old ideas and folkways are no longer persuasive enough to keep persons committed to their tasks and acting or behaving in the old ways. Inquiries must be made to determine why some people want what is not, at the moment, theirs. The analyst must "understand," in the Weberian sense, the intention of the social actors, inquiring into what they perceive to be their situation and why they are dissatisfied with the existing state of affairs.

The person is a social animal, and his or her behavior is a social phenomena. However the person acts, the act is a social act, be it an act similar to what others do and as the person is expected to do, or a socially different kind of act. Acts must be understood in social terms, as reflections of the demands and expectations of the society. What those expectations are, and how they are transmitted to the members of the society, are the defining and processing functions of what sociologists call the numerous agents of socialization. In abstract terms, perfect socialization occurs when the roles and jobs that the individual is called upon to play are taken to be a correct and proper participation in the larger social order. Things proceed as they are expected to, and when they do not, control and commitment of individuals to that larger social order are questioned. In a situation of what Durkheim would call "anomie" or "normlessness," the expectations of the individual are out of kilter with the demands or resources of the society: his or her wants and the social capabilities to deliver do not mesh. Where the individual accepts the given state of things, where he or she has what Durkheim calls "a wholesome moral constitution,"[11] the individual is content and the society is stable. He or she may strive to improve his/her lot moderately, but that individual will be calm and happy and the society will be, in the Durkheimian sense, healthy. There is a harmony between his or her expectations and the society's offerings; the individual is content and secure and the society moves along smoothly in its daily operations. But where the individual conducts himself or herself in a manner considered incorrect by certain approved social standards, where he or she wants or does what is not supposed to be desired or executed, the individual acts in what sociologists call a "deviant" manner. Where this deviant behavior is widespread, the society is experiencing disequilibration.

It is not being suggested here that during periods of "normalcy" persons are content with their lot and that, at a certain moment, they become disaffected. It may very well be that disaffection is a human constant. Moreover, one must beware of "oversocializing" the individual,[12] of committing that sociological fault of seeing the individual as imbibing social values without effort or resistance. Rather, one might build on Freud's insight and see the individual as mediating between his or her wants and socially proffered needs, for within each person there may be a battle between what he or she wants and what society — in the guise of social values — has taught him or her to want. Needless to say, this begs the question of whether personal wants are not also a consequence of social factors; certainly one can appreciate Marcuse's position that the ideology of the society can permeate the inner psyche,[13] and that the domination of the self-society process can be in the hands of an administered state such that persons come to want what others would have them want.[14]

In short, a social movement arises when disaffection is shared, acted upon and organized. Disaffection and pleasure are not to be seen as opposite sides of the same coin but stand, rather, in a dialectical relationship to one another: the scales are tipped, one way or another, at a certain moment.

Looked at another way, in any given society, there are certain values held by its members. These are what the sociologist calls the "definitions of the situations," the pictures persons have in their heads of how things are and how things ought to be. Values or value systems symbolically legitimate or make morally acceptable the particular pattern of interaction and stratification of the members of a social system.[15] Those who are entrusted with running the society depend upon the equation of these pictures so that people can be counted on to do what the social values ask be done; that is, the powerholders have as their job the extracting of compliance, the obtaining of consent through varied means, not the least of which may be coercion, overt or subtle. The notion of internalizing values means just this: the doing, by rote, what is expected of oneself, the non-recognition or non-consciousness of the way in which one goes about one's daily business. At this point, what is at issue is not from whence come these values (from a ruling class or a set of ethical norms?) but, rather, the awareness that they exist and prescribe behavior for oneself and others. Even in the writings of someone like Mead, who emphasizes the dialectical relationship between self and society, the constant change inherent in the behavior of social actors and the dynamic dimension of social acts, there is concern for the orderliness of ordinary behavior.[16]

Values are Marx's ruling ideas, Durkheim's collective conscience, Mannheim's ideology, and Kuhn's paradigms. The socialization process concerns shaping people to perform according to these collective notions which the social culture has prescribed, inculcating the shared values and guaranteeing support for them. Freudian theory also explains how the child comes to accept and internalize social and moral values, how ego replaced id as the arbiter of behavior, and how these values become a form, albeit necessary, of social control. Moreover, since it seems clear that not everyone has the exact picture in his or her head at the exact time, the legitimate authority must be able to extend its control and influence over a great variety of perspectives and it does this by its ability to balance and make integral a diversity of outlooks.[17] This can be done to the degree that diversity still accords legitimacy to those in positions of power; if not, there will be exhibited a range of behavior running the gamut from alienation and withdrawal to active rebellion and revolution. Diverse outlooks can be kept in check if they are understood in terms of the behavior which one can expect to flow from them. Power is responsive to the degree that it fully understands the depth and range of its diverse membership.

A social movement is indicative of there being a distinction between what "is" and what "ought to be." It has a set of values, an ideology, which does not accord with what is in effect. How great the disjunction will be is a matter of historical circumstance and why the dissension among certain persons and not others will require careful analysis. For those in the movement, roles are questioned or rejected, and the normal way of doing things is held up for examination or even dethroned. New ideas are patterned or put into place to explain, justify or rationalize the failure of the past and the need to redefine values for the future.

Change is the core of history and a social movement, be it conservative, reformist or revolutionary in intent, acts to alter the scope and direction by which the society realizes its aim and objectives. In this sense, the movement not only responds to social problems but is dialectically involved in defining and shaping what those very problems are,[18] although the political solution to the problem might not be the one envisioned by the movement architects.[19] The movement actively seeks to intervene in the historical process and to shape and mold events which are being given shape by those who already have the power to make decisions within an historical context that is in flux, for there are changes — new technologies, new scientific worldviews — always operative in the background.

One of the most interesting questions asked about a social movement is that of the personality (here used in the sense of behavior and character) of its membership. What has happened to allow its members to redefine the value system, or, if one does not want to go this far, to find the society's goals wanting and in need of redefinition? On one level, the sociologist can descriptively, not judgmentally, say that socialization has failed, that the society has not been successful in getting this particular group of individuals to do what is demanded of them. Or, the sociologist can point to the array and disarray of competing value systems and can come to understand a movement participant as following one tune played by one drummer in a band where other players are keeping their own librettos and scores intact.

Here one recalls the earlier discussion on the social construction of personality. Cooley writes that "the individual has her being only as part of a whole . . . separateness is an illusion of the eye and community the inner truth."[20] Mead speaks of the sociality of the self: "The self is something which has a development; it is not initially there, at birth, but arises in the process of social experience and activity, that is, develops in the given individual as a result of his relation to that process as a whole and the individual within that process."[21] He emphasizes the social interaction between a social reality and the I/me of the self. The self is always in the process of changing, of acting towards others or reacting to social phenomena. It is not simply responding but is interpreting social actors and social situations; hence, one regards the theory of society as one grounded in "symbolic interaction".

One learns, from a society into which one is born, one that is already there, how to be a person. Peter Berger will go so far as to call society "a gigantic Alcatraz,"[22] a prison of already constructed definitions. One's life is lived by learning from social others — significant others, generalized others, agents of socialization — what one must do to make it through the terrain of lived experience. Who one is — that is, the already existent class and status into which one is born — determines how the terrain is traversed almost as predictably as will one's eye color, or ear length, or predisposition to a genetic problem such as Tay-Sachs or sickle cell anemia. One's socially ascribed status is pre-set, "there," a vise into which one's particular self is placed and away from which one can move with varying degrees of ease or difficulty.

Peter Berger's "Alcatraz" is given an existential component when the prisoner, to continue the metaphor, realizes that he or she can say "no" to a social demand. The process of "realizing" that one is free is, at once, particular to the prisoner and contextually explicable; that is, the analysis must ask why this prisoner at this point in time and what conditions exist which make for successful recruiting of others to this newly awakened condition. Social movements arise when the old ways and explanations just will not do: the received values can no longer structure behavior and rather than retreat into a sub-culture which will glorify and reward what otherwise would be considered deviance,[23] movement participants press for social reforms.

It is too simple, and essentially incorrect, to speak of social movements as pathological or as repositories for the disaffected. Madness at one historical moment is exemplary behavior at another, and behavior which appears psychotic or neurotic is made comprehensible by an ideology which integrates dissent into a cohesive whole and thus becomes politically explicable. Ideologies are new mazes which enable one to translate disillusion into thought that is energizing and liberating; they also allow one to regard personal problems as public problems and personal disintegration as a manifestation of social disintegration.

The society will respond in various ways to the demand for social change; accommodation, disavowal, repression or annihilation are all options and it is only contextually that one can discuss the pathway that is selected. Writing on the Populist Movement in particular, but throwing his net much wider, Lawrence Goodwyn speaks of an "historical constant," the "rules of conduct" which subtly intimidate movements by calling out a sophisticated centralized bureaucracy to denounce and brand as " 'decadent', 'individualistic', and . . . culturally handicapped"[24] those who question the values of achieving what the system proffers as rewards. Writing on contemporary social movements, Jean Cohen criticizes those who brand the ecology and peace movements as narcissistic, regressive and infantile "revolt[s]against modernity."[25] The ability of the movement to counter-attack will be, in part, a factor of how strong its resolve is to hold onto its new perspective, rejecting the assumptions on which opponents operate. Those who reject the prevailing ideas and the ways in which certain bases of power result and benefit from present arrangements must do more than democratically discuss the fine points of their nascent and competing ideology. They must search for recruits, those who are potentially predisposed to make the "gestalt switch"[26] from one cultural mazeway to another, or those in a state of incipient insurgency if still unaware of the possibility of acting to retake their autonomy.

To fully understand the contemporary Women's Movement, one must trace its lineage far back into the country's history. A reading of women's history, which concerns itself with the emergence of social movements centered around issues of women's rights, is essential not only in order to understand more about the social processes of change, but also to see how certain themes appear and reappear at different moments in time.

The historical literature suggests four key moments in that history: the evangelical roots of the early movement and its relationship to the abolitionist movement; the move for voting rights initiated by the suffragists; the early twentieth century move to provide protective legislation for women (as part of a more generalized concern for social reform); and the contemporary phase, which follows two distinct paths. These sometimes, but not always, merge — the path arising from the National Organization of Women and the path originating in the Civil Rights Movement. Many strands and issues of the Women's Movement do not require examination. However, certain themes capture or illustrate how that Movement has faced commitments to equality and concerns with sexual differences. One can read the battle over the Equal Rights Amendment as the demand of the Women's Movement for equal treatment. One can read the abortion debate, related issues of reproductive rights, and a concern with violence against women, as the Movement's demand for recognition of women's uniqueness and aggravated status and the need for a legal redress of the latter.

Movements do not, in practice, fall into neat categories. Activists are certainly found in both equality and differences camps, just as political demands for equal treatment often accompany demands that a special interest group (women) be used to guarantee equal treatment (woman as president). Moreover, embedded in the very roots of the contemporary

Women's Movement are the complicating factors of class, race, religion and age.[27]

Complexity is not new to politics. The Civil Rights Movement and the Anti-War (Vietnam) Movement were diverse and saturated with complex policy debates. While the NAACP, the Southern Christian Leadership Conference, and the Black Panthers were in agreement that the condition of Blacks ought to be changed there was no consensus as to means or, necessarily, ends. The Dump Johnson supporters and the draft resistance movement held differing assessments on links to Third World revolutionary forces. And the opposition to female pornography comes from both those who have been in the feminist camp since the beginning and those who oppose feminists on most issues save this one of the immorality and sinfulness of erotica. Nonetheless, there has been a minimal commitment, by all of those who identify with the Women's Movement, to the idea that women are not treated as they ought to be under a democratic regime. While the causes of their mistreatment might not be agreed upon (that is, is it the economics of capitalism or the sexism of patriarchy that is to blame?), the recognition of some form of discrimination or oppression is understood to be the case.

When did a public constituency of and for women first develop? The 1790s was really the first time when women who were involved in the Evangelical churches could begin, as a group, to find the psychological and social space where issues of piety, health, and suffrage could be discussed together.[28] These churches were grounded in a religious ideology of the democratic relationships of people to each other and to their God. Women could read evangelism as saying that each individual was capable of receiving empowerment from God, that the theology converts all — men and women — alike, and that both sexes must work not only to improve the self but also the world. Church theology was seen by some as democratizing sexual relationships and legitimating women who were organizing to become more systematically concerned with women. Initially interested in discussing matters of the family, from the 1820s on these church women turned their attention — often through a variety of organizations such as benevolent and missionary societies, moral reform and temperance societies, and educational and anti-slavery societies — first to the question of slavery and then to the question of female suffrage.[29]

Slavery and racism exposed one to the even more general issue of inequality and the Republic's ideology was on the line in both instances. The nurturing of ideas on women which would fuel the suffragist movement occurred within the context of Jacksonian political development, itself evolving from the generality of Enlightenment ideas and the specificity of Revolutionary rhetoric. America was the practicum of Enlightenment theory, an alliance of liberty and equality that would be in sharp contrast to the traditional authoritarianism of previous political foundings. Add to this the economic development of the period, especially the move away from the agrarian life and its concommitant separation of the home and productivity. Women's power and influence were affected as they became less directly important to productivity and more central to domesticity. While initial intent of the Jacksonian spread of educational opportunities was to make women better mothers and teachers, it succeeded in producing a new breed of women, one perfectly attuned to a newly emergent movement for equal rights for themselves as well as for blacks.

The themes which colored the discussions on women, on their appropriate roles and their inappropriate treatment, can be read in the 1848 Seneca Falls document which demanded, among other things, the extension of the suffrage. Modeled after the Declaration of Independence, the Declaration of Sentiments and Resolutions detailed myriad examples of male oppression of the female: denial of the vote; inequitable treatment with respect to legal and economic conditions; exclusion from matters of property and education; and a double standard of morality and sexuality. The argument was made that women and men were equal in their capacities and, therefore, should be equal in their responsibilities: "The history of mankind is a history of repeated injuries and usurpations on the part of man toward women, having in direct object the establishment of an absolute tyranny over her."[30]

A movement to right these wrongs was needed.[31] While it can be argued that this movement arose out of the more generalized reform movements of the mid-1800s, in latching onto the voting issue there was a deemphasis of the central role that the family, the kingpin of women's private lives, played in keeping women from receiving equitable treatment. Perhaps the historical moment did not lend itself to a questioning of traditional sex roles and familial arrangements; suffrage, as an issue, was much more in keeping with the liberal, political culture of the day and interested in forming alliances with those seeking the vote for blacks.[32]

The themes laid out in the Seneca Falls Declaration — of universal human capacities such that all persons should be entitled to vote and of women's difference vis-a-vis men — would color the women's rights debate for at least the next fifty years. That debate is now well-documented.[33] Put most simply, the suffragists' demand for the vote was based on two ideas: (a) that it was owed them as citizens; and (b) that enfranchising women would transform the system along lines of progressive reform. Here can be seen a recurrent argument in the Women's Movement, that women qua women have a distinct way of thinking about political issues, that either their sentience or their outcastedness has enabled them to use their political vote in the best interests of the country. For, surely, women would vote as women: "Pure in spirit, self-less in motivation, and dedicated to the preservation of human life, female voters would remake society and turn government away from war and corruption."[34] Nonetheless, if the intent of the suffragists was to create a distinct interest group called "woman," this was not realized in fact. Why this is the case is grist for the historians' mill, but a tide of conservatism in the wake of the First World War that affected women as well as men, the passage of the Nineteenth Amendment to the Constitution which may have been considered by many in the women's movement as the completion of their political struggle, and the emerging similarity of male-female voting patterns, give credence to that argument that women were not the group that could radicalize politics, if indeed they were a cohesive group at all. One's sex, so the argument might be made, was tangential to one's voting behavior and views on political issues. In any event, the ways in which women actually did vote, usually in accord with established family patterns, allowed observers to look on the radicalizing potential of women with a jaundiced eye.

The period from the 1920s to the 1960s was one in which the feminist movement entered a stage of quiescence. This is not to suggest that women, active in the fight for the suffrage, got the vote and went home,[35] or that the ideas of feminism, which had been sounded at the Republic's birth, were now defunct. Women remained in the reformist struggles, playing significant roles in the debates over protective legislation for women and children as well as in the fight for other kinds of social welfare legislation.[36] They pushed hard for the acceleration of women's education; they joined forces with men in the labor movement to organize women workers, especially in the textile mils and factory systems. They also began to talk openly and vigorously about sex and sexuality, seeking to dispel myths inherited from the earlier, Victorian era. Feminists and businessmen alike were aware of the importance of women being involved in the marketplace, both as equal competitors in a highly individualistic market economy and as consumers, the buyers of goods and services.[37] The ideology of domesticity which assisted the growth of unparalleled consumerism depended upon women for its very existence. It is this ideology which colors the early twentieth century and which comes under criticism as "the feminist mystique," a way of entrapping those women who, for whatever reason, choose to remain out of the labor force.

In tracing the origins of the contemporary Women's Movement, historians highlight circumstances which created conditions conducive to the questioning of received and perceived sex roles. Women had been regarded as appropriately wives and mothers; single or unattached females were most assuredly present in the culture, but it was assumed that there were reasons for their not realizing their intended or appropriate role. When the cultural mazeways allowed women to accept their socially defined roles and when they chose to do so, there was an historical moment of serene calm, but when the roles were challenged and when there were demands to redefine role expectations so as to include a whole host of previous inconceivables, there arose the potential for a social movement to emerge and reidentify cultural mazeways.[38]

The Second World War required reassessments of the roles of both blacks and women in our society. It has always been the case that as industrialization alters the economic landscape, the contours of women's roles and their "place" are questioned. As the industrial replaced the agrarian society, women were removed from a direct role in the economy, from being what has been called contributing or productive laborers. Certainly, the argument on the use-value of housewifery, of taking care of house and family, could be documented;[39] but housewifery was not regarded as economic labor and the bearing and rearing of children was not seen, for the most part, as a contribution to the economy. Women were given no remuneration for the homemaker role which occupied most of the time of most of the women, nor was it considered appropriate that they should be paid for services rendered.

Returning from offices and factories once the Second World War was over and men returned to jobs entrusted to women in time of need, women began to reassess the value of domesticity. War took women out of the home and made their labor equality a factor of import; that is, when the society needed them to boost industrial output, no case was put that women ought not to be doing that which was more appropriately done by men. In this sense, the war legitimated new styles of work for women. Other developments were taking place: advances in technology began to reduce the number of jobs which required physical prowess; more women were starting to enter the labor force; labor-saving devices decreased the tasks of the housewife; and educational levels were increasing for all Americans. It is against this background that Betty Friedan wrote *The Feminine Mystique* and with which one dates the start of the contemporary Women's Movement.

Writing, or talking, of the Women's Movement in its contemporary phase is like weaving a tapestry of multicolor threads. At the most general level, feminism is an ideology that requires an explanation of sexual inequalities. Feminism, in all of its guises, assumes that individuals ought to have certain political and social rights in order to insure the realization of democratic principles. Where feminists may disagree as to how these rights ought to be achieved or even as to the nature of the rights themselves, to wit, whether they belong to the person by virtue of individual or social existence, they certainly invest their opposition to oppression and domination in a moral theory of liberation. Feminists want what they assume all or some others have by virtue of their inclusion in the work and politics of the society.

More specifically, there were two strands significant in the formative days of the contemporary Movement, and which colored feminist demands: first, the formation of the National Organization of Women (NOW) out of the ideas generated by Betty Friedan and assisted by women professionals who had been concerned with women's issues at the governmental level; and, second, the emergence of a part of the Movement out of Civil Rights struggles of the 1960s. These strands gave the Movement from its inception a predominantly white, middle-class membership, and the absence of both women of color and women involved in non-professional parts of the working class was apparent. The source of the strands — to keep the tapestry metaphor — are essential in understanding the breadth and diversity of the Movement as it evolved; the tapestry will have new strands added which will give it color and/or confusion — depending upon how one's eyes view the varieties of experience.

The Civil Rights Movement allowed one to compare the rhetoric of equality with the reality of racial discrimination; it also allowed those who thought in terms of racism (of whiteness as an opponent of blackness) to further dichotomize, now in terms of sex and sexism (of maleness as an adversary of femaleness). The Movement encouraged its participants to think in terms of autonomy and to look for social forces and practices that might impose barriers in developing this sense of self. One might profitably read Sara Evans's *Personal Politics*[40] as a work that traces contemporary feminism out of the Civil Rights struggles, and delineates the factors that encouraged sexism both within the organizational politics of the Left, and outside it.

The direction of the Civil Rights Movement was towards "participatory democracy," the dethroning of authority structures, the elevation of a kind of Rousseau-like "general will" achieved through consensus. In its distrust of others imposing their views, ideas of participation could only affect the ways in which the women in the Civil Rights Movement regarded their relationships with others. Evans quotes two SNCC (Student Non-Violent Coordinating Committee) activists on the conflict between the egalitarianism of the Civil Rights Movement and the replication of traditional sex roles in the Movement organizations: "[we] learned from the movement to think radically about the personal worth and abilities of people whose role in society had gone unchallenged before."[41] One can trace the feminist idea of the "personal is political"[42] out of the Port Huron Statement of the Students for a Democratic Society (SDS) which attacked the concentration of power in a military-industrial complex and the insidious way in which the ideology of corporate liberalism permeated the minds and hearts of all those enmeshed in its tentacles. The student Left, which paralleled and often overlapped with the

Civil Rights Movement, was, at the time, protesting against a growing bureaucratic society that alienated the person from him or herself and from others. Disaffected from an economy geared to an unwinnable nuclear confrontation and an immoral guerrilla war in Southeast Asia, the student Left was fascinated with both an existential philosophy that spoke of living in spite of social unreason and a set of Marxist categories that seemed to explain the oppressiveness of capitalist society. The Civil Rights Movement would integrate the religious opposition to segregation with the political opposition of movements of the Left and find in each of these a common preparedness to rest one's hope on the "people," those most oppressed and, as in Alice Walker's *Meridian*,[43] those not tarnished or stained by the larger social order.

In the South, the Civil Rights Movement had emphasized "the beloved community" and it was precisely this emphasis on a moral community, on a community as both a way of life now and a model for the future, committed to social change while itself abiding by the rules of the valued social order of the future, that was regarded as a distinctive mark of SDS. If "participatory democracy" meant a decentralization of power, where decision-making was relegated to those whose lives were affected by the decisions, where the objective was control of one's life, then the Movement seemed to some of its women participants to be hypocritical in its treatment of women.

Within this context, it will not be difficult to understand the centrality of "consciousness-raising" sessions as a core concept for that part of the Women's Movement that evolved out of SNCC and SDS. They shared a rejection of male authority, the perception of themselves as oppressed colonials, and the fear that the imposition of ideas would discourage leaderless discussions and keep participants from embracing or supporting positions that one had personally, through experience, come to see as true. Consciousness-raising was an admixture of theory and practice. Women gathered together in small sessions without a leader or authority figure to talk about how the private sphere replicated the larger social structure and how the understanding of one facilitated the understanding of the other. This "personalized approach to politics"[44] was coupled with a fear, understandable contextually, that being considered equal but different was a variation on the "separate but equal" phase of black history which had gone out with the Supreme Court's *Brown* decision of 1954.

For the most part, consciousness-raising was regarded as being a method of analysis particular or peculiar to women, centering as it did on what women qua women had experienced.[45] By starting with what women knew to be true, by validating their own experiences and sense of self, they could come to understand male oppression or patriarchy: they could start with the concrete and move to the abstract; they could start with the consciousness of their experience and "raise" their unconscious feelings about themselves and the world around them to that level. Consciousness-raising turned an individual into a social problem by showing the nexus that connected the two:

> what they thought was an individual dilemma [was] a social predicament and hence a political problem. [Involved was the] process of transforming the hidden, individual fears of women into a shared awareness of the meaning of them as social problems, the release of anger, anxiety, the struggle of proclaiming the painful and transforming it into the political. [46]

Consciousness-raising brought private lives out onto public stages. In effect, it argued that by keeping personal matters private one not only allowed immoral practices to continue but one also legitimated authority by covering it with the cloak of one's own confidentiality. The notion grew that the privacy of one's personal life could be part of a patriarchal ideology, a subterfuge, a male expedient to hide patriarchal practices of domination, subjugation and abuse. Moreover, consciousness-raising emphasized — although in practice it did not always work out that the women were equal participants in these sessions — what women shared in common, not how factors of race or class or religion or ethnicity might distinguish one woman from another. [47]

The Civil Rights struggles were going on when Friedan wrote *The Feminine Mystique* and helped to found NOW, but the incentives to raise questions of women's status were colored by very different factors. NOW pushed not for a reassessment of power relations in the United States but for equitable treatment with men, getting women into jobs and out of the housewifery trap which kept well-educated women harnessed to a consumer culture and enmeshed in family forms that were experiencing psychic stress. Friedan had links into the federal bureaucracy; the forces behind NOW included the President's Commission on the Status of Women, derivatives of the National Woman's Party and the National Federation of Business and Professional Women's Club, and attorneys in and around the Women's Bureau.

By the 1970s, the strands of the Movement were in place and there was a proliferation of feminist groups, with issues going beyond equal opportunities in the marketplace to include questions of marriage, family, reproductive choice, violence and pornography. Whatever the differences between NOW and the more radical groups — and often these revolved around the issue of lesbian politics[48] — one thing was clear: an earlier universe of strictly demarcated sex roles was no longer to be taken for granted.

*   *   *

The 1960s were marked by the emergence of the contemporary Women's Movement. It was also, at this time, that federal policy and legal enactments favorable to the equalization of the status of women were being formulated. In 1961, the President's Commission on the Status of Women created an official interest in issues of women's rights, making legislative recommendations which, in several instances, became law: The Equal Pay Act of 1963 spoke to the issue of discrimination on the basis of sex; the Equal Employment Opportunity section of Title VII of the Civil Rights Act of 1964 prohibited discrimination on the basis of race, color, creed, national origin or sex by any private employer or union; Executive Order 1246 (1965) prohibited discrimination by federal contractors in the aforementioned areas. In 1969, the President's Task Force on Women's Rights and Responsibilities made further recommendations for legislation to upgrade the status of women.

Within this context of an improvement in women's status, NOW grew in strength, there emerged the Women's Equity Action League (1968), and myriad organizations of the Left came into being—the Women's Radical Action Project, the National Women's Political Caucus, the Jeanette Rankin Brigade, Redstockings, to name but a few. Again, these strands of the Movement were themselves part of a 60s and 70s proliferation of movements—peace and anti-nuclear, environmental, consumer, communal, the elderly, the disabled, the gays, religious—all of whom were pressing for changes in government policy of one sort or the other.

For many in the Movement, it seemed a *fait accompli* that the Equal Rights Amendment to the Constitution would easily pass Congress and the respective state legislatures. If, in the 1960s, there were any reservations to its adoption, these came from some feminists themselves who questioned the need to expend Movement time and money on an issue of such questionable import.

The Equal Rights Amendment had been a devisive issue in the women's movement since its proposal in 1923 by the National Woman's Party. While some interpreted it as guaranteeing equal treatment by eliminating classification on the basis of sex, others regarded it as a threat to the protective legislation that women needed and a challenge to women's familial obligations; still others saw demands for its passage as a case of feminine hysteria, since it provided nothing that women did not already have.[49] In any event, the Amendment had been confined to the machinations of the Congressional committee system and while regularly introduced into Congressional sessions it was not until 1950 and 1953 that it was passed by the Senate and only in 1970 that it was favorably reported out of the House of Representatives. Congress passed the Amendment in 1972, cries for protective legislation which would guarantee women special treatment as a consequence of their being women no longer being made by supporters of the feminist cause. It was duly sent to the states for their ratification. By 1978, 35 states had ratified it and the votes of only three more were needed; Congress extended the ratification deadline to 1982 and a new chapter in the women's movement can be written on the failure to get that small margin of approval.

The battle over ERA revealed the emerging opposition to the Women's Movement and the reconsideration of feminist objectives by earlier allies and supporters. One could argue that an examination of the struggles over ERA—its formulation, its legal implications and the ratification struggles—unearth and deepen an understanding of both anti-feminist and feminist sentiments, for the debates afford a panoptic view of the kinds of issues generated by the Women's Movement.

The anti-ERA ratification struggles served as a window through which one could view an important segment of the public since those struggles were not only about legal issues but about how a segent of the population viewed feminist thought and action. The 1970s were marked by reassessments of the preceding decade and the even minimal gains made by blacks, students, and women. While the 1960s were characterized by an amalgam of political perspectives, those on the Left were both united by and vociferous in their demand for an extension of political rights and privileges to previously excluded segments of the population, not only blacks and women but also ethnic groups, gays, and the disabled. These demands, to be turned into political programs, required a commitment of Federal and state funds to new as well as existing social welfare programs and a concommitant reassessment of existing national priorities.

The erosion of confidence in government precipitated by Watergate, the failure to achieve a decisive victory in Vietnam, and the oil crises were the background for a public concerned with the reality of affluence and abundance and with America's changing fortunes in the international community. ERA came to symbolize the devaluation of authority, largely male, precipitated by the 1960s; experiments in social engineering that had begun with efforts to obliterate racial differences and were now to eliminate sexual differences; a movement for sexual liberation that was at odds with a certain reading of Christian, and even a more secular, traditional morality; the denigration of protective legislation for women; and the reaction to a movement seen to be dethroning women from their pedestal of adulation (the "cult of womanhood") by a small, vocifereous band of outsiders (sociopaths, misfits and miscreants) who were viewed as being traitors to the cause of femininity in general and betrayers of other women who held their distinctiveness to be a symbol of their identity and who did not want to be made equal to men.

The "feminist backlash" was a defense of traditional values which provided the basis for a moral community and which ought not be tampered with lest the society be plunged into bedlam and chaos. Feminists roiled and irritated those women for whom a traditional marriage and its consequential family were the mainstay of their existence. Women's rights—

especially the right to have an abortion (which became the acme of the women's rights movement in the 1980s) — were part of a larger crisis in consensus. The counter-attack on a backlash, which was seen as a conservative counter to feminism and which appeared to have an aversion to anything new, recognized that more was at stake than either the ERA or abortion rights. Zillah Eisenstein, joining issues of economic and sexual domination of women, wrote:

> The New Rights's antifeminist, antiabortion politics remains not merely a cover for right-wing militarism and interventionism, but is also a central aspect of this militarism, *the politics of restrengthening America is implicitly a sexual politics. Anti-feminism is simultaneously being used as a supportive rallying cry to create a morally strong society and is also a central aspect of how one will create the moral society.*[50]

In its emphasis on the private, in its opposition to government intervention into the private sphere and in its support of the traditional family, the New Right, it was argued, joined anti-feminism with an opposition to welfare liberalism.[51] In its defense of the traditional family, the New Right defended the hierarchy and authority of male prerogatives, especially but not exclusively as these had been institutionalized in the nuclear family.[52]

Feminist theory countered the anti-feminism that was itself a response to the Women's Movement, for that theory exposed the public/private dichotomy integral to conservative thought as a ruse for a bourgeois liberalism which refused to recognize that both the public and the private were related to issues of power and social class.[53]

In a sense, the case for the ERA was easier to state. If it could be argued that classification by sex is the denial of individual fulfillment and that an amendment was needed to guarantee, conclusively, that women be allowed to compete equally in an open meritocracy, it could also be argued that, like suffrage, ERA was an expression of one's individuality and human dignity.[54] Discrimination, whatever its intent, could create two kinds of citizens; moreover, since the reality of women's existence was increased participation in the labor force, ERA was a way of bringing feminism in line with the reality of working women. If ERA was, for its supporters, simply the logical end-point of the women's movement, for its opponents, ERA became the final nail in the coffin that obliterated sexual differences. In this context, one can read the import of debates on women, the military, and the draft as being more than a set of considerations on equitable training or the sharing of military facilities.[55] ERA was seen as the delegitimation of biological differences: one camp saw this as destroying women's "natural" roles, the other as declaring illegal dysfunctional sex-stereotyping.

Even if one could argue that part of the defeat of the ERA has to be laid at the doorstep of a Movement that waited too long to do the grassroots lobbying necessary to secure legislative passage, and which under-estimated the strength of the opposition, nonetheless, ERA's defeat was a legislative one since the courts continued to interpret already existing amendments (the Fifth and the Fourteenth) as guaranteeing women a status equal to that of men. Marriage and divorce laws were undergoing reinterpretation favorable to women.[56] And the Supreme Court, in a series of cases, held to the legal objectives of the Women's Movement, particularly by upholding abortion as a female perogative and a guaran-teed right: one need cite *Reed v. Reed* (1971) holding unconstitutional a law imposing sex discrimination; *Frontiero v. Richardson* (1973) hold-ing that married women army officers were to receive benefits equal to those of men; *Roe v. Wade* (1973), upholding the right to abortion; *Craig v. Boren* (1976), calling for something stricter than the "reasonableness test" in a case of sex discrimination; *Owen v. Brown* (1978), holding that barring women from naval ships violated the Fifth Amendment; and the Akron case (1983), reaffirming the *Roe* decision. However, it ought to be noted that in *Rostker v. Goldberg* (1981), the Court did uphold Congress's right to draft men only and that there appeared to be a chance that, were there a change in Court personnel, the *Roe* ruling might be overturned; certainly the Administration's presentation to the Supreme Court of the case for reconsideration of *Roe* was a blow to those who favored a reading of abortion as a woman's constitutional right and was an indication of an interest in reconsidering the abortion issue by a wider political con-stituency.

In traditional political terms, the pressure group tactics of NOW, which included the political demand for broadening the base of the Dem-ocratic Party to include consideration of issues of specific concern to women, and which began with the McGovern reforms of the 1970s, cul-minated in Walter Mondale's selection of Geraldine Ferraro as his vice-presidential running mate in 1984. Whatever else one might say of the choice (that is: did it really matter given the slim chances that any Demo-crat had against the incumbent president, Ronald Reagan? Did Ferraro represent the interests of all women, some women, which women?), the choice symbolized a major party's preparedness to treat women as equals and there is very little doubt that the choice reflected the recasting of par-adigms initiated by the Women's Movement. Here, too, there is the need to include in this assessment of the historic sense of the 1984 election, the fact that so many women did not vote the Mondale-Ferraro ticket: histo-rians will have to grapple with whether women voted on issues other than gender, whether they voted as a bloc, whether class was a more impor-tant factor than gender in how one voted, whether those women who voted Reagan-Bush had more in common than those women who voted the Democratic ticket.[57]

Encouraged by the political victory of blocking the passage of ERA, the opponents of the Women's Movement felt encouraged to move out of the insularity of their support groups. These were most strong in the South, in parts of the Southwest, and in states where fundamentalist Christian and Mormon populations were politically well organized. The opposition made its campaign into a national one, with their reservations on the purposes and intentions of the larger Women's Movement, not just those which had coalesced around ERA. In this context, the fight over abortion, characterized by public debates, Congressional hearings, marches, demonstrations, and the outbursts of zealots followed on the heels of the ERA defeat; and those feminists who had seen the ERA struggles as being over more than anti-discriminatory legislation were correct in their interpretation that far more was again at stake in the abortion campaign than equal opportunity.

Once feminism went beyond issues of equal rights and changing the world of work, which had been NOW's original intent, it raised issues of transforming the female sphere. Sexual issues began to be discussed more openly than in the early days of the Movement when they were confined to sectarian debates — questions of lesbianism, rape, abuse, harassment, prostitution, and pornography. Within this context, abortion became a major question and if in the first Reagan bid, in 1980, it was seen as an issue that revealed divergent ideologies,[58] by the second, re-election bid in 1984, it had become an issue of concern not only to the "New Right" but also to church groups, many of which had been the mainstay of the Democratic Party. Behind this ferment on abortion were other layers of agitation within religious groups as they became involved in the reassessment of women's roles; both within the churches and outside, lay theologians and others raised questions on the varieties of feminist experience.[59] The Catholic Church was asked to ordain married, female priests; parishioners wanted discussions on family planning, methods of contraception, and abortion; and inquiries were made about the feasibility of sex education in church-affiliated as well as public schools.

I wish to return to the abortion issue within the text of this book proper. Suffice it to say here that it became an issue of political import and one which was extended not only into a generalized discussion of the changing American family but also into a national inquiry into the meaning of human life itself. The abortion issue was part of a larger set of issues that asked not only how advances in technology, most especially in the field of reproductive technology, required a reconsideration of the traditional roles of mother, father, and child but also how technology was reshaping all aspects of human life. Abortion made concrete the paradoxes of a modern society.

One needs to point out that many of the legal and legislative advances of the Women's Movement affected middle-class and professional women; working-class women continued to suffer from low-paying, low-status jobs, sharing this with many comparably situated males, and their situation was compounded by minimal advances in federally assisted child care and homemaker support services. The data can be read as follows:

> Although strong legal basis now exists for *equal opportunity* in *employment* for *women,* women's *earnings* have actually dropped relative to men's. This holds true even when *experience on the job,* life-time *work experience,* and *education* are similar. Females are also still twice as likely as males to be below the poverty line. The impact of low female earnings may be of even greater significance today because of the increase in female headed families. *Equal opportunity legislation* has not been sufficient to end economic sexism.[60]

Discrimination is often not outright discrimination. Women have been socialized into going into professions which then become low paying even where the jobs require certain skills — jobs such as nursing and teaching; and it is this institutionalized sexism which requires political and social programs to undo and which explain the impetus of and rationale for arguments respecting "comparable worth." The profile of female participation in the labor force suggests the existence, still, of a dual-labor market; with female employment concentrated in clerical, secretarial, sales, health, and educational services. There has been an increase in the number of women working but not in the number of fields in which they are working, and where they are in fields with men, women still experience differential pay.

What is significant is the changing profile of the family, a theme to which I return later in this book. Of special interest is a change in attitudes toward motherhood and a reassessment of parenthood as a *part* of one's life,[61] although there are disagreements as to why these attitudes have changed,[62] if they have changed at all.[63]

If by the 1980s there seemed to be a counter-attack against what some perceived to be the earlier direction of the Women's Movement toward emphasizing equality and equivalences between the sexes, one does not want to forget that the debate over women's differences had been with the movement since its inception in the early suffrage struggles. This having been said, it is also important to note that movement events are not the same as the shifts in writing about women, although the way-posts of feminism find their literary sources: corporate feminism; socialist feminism; radical and/or lesbian feminism; Third World, black and Hispanic feminism, to name some Movement examples. The Movement must join these strands, while the theory can rest content with the variety of perspectives.

In a very general way, I should like to situate the Women's Movement within a cultural context of modernity as that has developed in Western society. There is a reading of contemporary history which seeks to capture the paradoxes of modernity or what may be called the underside of progress. I have been influenced by that reading as it comes out of the writings of the Frankfurt School, especially as members of that School took to discuss and debate the writings of Weber on rationalization and its consequences for the individual.[64] At the core of this discussion is the concern with the domination of social life by the apparatus of the state and the use of a scientific method and its practical, or technological, apparatus to control relationships between social individuals. The paradox for the Frankfurt School is that the material conditions exist for the improvement of the lot of the individual, but the cost seems to be a consequent loss of autonomy; while on the collective level, the advances in science and technology that could be liberatory have been used to perfect the Holocaust, make Hiroshima possible, and threaten the environment through either pollution and/or nuclear annihilation.

In a Mannheimian way, I am asking how this paradox affects feminist theory, that is, how the advances of science and technology are seen as either liberation and/or control. In the chapters to follow, I am more specific with respect to this *Zeitgeist,* this intellectual spirit of the times: for example, how do the debates on motherhood and reproductive technology reflect this concern? How, perhaps to a lesser degree, can the debates on sex education and even pornography be seen as expressing a concern with how information on sex expands one's vision or puts one into the hands of a "knowledge elite," be that elite William Masters and Virginia Johnson (sex therapists) or Larry Flynt (pornographic magnate)? How do the debates on science and the scientific method reflect the ordering and evaluation of reason, rationality, emotion, and passion?

It is best to situate the Women's Movement within the historical context of a system of modernity as a way of understanding both its bases of support, the obstinate resistance to its demands, and the writings that have evolved out of that spirited debate. It is a system marked by what Alain Touraine has called "two kinds of facts: the decline of reproduction and the progress of production," a system in which women spend less time being mothers and more time being consumers and in which men come to dominate women less but advertising comes to dominate them more, a system in which advertising and consumerism become the dominant class's means of controlling sexuality.[65]

It is not possible to support the assertion that the Movement is anti-technology, but one gets a sense of the milieu in which the Movement operates by seeing it as reacting to technological changes in life-world experiences. Certainly, one could argue that on the specifics of an issue, say "natural childbirth," one can read a back-to-nature romance; the para-

dox is that the birthing practices that are in opposition to modern obstet-
rics can be supported as a way of keeping scientific experts, who often
happen to be men, out of an area where they need not intervene or inter-
fere. Again, one could argue that a pro-choice or pro-abortion position
reflects a narcissistic concern with the self, and that self's own body; conversely, one could argue that the planning of one's family is based on considerations of communal needs as well as on one's own wishes. Could it
not be the case that the Movement is prepared to use science to liberate
the body from earlier biological demands by arguing that one can take
what one knows from science and talk about what people can now become, what ethical oughts can be realized to assure women of their
personhood?

As I have suggested, the ideas of the Movement and some important
part of the writings in feminist social theory which emerge out of a dialogic encounter with that Movement are resonant with certain themes of
Critical Theory. They are both addressing changes in life-world experiences that have been triggered by advances in technology and the
concommitant economic and social changes which have come out of the
increasing bureaucratization and modernization of the contemporary
social world. By detailing the penetration of a functional rationality into
the life-world, Critical Theory allows one to see a certain part of the
Movement as attempting to protect that life-world from becoming "colo-
nized," infiltrated by government support services in such a way that persons can no longer decide on their own how to live their lives. Habermas
sees the contemporary feminist movements as fearful of the administrative arm which is strong enough to push into areas where regulation
spells control, dominating "spaces" where people ought to be able to
make their own decisions on the basis of rational discourse which leads to
a consensus of how best to proceed with their own lives. For Habermas,
the feminist movement expresses women's objections to being controlled, and, in this sense, shows women resisting tendencies to colonize
the life-world; in addition, that movement provides a place where communication takes place, where women can look for both a personal and a
collective identity which now is buried but which has a potential for being
expressed genuinely and communicated.[66] Moreover, the movements,
for him, force one to focus on the important issues of the day: for while
they are movements for cultural change and ones in opposition to the "rationality of modernity,"[67] they are concerned that people are deprived of
a say in the ways in which their lives are ordered. The movements are
looking for a universal morality that would contribute to the integration
of individuals into a cohesive social community where ethical oughts
could be rationally arrived at and which community could counter the
disintegration of communal ties, while not precluding a plurality of life-
styles. Seyla Benhabib writes:

Today both the women's and the ecology movements are challenging the cultural legacy of modernity in the name of new ideals of autonomy and individuation in a non-patriarchal society and for the creation of new institutional structures in which the industrial exploitation of nature can be overcome.[68]

Critical theory expresses the hope that the Movement might steer a course between the protective encroachment and statism of neo-liberalism and the fragile and false ties of traditional collectivities like the nuclear family which, unable to fend for itself in a market economy, falls prey to whomever holds real power in the concrete social order that, in fact, does exist. In the steering, there must be rational discourse on what ought to be preserved, not a preservation based simply on tradition, on the past. There must be reflection by all parties concerned, not mere acceptance by some arguing the case for others.

The emphasis for Habermas is on process, on ways of arriving at answers to how persons ought to live. At its best, feminist social theory is part of that process. Extending Habermas's remarks, Cohen writes that movements "defend social spaces in which collective identities can form;"[69] they allow for ideas on how to democratically move to democratize the system. Movements wish to extend the benefits of democracy to those to whom they may not now apply, not simply to the monied or knowledgeable. Moreover, they are apparently, in the sense of potentially, a threat to or opponent of social order seeking as they do to raise questions about the routines of social action. Yet such movements need not be read as deviant or as threats to social cohesion but "as sources for new solidarities . . . for the further democratization of society."[70] They can build up traditional forms, not passively in support of the traditional forms, but rather as a consequence of rational reflection based on an understanding of both their practicality and their morality.[71]

I am interested in seeing, in a Mannheimian way, the place of the Women's Movement historically. An understanding of and writings about the Movement are part of the panoply of ideas seeking to understand the paradoxes of modernity. It is within this modern context that I understand feminism as an ideology which intends the obliteration of the oppression and subordination of women and, in this sense, their liberation.

* 5 *

Family: Contours of Change

In order to situate the social theory of feminism, one must account for the historical conditions that have led to changes in the status of women and, given their traditional involvement in childbearing and childrearing roles, the family. It is not easy to give a synoptic view of an institution which has not only been historically variable but which has been invested with such import both by those who are involved in its construction and those who use the language of analytic discourse to comment upon its significance for the shaping of social character. The family is an institution ostensively indicated by certain kinds of social relations, what Jane Flax has characterized as being integral to the needs of the species: production (the shaping of the environments in which persons live), reproduction (the creating and socializing of new members of the species), and psychodynamics (the structuring and regulating of those new members' internal life-worlds). Put differently, the family produces and reproduces the new members of the society and is an agent in the replication of social values and political ideologies. For the feminist, the family not only replicates gender images and is a site of female labor but is also integral to female identity, which has traditionally been thought of in terms of the mothering role.[1] Given this import of the family, I have chosen to begin this essay on the sociality of the "feminine character" with an analysis of works pertaining to the family, in general, and to the institution of motherhood in particular. For it is the way in which the institution of motherhood has changed, and the reasons for the change, that is at the crux of contemporary reinterpretations of the feminine character.

When sociologists talk about a crisis in the family, or the crisis of the family, they have in mind a catalogue of events: increased divorce rates; decreased marriage rates; decline of the birthrate; increased rates of birth outside of marriage; increased incidences of domestic violence, child neglect, incest, and rape; proliferation of non-traditional family forms; increased voluntary childlessness; increased number of two-career families; and commuter marriages.[2] To the degree that the family is losing its earlier significance, for better or for worse, one can speak of such changes as being part of a "legitimation crisis,"[3] a crisis in meaning, although interpretations of the changes and agreement on the old and new meanings are varied. Much depends on the kinds of questions asked: are there certain conditions which are necessary to produce the kinds of human beings one wants? Could one argue that children need the constant and passionate involvement of one or more adults, that they need to be under the aegis of one or more parent? If so, ought the society formulate those policies which would enable parents to have time for their children? Does one want to support or, if it has been lost, return to the father-dominated family? Are plans to support the traditional nuclear family viable in the economic system that prevails? Does one want to return to the family of a single male breadwinner, with a commitment to full-time mothering and housewifery for the female? Does one want to do away with the family entirely and with any kind of distinguishing gender roles? Does one want to go even further and have only test-tube babies, thereby eliminating the onus on woman that biology has traditionally placed?

What the analysis requires is a recognition of the historicity of social problems; the importance of analyzing and interpreting persons and their institutions in their historical context, of seeing how historical factors effect traditional psychological processes. By this one means asking historical questions about changes in family patterns: does the authority figure in the family change over time? Do patterns of childrearing change historically? How are parent-child relationships subject to the processes of democratization?

Writers as diverse as Tocqueville, Arendt, and David Riesman have asked those kinds of questions and their answers have been based on both an empirical reading of the data and a critical questioning of the logic of present practices. Tocqueville, in chronicling the effects of democracy on national character, called attention to new family forms that arise where there is no ordered, aristocratic hierarchy and where patterns of social and psychological equality evolve out of political principles.[4] Riesman, in relating characterological types to patterns of governance, subsumed a discussion of the family into his larger theme of changes in corporate lifestyles and their effects on personality. The peer group, he argued, came to matter more and the family less in the shaping of the child's personality: "The family is no longer a closely knit unit to which he [the child] belongs but merely part of a wider social environment to which he early becomes attentive."[5] Arendt spoke of the modern phenomena of the breakdown of authority and she was particularly concerned about the

> prepolitical areas of childrearing and education, where authority . . . has always been accepted as a natural necessity, obviously required by natural needs and the helplessness of the child, as by political necessity, the continuity of an established civilization which can be assured only if those who are newcomers by birth are guided through a pre-established world into which they are born as strangers.[6]

Historical considerations also suggest that one realize that practices become problems and the personal becomes political when a legitimating knowledge system so defines it to be the case. Feminism, as a political movement, has been successful in getting the power structure to address (that is, consider legitimate) issues on women and the family that might otherwise not have been considered as matters of public concern but, rather, matters of a very private nature. Within this context, it becomes permissible to question family practices which otherwise would have been considered personal concerns, of no business to the outsider. That is, feminism has opened up for discussion the practices of family life. The Women's Movement was integral to a process of obliterating public/ private demarcations, for reasons of noble and notable intent, so as to create a feeling of shared experience and to alleviate the realities of abuse and suffering. Raising questions about the family was not only related to apparent changes in family styles but it was also part of a "culture of self-exposure . . . a decline in an older etiquette of modesty and privacy about personal life . . . a new acceptability of a confessional mode."[7] It was hoped that by using the tools of social science one could demystify the practices of family life, exposing them for the power relationships that they were. An ideology of gendered roles would be seen as a cover or pre-text for male power. The politicization of the private, within a context that has placed import on the role that social factors play in the shaping of persons, epitomizes a modern paradox: in alleviating social ills one in-creases social controls which, in their wake, create a new set of problems; and in demystifying human relationships one not only strips away ago-nies but, perhaps, ecstasies as well, turning the sacred into the profane.[8] In an effort to help the family to do its job properly, patterns for state su-pervision of the family are established, often in unintended ways;[9] and in the guise of democraticizing relationships one may really be placing power in the hands of those who can define the relationship to begin with, those who have the "power to control the agenda."[10]

In that interaction between the Movement and the formulation of feminist theory, questions arose about socialization practices, about how gender is transmitted and learned, about how the child develops a sense of identity, a way of being able to say who he or she is.[11] The writings on motherhood are efforts to link this initial mother-child bond to ensuing socialization practices, to see the costs involved in an historical practice of women-raised children both for the women involved[12] and for the chil-dren, especially as this affects their sense of self, others, and sexual-gender identities.[13] There is a conscious effort to detail the ways in which traditional family structures become the nemesis of female liberation, imputing to patriarchal institutions a pertinacious power to shape per-sonality in ways that continue the historical domination of persons by men.

In the turn to the sociological consideration of socialization, of seeing the historicity of female forms and practices, there is an oft-unspoken emphasis on social determinism. Mark Poster writes: "In truth there is no *natural* sexuality, no *natural* stages of sexual fantasy; sexuality is defined for the child through his interaction with his parents, who are themselves unconscious agents of their class, society and emotional economy."[14] The only given-ness of the family is its locus, "the place where psychic structure is formed."[15]

In looking at the family, the question is raised as to whether the family is, in effect, a natural or necessary process, or an historical and, therefore, changing form. The contemporary debate on the family is, in its most direct form, the debate on the existence of an essential idea of humankind: is there any need for families at all? And what form, if any, need the family take? Joan Kelly has elucidated the historical varieties of family while holding onto a form of bonding based on support and commitment, passion and emotion, not biological or authoritarian controls.[16] She has offered historical evidence that refutes any notion of a nuclear family of idyllic proportions that existed in the past, while, at the same time, she has expressed concern about the disintegration and abolition of all forms that allow human communities to survive and flourish. There is a similarity here with the Frankfurt School's view of the family — how it contributes to a person's human-ness and to the formation of character.[17] Jean Elshtain, through the notion of a "social covenant or compact," has also tried to distinguish between a specific historical form of the family and an idea of the family as a form of symbiotic community and a site for nurturing:

> The ideal of the family is of an entity whose adult members have come together to create a mutual, ethical order; who acknowledge and accept the new identities that coming together forges, making them social beings of a particular kind; and who commit themselves to responsibility for the future, either through rearing their own children or through other generative activities that link them to past and future beings. A collection of people who happen to be under one roof at the same time does not make a family. Within the family . . . the animating ethos is to nourish humanity — not some vapid promise to fulfill an insatiably consuming self. This family is first and foremost an intergenerational institution, not first and foremost an intrapersonal association.[18]

In one sense, then, the writings on the family of both contemporary social theorists and feminists reflect the concerns raised by Bernstein when he speaks of the place at which philosophical thought finds itself today — at some distance from both the apprehension of objectivism and the spectre of relativism,[19] no longer exhilarated by the objective promise of Cartesian ontology, yet fearful of positing the logic of a relativism grounded in subjective experience.

I will detail further this crisis in the family by turning to some selected writings on the subject. In John Guare's *Marco Polo Sings a Solo*,[20] a young man, a transvestite, about to undergo a sex-change operation, deposits his sperm in the nearest branch of the appropriate bank. The operation successfully completed, she arranges for a bank withdrawal so as to become impregnated by his (now her) sperm. This transaction is similarly successful and she (formerly he) gives birth to a child. This ultimate act of "individualism" allows her (formerly him) to be both mother and father of the infant.

One might pass off Guare's story as the weird and eccentric expression of a playwright were it not the case that the present reality, shaped as it is by a scientific rationality using the tools of genetic engineering and reproductive technology, may allow for the realization of Guare's family-less family. For once the case is made that the family changes over time as a social institution, it can be further suggested that in an age of technological rationality the family will reflect the technological imperatives of the present moment. Peter Singer and Deane Wells open their scholarly book on reproductive technology[21] with a scenario of an imaginary twenty-first-century dinner party. Gathered together are a couple who have conceived their four children in the traditional, heterosexual way, and who find their dinner companions a rather odd and peculiar bunch; a couple who will have their baby through in vitro fertilization and who will parent, not mother, the child so that their academic schedules are not unevenly affected; a couple who will have their quadruplets one year hence from frozen sperm and embryo in an ectogenetic laboratory, and who cannot understand why having four children this way is either worse or better than the old-fashioned way; and a single female who, sans traditional male partner, will birth her own clone, thus assuring her of the child she really would like to have.

Whether Guare's compressed triad is simply a new historical form of the parent-child relationship, or the Singer-Wells dinner party the logical end-point of sexual liberation or humanity's conversion to a scientific barbarism or a way of allowing persons to use technological inventedness to fulfill their most rational and reasonable wishes, they are both dramatic and political examples to keep in mind in trying to gain some understanding of the transformation of family life.

If one takes as paradigmatic of the sociological literature most contemporary works concerned with the processes of socialization, one can see how they speak to the point of newly emerging forms of the family. Often their ideology is a form of truncated Marxism: first, they explain historical change as a consequence of structural changes in the economy; second, they omit Marx's philsophical presuppositions that the world, if not made by person, is shaped by his or her conscious actions, his or her labor, which ought to be imbued with a vision — an emancipatory interest — which will give direction to changing those conditions. In their descriptive format, they tend to equate that which is historically happening with that which is historically liberating and, thus, fail to ask the critical questions about the ideology of social relationships.

Letha and John Scanzoni's *Men, Women and Change*[22] chronicles the ways in which the family has been transformed over time. The picture that emerges is one of increasing equalization of the social and economic opportunities available to men and women, an evolution in sexual standards towards greater female autonomy and away from a double standard, and a suggestion, from their reading of the findings of the behavioral sciences, that persons not socialized into tight, traditional gender roles are characterologically more flexible. What they see developing, in line with a modern society characterized by rapid social change, is a "[p]sychological androgyny."[23] Changes in sexual relationships, changes in patterns of dating and mate selection, new styles of marriage (co-habitation, common-law, open, trial, gay), new styles of parenting (gay, single, communal), and new styles of birth control are part of what the Scanzonis see as a move towards a rational, in the sense of intelligent rather than sentimental, calculation of interpersonal relations. The inculcation of a bargaining process into the family, where relations are to be handled in terms of "negotiation and benefit seeking"[24] and where children are to be assessed in terms of costs versus rewards, is depicted positively. There is a liberal underpinning here: extend the options, amplify the ranges, remove the coercions and one increases human happiness.

Family studies define the family as an agent of socialization and look for the social factors which provide answers to the questions of why persons behave as they do and why and how they are socialized as they are. In *Aspects of Sociology,* which is indebted to the Frankfurt Institute's earlier (1930s) work on authority and the family,[25] the argument is made for studying the family as an historical institution, one which is not simply a natural arrangement of kin but one which is socially mediated, that is, effected by the particulars of the society.[26] Radical for its time in seeing the family as an agent of socialization, the Frankfurt themes have been incorporated into the conventional wisdom of mainstream American sociology: the demise of the family is part of a generalized weakening of traditional attitudes and attachments and of a growing rationalization of the society. The family is based on a principle of blood within an historical context in which that principle had been declared obsolescent. The family is ascriptive in a society of achievement; it is emotional in a society of rational calculability. Insofar as the system of economic production is the infrastructure on which society is built, rapid industrialization has declared the family obsolete in economic terms. At the locus of interpersonal relations, rationalization of psychological ties is declaring the family obsolete in emotional terms. In Marxist terms, one could say that psychological devaluation follows upon economic devaluation.

The Frankfurt critique does not stop where the Scanzonis do, but captures the dilemma Bernstein speaks of: in a society suspicious of universal values yet fearful of a relativistic epistemology that provides no direction for how one ought to live, how does one speak of the family? These are the protagonists of the critique: those who embrace the possibilities of a technological society and the liberality of changed sexual patterns of behavior; those who, hearing the death knell of the nuclear family, want to retreat to an idyllic age that precedes modernity; and those who, disenchanted with the form of progress that they experience, want to walk a tightrope between the ameliorative aspects of technology and its potential for human domination, looking along the way for new forms for human needs. For the Frankfurt School sees the emerging society as an example of reason turned into its opposite, a modern chimera; and, contextually then, the demise of the family has certain consequences fraught with danger, occurring as it does in a society of technological rationality, peopled by atomized, depersonalized individuals whose personal life-worlds have been invaded by the calculability of science. The family becomes increasingly less responsible for inculcating social values, once public agencies are considered more effective and efficient, in a very technical or cost-effective sense, or completing the socialization process. The technical effectiveness is, for the Frankfurt School, a technocratic invasion of the life-world, another "victory of the technological age . . . dimming the radiance of the person"[27] as social engineers and scientific managers manipulate human needs and human relationships. Evaluating the family in terms of functional and economic rationality is an intrusion of a technical method into the realm of the sensual, and the rationalization of inter-personal relations which accompanies the family's decline appears to be the result of what Horkheimer calls "psychoanalytic enlightenment,"[28] a euphemism for the conformity which the psychological experts are extracting. The family disappears and/or its socializing functions are taken over by the supra-state or the culture industry; in any event, it becomes absorbed by the administrative apparatus of the technological society.

Just as their reading of Marx allows the Frankfurt School to see the historicity of the form that the family assumes, so their reading of Freud supports their seeing the family as playing a role in the formation of the individual's personality or character. Critical theory is not blind to the exploitative aspects of patriarchy and to the weakening of the authoritative family by the processes of industrialization and democracy, nor is it unaware of the economic advances made by women as they have been emancipated from the subjugation of domesticity. A weakened family, weakened by the father's loss of moral and economic authority, the mother's growing economic independence and the child's development being left to outside agents of socialization, decreases what for Freud and for the Frankfurt School is a precondition for the emergence of an autonomous personality.

In holding onto Freud, the Frankfurt School holds onto a view of certain biological relationships between members out of which certain social and psychological consequences follow. Variable as historical circumstances might be, and varied as psychological traits might appear, the dialectical tension between parents and their children, grouded in both love and authority, is held by them to lay at the root of the human condition. If by autonomy the Frankfurt School means not unrestrained freedom (for that would be anarchy) but self-imposed restraints freely and consciously arrived at, then the paradox of familial life is that it is a biological relationship of kin which can potentially conflict with or negate the rational calculation by which the modern public realm is ordered and operated. Thus, Horkheimer writes that "the family suffers a fate that is not really so different from that of the corpse, which in the midst of civilization recalls to mind the conditions of nature."[29] The family may be a memory, in the Marcusian or Dinnersteinian sense, a way of being-in-the-world based on pre-scientific considerations of kith and kin. Or, looked at somewhat differently, in a society that is meritocratic and functionally rational, there is no social need for the biological bond that united individuals: "In the midst of a total condition defined by exchange . . . the family remains an essentially feudal institution, based on the principle of 'blood', of natural relatedness."[30]

To reiterate: Horkheimer specifically speaks of the demise of the family as part of a generalized weakening of traditional attitudes and attachments and of a growing rationalization of the society. He holds no romantic notion of an idyllic past and his assessment of the psychic costs attendant upon industrialization are not to be interpreted as longing for a return to any golden days. His argument is that as a society becomes enlightened, and as that enlightenment penetrates into the received knowledge system of human behavior, relationships move from ones of affect to ones of rationality, from ones bounded by emotion to ones constructed by techniques for good and appropriate behavior. Lovers are taught how to act; mothers are taught how to parent; children are taught how to respond and those doing the teaching — the purveyors of the techniques — while their intentions may be to alleviate pain and suffering and the ills of acting in destructive ways, become the new agents of social domination.

In addition to the loss of male authority as a consequence of changes in the economic conditions of late capitalism — family members are no longer as dependent upon the father for their economic well-being as had been the case earlier — Horkheimer sees an inherent tension within the contemporary family. There is a potential negativity to the family, since Horkheimer views the person, especially the man, as exemplar of the rational mode and woman as the passionate mode; therefore, one can appreciate his concern for what will happen to the family as women become more like men, when they are enervated of the vigor of motherly love that is not as integral to the economic system as the commanding authority of the father.

One can understand why contemporary feminism would reject Horkheimer's assertion that: "because it still fosters human relations which are determined by the woman, the present day family is a source of strength to resist the total dehumanization of the world and contains an element of anti-authoritarianism."[31] Jaggar is correct in seeing a Marxist perspective on the family as one that is gendered. Her interpretation of Marx and Engels would apply to Critical Theory as well:

> They waver between the radical ideal of full female participation in every area of life and the assumption that, while women's biology may allow for considerable participation, the complete achievement of this goal is impossible. . . . Certain unspecified biological differences between women and men would mean that there could never be a complete abolition of the sexual division of labor, either in the family, in the workplace, or in bed.[32]

The Movement is, by and large, eager for women to play whatever negating or revolutionary role they play in the realm of the public, not in the privacy of their own home. For the family has been used to legitimate a monogamous system that has kept women in a situation of subordination and the ethos of motherhood has been used in the past to deny women the full involvement in the public realm which is necessary if they are to have their interests justly represented.[33]

Marcuse was also concerned with control by experts and the illusory quality of socially programmed liberation. Both in *Eros and Civilization* and in *One-Dimensional Man,* he writes that under the bourgeois "performance principle" sex and love are defined and conducted in utilitarian terms, and lack the elements of spontaneity and playfulness necessary if they are to be forces of liberation. It is sex *for* reproduction, sex *for* physical release, sex *for* consumer consumption. Once libido is no longer a private affair, one between the individual and his or her psyche, the "private space" unique to persons is obliterated.[34] The person becomes a public object, and, in a capitalist society, regarded as a commodity and subject to processes of rationalization and domination.

Horkheimer well understands that female emancipation from the subjugation of domesticity is progressive, but he is equally aware that freeing women to be like men is making them, like their male counterparts, a calculus in an economic theory and an object in a capitalist market. Children lose the restrictiveness of the traditional nuclear family, but at the price of being turned over to other, non-familial, agents of social control at increasingly earlier ages and, for Horkheimer, being stripped of that long childhood which assisted the child in the formation of his or her character. Horkheimer refers to this as the "loss of . . . interiority" and writes:

> As interiority has withered away, the joy of making personal decisions, of cultural development, and of the free exercise of imagination has gone with it. Other inclinations and other goals mark the man of today: technological expertise, presence of mind, pleasure in the mastery of machinery, the need to be part of and agree with the majority of some group which is chosen as a model and whose regulations replace individual judgment. Advice, prescriptions, and patterns for guidance replace moral substance.[35]

The society has come to the point, he argues, where even marriages and children are evaluated in terms of functionality and economic rationality rather than in the humanly appropriate terms of sensuality and love. There was a time when the family was a place for withdrawing in order to catch one's breath, when how one's children fared was a matter for one's own growth, when memories and traditions were the basis for the continuing friendship of husband and wife. This, Horkheimer argues, is no longer the case, not in a society characterized by the equalization of the sexes, the leveling of the individual personality, the fusion of public and private life-worlds, the rationalization of the personal world. Technology changes persons in a most dramatic and revolutionary way.

The Frankfurt critique of the family builds on the moral dimension that is found in the writings of both Marx and Freud: if Critical Theory is nothing else it is a counter to cultural relativism and a value-free and ethically neutral social science. It accepts as natural, that is, in the nature of humanity, the biological relationships between members of the family and the social and psychological consequences which follow. At the same time, it situates the family socially and historically: like the individual, the family develops within history and its biological and moral dimensions are played out over time. The family is integral to a person's human-ness, and all queries about the family start from this domain assumption: how, historically, is the family mediated socially? How does the family assist in the formation of character? What are the social consequences that follow from this dialectic of nature and nurture?[36]

Others have explained the historical conditions out of which Critical Theory develops;[37] my interest in it here is that it lays out with prescience the themes that underlay many of the writings in feminist theory, a theory I interpret as caught up in a rapidly changing world where the older notions of appropriate sex roles and gender behavior just will not do. Before moving onto that theory, I wish to make one other intellectual point.

Very much in the tradition of Critical Theory, Christopher Lasch is a contemporary writer concerned with the changes in the family. *Haven in a Heartless World* chronicles the family's eclipse. He takes for his larger theme the invasion of the personal sphere of the individual by agencies of social control and the obliteration of a traditional private/ public dichotomy: advanced industrial society, specifically capitalism, has legitimated the invasion of private life by including the regulation of familial and sexual spheres in its orbit. Specialists and experts have brought rationality and, in its wake, order and control to matters previously considered private and spontaneous: through the "socialization of production" and the "socialization of reproduction", agencies of the society have increased their control over areas once left to the private domain.[38]

Women are stripped of their childrearing responsibilities; the ideology of consumerism[39] encourages their emancipation and liberation while double standards respecting jobs, morality, and political power still apply. Relations between the sexes have become exacerbated, for while, on the one hand, men and women are freed by the contraceptive revolution to be more open, intimate and avowedly sexual with one another, on the other hand, one sees this intimacy as "an illusion"[40] and the divorce statistics as well as a growing number of incidences of familial psychological problems bear similar witness. Womanhood and sexuality are stripped of their patina of awesomeness and reverence: this is what is meant by their demystification or exposure to the hard facts of life. The underside of this is the demise of emotion, feeling, and commitment. Since work has been degraded and communal life destroyed, sexual relations come to matter more. There is more riding on a successful interpersonal relationship and more likelihood given the demands of feminism — legitimate and moral though they may be — that it will fail. Again, one finds the paradox of honesty and openness and the data on sexual disappointment, sexual separatism, narcissism, the flight to drugs and suicide: "escape masquerades as liberation, regression as progress."[41]

Childrearing is given over to experts and the definition of the family to the knowledge purveyors within sociology: the cost to the individual is his or her loss of self-help and self-direction. It is not that the family, in the past, was rigidly distinct from the public world but that in some sense, it was a haven from the rigors of the modern, abstract, impersonal society. By the turn of the century, the passionate and emotional aspects of life — sexual relations, marriage, childbearing, childraising — became subject to the scientization already evident in the economic and political domain. This "rationalization of emotional life,"[42] intended to improve one's mental health, appropriated roles previously left to the individual. Science and technological rationality, in holding onto the belief that by applying their methods they would alleviate the plight of individuals, shared with the cultural relativists a disdain for what they read to be Freud's ideas on biological determinism and the primacy of libidinal drives. In so doing, they had to dethrone Freudian theory as the key to the problem of the family and cleanse or expurgate his theory of instincts.

The family, for Lasch, is the place where a strong sense of self — not selfishness and not individualism but an autonomy capable of handling relationships with others — will be formed. The consequence of allying feminism with the culture end of the nature/nurture dichotomy is to undermine the Freudian tension between culture and instincts and, as a consequence, undermine Freud's seeing the family as the psychological mediator between the two, the place or space where children acquire and internalize culture. In holding onto the family not only as an agent of social mediation but also as an essential human structure, Lasch must take issue with those in the Women's Movement who want either to democratize the relations of parents to their children or obliterate the sexual bond that ties members of the family to each other.

Where Lasch speaks of the politicization of the family, in the sense that its chores are now handled by a series of state agencies be they schools or social welfare offices, Marcuse offers a more general explanation of the loss of self as a consequence of modernity. In *Eros and Civilization,* he argues that psychological categories become political categories, as individuals come to want and desire what the society wants and needs.[43] Privacy, which the psyche needs to keep itself from a situation of total domination, is diminished in contemporary society. Since the individual can no longer forge his or her own personality, the person becomes enmeshed in a public vise. The "introjection" of social needs is a consequence of the private sphere's merging with public demands. A diminution of an opposing, inner self leaves the individual unprotected, without any consciousness of negation.

Lasch critiques the feminist movement in arguing that it is misdirected in its attack on the family. He understands the reasons why, in the 1960s, the family was seen as a place where women were oppressed, for the attack on the family was but a single salvo in the attack on the privatism, individualism and anti-communalism of the United States that the cultural revolution hoped to undermine. It would be incorrect to say that Lasch wishes to dispute the facts of female subordination and domination, nor does he intend a glorification of the nuclear family which asked too much of women. Yet he sees in the Movement a narcissistic concern with the self and an emphasis on consumerism and improving the lot of women that ignores the larger issues of the needs of children and the meaning and meaningfulness of work in advanced industrial society.[44]

One can situate Lasch's work both with respect to the debates on the crises in the family and the reassessment of Freud that had been in process for a good part of the century. While there has been a strand of feminism that has argued that Freudian categories could be used to show how women develop differently from men,[45] there have also been attacks on Freud for his alleged sexism: his views on the determining qualities of biology; his writing about the neuroses and psychoses of men, even where the data for his theories has come from women patients; and his apparent rejection of cultural factors as having an equivalency with biological factors.[46] The latter position, when it has not spelled the wholesale rejection of the Freudian paradigm, has joined forces with a revisionism that was influenced by theories of cultural relativism as these came out of twentieth century anthropology and with a political revisionism that sought to make Freud more palatable to a democratic society and of greater use value to social reformers.[47]

Feminist critics of Lasch and, to a lesser degree, of the Frankfurt School, do not take issue with the portrayal of the family as a social institution in crisis, but they find fault with what they regard as the defense of traditional patriarchy for the role that it has played in the development of one's character and sense of self. Finding Lasch's support of patriarchal authority one-sided, and his model a male model that has in mind only the relationship of father to son, the argument is made that: "For Lasch, the collapse of traditional patriarchy is an unmitigated disaster. As women we do not share his nostalgia for patriarchy's heyday nor his sorrow with its passing."[48] His views, the argument continues, are akin to those of the Frankfurt School in that like the latter he emphasizes character development as a consequence of rebellion against the male parent, and, in this, his psychoanalytic critique supports the exclusivity of a male form of relationship. Were he to explore, as feminists are doing, the nature not only of mother-daughter relationships but also the import of pre-Oedipal relationships, he might see the way in which individuation and autonomy can develop shorn of the repression integral to the traditional Freudian schemata: "The struggle with the father is not the only source of values within the family. Cultures of resistance centered around women sustain values, relationships, and communities which can be a basis for rebellion."[49]

It is to these feminist writings on motherhood that I now turn.

* 6 *

Motherhood as a Social Institution

The ways in which one approaches a social text are manifold. In choosing to use a sociological lens to focus on sexual arrangements and the fate of humanity, one is attributing value to a certain method of analysis that affords one insight even if at the price of not being judgmental. A sociological reading concerns itself with text as social artifact, with argumentation as the legitimation and delegitimation of certain historical ideas. As opposed to or distinct from a literary or psychological reading, a sociological reading seeks to understand how the text is part of its culture, both with respect to its general social criticisms and its particular feminist perspective.

This etiology of ideas asks questions about the historical specificity of social texts. It also analyzes the role of legitimating or critiquing ideas that these texts play. To maintain the social order, Berger and Luckmann argue, there must be social structures functioning to do so:

> It is correct to say that theories are concocted in order to legitimate already existing social institutions. But it also happens that social institutions are changed in order to bring them back into conformity with already existing theories, that is to make them more "legitimate." The experts in legitimation may operate as theoretical justifiers of the *status quo*; they may also appear as revolutionary ideologists.[1]

Knowledge, and text as knowledge, is, then, a form of legitimating device.

It is with this framework that the sociologist reads the feminist texts on motherhood; deconstructing them, situating them historically, placing them within a social context that uses particular colored lenses. Mannheim would have one unpack and historicize the texts, a task to which we now turn.

Dorothy Dinnerstein's *The Mermaid and the Minotaur* was begun in the 1960s, at a time when the Civil Rights Movement had brought intellectual discourse about the nature of equality to center stage and when the Anti-War (or Anti-Vietnam) Movement had forced a reconsideration of a wide range of topics, from the nature of imperialism to the possibilities of limited warfare in a nuclear age. While part of the Women's Movement came out of these struggles, all of the ensuing discussions of sexual liberation, which participants in the Movement engaged in, need to be understood against the background of issues of political re-direction and political legitimacy generated by the New Left in their critique of authority.

The intellectual background in which Dinnerstein writes is the sixties' questioning of authority and the relationship of self to society. Yet at another level, *The Mermaid and the Minotaur* contributes to the debates and dialogues which have historically colored the discussion of women; that is, what factors of biology and which of environment contribute to the shaping of the "feminine character," to the philosophic disputes over essentialism. Once one accepts certain Freudian principles, as Dinnerstein does, one is giving credence to the argument that the body has an effect on how one behaves. Even if one does not maintain the "anatomy is destiny" position, one is certainly not at the opposite extreme of saying that the body is only what it is constructed to mean. In reading Freud (as other neo-Freudians do) as allowing for the integration of biological and sociological concerns, Dinnerstein restrains certain assumptions of Freudian psychology while emphasizing (more than Freud did but very much in the spirit of contemporary sociology) the cultural factors that condition, effect, and modify behavior, getting persons to behave one way and precluding their behaving another. Human developmental stages are, in effect, played out in varying cultural ways; the unconscious, infantile sexuality, the Oedipus Complex, and the Life and Death instincts are givens that preclude the perception of persons as *tabula rasa,* a view central to behaviorism and liberalism, but which need not lead to a determinism that precludes the idea of human action.

Dinnerstein's perception of motherhood is colored by this recognition of the body's effect on behavior as well as on the belief that the specifics of behavior change as a consequence of new political and technological requirements. The question of why women mother is to be answered psychologically, but the answer need not be static or without concern for the changing fortunes of women. There is here that affinity with de Beauvoir's thesis, indebed to Marx, that there is a dialectical relationship between what women make of themselves and the specific circumstances in which this project takes place. In this sense, what it means to be a woman, or gendered, is neither fixed nor indeterminably variable, but that interaction between how one defines oneself and the historical circumstances which encase the act of selfhood. The rooting of a "feminine character" in time and place allows us to see it as political, as subject to the social arrangements of the particular society.[2]

Friedan's *The Feminine Mystique* argued that women had been socialized into accepting a role as a domesticated housewife whose place was away from public and exclusively into private matters, concerns of the heart, hearth, and home. The Women's Movement, in unearthing different treatment accorded men and women in American society, had set out to correct the sex bias which affected the ways in which persons were socialized and the ways in which women, in particular, were held in esteem.[3] Correcting bias was piece-meal, having as its design the bringing of certain aspects of women's treatment into line with that of comparably situated men. There still remained the question of why these differences existed at all and whether they reflected differences between men and women that should or should not be eradicated.

Dinnerstein sets out to look at the reasons why women are regarded as not only different from but also inferior to men. She seeks her answers in psychology; more precisely, in a psychoanalytic theory which takes its roots in Freud and which is not only descriptive of the condition of women but also explanatory in terms of certain moral ideals of equal treatment for persons irrespective of gender. Her main purpose is to use Freudian categories to study the love/hate relationship men and women have towards each other and to demonstrate not only how deep-seated these feelings are but also what consequences follow from individuals not confronting and changing practices which cause and legitimate these feelings. Underlying the pessimism, that is, beneath the recognition of how deep-seated feelings of ambivalence towards women are, is the optimism of a person who allows for the Enlightenment project — the use of reason — here understood as rational reflection, to free persons from the shackles imposed by their own passions.

In looking at Dinnerstein's views on women, and most especially on motherhood, one wishes to see how these views are affected by the climate of the times — how motherhood, as a constellation of ideas, is, in Mannheimian terms, an ideology and, if one is to be fair, how its replacement with parenthood, or any other structured set of childcare arrangements, is a similarly constructed set of beliefs explicable in historical terms. As women returned to the work-force, their role as mothers underwent re-examination, that is, what was taken to be a socially approved and socially set role that reflected what "nature" had "intended" women to perform was seen as being one subject to historical change and redirection. This reassessment of the role of women as mothers has been a continuous one in women's history, but it makes its sharpest impression during the years of the new wave of the Women's Movement, the post-1960s period.

Questions of motherhood raise questions of intent: are women intended to be mothers? Are women intended to be anything in particular? Does physical anatomy intend a particular result? Is biology destiny after all? Does biology restrict what one can and cannot do? Is the mothering of children by women one such restriction? Distinctions can also be made between mothering and motherhood, one an act of caring for young ones and one the institutionalization of prescribed rules and regulations by which this caring is to be undertaken. Further distinctions can be made between childbearing and childrearing, and whether biological sex is or ought to be a factor in one or both of these roles.

Much of human thought, both written and elaborately debated in dialogic discourse, concerns the relationship between the individual and his or her society. One may be positing an erroneous *dichotomy* if one thinks of two independent spheres, that of the individual, on the one hand, and that of the society, on the other. Theorists have elaborated upon the epistemological consequences of this dualism in Western philosophy, calling attention to the dangers of an abstract individualism, one that does not situate the person within a concrete social place, and calling for replacing the dichotomy or dialism with a "dialectical conception of the relation between individual and society"[4] which is more in accord with how persons experience the world, that is, as one which shapes and structures their individuality. Unless one wants to deny the notion of a self, a human being who exists in space and in time and who is conscious of having an identity particular to himself or herself, an " 'I' — the most elementary affirmation of identity"[5] — there remains a tension between persons and the social surroundings in which they find themselves. Even unuttered musings deal with how one can be an individual, one's own person, and live within a social milieu that not only makes demands upon one but also indicates, usually in no uncertain terms just what being one's own self ought to entail. This struggle between the individual and the society is consonant with a Western intellectual heritage and it takes on a particular set of garments in contemporary society.

One of the major contributions of American social theory to the contemporary intellectual climate of which Dinnerstein is a part is the idea of the social genesis of the self: the turning of Marx into conventional wisdom. One could make the case that an understanding of the social and historical roots out of which sociology as a discipline arises — the Enlightenment period of Western society — allows one to see why, in contrast to the individualism that colors political thought as it comes out of that initial age of capitalism, social theory rejects the idea of individuals preceding a social order. Meadian sociology, as the first important contribution in the American context, developed this Marxist notion that the self was to be considered as essentially social, growing out of the specifics of social experience.[6] One of the assumptions made by social constructionism, or by those branches of phenomenology which, like symbolic interactionism, credit social interaction as the means through which reality is constructed, and which assumptions are shared by many of the writers who have come to write on feminism in the period with which this study is concerned, is that everyday life appears to be ordered, that prior even to one's consciousness of it, it is ordered by institutions, by habits, by expectations which inform traditional ways of behaving and which take on, over time, the appearance of being natural even if they are ways of doing things which are person constructed.[7]

Everyday life is subject to a continuum of typification, of coming to know both intimates and strangers by the typical roles they come to play: "Social structure is the sum total of these typifications and of the recurrent patterns of interaction established by means of them."[8] Social order is a human product, arising out of biological necessity: "institutionalization occurs whenever there is a reciprocal typification of habitualized actions by types of actors."[9]

Following this, one would argue that the ideas that are held to be feminine become the feminine: the role shapes the individual's behavior, fitting personality to role demands the way Procrustes was fitted to his bed. When it is said that there is a social construction of reality, it is assumed that there are psychological mechanisms for internalizing that reality, mechanisms that can be understood in terms of role theory and generalized and significant others.

If the sociality of the self is a significant influence in social theory, which finds certain parallels in behaviorism with its emphasis on the role of environmental factors in shaping human action, the ideas of Freud, with their emphasis on male and female patterns of living in and relating to social conditions, has also had an impact on the ways in which writers handle questions of sexual roles and relationships. Within the context of an emerging feminist movement, Freudianism seems to many a system of ideas that is at best in need of reworking and at worst a candidate for the trash heap of history given, if not the theory's biases, what is taken to be Freud's own overt sexism and legitimation of male domination of women. Whatever their assessment of his work, feminist writers certainly felt the need to respond to the Freudian notion that "anatomy is destiny"; and in their responses one comes to see the ways in which their writings were shaped and given direction by Freudian canonicals.

Freud contributed to social theory by extending his analyses of the individual to groups and by interpreting his findings in ways that emphasized the import of cultural factors and the ways in which societies mold the specifics of personality. One has in mind most especially, *Totem and Taboo*[10] and *Civilization and Its Discontents*,[11] with their themes of Oedipal conflict, incest, totems and gods replacing all-powerful but deposed fathers, and the emergence of authority figures and aggression and the need to sacrifice and renounce those demands and wishes which contribute to social disorder. Freud offers a social theory where guilt and unhappiness, not doing what one may wish, are part of all social life, and it is in the debates with Freud on this point that one finds some of the most important writings in contemporary social theory.

The Mermaid and the Minotaur is an excellent starting point for an examination of contemporary ideas on motherhood and on the sexual relationships that accompany the kind of childrearing arrangements that proceed from that social institution. Dinnerstein's intent is not only to raise questions about the social ways in which children are reared and the consequences of these arrangements for both men and women but also to suggest that these arrangements produce or contribute to a set of consequences which affect how the human planet is administered. For, she argues, these patterns of rule have brought humanity to the point of nuclear annihilation and, yet, it is the precise nature of these rules being social and subject to change that can allow one to move out of this historical morass.

Dinnerstein's book is purposely interdisciplinary and, while she herself is a psychologist — trained in Gestalt psychology, involved in research on perception and cognition, and holding an academic appointment — she does not offer the work as a scientific treatise but as a form of social criticism, an argument distilled from her readings in a wide variety of sources which coalesce into an argument on the gender predicament created by an historical occurrence which still predominates for most persons today, the rearing of children by women. In addition to a certain kind of psychology which grows out of her studies with Max Wertheimer, Wolfgang Kohler and Solomon Asch, and which sets her apart from the more dominant behavioral tradition that takes its roots in the work of B.F. Skinner, Dinnerstein wants to hold onto certain aspects of Freudianism, some of which is filtered through her reading of Melanie Klein, without embracing a conservative, tradition-bound Victorianism which she sees Freud as manifesting. Nonetheless, Freud leaves an indelible mark on human thought: it is the mark that exposes the importance of infancy and childhood for one's later social and sexual development, the role that sex plays in one's life, including the life of the infant and very young child, and the import of one's male and female parents for character development. This revolutionary departure in viewing individual development is interpreted conservatively, Dinnerstein argues, as a human given that is not subject to change and redevelopment but that is "there" to be responded to and accepted. Freud requires that one reflect on whether the psychic structures are biologically grounded or biologically influenced, and Dinnerstein, in order to avoid the conservative implications that accompany any position of biological determinism, will have to argue for social structures affecting the dialectical relationship between the biologic and the psychologic.

Her argument, incisive and biting, is that the main human presence for the young child is the female, but this unarguably historical given can be read and assessed in a variety of ways. Moreover, these traditional sexual arrangements can be altered by humans themselves who can create a new set of arrangements, what might be called the replacing of mothering with parenting and the obliteration of motherhood and its replacement by parenthood as a social institution. Implicit in her argument is that historically this replacement is on its way. Technology affects childcare arrangements in the following ways: first, women's nurturing relationship to children is altered (by food formulas, for example) such that one could bring up children, if one opted to have them (itself a technological possibility), in a healthy, to wit, masculine and feminine way of parenting; and, second, adults are now able to participate in public and private realms in a new way, in that they are freed from the tasks of the private realm to work in the public realm, although considerations of class, race, and gender will affect the quality and quantity of that participation.

What Dinnerstein wants is that one see the import for the kinds of persons one wishes to create that this ending of female domination of childrearing will offer: men will be able to accept women on more equitable terms and women will be able to bring their nurturing capacity into the public realm.

I will explicate, in some further detail, the contents of Dinnerstein's book, delineate the history of some of its themes, unpack the embedded assumptions, and ask to whom her argument might appeal and for what reasons.

Dinnerstein asks that we recognize that the centrality of human sexual arrangements or the division of human sex roles rest in the fact that women are the primary caretakers of children. This arrangement has certain consequences, most especially of a psychological dependency type, that is, this female monopoly of early child-care means a very early dependency on and tie to women by both boys and girls, each of whom will resolve to go beyond this tie in different ways. These arrangements need to be changed. But before this task can be undertaken, one has to see how the society continues these arrangements and how they are legitimated by psychic factors, which, in dialectical fashion, grow out of them and are so deep-seated—they are "buried foundations"[12]—that one assumes, even if with fear and trepidation, that they must be continued and one is cautious about any efforts to change or restructure them.

These forms have a tenacity that must be challenged. It is not the bonds of primary groups that all humans need which is at issue, but the specific forms of bonding which women-raised children have. It is a specific or exclusive kind of tie that she wants to critique, the mother-child bond especially as it is manifested in the pre-Oedipal stage; the attachment of persons for others is not to be repressed but, on the contrary, is, owing to its beneficence, to become the model for other human relationships. It is the dualistic arrangements of mother as private nurturer and father as public authority that she wishes to make into a dialectical relationship.

One can recognize certain continuities and differences with the world of animals; hence, there is a literary fascination with mermaids and minotaurs, creatures who are less than fully human because of their insatiable need to lure and destroy or wreck havoc on the opposite sex:

> The treacherous mermaid, seductive and impenetrable female representative of the dark and magic underwater world from which our life comes in and in which we cannot live lures voyagers to their doom. The fearsome minotaur, gigantic and eternally infantile offspring of a mother's unnatural lust, male representative of mindless, greedy power, insatiably devours human flesh.[13]

Dinnerstein wants to suggest ways in which persons can live with ideas of mermaids and minotaurs without equating these mythic creatures with the flesh-and-blood persons one lives with in the empirically constituted, or real, world; in short, she wants persons to come to terms with their dreams and fears, the underside of their goodness, and move on to arrangements which keep these in their place.

Until now, one has not been able to change this relationship between women and their offspring. The species being what it is, children remain dependent upon adults far longer in the human than in other animal species. Now, however, advances in technology enable one to alter these patterns of sexual relationships and relatedness; thus, persons have the freedom to change the present arrangements and institute relationships that are not suffused with layers of hostility. Technology has made caretaking options available that were, at best, utopian possibilities at other historical moments. Before such changes can be undertaken, however, it must be made clear that while they are necessary, they will not be easy to make. The feelings of men and women toward each other are deep-seated, rooted in the sexuality of early infancy that consists not only of erotic feelings but also of conscious and unconscious awareness of those passions. New gender relationships, which will alter the prevailing symbiotic relationships between men and women, can evolve out of species awareness just as readily. Or, if one is pessimistic, they can evolve with as much difficulty as can other forms of human awareness — awareness of the self's mind, of the self's body, of the self's relationships with other persons. All such projects towards liberation from unawareness to liberation for a more perfect realization of the self are ways of countering "human malaise";[14] but all are possible given the species ability to make of itself what it will.

Dinnerstein accepts certain Freudian notions about the nature of human nature: the fact that there is such a thing; that it involves a penchant for and is an inner struggle between certain contrasting forces of life and death, Eros and Thanatos; and that it allows for or burdens the individual with the power or ability to direct the course that his or her life may take. In many ways, her reading of Freud is spiritually akin to that of

Bruno Bettelheim who, in seeking to reclaim Freud from the hands of narrow-minded scientific technicians and replenish his theory with fresh meaning, speaks of Freud's interest in man's "soul,"[15] of his struggles to explain that which humans have in common with one another, and how persons can, through reason and culture, tame the dark underside of their nature. Dinnerstein adds the kind of historical dimension to Freud that Marcuse so brilliantly demonstrates in *Eros and Civilization.* She is influenced by both Neo-Freudians and Freudian Revisionists (and especially by Norman O. Brown), who attempt to situate Freudian insights into the human condition within the contours of specific economic systems in specific stages of technological development. She speaks of the biological factors which equip women to bear and nurture children, who, owing to their evolutionary legacy, require care and attention for an extended early period of their lives. What persons have in common is this extended infancy; this period affects all later ideas which persons come to hold, although this period is culturally variable. The "handicaps to . . . mobility"[16] are, she argues, affected by developments in technology which could alter the caretaking roles played by women and allow the latter more involvement in the public sphere now dominated by men. Why, Dinnerstein asks, has this not then occurred? Could one not benefit, she continues, from de Beauvoir's preparedness to think in terms of the One and the Other and ask what it is in male-female relationships that preclude one's thinking of them in terms of this interacting dyad?

In detailing the infant-parent tie, the infant's dependency on the adult, which is usually female, Dinnerstein emphasizes the significance of the role that women are called upon to play in the lives of children of both sexes, acting as the source of all forms of early social relationships, both those that are pleasurable as well as those that are painful. Biological and emotional needs, of a kind of intensity that will surface again only with the onset of puberty, are met by the female care-taker: "The child's bodily tie to the mother . . . is the vehicle through which the most fundamental feelings of a highly complex creature are formed and expressed. . . . This tie is the prototype of the tie to life,"[17] for it captures joy and security, dismay, disappointment and fears of all kinds of loss.

This early tie sets the cadence and the rhythms of the sexual double standards, adult infantilism, and both male and female antagonisms toward women. The child wants to possess the mother to himself or herself, and much of the frenetic movement of adult life, Dinnerstein argues, will be spent in repressing the remembrance of an earlier, erotic relationship with the mother while at the same time acting to realize those first early times when the child needed the mother were she or he to survive at all. The boy's need for mother becomes his need for and, hence, his possessiveness of all women, never wanting to share female loves with others; the girl, seeing herself as a mother-figure, comes to recognize how much others need her and she is less troubled by sharing loved ones with others. Such, Dinnerstein argues, is the psychological foundation of a double-standard of sex that is enhanced by factors of male strength, male scarcity and the asymmetry of biological parentage which allows women to know who their children are in a way not granted to men.

The girl, being of the same sex as the mother, has a greater burden than does the boy of transferring sexual allegiance away from the mother and to the father, for as she has to learn to transfer her homo-erotic love — a form of love on which there are social bans — from the mother, she feels unfaithful in this transference in a way that the boy does not. The girl's Oedipal jealousy is colored by this homo-erotic bond, and she becomes embroiled in battles with the mother that the boy does not. The boy, able to bond sexually with the father, can, like him, move to possess the world since he can no longer possess the mother; the girl, were she to try to possess this public domain, would find it blocked to her in ways that are not the case for boys.

> Early rage at the first parent. . . is typically used by the "masculine" boy during the Oedipal period to *consolidate* his tie with his own sex by establishing a principled independence, a more or less derogatory distance, from women. And it is typically used by the "feminine" girl in this same period to *loosen* her tie with her own sex by establishing a worshipful, dependent stance toward men.[18]

Heterosexual relations in adult life are played out differently by men and women, women becoming the mothers they once had to give up and men becoming secure and dependent upon the mothers they, too, once had to give up. Women are also more prepared to mute, or play down, their sexual wants so as to keep from remembering what giving up of mother for father seemed to them to be: an act of betrayal of one like oneself.

The bond between women and children, so strong and so exclusive, allows all of those children who, one day, grow up to act as if mermaids and minotaurs really did exist, Dinnerstein argues. The bonds between mothers and infants are too strong and those between fathers and infants too fragile; one makes too much of one and too little of the other.[19]

Out of the childhood experiences and the particularities of children's relationships to women, people come to see women as mother and other as woman and each as a kind of quasi-person, a creature imbued with qualities beyond human-ness. Men, on the other hand, are seen as real persons, authoritatively operating in the public domain. Both men and women share an ambiguous set of feelings towards women, for both have been in an early, intense relationship with that first woman who raised them:

> our ambivalence toward the parent who is the first representative of nature consists not only of unstable, conflicting feelings of envy and gratitude, rapacity and compunction. It consists also of unstable, conflicting percep-

tions of her sentinence [of her having] an autonomous awareness corresponding to our own.[20]

Dinnerstein, building upon the analyses of Marcuse and Brown, goes on to argue that the child's pain at having to alter his or her relationship to this first female presence grows into the adult's pain of having a conscious awareness of his or her limited mortality and of the fragility of the flesh in the face of worldly pressures.

Learning of the body, of its joys and of its limits, in the presence of that first woman, Dinnerstein continues, lends itself to both a conscious and unconscious association of bodily fragilities as somehow being associated with women. By altering gender relationships, most specifically, by changing the female monopoly over early childcare and allowing for equal participation in such childcare by both men and women, one can cut that link between women and mortality, women and the flesh, women and bodily restraints and bodily pleasures. If men and women were both allowed to be the primary caretakers, they would both have a different relationship with nature and they would be less prepared to assault and "murder . . . nature".[21] There is, then, a chance that persons could handle the tension of human existence better than if these are inextricably linked to one sex and one sex only. Only when one can recognize that all persons are both part of and distinct from nature will one be able to treat all persons equitably, and this will come about when that "first" is both mother and father, she who mothers and he who fathers:

> When the child, once born, is as much the responsibility of man as of women, the early vicissitudes of the flesh — our handling of which lays the basis for our later handling of mortality — will bear no special relation to gender. Both sides of the double fact that we are born mortal and born of women will then change their meaning.[22]

In other words, if parented, that is, if the early human presence were both male and female, the child could less readily imbue a particular gender with the problem it is having of both wanting and fearing independence from the caretaker. The child could learn to live with ambivalence and ambiguities much more readily if there were not those simple dichotomies which equate gender and strength. The child would come to recognize the importance of the male for his or her being like he or she is; and "When males are as directly involved as females in the intensely carnal lives of infants and children, the reality of the male body as a source of new creatures is bound to become substantial for us at an earlier age than it does now, and to remain emotionally more salient forever after."[23]

Dinnerstein writes: *"the most urgent present reason for outgrowing our traditional uses of gender is that they have helped us postpone. . . steps. . . toward adult acceptance of the responsibilities intrinsic to humanness: responsibility to and for each other, and joint self-responsibility, as a species, for our position in nature."*[24]

In fearing the will of women and in fearing becoming infants again, in the ambiguity one has towards she who was the first person to socialize the child and, thus, to make for its entry into and access to the world of other persons and social objects, persons are predisposed towards handing all power over to men, to those who did not have such a hold over them in those early, crucial days of infancy. Surely, Dinnerstein continues, persons come to resent paternal authority in particular and male authority in general, but one comes to resent it in a different, less infantile way. One comes to reject it when one is better suited to handle it and its rejection, when one is older, wiser, and able to view the world without the magic that the eyes of children bring to the viewing process and at a psychic moment that does not imbue it with the trauma associated with the separation from and rejection of that early female presence. Paternal power is seen as *"a sanctuary from maternal authority"* operating in the realm of pure and enlightened reason and not the "mysterious . . . omniscience . . . of the nursery goddess."[25]

Male domination of the public realm, as well as double standards in respect to both socialization and sexual expectations and demands, can be explained, Dinnerstein argues, by this monopoly on child-care by women. Certainly, this is the "emotional" explanation for the phenomenon of male power, that is, there are psychological reasons why the ways in which children are raised by women encourages and legitimates men moving into positions of power at a later moment in a person's life:

> woman's exlusion from history is based on something more than sheer force. It is not a simple matter of some massive coup d'etat. It is woven into the pattern of complementarity between male and female personality that emerges from female-dominated early childhood. An exclusion like this is necessarily *buttressed* by societal coercion. It could not be maintained without external force since it violates profound impuses in both sexes. But force alone could not maintain it if it were not at the same time supported from within by a powerful web of emotional factors.[26]

Both in the ways in which men relate to women and in the public performance of their duties, men and women act in accord with needs and desires which were set at a much earlier moment in their lives. The patterns of male domination-female subordination place a heavy burden on men and women, taxing one set of capacities — execution of jobs in the case of men and caretaking skills in the case of women — and under-utilizing others — public performance in the case of women and nurturant capacities in the case of men. It constricts and deforms, Dinnerstein argues, rather than contributing towards the self-actualization of the total person. It allows women to escape, or be immune, from the difficulty of making decisions necessitated by power and it burdens men with this responsibility; at the same time, it deprives men of another, different voice to assist them in their deliberations and shuts a feminine perspective and presence out that may offer some new and vital way of looking at and handling a set of problems. Its consequences are, thus, pathological, for the division of sensibilities that ensues allows men and only men to act on behalf of all of the species in its need to effect the dilemmas imposed by its awareness of the limitations to what its bodies can and cannot do, that is, by the limitations imposed by mortality. Insofar as women, in their capacity of taking care of children, are the infants' first encounter with reality and the ones who shatter their "illusion of omnipotence,"[27] they become "scapegoats" for the anger and resentment that all humans feel towards being human—"*human resentment of the human condition,*"[28] as she puts it.

By keeping women outside of the realm of public affairs, men enable both women and themselves to vent their anger on the sorry condition of humankind. Women can feel divorced from a set of affairs in which they played no part, and men can use the knowledge that things might have been different had women been involved as a salve for the wounds inflicted by their mess-up. Dinnerstein writes:

> Her outsider position has enabled us all to keep the vital insight she embodies sealed off from the historic realm. . . . It has let him live vicariously with this insight, which some part of him wants again and again expressed. And it has let her live vicariously with those deeds, which some part of her wants again and again done.[29]

Keeping women out of history, that is, out of the public realm, caters to "the ambivalence which both sexes feel toward the self-creative enterprise that human history is." Her exclusion is the "safety-valve" of keeping alive a "vital vision of sanity."[30]

Dinnerstein, then, is actually a feminist neo-Freudian, more akin to Marcuse than to Fromm, and like both of them and Brown, concerned with examining the relationship between sexual identity and social factors. While this neo-Freudian perspective is the least developed part of her work—and the reason is her omission of any significant discussion of Marxism which, for those she finds herself in agreement with, is a lynchpin in their presentations—she does try to historicize Freud by asking whether certain kinds of societies encourage or inculcate certain sexual styles. Like the neo-Freudians and, if one categorizes Fromm accurately, the Freudian Revisionists, Dinnerstein assesses the effects of social structure on personality. Like Marcuse and Brown, but in departure from Fromm, she wants to hold onto the Freudian categories that see the neurotic underside of the human personality as being a given and social categories as ways of handling these neuroses in ways that are socially productive. As Jaggar puts it, she views "the acquisition of gendered character types as the result of specific social practices, particularly procreative practices, that are not determined by biology and that in principle, therefore, are alterable."[31] Marx can be used, as he is by the

Frankfurt School, to take the seeming inevitability out of Freud without sanitizing the latter as Marcuse accuses certain Freudian Revisionists — Fromm most directly — as doing.[32] Put differently, Dinnerstein wants to ask what price repression for what kind of civilization — the very question asked by Marcuse and Brown in their dialogue with *Civilization and Its Discontents*.

Dinnerstein does not go the route of those social constructionists who assume that all sexual differences are socially constructed. In this sense, her thesis is a rejection of the behaviorism that underlies socialization theories, with their emphases on learning to play roles which are deemed socially appropriate. It is not that one does not "learn," but in grounding her arguments in identification and bonding literature that comes out of a Gestalt and a Freudian tradition — and it is not always the case that these two traditions find themselves saying the same thing — she places learned behavior on certain biological and psychological foundations which for better or worse, make it extraordinarily difficult to change the ways in which people behave.

Dinnerstein is certainly not suggesting that the moral idea is an androgynous person who is rid of the neuroses which all persons have, by virtue of being human, and who are engaged in a struggle against civilization. There is no hermaphroditic solution here. Nor is hers a rejection of sex and sexuality — quite the opposite. Dinnerstein wants to hold onto certain trans-historical sexual categories or sexual properties, and while she sees certain sex roles as being restrictive and psychologically damaging to all concerned, she does not go the route of arguing that one can become just about anything one wants to become. In her building on de Beauvoir's work, she not only accepts the idea of humanity but also that of womanhood, a category of being-in-the-world that is distinctive and in sharp relief from its dialectical Other but which like that Other starts with a *body* and is *embodied*. She shares a perspective with contemporary French feminism — Julia Kristeva, Luce Iragary, Helen Cixous, Monique Wittig[33] — on the importance of the body in both its erotic dimension and engendered aspects. Because of her indebtedness to Freud, she, like them, is trying to ground sexuality in ideas of the body.

The sociologist finds in Dinnerstein a concern shared by others that the observer of persons must look for the most basic conscious and unconscious ways in which gender is seen in a particular culture. He or she must start with the infant-adult tie as it is experienced in its immediacy by the person involved. Dinnerstein takes the child's perspective, seeing, as a phenomenologist might, the world of men and women as the child sees it, as the child gives it meaning: on one level, *Mermaid* is a phenomenological accounting of primary relationships. One might, in fact, argue that *Mermaid* is not so much a feminist challenge to male perception but a child's challenge to adult perception. In starting here,

Dinnerstein allows her reader to understand how it has come about that women are held in positions of subordination.

Sometimes Dinnerstein writes as if women, having certain properties, say a nurturing capacity, could enrich men's lives which lack these properties by engaging in some form of activist dialogue with them. At other times, she writes as if each sex has certain virtues particular to it and that the female virtues, of nurturance and caring, are the ones that ought to be built upon and that women, therefore, ought to be in the forefront of efforts for meaningful social change. She has been regarded as having contributed towards "feminist discourse," defined as a way of speaking on and of women which, in the case of some commentators, builds on woman's primary role as "caretakers, nurturers, and providers for the needs of others."[34] These are considered to be roles played at some point in their lives by most women and relatively few men. The embedded assumptions, when one speaks of "feminist discourse," are women's sameness, their shared status, arising either out of their being essentially like all other women or their being socially defined as being like all other women. Even allowing for factors of class, race, and sex, women are treated alike in certain significant ways by institutionalized practices, alike enough to be catalogued or characterized as being a distinct entity. Much of the literature on prostitution, as well as on rape and pornography, builds upon this shared sense of being women, such that prostitutes are more like other women than either of them are like men, and all women are the victims of pornography and rape.[35]

Out of these likenesses or shared identities come a morality and a politics particular to women. Just as infants connect with their mothers, or those who mother them, so women identify themselves in terms of this connectedness, for they remain like that person with whom they identified in early life in ways that men, for obvious sexual reasons and for the psychological or emotional reasons that follow from those sexual reasons, do not. The work of Carol Gilligan,[36] a psychologist out of another tradition, is the most explicit on this point when she links differences to moralities. Dinnerstein is often seen to explain what Gilligan describes: women thinking differently from men; women being more concerned with the bonds of emotion than are men; and women more concerned with the feelings of concrete others, with having solidarity with others, than they are with certain abstractions no matter how noble these abstractions may seem to be.

Even if one does not want to view Dinnerstein as distinguishing between the sexes on the basis of forms of moral reasoning — and I do not read her as saying exactly what Gilligan says — one can find in her writings the argument that women will bring to the public realm certain views which can benefit that realm and that these views come out of their being women and resolving their relationship with that early female presence in a feminine rather than a masculine way. She writes: "What women have tended to develop, because they have been expected to become nurturers of children and because they have identified from the outset, as females, with the female person(s) who nurture them, is what Ruddick calls 'maternal thinking'. "[37]

In this respect, her argument is very much akin to that made by Marcuse when, in speaking of the possibilities for a new social and political reality, he speaks of an aesthetic dimension to its material base, that is, the joining of the necessary and the beautiful, tasteful and artful. Marcuse sees in Marx's analysis an aesthetic dimension that is peaceful, disinclined towards domination, not restricted simply to "High Culture" or "The Arts," and creative without necessarily being productve in the materialist or economic sense of that term. It is in this sense that a new reality would negate masculine values and proffer feminine ones. It is not a society of matriarchs or one which would glorify motherhood: "At stake is rather the ascent of Eros over aggression, in men *and* women; and this means, in a male-dominated civilization, the 'femalization' of the male."[38]

The decline of patriarchal society, which would accompany the changed relations found in advanced industrial societies, entails both the reduction, loss, or possibly obliteration of the family's role in socializing its young. But this loss makes it possible for women to be freed from the subjugation of their husbands or other males and free to enter into more equitable economic and political relationships with men. It is not that advanced industrial society automatically becomes an improved society. *One-Dimensional Man* is Marcuse's critique of a potentially liberating set of circumstances changed into their opposite, but a post-scarcity society provides the pre-conditions for a new reality that allows for relations between individuals and between individuals and their environment that are "eroticized," in Marcuse's specific sense meaning the infusion of sexuality into all parts of the life-instinct.[39] Libido would not be displaced onto commodities: sexuality would be genuinely diffused as the humanly destructive elements would be transformed. Life, Marcuse argues, would become *feminized,* as the sensual qualities unleashed would be made to counter the now-dominant aggressiveness of the present form of industrial society: Eros would take precedence over Thanatos.

What are these feminine qualities that Marcuse perceives as the handmaiden of the aesthetic? A careful interpretive reading of him allows one to see that certain natural, physiological differences, certain socially conditioned attributes so long in the making as to appear to be natural characteristics, and certain general ways of being feminine are what he has in mind. Men and women, for deep historical reasons, have come to embody different personality types. The qualities of women can become ascendant when the social conditions of a post-scarcity, aesthetic society are historically present. Natural, that is, physiological, differences would remain and would provide the tension inherent in and inherently necessary for male-female relationships. However, the mental qualities of the two sexes — and he almost, but never quite, suggests that males are aggressive and destructive while females are sensual and serene — would be fused, so that neither sex would be allowed to dominate the other. With a dialectical mode of analysis in mind, he wants to argue that the traditional male-female antithesis would, at a certain historical juncture, lead to an androgynous synthesis. I see this in his designating feminization as "feminist socialism":

> Socialism, as a qualitatively different way of life, would not only use the productive forces for the reduction of alienated labor and labor time, but also for making life an end in itself, for the development of the senses and the intellect for pacification of aggressiveness, the enjoyment of being, for the emancipation of the senses and of the intellect from the rationality of domination: creative receptivity versus repressive productivity.[40]

Marcuse is calling for a critical reason, a reason not tied to domination. The route to this reason is through memory, a remembering of what it was like as a sensuous infant, where the individual obtained gratification; thus, the *"recherche du temps perdu* becomes the vehicle of future liberation."[41] Dinnerstein also places responsibility on what one has come to be through memory; her thesis is that how women come to be regarded is a consequence of their involvement with children in the child's early life. Marcuse wants to take the sensuous aspect of this involvement and build upon it, such that feminism as sensuality becomes feminism as negation, feminism as "a change in consciousness."[42]

It seems appropriate to read Marcuse as saying that there are psychological and political reasons why women become a necessary and potentially active agent of negation in advanced technological society. Their potentiality has to do with certain qualities of being female and their historical exclusion from positions of domination in the society or their less than full integration into the economic and political life of the society.[43] Their vitality, in the sense of importance, also stems from certain sensual qualities which are part of their being-in-the-world as well as the historical role which they have played in the family and in the development of children. Insofar as the present society is one of technological domination, and insofar as sensuality and the self are themselves in the process of undergoing a rationalization and scientization that is antithetical to their very being, women may provide a "locus" — I am careful not to choose the word "refuge" — for the inculcation of critical, alternative values. Thus, for Marcuse, femininity is a form of praxis.

It should be pointed out, however, that there are serious disagreements between writers like Dinnerstein and those, like Marcuse, who formulate a "critical theory" of society which questions the forms of rationality and rationalization which have come to characterize advanced industrial society. Feminist critics of Critical Theory see in the writings of the latter a concern with the individual — with his loss of self, his loss of identity, the demise of his ego — that is resonant with bourgeois and patriarchal thought.[44] It is not that Critical Theory is not cognizant of women's subordinate status; it is, I should suggest, that those writing in that tradition concentrate on the individual's loss of autonomy and that, coming out of a Marxist tradition, they are attuned to the failure of the technocratic establishment to enlarge and make meaningful the social and political arena of discourse that would be the basis for a genuinely democratic society. Certainly, they, like the Marxist heritage from which they draw their sustenance, are not sensitized to a gender perspective even where they are critical of gender discrimination.[45] For, women's subordinate status does concern writers like Marcuse and Habermas who see a relationship between the treatment of women and the more general treatment accorded persons; both are regarded as objects in a world of commodities. Critical Theory has always tried to avoid the romance of looking backwards, and their criticisms of technology are always in terms which do not try to reify it, to make "It" into "An Evil," but which suggest how forces unleashed by scientific advances have been used for oppression, not liberation. They would reject what would be taken as romanticism, Fromm's embracing of a theory of the matriarch.[46] For while they would appreciate his positing of a relationship between capitalism, patriarchy and the authoritarian family, they would find his argument that feeling and compassion were to be found in matriarchal societies simplistic.

Dinnerstein's thesis, that patterns of child-care affect the ways in which one comes to regard men and women, demands a dismantling of gendered institutions, and one could argue the further point that in the process of dismantling, one could begin to allow for the creation of personalities with the very kind of strong and healthy egos for which other social critics have been arguing. It is almost as if feminist theory becomes the practicum for Critical Theory — although here, too, one does not want to make a very complicated set of intellectual legacies into pat formulas for social change.

Nancy Chodorow, in her *Reproduction of Mothering* (1978), written out of her experiences as both an academician (a sociologist) and a member of the feminist movement, asks the same kinds of questions that Dinnerstein does: how does one come to learn about society? How does one internalize, or make a part of his or her being, what the society sees as being true? Why is the role of mother restricted to women in our (by which they both mean Western, advanced industrial) society? Is it biologically necessary? Is it a result of processes of socialization? Is it a result of cognitive learning? Like Dinnerstein, Chodorow sees childrearing, or the mothering role, as having been implanted in the psyche of women: women *want* to mother for psychological reasons, not because their bodies are *intended* for this or because they are coerced into doing it but because they have "the capacity and sense of self as maternal to do so."[47] Chodorow also values Freudian theory: for the help it can offer to explain why social relations are grounded in psychic foundations; for its insights into the psychodynamics of the family which insights then allow one to see the family's role in the construction of gender; for systematically investigating the role that the unconscious plays in human life. This respect for Freud that both Chodorow and Dinnerstein display is similar to that of Juliet Mitchell who argues that Freud's is a descriptive theory of patriarchy, of the processes by which males and females learn of the gendered power relations which make for their manliness and femininity.[48]

Just as Dinnerstein supplements her Freudian categories with the language of Gestalt psychology, Chodorow uses object-relation theorists (John Bowlby, D.W. Winnicott, W.R.D. Fairbairn) for subsidiary and complementary explanations. Drawing upon her background in sociology, she selectively uses writings on the family as these come out of Parsonian functionalism and the Frankfurt School to see how social factors affect the psyche and how asymmetrical patterns of psychological development affect the prevailing social order. She draws upon Talcott Parson's work to see how the roles of mother and father are reproduced within the family; specifically, she finds of use his work on how certain kinds of families, for example, middle-class families, use socialization practices which encourage children into patterns of achievement. She integrates this functionalist approach with Horkheimer's work on the family, on the authority patterns established in families operating in capitalist societies, and in the psychic and economic factors involved in getting children to comply with the demands of the system.

Adrienne Rich, a poet and essayist, had distinguished between a woman's potential to mother or bear and care for the young and the institution of motherhood which she saw as a set of practices which allowed men to control that potential.[49] Chodorow argues that boys and girls suffer from exclusive parenting by women, that is, both from mothering and from motherhood. Where Rich uses literary references in support of her position, Chodorow takes from psychological theory and psychoanalytic practice the data to make the same case.

Girls remain attached to their first object relation, mother, adopt feminine traits of empathy, are concerned with relations between persons, and desire to bear children. In their preparedness to be like other women, girls and later women are prepared to do mothering-type things: they are prepared to care for others and be intimate with others. Boys, forced to renounce their primary identification with their mothers in favor of their fathers and having to form their egos with masculine role models in mind, suffer throughout life with an ambivalent set of love relationships. Even if one does not want to evaluate this male rejection of female caring and intimacy, and one does not want to say that boys and men suffer from not being like girls and women, one can still be asked to accept, on the descriptive level, men not either wanting to or needing to have relationships like those of women. Certainly, one might argue, as Chodorow does, that it is easier to learn how to be female, whatever other problems may be attendant upon being woman in the society, than it is to learn to be male, for it is a more direct, one-to-one learning experience if one learns from the mother that one is like. Boys, who have more distant role models, learn how to distance themselves from their families and invest their energies outside of the private sphere. Contextually, their detachment from emotion as well as from themselves may act to serve them well in a society founded on the division of labor and principles of rationality which encourage objectivity and distancing, but each sex pays a heavy toll for the existing, highly differentiated roles used to bring up children. She writes:

> Women, as mothers, produce daughters with mothering capacities and the desire to mother. . . . By contrast, women as mothers (and men as not-mothers) produce sons whose nurturant capacities and needs have been systematically curtailed and repressed. This prepares men for their less affective later family role, and for primary participation in the impersonal world of work and public life. [50]

Anthropological data suggest limitations to the thesis that women are always the sole providers of child care while "psychologists have demonstrated unequivocally that the very fact of being mothered by a woman generates in men conflicts over masculinity, a psychology of male dominance, and a need to be superior to women." [51] All across the board, from the different ways in which men and women respond to their children to their economic and political styles, the imprint of the feminine monopoly on child-care leaves its mark.

Reminiscent of the arguments made by Rich when she also speaks of the contradictory ways in which the individual comes to regard she who has mothered him/her and when she suggests the consequences of women socializing their sons into maleness and daughters into femaleness, Chodorow also traces the roots of sexism and patriarchy to early childhood and the relatively little involvement of men in the traumas of children coming to an awareness of who and what they are and how and why they may do what they can and cannot do. Rich argues that "the male mind has always been haunted by the force of the idea of *dependence on a woman for life itself*" and that men spend their ensuing lives coming to terms with being "of woman born." [52] The institution, subtly connected, needs to be destroyed but not the capacity to mother; that has to be changed, and mothering has to become a task that one freely commits oneself to do but that is not the sole *raison d'être* for women.

In explaining why men and women perceive the world differently, one has to recognize that certain developments in the child's psyche occur as a consequence of the ways in which children are raised, to wit, their being raised by women. Girls relate to the women who raise them differently than boys. Girls see themselves as being more like their mothers than do boys and mothers see their daughters as being more like them than they see their sons as being like them. They see less of a need for their daughters to outgrow their bonding—their attachment—than they see their son's need to do so if they are to become their own persons. Thus, girls achieve selfhood much later and in a different way than do boys, if at all: they continue to bond where boys begin to separate; they define themselves more in respect to other people than do men; they have a different sense of ego.

Chodorow writes:

> Children first experience the social and cognitive world as continuous with themselves; they do not differentiate objects. Their mother, as first caretaker figure, is not a separate person and has no separate interests, and one of their first developmental tasks is the establishment of a self with boundaries, requiring the experience of self and other as separate. . . . The father, by contrast, has always been differentiated and known as a separate person with separate interests, and the child has never been totally dependent upon him. He has not posed the original narcissistic threat (the threat to basic ego integrity and boundaries) nor provided the original narcissistic unity . . . to the girl. Oedipal love for the mother . . . contains a threat to selfhood which love for the father never does.[53]

As boys grow up, they learn to make distinctions between themselves and others, to deny instances of relationships built on affect, and to think in terms of generalized ideas and ideals of being male. Girls grow up to think differently than this; they learn to think in terms of others and in terms of themselves in relationship to others: "Feminine identification processes are relational, whereas masculine identification processes tend to deny relationship."[54] This is the case even though both the boy and the girl child, as infants, "achieve[s] a differentiation of self only insofar as its expectations of primary love are frustrated."[55]

Like Dinnerstein, Chodorow is a discerning critic of contemporary sexual arrangements. She sees this early pattern of women bringing up children as having consequences for one's adulthood. In recalling the intimacy of one's childhood, one wants to return to it and one wants to recreate those instances in which one will be taken care of by women. This care has the underside of dependency: "It is aspects of the relationship to *her* that are internalized defensively; it is *her* care that must be consistent and reliable; it is *her* absence that produces anxiety."[56]

This is but another way of explaining what Dinnerstein means when she says both men and women *"fear the will of women,"* the fear of becoming, once again, as helpless as one was when one was an infant: beware "the hand that rocks the cradle." The person's first encounter with power has been that of the power of women: *"Power. . . concentrated in one sex and exerted at the outset over both . . . is far too potent and dangerous a force to be allowed free sway in adult life. To contain it, to keep it under control and harness it to chosen purposes, is a vital need, a vital task, for every mother-raised human."*[57] Only by giving up this initial unilateral power, or only by having it taken away from them, will women be in a position, Dinnerstein continues, to get out from the yoke of power-as-control which contemporary childhood practices place them in. In other words, infancy stamps an indelible set of attitudes onto one's thinking about women, so infancy must be changed before those attitudes will change. Unchanged, gender arrangements will be a factor in leading humankind to the nihilism of nuclear destruction; unchanged, they presage disaster. Were men to be intimately involved in the child-care role, they would come to think more of the importance of the role and, thus, they would come to think more highly of women; women would be able to establish better ego boundaries were they to have both a female and a male presence around in their early years. Cultural and, in this sense, environmental factors affect the ways in which the representations of male and female sexes are perceived. At the same time, however, these perceptions are so deeply embedded in the individual's psyche that they appear to be inalterable.

In distinguishing her own work from that of Dinnerstein, Chodorow has emphasized the need to situate discussions of motherhood within a specific historical context. Were one to do this, Chodorow argues, one would see that the separation of the mother-child dyad from the rest of the family and the outside community is of fairly recent (nineteenth century) historical origin: moreover, this separation or isolation had as its intent the producing of moral children for their rightful place in a moral world and is intimately connected with the rise and growth of capitalism. The historical occurrence of an isolated mother/child unit becomes the lynchpin in Freudian psychology and developmental theories of bonding, and this unit is invested with extraordinary import both for society and for the child's future development. The success or failure of the child's socialization is laid at the feet of the dyad. Chodorow finds that this view of "the all-powerful mother"[58] turns into the ideology of motherhood, such that the particular arrangements of early child-care and the female monopoly on such child-care, which are historical occurrences, become ahistorical psychological explanations for infantile fantasies. Dinnerstein, Chodorow continues, confuses infantile fantasies of the mother's power with the mother's actual power which is really not so all-consuming; and in blaming mothers for as much as she does, Dinner-

stein is too "apocalytic."[59] The antidote to this psychological interpretation is the infusion of history; seeing personality as socially produced, seeing the self as more than an anatomical self. There is the need to see dynamic elements in mothering; for example, how children affect the bond, how social conditions affect the bond, how other aspects of growing up are equally as important as are these years colored by mother-child intimacy.

One could argue that in her emphasis on the need to change these patterns of bonding, Dinnerstein recognizes the historical dimension to the mother-child relationship. Some have seen an explicit political ideology underscoring women-raised children, referring to such patterns as an example of "patriarchal childrearing practices."[60] Childbearing is seen as biological and childrearing as political: "Patriarchy seeks to maintain the myth that patriarchal motherhood is a biological reality rather than a politically constructed necessity."[61] It is not that women naturally belong in the home, but rather that their being there serves the needs of the political and social system.

Rich writes:

> Even if contraception were perfected to infallibility, so that no woman need ever again bear an unwanted child; even if laws and customs change — as long as women and women only are the nurturers of children our sons will grow up looking only to women for compassion, resenting strength in women as "control," clinging to women when we try to move into a new mode of relationship. As long as society itself is patriarchal — which means antimaternal — there can never be enough mothering for sons who have to grow up under the rule of the Fathers, in a public "male" world separate from the private "female" world of the affections.[62]

I do not intend to suggest that on all counts Dinnerstein and Rich would find themselves in agreement, only on the consequences of females-as-mothers and the intensity of the early relationship with those who do mother. Rich has criticized Dinnerstein and others for uncritically accepting heterosexuality and not seeing it as being as much an institution as is motherhood. Rich's ideas on the particular attachment women have to women, traceable to early child-care practices, and of the enforcing of heterosexuality so as to reinforce male power and keep lesbian experiences, both those which are sexual (genital) and emotional (woman-centered), out of reach, are also ideas on which she and Dinnerstein might come to disagree.[63] They also have different reassessments of the psychological cost to the daughter of "losing" that early bond with the mother; where Dinnerstein finds the loss equitably felt by both sons and daughters, Rich is more concerned with daughters' experiences.

Chodorow is concerned with the political consequences of a pattern of familial relationships centered around the privatized nuclear family in which the rearers of children are mothers or other females; such arrangements encourage individualism at the expense of communal concerns and allow parents to think of their children as products of their sexual activity. She does not speak of eliminating all kinds of familial forms, for the need for attachment is demonstrably there in children. "Mothering" is necessary if the child is to develop a sense of self, she argues, that ability to grow away from its original source of nurturance. Nonetheless, there are other less overt but still political consequences with the present arrangement of women-reared children. Insofar as boys experience differences between themselves and the women who raise them at the outset and girls experience relatedness and connectedness with such women in their earliest, even pre-Oedipal moments, boys experience an individual self in a way that girls do not. Therefore, boys are more prepared for or predisposed towards a philosophy of individualism than are girls; for the latter, the sense of self is not as strong. As Naomi Scheman puts it, in referring to the implications of child-care practices:

> our moral notions reflect the socially dominant view of the nature of persons: if individuals are distinct and not essentially connected with one another, then morality can be expected to concern itself not with the particularity of relationships among people, but with abstractly characterizable features of interactions among individuals whose natures are taken as given.[64]

Chodorow, reflecting the concerns for community and communal life-styles that were an expression of the New Left and the counter-culture of the 1960s and 1970s, argues that the exclusivity of mothering which characterizes the nuclear family in contemporary society is not necessary if the child is to develop along pathways that are psychologically healthy. Such exclusivity, she continues, benefits the particular capitalist system, by producing more persons, mostly male, who are individualistic and achievement-oriented. Such exclusivity contributes to dichotomizing public from private spheres, productive from non-productive work, and male and female contributions to the economy. She suggests that parenting, by altering the period of infancy from what it now is — the exclusive preserve of women — and by enlarging the number of relationships that the child would pleasurably experience in the early years would encourage people to relate to others differently, and, by implication, more positively, but this might threaten a social system that depends on individualistic, achievement and goal-oriented, and non-cooperative forms of worker relationships.[65]

Both Chodorow and Dinnerstein, in enculturating Freud, reject seeing him as a biological determinist; that is, they emphasize the variability of what could constitute "good mothering" and the importance not of the gender of the caretaker but of the quality of care that he or she renders. Their work belongs to a tradition that rejects any strict dichotomy between culture and biology, one that not only sees the social as being built on the concreteness of the biological but which also recognizes how much of the biological is socially constructed — that is, how important social factors are in structuring perception of how to regard or interpret matters of the body. Chodorow emphasizes that psychoanalysis, as a method, allows one to understand how a specific individual, rooted in a particular moment of historical time, comes to regard himself or herself. Even if one would agree that one's genitalia play a key role in one's destiny to reproduce or not, it is one's social existence that conditions how one comes to understand this destiny. Having rejected any idea that there is a pure biological instinct particular to mothers, that is, that women's reproductive and lactating capabilities provide women with a sense of caring that is biologically rooted — "There is no one-to-one correspondence between genes and behavior"[66] — she is, nonetheless, prepared to argue that sex roles reinforce what is going on at an unconscious level. She wants to establish patterns of interaction, dialectical relationships, but not examples of mechanical causation.

One could argue that just as phenomenology was directed at moving away from seeing a dichotomy between the individual and society, so certain developments out of Neo-Marxism and Neo-Freudianism are arguing against any simplistic demarcations of the cultural and the biological. Writers like Schutz and Maurice Merleau-Ponty have taken the Husserlian idea of a subjective understanding and interposed it with a sociological concern for the objectivity of a particularly constituted social world. If consciousness is always consciousness of something, individuals are always in a society, a society that has a specific set of values which structure the perception of that individual, that is, which inform the way in which he or she comes to see the world. The key word for phenomenologists is inter-subjectivity, communication between persons, each of whom is grounded in a world already there. In this sense, the psychoanalytic method is the means by which one comes to understand both oneself and the other subject as each acts in a socially constructed life-world.

The Dinnerstein-Chodorow thesis assumes the importance of bonding or attachment of the child to another — to the mother or to another child-rearer. Just as one could argue[67] that it is ideological to say, as the sociobiologists do, that parents care for their children in order to guarantee their investment (their own genes) and to ensure their future legacy (genes making it into the next generation) and that women invest more in their children than do men because they are more certain of the children's parentage than are the men, so one could say that arguing that it is good for a child to bond with his or her mother is also ideological in that it legitimates a woman's being with her child and that that relationship has consequences for a woman's involvement in non-familial spheres of human life. The argument has been made that bonding theory shores up or legitimates practices that are in the process of being revised, that is, the relationship of children to parents.[68] Without reform, that is, without such theory informing policy which puts a premium on strong relationships between children and their parents, especially their mothers, these familial forms or "institutions would succumb to the challenges presently mounted against them."[69] In other words, bonding is a political ideology, a new form of the "maternal instinct" that can be and is used to keep women in their place, legitimate patriarchal relationships, and keep the family from undergoing the metamorphosis made possible by the concrete conditions of an advanced industrial society. The idea of bonding is functional for a society that has designated the home as the appropriate place for women to be, but its days are numbered to the degree that a new political movement, the Women's Movement, is beginning to question the utility of asymmetrical gender relationships that reserve to one sex the private sphere of the home and allow to the other sex full participation in the world of work and the world of public politics. Bonding literature, so the argument continues, is a form of scientific knowledge which tells persons, especially women, how they ought to live their lives. Like any form of knowledge which is used to legitimate certain social and economic relationships, it is an ideology that functions as a form of social control, paternalism of a sort, a pattern of ideas which keeps one from giving one's own meaning to one's own life, of structuring one's own world of social relationships.[70]

The evaluation of the Dinnerstein-Chodorow thesis opens up two kinds of issues. The first concerns what is assessed to be empirically the case: what is the relationship of parents to children at any given historical point in time? Who does raise whose children? What kinds of jobs do women now hold in the labor force? Do both men and women relate to their jobs in the same way, that is, do either or both of them invest jobs with importance? Do changing patterns of participation in the work force effect the authority structure(s) in the family? Does the male still have authority in the family? Do either parents have any real power over the child? By what criteria are these present sets of relationships found to be functional or dysfunctional? The second set of issues is normative in form: what is the kind of person one would like to see in one's ideal society? What kinds of childrearing practices ought one to institute to arrive at that political and moral goal? Is nurturing or caretaking a value that all ought to embrace?

Akin to the Mannheimian argument that ideas reflect the social conditons out of which they arise, one could begin to understand the appearance of new personality types as a consequence of the technological revolution to be seen in advanced industrial societies. In the way that Fromm speaks of the acquisitive personality evolving out of capitalism and Scheler offers the bourgeois man as a creation of a society governed by rules of functional rationality, Marcuse argues that in an advanced technological society governed by economic conditions of post-scarcity it is theoretically possible, if politically unlikely, that a new kind of person could emerge, one with a "New Sensibility."[71] Marcuse's support for values traditionally associated with the feminine is integral to his thesis that the progressive forces of advanced industrial society, if they are to resist the processes of bureaucratic rationalization, must demand the radical restructuring of basic human instincts, such that new patterns of relatedness, based on aesthetic principles, will direct persons lives.

I would argue that Dinnerstein and Chodorow offer parenting as an idea appropriate to a redefined historical situation where women no longer have to care for and feed their own children or work at tasks which keep them near to the home and where the continuation of traditional child-care patterns have deleterious effects on all involved. At the simplest level, they mean by parenting shared child-care, but at a more sophisticated level they are arguing for the recasting of personality so that traditional male-female characteristics will be radically reformed: it is the nurturing dimension of motherhood that they wish to see transposed from its conventional association with women.

The present form of the market society enables women to leave the household and it would, therefore, seem to be the case that, if women are to be treated equitably with men, if they are to move into the public realm, the familial arrangements of an earlier time will have to be replaced. Domesticity having been defined as ideology and a movement having been set in place to raise questions of housewifery and motherhood — at least for a certain class of persons — a new consensus is sought on ideas appropriate to the role of woman as worker, a role borne out by the labor statistics on the number of women, including women with small children (under the age of three) who do work. The conditions exist for a reevaluation and reinterpretation of motherhood as an institution, but there is no inextricable logic that will bring these economic developments in line with theories of parenting that make the case for involving both sexes in the care of young children.[72]

What I am suggesting is that one can explain the appeal that the argument on parenting has to several groups of people: to those who want to legitimate women as involved workers in the public sphere and who recognize that the child-rearing practices which support motherhood as an institution act to keep women out of the labor force or, at least, involve them in that force in ways that are not comparable to the patterns of work undertaken by men for whom there is no equivalent fatherhood responsibility; to those for whom Freudian categories are meaningful and the present child-care patterns act to reinforce inequitable appraisals of men and women; to those who want childrearing to be a responsibility of both sexes and who do not simply want to replace one category of females (the mother) with another (a paid female worker) for the same job but who see in the demise of motherhood an opportunity to radicalize human relationships in a way that would invest those relationships with highly prized moral values.

In the writings on motherhood of Dinnerstein and Chodorow, as well as in the writings on the effects of developments in reproductive technology on the ways in which families are constituted[73] — to which I will return, in greater detail, later — there is concern with the social construction of child-bearing. The argument is made that the kinds of practices that a society engages in to assure that children will be both born and reared by women are ideological in consequence, if not in intent. The rearing of children by women is integral to the prevailing sexual arrangements, but these are both historically constituted and socially rationalized, with serious consequences for all concerned.

The issue of motherhood is part of a larger set of issues that are discussed by social theorists, to wit, what limits, if any, do certain natural or human givens, if any, place on the reconstruction of the family as a socially constituted group. The controversy, which seeks to get beyond what may be both the historicity of classic models and the ephemera of current family styles, is grounded in a concern for human needs, but the participants in that controversy are not insensitive to the ways in which ideology can color discussion. If Dinnerstein and Chodorow, and other writers who make the case for a major reformation of child-rearing roles, are to be understood as responding to changes in what women can technically and politically do with their lives, so, too, can one find others whose work can be historically situated within the context of changing familial needs and wants. I wish to look at the writings of sociobiologists, on the one hand, and certain feminists, on the other, who raise oppository arguments to those for radical parenting.

A social analysis of sociobiology is concerned not with the truth value of its theoretical model but with the arguments derived from its premises and the ways in which these are formulated and read within the specifics of an historical context. For if sociobiology is seen to consort with those who are opposed to feminism, it is because certain ideas at certain moments in time are read one way and not another, a position, a Mannheimian would have to say, from which there is no escape. Given that interplay of economics, science, and politics which allowed for the receptivity to the ideas of the Women's Movement, it is understandable why oppository ideas would arise in reaction to the same confluence of circumstances. The factors of birth control, infant feeding formulas, changing labor conditions and advances in reproductive technology would affect all writings on families and familial relationships.

Science, as it developed out of Galileo's world, played a very different social role than is the case with science in contemporary society. In its

Enlightenment origins, science stood for the demystification of tradition and power, a tool by which one could strip away the cultural blinders by which those entrusted with safeguarding the cultural mazeways were able to order the patterns of lived experience. Comte's faith in, or commitment to, the natural science model for studying social phenomena was also rooted in replacing the chaos of diverse interests with the order imposed, or revealed, by a scientific truth. Science was regarded as having a pristine quality, one unsullied by material interests. It was a method — but far more than merely a set of techniques — which would allow one to see or unearth the natural limits to biological givens; it was to lay bare the laws of the social world and play the social role not of detached observer but of involved benefactor to humanity. For Comte, science allows us to see how we are to act. Truth is revealed not by the clashing of interests, as liberal theory out of Thomas Hobbes, John Locke and John Stuart Mill would have it, but by scientific revelation. Even where there is a commitment to liberal principles which allows for interests arising out of the diversity of one's social and economic position, there is still a belief that through scientific reasoning one can uncover the ways in which one ought to govern and be governed — it is this Newtonian spirit that underlay the efforts of the founding fathers to write a constitution which would assist those who fell within its jurisdiction to behave as they ought.

Even at the time of which Klein writes in *The Feminine Character,* science was seen as an opponent of the religious percepts which accepted and defended the subordinate status of women, although Klein reads the natural sciences, and most especially biology, as emphasizing the ways in which men and women are irrevocably different, that is, physiologically determined to be one but not the other sex.[74] It appeared to many concerned with the status of women that science took surprisingly little account of the social factors responsible for women's condition, but, instead, accepted the given-ness of sex roles, seeing them as an outgrowth of the behavior dictated by anatomy and physiology. Thus, from a challenger to the absolutism of the age, science, once it claimed to be the sole arbiter of truth and became entwined with the economic and political interests of the industrializing state, came to be regarded by many as a defender of existing social relationships and, consequently, as a legitimator of the new priests of power, those in charge of the technocratic establishment. When one speaks of Comte as the first technocrat, one means that he, like they, will regard science as the new authority which dethrones tradition and becomes the arbiter to which people will pay homage. Eric Weil has pointed out that one defers to science on questions of how one ought to live not because science has expertise in this area but because people believe science has the ability, or wisdom, to give them the right answers. This is another way of arguing that science has come to replace religion and has been seen as a practical way to improve the condition of humankind. Weil continues (and in this is very much akin to the feminist critics of science to which we will come) that what is now regarded as value-free science is really a science with the practical intent of dominating nature, and as science becomes fused with technique and moves from a concern with pure theory to applied technology, it becomes "scientism."[75]

In writing, then, about attitudes toward science, one must chronicle if not a growing disaffection with science, a recognition that it was a double bind; it did alleviate the condition of humanity through advances in medicine, wipe out diseases, make it easier to produce more of the goods and services that people wanted, allow for advances in chemical and nuclear weaponry, and change the nature of warfare. Weil allows us to see how science came to be reified, became an entity unto itself: it was not seen as a practice or set of techniques used by persons living within the specifics of a time and a place. The enemy is not the tools but the uses to which these could be put, and the devices of the Second World War (both those used by the Nazis and the Allies) made individuals question the uses to which science could be put.

If the ideology of scientism, then, is part of the intellectual background against which feminism develops, there is as well a growing interest in how other social factors affect social and political relationships. Klein is prescient in suggesting that a turn toward social explanations of sexual differences, for example, will come to replace or, at least, critique the earlier hold of biological explanations of the feminine. There was a turn to anthropological and ethological studies — Klein's essay on Margaret Mead suggests the import of this — to support theories of behavioral flexibility and cultural diversity. Colin Turnbull writes: "The IKung teach us that our vaunted human values are not inherent in humanity at all, but are associated only with a particular form of survival called society, and all, even society itself, are luxuries that can be dispensed with."[76]

At the same time, not all who used anthropological evidence used it to support limitless diversity. Starting with Konrad Lorenz,[77] there were ethological theories of human behavior[78] which compared and contrasted human behavior with that of animals, seeing in matters of sex and social organization similar examples of male supremacy and female subordination. Robert Ardrey's *African Genesis* predates the arguments that were later to be found in sociobiology. Male and female sexual patterns, Ardrey would argue, are genetically determined, having evolved from ancestral animal species. Humans are more complicated and sophisticated about their instinctual behavior, but the "demands of the loin must be satisfied."[79] Played out amidst the struggle for order or anarchy, cooperation or conflict, the human drama becomes confused by a num-

ber of illusions, as Ardrey calls them, which detract from the animal behavior which individuals share with other species: his uniqueness, the Illusion of Central Position; his benevolence, the Illusion of Original
Goodness; and his inordinate faith in the ability of the environment to
shape and mould behavior along lines compatible with moral innocence.

In this context, Ardrey bemoans the contemporary woman's plight:
encouraged by a romanticism at odds with the findings of natural science, the American woman:

> lives in a feminine Utopia. She is educated. She has been freed of the
> dustmop cage. No social privilege is denied her. She has the vote, the bank
> account, and the entire family's destiny gripped in her beautifully mani-
> cured hand. Yet she is the unhappiest female that the primate world has
> ever seen, and the most treasured objective in her heart of hearts is the psy-
> chological castration of husband and sons. The emancipated woman of
> whatever nationality is the product of seventy million years of evolution
> within the primate channel in which status, territory, and society are inva-
> riably masculine instincts, in which care of children has been a female pre-
> serve, and in which social complexity has demanded of the female the role
> of sexual specialist. Yet she must somehow struggle along in a human soci-
> ety which idealizes in her behavior every masculine expression for which
> she possessses no instinctual equipment, downgrades the care of children
> as insufficient focus for feminine activity, and from earliest girlhood
> teaches her that a rowdy approach to the boudoir will bring her nothing
> but ruin.[80]

All is mixed up, and amid this potpourri of social roles, individuals have
a heightened consciousness of self that makes them even more aware of
the mix-up.

There is, therefore, in feminist theory, as there is in sociobiology, an
on-going dialogue on what weight one ought to place on biological factors in explaining human behavior: on what kind of dialectical relationship does exist between nature and nurture; on whether or not it is a dis-
service to think even in terms of such interactive dualisms, lest one come
to believe that there is, in fact, some pure realm of one or the other. Certainly, social explanations of human behavior are much more highly regarded now than they were in Klein's time; the data of sociology and psychology emphasize the ways in which social and cultural roles structure
behavior and, in so doing, the data is used to question ideas of innateness
or physiological supremacy of sexual characteristics. At the same time —
and this clouds the picture — there is the growing recognition that science, in the guise of technological innovation, affects sex roles, and not
necessarily in ways that interpretors approve of: mother-child relationships are altered by the invention of infant feeding formulas; sexual mating patterns are colored by advances in contraception and conception;
sex change operations affect the most assumed givens. It may very well
be the case that there is no way or ways to be men and women, but that,

rather, the being is whatever is technologically possible. Certainly contemporary sociologists, by and large, share with the Women's Movement a suspicion of theories that emphasize the fixidity of sex role behavior, preferring instead to demonstrate the ways in which circumstances, as well as the particularities of the life-cycle, change those roles.

Because of the political dimension of feminism and its concern with the oppression of women, one can appreciate why feminist writings have concerned themselves with an understanding of the nature of sex roles: What, if any, are the biological differences between the sexes? How important are these differences in terms of behavior, that is, in terms of how persons act? Do these differences reflect social and cultural arrangements? How are these differences regarded by the particular society? What valuation is given these differences? Are the biological differences set and irreversible? Can the biological differences be altered or affected by deep-seated psychological factors? Are sex roles rooted in nature or culturally determined, set or made stereotypic?

The view of the feminine as distinctive, that is, as being in contrast to the masculine, was part of a more generalized view of sexual dichotomy, although especially since the Enlightenment this diversity has always been in tension with another idea, that of equality of person. Diversity and equality are themes carried through to the present day and the sociologist is interested in how the revelation of scientific data is assessed differently according to the ideological prism of uniqueness or sameness that one may be holding before one's eyes. Feminists draw upon science in a variety of ways. One might suggest that the prevailing intellectual paradigm, certainly the one that marks academic discourse, is now sexual equality and that this paradigm is brought to predominance not by a scientific discovery of sexual equality but by a moral and, therefore, political reading of the democracy and equality that is embedded in Enlightenment thought by both liberal and socialist thinkers. The revelations of science are, it seems, made to accord (through interpretation, not coercion) with the egalitarian paradigm. In this sense, the thrust of science, in the United States at least, seems to be in the direction of affirmation of equality, which is made easier by a technology that minimizes or obliterates differences that in the past were not subject to change or alteration.

In turning to a discussion of sociobiology and its critics, one is able to see precisely what feminist thought reads out of a certain kind of scientific theory and why it comes to tar that theory with the brush of sexism. At the outset, it ought to be made clear that, by and large, feminist thought is not anti-science. That is, it is not a Luddite reaction to the kind of changes science can make possible. It is critical, rather, of the uses to which scientific data has been put as well as to the accompanying attitudes that go with being "scientific." Ruth Bleier, a biologist involved in the feminist movement, has expressed her concern for the ways in which science has been used to create myths, which pass themselves off as theories, about the ways in which women's biology requires that they play subordinate social roles.[81] In this sense, Bleier would come to regard sociobiology as ideology in the guise of science, a new form for defending an old ideal.

Given the aspects of human behavior that sociobiologists look at — heredity, aggression, sex and religion, to cite but a few — and the time frame in which the theory was being formulated — the 1970s — it is not surprising that their work generated debate, much of it controversial. The controversy is of interest to the sociologist, who seeks to situate their ideas within the context not only of academic discourse but also of the feminist movement; one cannot ignore the fact that sociobiologists talked extensively about sex roles, about sexual practices, about sexual displays and sexual strategies at precisely that moment when the Women's Movement was engaged in a struggle over the Equal Rights Amendment and when the institution of the family and the role of women within that institution was being questioned.

I will discuss the general idea of sociobiology, especially as it concerns areas of interest to feminist theory; specifically, I want to interpret how sociobiologists formulate ideas on sexual relationships, the family, the incest taboo, and homosexuality. Then, I wish to turn to the critique of the theory made from the perspective of feminism, trying to discern the ways in which sociobiology is antithetical to much in that set of ideas.

I intend to take as central to the arguments of sociobiology the writings of the biologist E.O. Wilson, especially as these bear on issues integral to feminist social theory. Wilson wrote his "speculative essay"[82] *On Human Nature* in order to continue the argument on animal behavior that he had begun in *The Insect Societies*[83] and *Sociobiology: The New Synthesis*.[84] That argument deals with the biological bases of behavior and, borrowing from ethnology, population biology and evolutionary theory, seeks to ground a description of how insects, non-human animals and humans act. Wilson, like W.D. Hamilton, [85] Robert Trivers,[86] and Richard Dawkins,[87] seeks to establish an explanation of the Darwinian thesis on evolution in terms of the gene by explaining both animal and human behavior through gene selection. In the final chapter of *Sociobiology* and throughout *On Human Nature*, Wilson argues for a merging of the social sciences, including social theory, and the biological sciences into a new synthesis or master science, and, insofar as it has been the biological sciences that have made the most dramatic advances, they are the ones to take the lead in describing how it is that humans behave in the ways that they do. The knowledge acquired from advances in the natural sciences is to be used to describe and explain the problems traditional to the study of societies. Even such matters as art and religion are to be described in terms of their adaptive or functional value;[88] that is, all behavior is to be understood as being bound or limited (the terms vary) by biological possibilities which help to keep the gene structure intact.[89]

Human existence is, for Wilson, a scientific question, a question of "how" — how natural selection operates, how genes reproduce, how DNA works. Human existence is not a philosophical dilemma of why — why am I as I am, why should I continue to live. In terrain traditionally traversed by philosophers, theologians, artists and poets, Wilson puts on the sturdy boots of the natural sciences and marches over and around centuries of inquiry, discussion and debate on the question of what it means to be human. He is not troubled by the epistemological concerns of others that one needs to be very explicit in asserting what one takes to be true; by reading in certain fields of science, one can come to know that which scientific inquiry has found to be true. It is not mere chance that *Sociobiology* begins with a rejection of Albert Camus and *On Human Nature* with an invocation to David Hume. Brains, for Wilson, are the summation of nerve cells, and minds are a complex of chemical reactions. Personhood is a biological state of being: what one now knows about the mechanics of the brain will be complemented by a scientific and empirical understanding of values and ethics. Camus, it would seem, must be disputed because of his search for being human in a world which, like Wilson's, has no purpose and in which, through being and doing, living, acting and even rebelling, one makes one's own purpose. There is an individualism to Camus with which Wilson must take issue; he writes to counter the theory that human beings are *social* products which, in the way he has come to understand the social sciences, disavow innate tendencies to behave one way rather than another and dispute the notion of inbuilt propensities to act as one's body is constituted to act.

Wilson's works encouraged the creation of a new paradigm (to borrow Kuhn's term) that would reorder and reassess previously held interpretations on the nature of human nature. They have also suggested, in terms laid out by Kuhn, new ways to solve puzzles that have defined solution by earlier paradigms. Following Wilson, one could explain the biological roots of such forms of behavior as nepotism, altruisim, celibacy and promiscuity in terms that do not reduce these to behaviors peculiar to any particular culture. In opposition to social theories that emphasize the role that social and environmental factors play in shaping the person, sociobiology highlights the decisive role that heredity plays in making people what they are; it is a delimiter to cultural styles and, in this sense, a constraining factor on how people behave.[90] One could deemphasize the socio-historical factors and elaborate upon the physical and chemical properties that bind humans together, as a class or group. Behavior which might be interpreted in Marxist, Freudian or religious terms could now be interpreted in genetic terms, and, as is the case with new paradigms, sociobiology would displace earlier explanations and its reading of the data would be considered true and definitive.

Wilson, building upon the Darwinian model of evolution and natural selection, seeks to do nothing short of explaining human nature in the physical and biological terms appropriate to the natural sciences. Untroubled by differences between description and understanding, in fact, negating the very power of intellect when he says that it "was not constructed to understand atoms or even to understand itself but to promote the survival of human genes,"[91] he barely pays lip-service to the centuries' old debate on whether one can, in fact, know the social world of persons in the same way that one can describe the natural world of inanimate, physical objects. He wants to uncover the "deep structure of human nature"[92] through the turning of biological keys. There is, he suggests, no soul in the theological sense, no freedom in the political sense, and no spirit in the metaphysical sense: "no species, ours included, possesses a purpose beyond the imperatives created by its genetic history."[93] Religions and other ideologies — reason itself — are "enabling mechanisms for survival"[94] master-minded by genes, for "the human mind is constructed in a way that locks it inside this fundamental constraint [its genetic make-up] and forces it to make choices with a purely biological instrument," certainly not through "goal[s] external to its own biological nature."[95] David Barash, a zoologist, writes: "Our genes have programmed us and every other living thing to do what is best for them. . . . We are free it is true, but free only to maximize our fitness and that of our silent genetic riders."[96]

Some will be troubled by Wilson's expropriation of the study of person into the biological orbit and the authoritative role afforded empirical science as the arbitrator of truth; others will question whether Wilson can deliver what he promises, that is, whether he may be but a poor practitioner of his trade. For Wilson argues that genes, the biological building blocks of the species, predispose persons, who may not be conscious of what is going on, to act in a way which will assure species survival: those genes survive which can adequately adapt and in so doing guarantee their replicability; the social structures of any society exist to "serve ultimately as the vehicles of individual welfare;"[97] morality exists to keep "human genetic material . . . intact;"[98] religions function to "enhance the welfare of the practitioners."[99]

In this schema, there need be no idea of human purpose, only a carrier for genes from one generation to the next. Genes act in their own self-interest; they act to protect their kin, those whose genetic make-up is similar to their own. Ethical choices — altruism, for example — are biologically grounded and are those which one is programmed to choose on the basis of their maximizing not one's personal but the species' fitness. While at the gene level altruism, "self-destructive behavior performed for

the benefit of others,"[100] is bad and selfishness is good, at the kin or species level, altruism may be a strategy for ensuring gene survival. Altruistic behavior may appear to be self-less and at odds with genetic self-
interest, but it is really, for the sociobiologist, a more implicit way of
potentially keeping alive one's genes by looking out for those who may in
turn look out for one's kin.

Seeking to ground the behavioral differences between the sexes in biology in general, and evolutionary theory, in particular, Wilson argues
there are genetic reasons why the sexes behave differently and that behavior is necessary for the survival of the next generation. Thus, parental
care can be seen as kin altuism in that one is selflessly looking after one's
own genes. Wilson argues, to cite another example, that the incest taboo
is not merely a culturally devised sanction whose purpose is to safeguard
the authority structure of the family, preserve its integrity, and avoid
role confusion, nor merely to prevent familial disintegration or to secure
the exchange value placed upon women, as Claude Lévi-Strauss argues.[101] The taboo is a universal of human behavior, a way of protecting
genetic fitness and is, in effect, an instinct encoded in the genes. By looking to biology and neuro-physiology one should be able to tell "why," in
functional terms, individuals make the moral choices which they do.

If sociobiology has a role to play, once it uncovers the biological basis
of behavior, it is not to denigrate persons' ideals but, rather, to alert individuals to what is expected of them. It — not philosophical dogma, or theology, or political programs — would reveal the biological underpinnings
of sexual behavior: of courting, bonding, bodily appearances, aggressiveness, monogamy and polygamy, nuclear families, male dominance,
and the altruism of homosexuality. It would take the mystique out of
these behaviors, explaining them in terms of gene demands. For example, in the case of incest, sociobiology would help persons rationally assess the consequences of their violating the instinctual aversion to close
sexual relationships to kin and the dangers of reducing their genetic fitness. In the case of parenting, it would indicate the limits to behavioral
learning theories which may be at odds with mother-child bonds; it
would move one in the direction of the different parental investment actions particular to men and women and explain, in no uncertain terms,
why each sex relates differently to its offspring. Thus, the biological replaces the moral, political or theological in the test of behavior by, among
other things, showing the limits to what persons can know of and do to
themselves. Wilson writes: "The principal task of human biology is to
identify and to measure the constraints that influence the decisions of
ethical philosophers."[102] Put succinctly, persons are their heredity; they
are what they inherit, what has evolved and successfully survived over
time. Individuals are not Locke's *tabula rasa,* entering the world as if
they were totally malleable and could be shaped by the environment,

their behavior socially conditioned; rather, people come into the world predisposed toward behaving in accordance with their genetic make-up — a particular eye color, a specific length of ear, a predictable height, a most likely hair color and, even, a possible personality, temperament, sexual proclivity and intellectual ability. People are constrained by certain behavioral predispositions which are influenced by the genes; thus, there are limits to what one can be and what one can do. One exists in order to play out one's genetic history: free will is philosophical hog-wash, or, put in a more refined way, "spirituality becomes just one more Darwinian enabling device."[103] Cultural determinism or any form of social constructionism becomes Wilson's *bete noire*. For it asks that persons consider becoming what they are not. By extrapolation, it asks that someone who is short try to become a basketball player, that someone who is homosexual try to become a heterosexual, that someone who has problems with mathematics excel in calculus, that someone who is male learn to mother. Assuming that "we are what we are," sociobiologists distrust ideologies that place a high premium on human agency and action.

One can appreciate the sociobiological argument on sexual characteristics provided one understands the framework of biological or genetic determinism with its accompanying argument for the grounding of ethics in biology. One may wish to object to the bases of Wilson's paradigm, rather than quibble over points that evade the import of the thesis. For while there are times when Wilson emphasizes his opposition to determinism, the number of instances in which he speaks not of predispositions but of determining factors is tantamount to making the case for biological determinism. He has certainly been read this way by most of his critics.

Wilson makes three kinds of arguments: by extension or extrapolation within the human species; by analogy with other species; and by identifying behavior by its adaptive value. Questions will be raised over which traits are inherited (eye color and sexual proclivities?), which behaviors are innate (the infant's grasping of objects and mothering?), and which are homologous, (protection of the young and sexual displays?) that is, have the same function in humans as in other animal species and for the same reason.

Wilson argues that males and females are differentiated one from the other chromosomatically, hormonally, anatomically and culturally and that the cultural behavior proceeds from the biological parameters set by genes, hormones and anatomy. People are their genes, behaving as the genes direct them to and these genes were designed to provide for sexual diversity. Owing to hormonal and anatomical factors, men are, as a rule, bigger, stronger and more aggressive than women. Given the historical needs for societies, these factors have led to male cultural dominance, and it would only be through measures of social control and behavioral engineering that this diversity could be altered. Even a cursory reading of Wilson allows one to see how he abhors this use of social policy to alter evolutionary patterns of development.

Wilson offers a description of male dominance. Males have a certain capacity to develop traits which have come to be dominant. Like his female counterpart, man is not a Lockeian clean slate, able to do or be anything he pleases, for his biology restricts his choices and guides him into accepting certain options and rejecting others — "at birth the twig is already bent a little."[104] Males may differ from one another, but the range of biologically accepted behavior is similar enough so that one can speak of being male, or being female. These are implicit in Wilson's position: first, a notion of a biological structure which is trans-historical and trans-cultural and which defines one's sex; and second, a recognition of a relationship between sex traits and cultures, such that as societies change and evolve there is the possibility that these traits could come to be valued or regarded in a different way.

In explaining why certain sexual practices seem to continue over time, sociobiologists turn to species behavior as it is grounded in the genes. Barash argues, for example, that the sexual double standard relates to the need to assure that one's genes will survive. The begetting of children, their preservation and protection, are affected by the different reproductive strategies and parental investment theories of men and women. Men, to maximize gene replication, consider increasing copulation with as many women as possible and weigh the limitlessness of this against their need to protect as many of the resulting offspring as possible; hence, it pays genetically for men to be philanderers. Women have to be more selective, since impregnation removes them from the reproductive pool for nine months plus; therefore, women ought to be selective, or coy, about whom they will mate with, since a wrong choice is more costly for them than it is for a man. Implicit in the argument is the role of reason, here understood as the mind's understanding of the body, in getting one to behave as one biologically ought; sexual and reproductive strategies are biologically based and different, and if one were to "listen" to one's body, the "whisperings within" would tell one how to act. Genes "whisper" to persons that sex exists neither for purposes of reproduction nor pleasure but to guarantee genetic diversity and adaptability; not all persons are intended to reproduce, and those with homosexual tendencies, for Wilson a biological condition, play the role of assisting the kith and kin of their heterosexual brethen, what is called an "altruistic impulse[s]."[105] For Wilson, the contemporary ideology of sexual equality belies the reality of different sexual strategies: the verities of behavior are grounded in the genes not in the proclamations of a misguided social movement.[106]

In one of his responses to his critics, Wilson confessed surprise that the import of sociobiology was its conservatism. In what may strike the observer of ideological battles as a most strange line-up, Wilson contended that he was working the same side of the street as Marcuse and Noam Chomsky, neither of whom could or would be accused of advancing a position that was racist or sexist in the way that Wilson has been. One can understand why Wilson sees himself as arguing Freud's "biology is destiny" theme and why he quotes Lionel Trilling's *Beyond Culture*: " 'there is a hard, irreducible, stubborn core of biological urgency, and biological necessity, and biological *reason* that culture cannot reach and that reserves the right, which sooner or later it will exercise, to judge the culture and resist and revise it.' "[107] One can also see why he associates himself with Chomsky's work on deep structures, Jean Piaget and Lawrence Kohlberg's stages of moral development, and Marcuse's disputes with Fromm on the relationship between instinct and culture. Like Wilson, these thinkers have serious reservations about a position of radical environmentalism, one that allows for few, if any, limitations on social policy changes.

One can understand, further, why Wilson can be read as being in agreement with someone like Erik Erikson, in that both want to hold onto certain essential differences between men and women; one can also understand why Erikson himself has been criticized by some feminists for accepting stereotypic views of women. In his essay on "Inner and Outer Space,"[108] Erikson speaks of a new set of historical factors that call into question the kind of maleness personified by a certain political and technological hegemony. Introduced this way, Erikson is already assuming the historicity of personality types, yet a historicity that is conditioned by a universality of maleness and femaleness that has evolved and unfolded. Thus, he writes that "a new kind of political and technological ethics" would be available if women brought to the political arena "what they have always stood for privately . . . realism . . . responsibility . . . resourcefullness . . . and devotions to healing."[109] Women becoming equal to men, in the sense of their becoming like men, allow men to impose their notions, misguided and incorrect though these may be, of what is humanly desirable and humanly possible on women. This imposition enslaves women, continues to entrap men, and precludes any genuine dialectic of an ideal of being human. This is very close to the ideas of woman as negation spelled out by Marcuse, Dinnerstein, Elshtain, and Sara Ruddick, and which I have previously discussed. However, there is a universality which Erikson assumes as a starting point in understanding sexual differences out of which spring sexual identities of a given time and place. It is not simply that "anatomy is destiny" but that "anatomy, history, and personality are our *combined destiny*."[110] Being female has its roots in what he calls "somatic design," to wit, the female *predisposition* for internal concerns and a *potential* for bearing children. This "inner space" carries with it consequences that are biological, psychological, and ethical in import. Females come to understand out of anatomical differences, not differences that are missing or envied but those that are there: they come to recognize the "existence of a *productive inner-bodily space* set in the center of the female form and carriage."[111]

In this connection, it is worth noting Joan Smith's equation of the essentialism of sociobiology and the essentialism of certain strands of feminist theory.[112] Both, she argues, are predicated on a notion of person outside of history and both are guilty of reification. Both are ahistorical treatments of women which avoid the contextualism in which examination of human behavior must be grounded. The abject denunciation of men that is found in patriarchal critiques of female subordination castigate men irrespective of the economic arrangements of the society that have legitimated their treating women as they do: one can hear her saying that it is not all men that oppress women but some men at a specific time and place and it is, therefore, not all women who will bear and rear children but only some at a similarly constituted time and place. A dialectical method, often absent from feminist theory and never found in sociobiology, would be the corrective to or antithesis of each of these paradigms and would counter a universalism that is historically untenable.

Critics of Wilson and other sociobiologists have run the gamut, from those who see in sociobiology the antithesis of properly conducted science, to those who find the position basically sound although often an overstatement of the determining nature of the biological and, more specifically, the genetic. Some have taken Wilson to task for his model, arguing, among other things, that his comparisons with the animal kingdom discount the notion of human agency which distinguishes the person from other species of being; that is, he makes analogous what is really disparate behavior. Even if the case is made that sex roles evolve out of the biological differences between males and females, and that if one looks to the animal kingdom one can see how this evolution has occurred, that is, how it has grown out of innate behavior, might it not be the case that (a) men and women are more alike than they are different and certainly more alike than they are to a non-human primate, and (b) that one anthropomorphizes or imposes a pattern of behavior on animals that is not really there. Some critics of sociobiology have argued that one can read the data from the worlds of other primates, as well as other peoples, as indicating the malleability and diversity of sexual arrangements.[113] In this way, that is, by finding fault not with the zoological or ethnological data but with the way in which it has been read, there is no inherent contradiction between the tenets of biology and feminism: it is simply a question of how the data is incorporated into the larger thesis. The feminist concern is with the notion of "innateness," which is certainly stressed in Wilson's construction of sociobiology. Bleier, taking issue with Wilson, writes in a way that expresses a theme resonant to the Women's Movement, although we have already seen how there is disagreement among feminists on this point: "If anything is innate and inevitable, it is our behavioral plasticity — the potential to develop in any of the infinite variety of ways in response to environment and culture."[114]

Critics of sociobiology have also found fault with the mechanistic quality of the model: in some instances, genes affect behavior, as do hormones, but neither genes nor hormones determine gender, nor certain aspects of intelligence or skill, as Wilson suggests that they do. In some instances, there has been a scientific demonstration of the relationship between the genes and a particular quality, eye color, for example. But there is no "gene" for homosexuality and no "gene" that warns against incest. While scientific data might demonstrate that certain behavioral differences do exist, it does not prove what causes these differences, that is, whether they are innate or the result of long established social practices.[115] Again, one must reiterate that sociobiology deals with issues that the Women's Movement has dealt with since its inception — what are the significant differences, if any, between men and women? Are these differences primarily biological or a result of sex role socialization? Can biological differences be altered? Ought they be? Within the context of that Movement — and one could raise a similar set of considerations respecting sociobiology, race relations, and theories of racial differences — statements which seek to ground sex role behavior in terms of either biological givens or predispositions are bound to incur opposition, especially when the issues are why women raise families, why men rape, why women are less aggressive than men, and why there are double-standards in matters of sexual behavior.

Sociobiology appears conservative in so far as it emphasizes the boundaries or limits of human action; this emphasis on parameters puts sociobiology on a collision course with the emphasis of the Women's Movement on the ability to construct socially the world in which women find themselves. It is not that writers are questioning the validity of the Darwinian theory of evolution or that there is a rejection of the thesis that the building blocks of humankind are the genes. Rather, it is the speculation that all forms of social behavior can be attributed to genetic differences that is at issue as well as the implications drawn from data which suggest differences between males and females. It is not that sociobiology is indistinguishable from all forms of political conservatism, for on another set of political axes, sociobiology crosses swords with those conservatives who oppose Darwinism with Creationism and who equate homosexuality with sin and sedition. What is demonstrable is its affinity with political views that wish to uphold a more traditional view of sexual arrangements than is to be found in the literature of the Women's Movement.

When one comes to the more recent writings of Alice Rossi, who will be discussed later, one will see how a feminist tries to build on similar data to that used by sociobiologists while avoiding the rigidity found in much of that theory. Rossi writes: *"A biosocial perspective does not argue that there is a genetic determination of what men can do compared to women: rather, it suggests that the biological contributions shape what is learned, and that there are differences in the ease with which the sexes can learn certain things."*[116] It is certainly the case that one can reject sociobiology on any combination of grounds — the inappropriateness of anthropomorphizing animal studies, the limitations of biological determinism, the implicit racism and sexism of its reading of gene theories, the use of sociobiological writings to legitimate, protect, and preserve those inequities which exist in the society — without dismissing the import of biological factors in structuring human behavior. Stephen Chorover, for example, spells out the conservative consequences of linking marginality and deviance to underlying biological causes as sociobiology does, but, at the same time, he wants to hold onto certain biological givens, to preserve certain biological laws which would allow for a more satisfactory relationship with factors of human and physical nature.[117] Richard Lewontin, a population geneticist and an outspoken critic of sociobiology, has argued that one can turn biology away from conservative implications, both by recasting its mechanistic mold and by using its findings to create the kind of mental and physical environment conducive to a liberated existence. Lewontin argues that the model of biology that Wilson erects proffers a Nature far more deterministic and far less influenced by human intervention than is the case. Radicalizing biology, by making it dialectical, involves taking from Marx the philosophical presupposition that the world, if not made by individuals, is shaped by them: by their consciousness, their actions, and their labor. Individuals are potentially more than a product of their circumstances; their visions of an emancipatory interest allow them to change those conditions.[118]

As we shall see, feminists have reacted quite strongly to Rossi's position, critically assaying the emphases she places on the anatomical and hormonal constitution of female behavior and the consequence of these for theories on the social construction of personality and suggesting that it is only hairsplitting that distinguishes her position from that of Wilson's. Feminists are on guard for arguments that tend to equate historical sex roles with behavior grounded in hormones and anatomy, and, therefore, research on differences in brain structures, like a Wilsonian sociobiology, is looked at very carefully lest it jeopardize the political program of the Women's Movement.[119] Nature or nurture, genes or environment, biology or society are, then, not only pointless dualisms but legitimating devices for the continuation of a patriarchal structure. What matters, nonetheless, is not the scientific correctness of sociobiology but rather its political import, the ways in which it is used by individuals to orient their behavior, and by political agencies to order their priorities to accord with the assumed innateness of sexual characteristics. Many feminist critics of sociobiology have feared that Wilson will be understood as validating a biological determinism that becomes the handmaiden of Social Darwinism, legitimating social arrangements in terms of an assumed evolutionary intent.

Feminism that has been influenced by the Marxist emphasis on the political restructuring of the environment will be on a collision course with sociobiology. In this emphasis on a person shaping his or her life according to a moral or political vision that is not grounded in any fixed idea of a human essence, Marxism would view sociobiology as conservative. The argument is that:

> It is not that it is difficult to conduct a proper scientific experiment which will determine how much of an influence is "innate" or "genetic," how much "environmental," and how much "interaction between the two"; rather, the distinction makes no sense. . . . Personality is both personal *and* social . . . neither exists without the other.[120]

Genes interact with particular social systems and it is this relationship and not any nature/nurture dichotomy that ought to command one's attention. The body is "presented," or "written" or assessed within the context of a social framework and not in any kind of isolation. While it may be the case that behavior is circumscribed, in the sense of affected, by biology, it is too simple to equate this with genetic determination. Factors of birth, be they the genes with which one is born or the class into which one is born, effect the kind of person one might become, but in either case, allowances must be made for human action to effect the ways in which these are presented and played out.

Wilson writes as if science were objective and neutral and that sociobiology is only concerned with demonstrating how human nature has come to be what it is. He does not ask, except in a very perfunctory way, what the presuppositions of sociobiology are, what metaphors or models are used to focus that data, or what social purposes are served by its revelations. He does not ask how his work will be understood and the uses to which it will be put and the social interests which will or will not be served by his data. He abstracts sociobiology from history and, in so doing, removes the scientist artifically from social activity. One could argue that the import of sociobiology is precisely its conservative political agenda that substitutes genes for an earlier Divine Will and its appeal comes at a time when there is the growth of neo-conservative thought on matters on both race and sex and a public backlash to those social movements pressing for equality. It is the myth of science as neutral that Wilson's detractors seek to expose, the belief that science is objective, that it can be separated from the social context out of which it develops and is nurtured, and that there is no obligation on the part of the scientist to consider the consequences of his or her research, that is, the uses to which it will be put.

The debate over motherhood has been part of a larger debate over what it means to be a "gender." It has been suggested that a reading of the history of the women's movement, if taken back to the earliest days of the Republic, reveals a constant theme: whether "femaleness" and "maleness" are essentially distinct spheres. In its contemporary phase, the Women's Movement centers its political activity on securing legal equality and full rights of personhood, the latter coming to include the right of women to have ultimate authority respecting questions of their bodies, which, in immediate terms, means the right to terminate pregnancies.

It is in the literature about the Movement, that is, in most of the feminist writings, that one finds the theoretical explorations into the question of gender distinctiveness. Two kinds of questions are asked respecting this distinctiveness: one is empirical; the other is normative. The empirical question is: are there significant differences between the sexes and are these biological and/or psychological? Here the following kinds of questions are raised: Is there a physical syndrome that constitutes the feminine? Are there mental characteristics that accompany it? Are sex roles, defined as role performance by a particular sex, biologically and/or historically set? Does the person performing the role have to do so? Can others perform the role in their stead? What if the person chooses not to perform the role? When does motherhood, for example, become pronatalism? When does what one takes for granted become ideological, that is, a way of structuring perception of how one ought to be in the world? Is sexuality, which may or may not stem from sex differences, natural? It could be argued that sex roles, in their empirical dimension, are regarded as factors of temperament, interests or abilities which may be due to any number of factors — differences in the nervous system, hormonal substances, variations in brain structures, different ways of regarding one's body.

The normative question is whether in an ideal society, or a society to be constructed in theory or in practice, certain sex roles ought to be assigned to females and others to males. The normative may follow upon the empirical: one may find that one's reading of the empirical data suggests significant differences between the sexes, which differences ought to be protected, preserved, modified, or changed through policy initiatives that will achieve the normative end one hopes to achieve. Or one's reading of the data suggests few, if any, significant differences between the sexes, such that one ought either write policy to enhance those differences that do exist or moves to eliminate the few vestiges of differences that are to be found.

Of course, it is reasonable to argue that one might not wish to structure any future society that disregards the empirical data, for to do so would be to fly in the face of facts and appear to be a fool. One could also argue that classifying questions as empirical prejudges the case and assumes verification where none may be possible. I do not wish to undertake an excursion into the philosophical debates over the nature of verifiable data, the fact-value dichotomy, the politics of classification. Rather, I intend merely to indicate that the discussions concerning women as child-rearers provide a case study in whether this rearing is to be regarded as biologically and/or socially constructed—that is, whether it is, as Dinnerstein and Chodorow argue, a factor of historical arrangements that those who bare children come to rear them or whether it is, as Rossi would argue, the case that a woman's biological condition suits her for both bearing and rearing roles. It is to this case of motherhood as inherent in female biology that I should like to turn.

Before doing so, however, two other factors, both a matter of historical record and both necessary to an understanding of the context in which ideas on motherhood have to be understood, ought to be noted. The first is that as a consequence of the Women's Movement, academicians (researchers, scholars) began to study the process of mothering and the institution of motherhood from the point of view of the mother or caretaker and not, as had previously been the case, from the perspective of the child.[121] In addition, the confluence of the movement, the questioning of authority initiated by the sixties, and an emerging neo-Freudian literature encouraged scholars to rethink certain aspects of Freud's theses on the role played by the father in the formation of the child's personality, what one critic calls the "patricentric inflation of the power of the father."[122]

This illustrates a point made earlier in the discussion of the social construction of knowledge: that what one takes to be of intellectual importance is most often a consequence of historical circumstance; that the scholarly interest in what being a mother entails is generated by the changing conditions of motherhood, which conditions are brought about by concrete changes in the possibility for and encouragement of women to choose options other than child-rearing for themselves. Options are real possibilities to the degree that technological and economic changes, themselves interrelated, have been or can be instituted. For example, infant food formulas make it possible for women with young children to remain in or return to the labor force without the same set of concerns as exist for women who are their child's sole source of nutrition. Reassessments of which jobs women are physically and legally able to hold require changed political and economic attitudes; and it is no simple matter to arrive at a social agreement on which jobs women could physically hold — truckdriver? firefighter? construction worker?

To add a necessary layer of complication, it certainly appears to be the case that what changes a society works for, that is, what efforts it puts into making certain technological and economic breakthroughs, is affected by ideas and values which at least those in charge of the technology and the economy come to regard as valuable. This does not imply that anything is possible: certainly, it seems that the laws of gravity are there to prevent persons from flying (without the aid of artificial wings), and, certainly, long-entrenched social values and biological possibilities are there to keep men from bearing babies. But as Shulamith Firestone suggests,[123] one ought to be researching the ways to alter this biological situation if one is to realize a genuine equality between the sexes. It certainly had been the case that social ideas were there to prevent women from holding jobs that seemed impossible for them to hold given social attitudes towards and scientific data on male versus female physical strength.

What I wish to argue, however, is that being there varies according to whether the thereness is physical or social in nature, allowing as one must for the dialectical relationship between the two. Social facts are there, as Durkheim argued, but in a different way than biological facts. If one says, as Rossi does,[124] that one's age and sex are things that one is born with, certainly one has less control over one's age — perhaps none at all if one takes into account the very fact of human mortality — than one has over one's sex. Maybe this will not always be the case; certainly the level and degree of technological control of sex was not always possible in the shape and in the form that it is now, and it is in this sense that one could argue that technology helps to define the "feminine character" in a way and to a degree that it does not define age — although cosmetic surgery makes incredible alterations in what one appears to be and social values do redefine expectations of how any particular person of a particular age ought to act or ought to be regarded.

A second factor to bear in mind if one is adequately to understand the tenor of the debate over the nature of motherhood is the profile of changes in family structures that the demographic studies reveal. One finds the following: a decline in the number of children born and in the size of families, although the vast majority of women are still continuing to have children; a decrease in the number of unwanted pregnancies; child-bearing occupying a smaller time period in a woman's life, while at the same time coming later in life for more women and, therefore, reflecting and contributing to changes in women's participation in the labor force; and an increase in the number of single-parent families as well as in the number of alternative patterns for raising children — single-single parents, unmarried and often same-sex families, communal families, step-families, reconstituted nuclear families. [125]

These changes in the family involved reassessments of what the family was and ought to be. The reassessments are of two kinds: those made by the social participants, that is, by persons acting in their everyday life-world; and those made by analysts of that social world. Rossi's depiction of a changed perception of the family, as it respects the formulation of theory, strikes me as correct. She asks why there is a change in assessing the family after the 1960s, why there is a move from seeing the family as a structure of integration, charged with the socialization of the newborn, to seeing the family — most expressly the nuclear family — as a confining, controlling and restricting mechanism contriving to shape up those free spirits who are waiting to break loose. And how is it that the "deviant" style of sexual relatedness becomes the "variant"?

Rossi suggests that at an earlier time, functionalism, as the prevailing sociological paradigm, required that one look at factors of age: persons were different because some of them were older, others younger, and these age differences made for generational differences in role behavior and role expectation. Functionalism was not concerned with sex differences perhaps, if Rossi is correct, because these were taken-for-granted differences. The contemporary mode of analysis, which is still at one level empirical descriptive even if purged of the Parsonian terminology, utilizes role theory as its orienting perspective and looks at the family in terms of female and male actors and sees these attributes as less-than-natural and more as the consequence of specific instances of socialization. This contemporary writing on the family, written after the political struggles of blacks, women and gays for equitable treatment, flattens out sex differences in the family, and, in so doing, suggests an historical conservatism to holding onto motherhood and fatherhood as one can come to know them.

Functionalism, then, supports family units based on age assignment, while a sex-centered analysis supports a sexually egalitarian grouping of peoples that extends the concept of family into heretofore unchartered waters. It departs from earlier views that confine the family to units which reproduce themselves and then care for the product of that reproduction. Rossi seems correct in arguing that while age and sex have been seen as ascriptive characteristics — ones with which one enters the world — the unalterability of sex is being questioned. The new mode of family analysis wants sex to be like class, that is, a condition that is culturally determined and politically alterable. While how much of an alteration is being debated, the parameters are being set around questioning the conventional wisdom of one's understanding of sex roles.

Two examples might help to clarify what I take to be a dialectical relationship between changing ideas and ideals and structural changes. First, more women were to be found in the ranks of the labor force, but their reasons for being there might not be all of a kind. Factors of class, for example, might affect an economic need to work for some women while for others a psychological need for self-expression through a craft might be the primary reason for working. The valuing of one's work, that is, how integral to one's sense of self it is, might have to be taken into account, for it might be that having to work as opposed to wanting to work — if one allows for that simple distinction — might affect how one comes to regard the child-care role. Yet, a simple reading of the employment figures would not reveal how persons value work and family. Second, there are now more varied ways to bear as well as rear children: another dialectic of technology and values was redefining what "having" children meant as well as what "raising" them meant. The family was subject to the kinds of crises — crises of "legitimation" or "motivation"[126] — which Habermas regards as characteristic of advanced industrial societies. A crisis would exist if people withdrew their support from the family because they no longer believed in its normative ideals, a bonding through ties grounded in blood or agreements. A crisis would exist if no one knew, any longer, what the family was either expected to do or ought to do. For if other institutions began to take over functions that were previously held the family, then the family could either welcome a redefinition of its role, or accept the emerging new reality with disquietude, or exhort those in positions of power to return to the family those tasks of socialization previously considered legitimately theirs. Lasch's exposition of the ways in which the state has taken over functions previously held by the family, most expressly by the father, speaks to just this point.[127] A crisis exists when persons lose their sense of understanding about the ways in which social processes are occuring, or, put somewhat differently, when institutions lose their meaning.

Habermas allows, however, for situations in which if persons could be made better off by the failure of institutions (personal incomes increase as family form undergoes change) or if persons did not experience crises as such (collapse of family seen as obliteration of an oppressive institution), the system could move to a new stage of development.[128] How one might regard these crises is ultimately a moral question, and one can certainly make a moral case for the family, as certain feminists have done.

The idea of motherhood being socially constructed is questioned by Rossi, a sociologist whose professional work has been concerned with the status of women.[129] She grounds her argument for motherhood's biological dimension in her reading of scientific data on sex and hormonal relationships. She intends to offer an empirical answer to the question of what being female entails by reference to data from evolutionary theory, biology, and psychology. In her paper "A Biosocial Perspective on Parenting," she argues that social attitudes toward the family have changed: its variations are no longer considered deviations and its worthwhileness is now held to be oppression. Under the aegis of an egalitarian ideology, there is a questioning of a traditional division of labor in the family along sex lines, most especially with respect to how mothers and fathers ought to relate to their children. This ideology, she continues, emphasizes the degree to which sexual roles are culturally determined, and it finds a companion set of beliefs (an ideology, too, perhaps?) in contemporary social science which fears what it takes to be the conservatism of biology. She wants to steer a course between a view of humans that allows them unfettered freedom to be whatever they and their economy allow, and a view of humans as totally constructed by whatever belief systems happen to be fashionable or powerful. For her, "sex . . . is a biological fact . . . while equality is a political, ethical, and social percept." It is biologically the case that families are to reproduce and rear children and it is against this given — what she calls "innate physiological factors" or "the biology of our species"[130] or "underlying biological processes"[131] — that she examines the sexual and parental "scripts" which govern social rules of behavior.

Basic to her argument is the heritage which humans have with other primates, for while technology has altered the social conditions under which humans live, their genetic equipment is still the same as that of their earliest mammalian forebears. The roles of women and men in respect to work have changed, but the bearing and rearing of children have still remained the same; it is in this sense that the maternal quality has evolved. That this is the case is a consequence of certain biological predispositions which women have, to mother or care for the young; it is not that men cannot learn how to do these things but, rather, that women are biologically predisposed towards these tasks in ways that men are not. In other words, because of their bodies men and women respond to their children differently:

> *A biosocial perspective does not argue that there is a genetic determination of what men can do compared to women; rather, it suggests that the biological contributions* [what she will elsewhere call the "unlearned responses" or "propensities"] *shape what is learned, and that there are differences in the ease with which the sexes can learn certain things.* [132]

There are male and female "parameters" that color what is learned. A society could move toward "unisex socialization", but it would require extensive "compensatory training that would have to be continually monitored lest there be a return to those things that come easily to the respective sexes, to wit, mothering to women, based as it is on a mother-infant tie that evolves out of birthing that is biological and social in a way that fathering is not. Were a society to move away from mothering and towards parenting, it would have to recognize that the two bonds are not of equal strength, that the mother-child bond has a biological (to wit, hormonal) basis that the father-child bond does not, and that men would have to be compensated, in the form of training programs in child-care, for mothers' physiological advantages. One might interpret this to mean that parenting goes against the biological grain and if it is to be undertaken, it will be costly and difficult to achieve.

Rossi is not simply saying that men have evolved to be providers and women to be caretakers: she takes great pains to distinguish her argument from the rejection of cultural factors and a tendency to equate differences with inequalities which she associates with such writers as George Gilder, Robin Fox, and Lionel Tiger. Differences have a basis in an unalterable biology while the equitable treatment of persons with differences must be built into a social and legal system. Hers, she argues, is not a position of genetic determinism, but, rather, biological predisposition: a biosocial perspective and a sociobiological perspective are not the same thing, either with respect to their comparisons of different species or in their regard for biology as a master science.[133] One should point out, since Rossi does not, that even in the writings of a sociobiologist like Wilson, whose work can be interpreted to mean that biology intends men and women to play different roles in the bearing and rearing of children, there is a recognition that a society can underwrite programs that would redirect biology. Wilson would regard co-parenting programs not only as massive experiments in behavior modification but also of dubious economic value: the "price . . . required for training and enforcement that must be spent to circumvent our innate predispositions may well be too great to outweigh the advantages of sexual equality."[134]

Training for parenting is not, then, a biological question, but a policy question: is the value of sexual equality to be reached through co-parenting? Dinnerstein and Chodorow would be most empathic in saying yes, while Rossi would suggest other ways to achieve the same goal; each would recognize the economic cost of this to the society. Rossi would part company with Dinnerstein and Chodorow on whether the cost would arise from the deep-seatedness of mothering in psychic practices or in biological factors, although each would be wary of any simplistic efforts to make distinct categories out of the social, the psychological and the biological.

Similarly, the question of fertility, fertility rates and fertility transformations is not simply biological. Those concerned with the drop in fertility rates of a certain class of women and the rise in another class wish to see society structured in one way rather than another. Those who do not share those concerns also have political values but they are of a different ideological cloth. Likewise, resolutions to the problem of infertility also occur within a given social context. If, for example, in vitro fertilization is a costly process and the availability of medical services is dependent upon one's financial resources, then infertility falls differently on those with money and those without, unless, of course, social policy is written to make readjustments in fertility an entitlement and not a privilege. One could also argue that keeping women out of certain jobs (for example, jobs in which the work might endanger their reproductive ability) is not a question of women's biology but, rather, of the willingness of industry to expend the monies necessary to make the work safe and of society to forgo using those products whose production endangers lives, even if the products themselves enhance lives. [135] It is not that there are easy answers to these questions, but, on the contrary, their complexity which makes it erroneous to reduce them to biological questions.

Rossi, not prepared to leave biology to the conservatives, argues that one must counter an understandable hostility towards the biological sciences which social scientists have, for the latter remember an earlier era when biological data was used to advance the cause of biological determinism in general and Social Darwinism in particular. Rejecting all physiological data as having a bearing on sex roles and sex role socialization, or minimizing the import of differences which appear to result from reproductive functions, or arguing that technology will soon eliminate what differences do exist, is dangerous:

> The reproductive and endocrine systems that underlie child-bearing and lactation are functioning systems within the female throughout her life cycle, and to deny their significance to female psychology or to the organization of family systems is to devalue a central fact in human-species survival for which the human female plays the most critical role, to reveal the profound degree to which many women accept masculine technocratic thinking, and to by-pass the significant findings of science pertaining to reproductive and endocrine functioning. [136]

In short: the minimization of one's biological condition plays into the hands of technocratic control and this has the added consequence of minimizing a female contribution and maximizing a male sphere of influence. It is almost as if biology, or the biological, becomes the political weapon against technocratic take-over. In this spirit, she refers to her position as a "radical vision"[137] of a social order that would be more in accord with Nature, with one's body, and with the need to balance the world of work and the world of intimacy.

This theme of the "natural" as a counter to technocratic domination also runs through Germaine Greer's *Sex and Destiny*. Concerned with feminist theoreticians and male technocrats who consciously or not act to tell people how to live their lives, Greer, a feminist writer on women's issues, sees great danger in the devaluation of both fertility and motherhood which characterizes Western society, a devaluation imposed on

Third World countries as a consequence of the "cultural hegemony of Western technology."[138] Greer says that the desire to reproduce is instinctual, something the body urges one to do. She asserts this to be the case, and were one to ask her where her evidence is, she would argue that one's common sense tells us what science is not and never shall be able to prove incontrovertibly. In the West's quest for reason, she argues, it has used the ideology of rationalism to demystify and rationalize, mechanize and pharmaceuticalize, aspects of life that were meant to be carried on in a manner that precedes and precludes scientific theorems. Rossi, like Greer, and both having a like consignification with some of the themes out of Horkheimer, Habermas, and Lasch, are responding to the consequences for sex of the modernization processes, often referred to as the technological invasion of the life-world.

Rossi argues that the handling of biological data is affected by political considerations. If it were the case that in the past biology was used to keep certain status groups in their place — and there is an entire literature on the ways in which biology has been so used[139] — it could equally be the case that the rejection of biological data is also rooted in one's ideology, albeit an ideology of sexual equality. A liberalism or a psychological behaviorism that places inordinate weight on the role that environmental or cultural factors play in shaping the person wishes to consider humans as coming into this world as blank slates and the personalities which they develop are seen as a consequence of the social values and social policies of the societies in which they come to maturation. The democratization and egalitarian thrust of this position, which aims to de-emphasize ascriptive characteristics and enshrine the potential merit and achievement to which all persons can equally aspire, has as its underside a set of unlimited possibilities which may demand of persons more than they are genuinely able to deliver.

Rossi, like other contemporary writers, asks a contemporary question: what data does biology offer and how does it affect one's perception of the "feminine character"? Biology, as a discipline, provides evidence which Rossi sees as helping one to understand human nature and setting down the basics out of which cultural diversions emanate. Advances in bio-evolutionary theory and in neuro-endocrinology have increased one's knowledge of what being human means and they have provided one with answers to the question of why women are in charge of child-care and domestic operations. They provide the data for ideas like maternal instinct and mother-child bonding. Biology, however, only seemingly appears to explain sexual inequality; differences, for Rossi, do not logically lead to inequities, even if politically they may appear to do so.

Rossi argues for an "interactive-influence model,"[140] one that focuses on the relationship between socio-psychological and biological factors, to explain human behavior. Sociology must take into account the reality of the body, just as biology must note how social factors influence and affect seemingly independent processes of a physical nature: "Biological processes unfold in a cultural context, and are themselves malleable, not stable and inevitable. So, too, cultural processes take place within and through the biological organism; they do not take place in a biological vacuum." She is supportive of the work being done to integrate biological data and a sociological approach to knowledge and understanding, and the concomitant critique of determinism and reductionism, which is to be found in the writings of biologists who have been influenced by Marxist notions of the dialectic, social change and human praxis. She finds that: "organisms are not passive objects acted upon by internal genetic forces . . . nor are they passive objects acted upon by external environmental forces. . . . Genes, organisms and environment interpenetrate and mutually determine each other."[141]

Rossi attacks current sexual mating practices finding them concerned with sex and mating but not with matters pertaining to families and parenting. There are ideas similar to those of Lasch in her critique of the narcissism and individualism that prevents the caring for others essential to family relationships. It is the case that the sociologist finds "recreative sex" to have "contemporary ascendence over procreative sex and parenting." Characterizing the new forms as examples of "ego indulgence and immediate gratification," she is concerned lest these affect parent-children bonds, either by allowing these to become the kind of on-again/off-again relationships that fathers often have had to their children (the adoption of a male model of relatedness replacing the highly-valued mother-child tie, based as it is on "innate predispositions" of each to "relate intensely"[142] to the other) or by ignoring the biologically grounded emotional needs of mothers and children for which she had already offered evidence from endocrinological studies and which needs have already been affected for the worse by the introjection of technology in the birthing process in the form of obstetrical intervention.

Certainly, Rossi does not value a plurality of life-styles in and of themselves: there is no equivocation with respect to the ethical value of family and human relatedness. Her reading of demographic data suggests to her that women are still expressing an interest in having and raising children although the patterns in which they are doing this have changed, with an increase in parenting outside the bonds of a traditional heterosexual marriage and often in a single-parent pattern. These changes, when linked to other changes — fewer number of births, births later in one's life, greater emphasis on personal independence and self-fulfillment — will affect not only the profile of the family but also the bonds between the family and the outside community, that is, the family's sense of communal obligations and the feelings of integration, of ties and belonging, that grow out of familial relationships. Solo, or single, parenting has both individual and social consequences that Rossi suggests are matters for deep concern.

She substantiates her argument on differences in the ways men and women parent by examining studies where fathers have been placed or freely elected to be in a caretaker role; she notes that men "distance" themselves from early childcare responsibility while women "embrace" such demands. Persons bring to parenting gendered personalities; men are more impersonal and women more intimate in their relations with children. She reads current research to suggest that these differences are more than a consequence of socialization and more a result of " 'pre-cultural sex differences' "; and she is critical of those like Gilligan who do not postulate why this is the case. It is in the very biology of sexual differentiation that men and women are distinct and that these distinctions effect the ways in which they are and act in the social world. It is certainly the case that the differences are not all of the same kind, some bearing a more direct relationship to body structure than others; nonetheless, the sensitivity of the senses, activity levels, cognitive skills and parenting are all based on sexual dimorphism. It is in this context that she distinguishes herself from those like Dinnerstein and Chodorow, who would move to make parenting a task for both men and women, since certain things will still remain even if there are changes in gendered attitudes of childcare patterns, a certain disjunction between thinking like the primary caretaker and acting the role.

Rossi says that the evidence out of the neurosciences suggests sexual differentiation while there is a growing social trend toward sexual equality and, in the area of child-rearing, toward co-parenting. The child is predisposed toward a certain gender at birth, and these predispositions interact with parents (or caretakers?) who are also gendered. Being "gendered" means being what the interplay of one's biological predisposition and prevalent social-sex role results in, remembering that social roles can either accentuate or devalue biological predispositions. Co-parenting could lead to greater instances of androgyny, where male and female characteristics are found in equal instances in both males and females. This, she argues, has much to commend it, but, at the same time, the society must recognize that which the body is biologically predisposed to do and it must assure compensatory measures if it wants to redirect or change this in order to achieve a political or moral goal that it has deemed necessary or worthy. One can "actively encourage children to absorb the socially desirable attributes of both sexes,"[143] for example, encourage men and women to value intimacy *and* impersonality, competitiveness *and* cooperation, self-interest *and* communal interest. Rossi suggests that a more traditional family structure than the one envisioned by Dinnerstein or Chodorow or than those varieties being carried out by the sexual arrangements and liasons in practice at the present time still allows for building on the best that each sex has to offer. Similarly, cooperative efforts by women to rear children with group supports, usually of other women, necessary to assure that they do not suffer the isolation that has often accompanied the nuclear family in modern industrial society, also allows the women remaining in that biological role which would be most psychologically beneficial to the child.

What characterizes the period about which I write, as it had characterized Klein's period, is the presence of science as a paradigm for truth. The question of "what is a woman" was regarded by many both in and outside of the Women's Movement as a scientific question, and it was to the sciences, most especially to biology, that many turned to look for the data that would validate their hypotheses on the "feminine character." Not all read the data the same way, in large part because not all looked at the same data. One has already seen, in the discussion of motherhood, Rossi's position that a careful reading of the findings of the neurosciences would reveal that there were essential morphological differences between the sexes, out of which differences flow certain propensities to behave in a way one had come to define as feminine or, for that matter, masculine. Social practices and policies either reinforce or inhibit those propensities, depending upon the political goal they are hoping to reach (for example, equality) and the ways in which they define these goals in relation to biological differences (that is, differences need not lead to inequities).

In some sense, Rossi sees biological propensities as structuring the givens. There is in her writing no apologia for her reservations about socially constructing sex roles without regard to what she takes to be incontrovertible evidence that males and females are not similarly constructed. In this she has been read as being either too mechanistic — almost as if she sees a concrete biological structure or hormone, if not gene, for a mother's advantage in parenting, or too like those sociobiologists who are troubled by cultural mores which disturb what they see to be an evolutionary design. Rossi's essays on parenting, following upon work that had been heralded as championing the cause of sexual equality, evoked acrimonious responses, and in the caustic and bitter way in which her defense of motherhood has been received, one can understand the centrality of family relationships to emerging definitions of self and the reconstruction of social relationships. Some of her critics have interpreted her work as a "startling rejection of feminist cultural analysis,"[144] one of "retrenchment." Rossi is criticized for abandoning efforts to restructure personal relationships, especially those which arise out of familial arrangements which are perceived as being: (1) essential to female subordination; (2) historically, not biologically, grounded, and; (3) not determined by biology but constructed by human activity which is itself shaped by the constellations of humanly structured power relationships. Once it is conceived that the family is not located in history but in biology, one reduces, if not eliminates, any chance for correcting patriarchal family practices and the subordination and domination of women that follow out of those practices. Rossi's critique of social constructionism, in effect, contributes to an "anti-feminist backlash"[145] with its accompanying denial of the need for social policies that will act as a corrective to the historical situation of disempowered women.

Rossi, in her emphasis on the dialectic between culture and biology, distinguishes herself from those who speak of designs, or purposes, or intents, preferring instead to speak of socially alterable predispositions. She recognizes the correctness of the claims of both feminists and social scientists that a reading of history reveals the ways in which biological data has been used to legitimate the status quo, but she wants to reclaim biology from its entrapment in the conservative camp and see how its data can be used to achieve a different set of political objectives, and to do this she allies herself with those in biology who recognize a dialectical quality to natural as well as social phenomena and for whom the word "destiny" is anathema to the human project of praxis. She certainly is at odds with those who devalue biological considerations, arguing that what really is at issue is how the data is assessed. She is not prepared to say that the data itself is of little import and that the biology is not what is at issue but how the biology is assessed. Rossi does not want to give up some objective import of the biology.

The debate over biology is one of emphasis, of where the interpretor seems to place his or her stakes on a continuum. What interests the sociologist is the social context in which the continuum operates: in the background is a recognition that science reveals certain pieces of information which affect, or can affect, the ways in which one regard the sociological. In an historical context in which social movements, both of the Left and of the Right, have come to be fearful of or suspicious of science, its revelations—its data—are often made to accord with other values. Firestone, Rossi and the sociobiologists—Barash, for example—read data differently, or read different data. The question of what women are intended to do is not a scientific question but a moral question: for Firestone they are not intended to do or be anything other than authentic persons; for Rossi they are biologically predisposed to be mothers, but this need not occur; for Barash they are intended by nature to be mothers and they are going against their bodies to do otherwise, not to hear the "whisperings within."

The varying views on motherhood are but a further confirmation that science and scientific data are not "neutral," in the sense that one can place the findings of science on the table and all who sit down will read them in the same way. Similarly, debates on what is natural and what is cultural are revelatory not of what is really natural but how the concerns and fears of an age are expressed in attitudes on these issues. It is the fear of a technological take-over that makes Rossi's position intriguing, as it is Dinnerstein's and Chodorow's search for a solution to the problem of "human malaise" in the institution of patriarchy that interests the social theorist. [146]

Motherhood and Technology

In arguing that one can trace the ideas of feminist social theory to their provenance in the historical moment in which feminists are to be situated, one supports the thesis of this book: that ideas are restructured as a consequence of changed social conditions. This is a rendering of Marx's dialectical relationship between facts of mind and facts of matter. In Horkheimer's words: "That new views in fact win out is due to concrete historical circumstances. . . . Modern theoreticians of knowledge do not deny the importance of historical circumstance." There is no presumed judgment, on the part of those who follow this reading of history, that what evolves is necessarily what ought, in any moral sense, to evolve. Horkheimer, in fact, warns that if such a theory "conceives of reason as actually determining the course of events in a future society . . . [it] is also a camouflaged utopia," or a dystopia. What evolves, in any event, is shaped by humans acting on their material conditions. Everything that concerns persons reflects the impact of human activity on nature, not only cultural artifacts but also what one perceives: "The facts which our senses present to us are socially preformed in two ways: through the historical character of the object perceived and through the historical character of the perceiving organ."[1]

It is the case that many of the writers that I have selected to look at concern themselves with the issue of motherhood. For historical reasons, the debate over the status of women and over the appropriateness of their assuming certain roles coincident with or to the exclusion of other roles has often had to confront the structuring of women's life-worlds around the bearing and rearing of children. Thus, the case for a redefinition of feminine behavior, which is the subject matter of my inquiry, most often touches base with this issue. Writers on the feminine, even those who argue for the reevaluation or reassessment of th importance of mothering, nonetheless direct their gaze on the way(s) in which a female biology is either socially constructed or biologically grounded in principles and practices of child-bearing. I see the argument on mothering as a form of nurturing or caring, or caring and nurturing as quintessentially feminine ways of being-in-the-world, as integral to the discussion of women's sexuality and to issues as apparently remote as comparable worth where the question of equitable treatment for different performances echoes a concern of feminists respecting ways in which women are not or do not act like men.

In another guise, the issue of the import of mothering for women is part of a continuing philosophic inquiry into the nature of equality, to wit, whether men and women are alike and, therefore, to be accorded similar treatment. Put another way, one questions whether people can be treated equally while allowing for their differences. To the degree that the question of a "feminine charcter" is derivative from the ontological question of what constitutes humanity, it is at the crux of Enlightenment and post-Enlightenment enquiries. To the degree that historically all mothers have been women and most women have been mothers, the discourse on women has revolved around the historical conditions which have accorded motherhood a central role. Yet it has been the legacy of the Enlightenment to use reason to question that which has been taken for granted and that which power has named, codified, classified and grouped together under one rubric rather than another. It is in this context that I should argue that motherhood, reproductive technology and abortion are concerns that need to be understood historically, just as they need to be placed into a social context.

The Women's Movement occurs and is a contributor to an ongoing sexual revolution, one that is affected by the kinds of changes already suggested: changes in economic conditions, especially in the nature of work and the increased presence of women in the labor force; and changes in technology. These affect not only reconsiderations of such issues as life and death but also changes in sexual behavior and activity (including issues of child-bearing and child-rearing as well as issues of sexual gratification and diversity, or hedonism and exhibitionism, depending upon how one comes to regard freedom from restraint). Lasch's books on the self, in both its diminished as well as narcissistic forms, explore the ways in which an individualism without communal ties devalues all forms of authority, and, within this context, whatever the intent of feminism's theoreticians, it might be the case that sexual liberation is interpreted as assisting women to become concerned with self, as the ideology of American individualism and consumerism—which has been seen as working so well in the past—encourages them to be. Leave aside for the moment that this message of individualism, consumerism and success may leave out of the picture a class and race of women passed over when the goods were being distributed, and that very few can "have it all." Lasch's concern, which one can read out of Rossi, as well, is that this individualism has certain consequences for the notion of political community, of a politics shaped by us all, so essential to a certain reading of democratic theory. It appears to these critics of modernity that there occurs a demise of a civic public, which may, in turn, lead in the direction of a new kind of dictatorship or totalitarianism in which there is a devaluation of the person. Horkheimer fears the "crisis of the individual"[2] and Arendt sees in the modern style of Naziism a declaration of the individual as superfluous.[3] Horkheimer argues that persons are no longer conscious of themselves as persons and they no longer direct, in the sense of see or understand, their lives; machines determine what people shall both want and need. There is the destruction of cerebration — the self is lost: there is no " 'I' — the most elementary affirmation of identity"[4] and there is an involvement not with other selves but with either one's own self — what Lasch will call the "culture of narcissism"[5] in which one gets erotic gratification by admiring one's own attributes — or with machines, which involvement effects the self, making it more machine or automaton-like.

A contemporary rendering of these themes can be found in Elshtain's writing on the family as a form of community based on a certain kind of social compact that counters the atomism of liberalism, and the consumerism and "possessive individualism" of ultra-liberalism and utilitarianism. She writes: "the atomistic, contractual frame exudes a politics of self-interest undertaken by a freely choosing, rational agent who, within the present order, is reborn as a sovereign consumer."[6] She counters this with the individual in what she calls social compact theory, who sees him/herself as part of a tradition to which he/she is indebted and from which he/she ought not cut him/herself off: one is respectful of diverse life forms and of one's natural surroundings and one is "organized to defend and sustain what remains of a way of life not permeated by the forces of atomism, consumerism, and technological forms of control."[7]

The feminist fear of technology, in the way it is put by Greer or Rossi, or even Dinnerstein, comes out of these contemporary concerns for the consequences of a machine culture to the assumed sense of self. It is not a simple Luddite reaction or a call to return to some golden, non-technological past, but a fear based on technology's determining how one ought to live, to its subsumption of one's life under a series of mechanical demands. It is directing one's life through what is possible, not what is desirable: what can be done is done, as opposed to what ought to be done determining what is pratically done, and, as such, it is the loss of the sine qua non of personhood. Bureaucratic rationalization involves the intrusion of technical expertise and methods of analyses into one's life. Horkheimer puts it this way: "The machine has dropped the driver; it is racing blindly into space."[8]

One could catalogue areas in which technology, especially what some regard as that bright and "brave new world" of reproduction, shapes issues in ways previously unknown: abortion; contraception; artificial insemination; embryo transfers and embryo adoption; genetic screening; prenatal screening for sex; in vitro fertilization; sterilization. Some of these areas contain technological advances of long standing; others are part of a nascent movement towards a wider range of fertility planning technologies, the logistics and ethics of which are being widely debated. The Office of Technology Assessment of the United States Congress has catalogued such changes according to their availability during the twentieth century. Of those highly likely before 1990, one finds: safer oral contraceptives; improved IUDs; improved long-acting steroid injections; improved ovulation-detection methods; steroid implants; steroid vaginal rings; and the prostaglandin induction of menses. For those technologies which are possible by 1990 but doubtful, one finds: monthly steroid-based contraceptive pills; improved monthly steroid injections; new types of drug-releasing IUDs; anti-pregnancy vaccine for women; improved barrier contraceptives for men; sperm suppression contraceptives for men; reversible female sterilization as well as simplified female and male sterilization techniques. And, as a final category, they list those technologies which while unlikely before 1990 are possible by the year 2000: anti-fertility vaccine for men; anti-sperm drug for men; lactation-linked oral contraceptives for women; new types of anti-ovulation contraceptive drugs for women; contraceptive drugs for women that disrupt ovum transport; reversible male sterilization; and pharmacologic or immunological sterilization for both men and women.

In analytic terms, these new forms of reproduction change the sexual landscape which provides the background against which traditional ideas on birthing are discussed. Reproduction has been moved more into the public realm and, in this sense, has become subject to greater control by public forces, which may or may not bring desirable results. At the outset, it has demanded answers to new questions: Do these new directions affect who controls whose reproduction? For what purposes, if any, do these new changes occur? Do these give new meaning to notions of person, of person as embryo, of rights of persons and/or embryos? Is the desire to have children in a form that requires the assistance of science one that ought to be encouraged? Is childlessness a socially constructed problem? Is infertility a problem that ought to be solved and at what cost and to whom?

Sexual relations have always been affected by the state of the technological art, although technique does not "cause" changes in social, political and economic arrangements. Linda Gordon has argued that the control of women's fertility was not due to changes or advances in contraception but, rather, was the result of political needs for population control.[9] The technology is played out in a given historical context, although the social and economic conditions are a background for scientific inventiveness and public acceptance of such inventedness. If Gordon is correct that the decline in fertility preceded the advances in contraception and that women were receptive to the birth-control pill and other devices to limit or control family size because of their changed economic situation, then one might argue that further advances in reproductive technology may follow the same pattern: it is not that such technologies will cause new approaches to reproduction, but, rather, that the success of the Women's Movement, its part in the redefinition of women's social roles and sexual morality, coupled with the ideology of secularism, consumerism and material success, will encourage women to alter traditional child-bearing roles. Furthermore, in a society of technological rationality, such advances seem to be a perfect fit for a cultural landscape in which the functionality or adaptability of individuals to systems needs is already considered legitimate.[10] These feminist writings open up the question of the relationship between politics and contraception: What happens when one transfers such contraceptives into a sprawling biomedical industry with all of the considerations of profit, cost-effectiveness and consumer protection that ought to be asked of such industries? Might not these new reproductive technologies effect and possibly even counter alternative technologies, such as natural childbirth and midwifery practices?[11]

This century has seen not only a dramatic increase in the number of persons who choose to be sterilized but it has also seen the refinement of sex without contraception and the perfecting of conception without traditional sexual relations. Artificial insemination by a donor (AID), in vitro fertilization (IVF), and surrogate embryo transfer (SET) have altered traditonal patterns of reproduction regardless of whether one comes to regard these practices for reproducing as extending parenting to persons previously denied the possibility or of invading the life-world as that world has been constructed over time, of assisting persons to realize their desires or as controlling the contours of human life and human existence.

For the sociologist, these advances affect ideas about individuality in general and parenthood in particular. In social terms, one finds genetic parents and legal parents. In the case of AID, the genetic father donates his sperm to another man's wife, the genetic and legal mother. Which man is the child's legal father? Is it the legally constituted father who will have responsibility for the child? Does this society not presume that the sociality of parenthood is greater, say, in an AID case, than the genetic or biological dimension? What of instances in which the legal father (husband) disavows that the child is his and does not, like an AID father, want the child? Might obligations, then, not revert to the genetic father? Might not these changes bring about new kinds of paternity suits? In SET cases, the genetic mother is not the same as the gestational mother — she who gives birth to the child and, if the child is given up for adoption, each may differ from a legal mother. The rearing mother, most often the gestational mother, is usually considered to be the primary mother: what values are at play here?

There are at least two ways to look at this social/technological nexus: either the technology is outstripping the society's moral resources or the society's social thinking has not kept pace with the technology.

When in July 1978, a baby, Louise Brown, was born who had been fertilized in a glass dish by doctors who had co-joined her father's sperm and her mother's egg, each of which had been surgically gathered, a new stage in a constantly changing technological drama had been recorded: a child had been fertilized outside a woman's body. Technology changes the world and one has to ask what changes are intended by an invention and what changes may be realized or thwarted by it.[12]

Humanity can be defined, redefined, and reformulated by technological advances: organ transplants, mechanical hearts, screening for Tay-Sachs, and electrode implantations in the brain are some of the means by which human misery can be alleviated. In the process, these devices alter the means and manner of discourse used to discuss being human, male and female, mother and father. As one writer suggests: "Man is partly defined by his origins; to be bound up with parents, siblings, ancestors, is part of what we mean by 'human'. By tampering with and confounding these origins, we are involved in nothing less than creating a new conception of what it means to be human."[13] Moreover, he or she who has the knowledge of how to alter traditional sex relations has a power advantage even if the case is made that the knowledge is only to be put at the service of individuals who ask for it: "the power rests only metaphorically with humankind; it rests in fact with particular men — geneticists, embryologists, obstetricians."[14]

The fear is that those who have access to the knowledge of genetic and reproductive technology come to have control over others, that various forms of prenatal testing and fetal monitoring might counter dangerous pregnancies or be integral to the practice of eugenics or both. Preventing certain births from occurring means assuring that other kinds will succeed: the question is which fall into which category. Eugenics might conjure up the Nazi legacy of the Holocaust or fears of creating a race of androids, but it is also a democratic way, one could argue, of allowing a person or persons to decide what kind of child they want to have. The same might be said of sex pre-selection. Feminists have been of several minds on these issues, none wanting to get on the "slippery slide" of beneficent reform that ends in totalitarian control.[15]

Procreation, the act of specific individuals at a specific moment in time creating the life of another, is changed to the degree that scientific locations and scientific experts enter into the picture as active agents in the process. Some see this as extending life — heterosexual or homosexual persons who might otherwise not be able to have children now can do so. Others see such technological innovation as improving life — surrogate mothers may be a rational and intimate alternative to adoption agencies. Still others, often speaking at another level of discourse, see scientists as having an attitude which, as it is applied to persons, can be intemperate in treating subjects as objects, putting them through a dehumanizing and depersónalizing set of processes, a labyrinth of bureaucratic detail; this is the case even though, paradoxically, science, when put into the service of humanity, is invested with a countervailing potential to alleviate human misery and suffering.[16]

That the craft of childbirth undergoes radical alteration, in that it involves persons other than the traditional dyad, may be only one perspective on new techniques. It may be the case that these technological innovations are but new options and that what matters is not the technology but who controls it and for what purposes. In other words, one must empirically determine which interests are being protected and for what purpose, and whether those involved in the technological nexus, be they doctors or patients, researchers or beneficiaries, are aware of what is involved and why.

In *The Dialectic of Sex,* Shulamith Firestone, a feminist activist and theoretician, underscores the import of the biological in the social construction of gender. Going further than most feminist writers in her preparedness to see even biological structures as essentially historical, that is, shaped by the technological contours of the specific moment, Firestone speaks of the need to change a fundamental biological condition. Technology offers the material possibilities for eliminating all gender differences, thereby ending the biologically rooted war between the sexes. Empiricism and the empirical method allow for the "total understanding of the laws of nature;"[17] they provide the tools through which one could build an ideal yet real world in the here and now. Her reading of Marx—and, even more so Friedrich Engels's *The Origin of the Family, Private Property and the State*—whose ontology she adopts for her feminism, is that one must understand Nature in order to control it; that is, one must use the scientific method to make the break-throughs in knowledge which will allow individuals to create the kinds of lives which are free from restraint, providing them with the self-sufficiency at the root of personhood.

In line with using technology for humane purposes, artificial reproduction, which "is not inherently dehumanizing,"[18] is seen as freeing women from their female roles. Not only do women no longer have to depend upon men for their well-being, but they no longer have to subordinate their desires to their biology. Women must seize control of the processes, both political and technological, by which they bear and rear children as a first step towards the elimination of the distinction between the sexes itself. Sex, not class, is the primary divisive category and "a materialist view of history based on sex itself"[19] allows one to see how one must obliterate that upon which tyranny and oppression are grounded. She writes:

historical materialism is that view of the course of history which seeks the ultimate cause and the greatest moving power of all historic events in the dialectic of sex: the division of society into two distinct biological classes for procreative reproduction, and the struggles of these classes with one another; in the changes in the modes of marriage, reproduction and child-care . . . . in the connected development of other physically-differentiated classes (castes); and in the first division of labor based on sex which developed into the (economic-cultural) class system.[20]

To end the "tyranny of the biological family," with its inequitable power relationships, where women are dependent upon men and children upon both men and women, pan-sexuality would have to replace heterosexuality, homosexuality and bi-sexuality: "genital differences between human beings would no longer matter culturally." She writes: "The reproduction of the species by one sex for the benefit of both would be replaced by . . . artificial reproduction: children would be born to both sexes equally, or independently, or either."[21]

By eliminating the family, which technology now or in the immediate future allows one to do, one could undo the Freudian categories — the Oedipus complex and the incest taboo — which now constitute mechanisms of repression. In addition, once biology is freed from restraint, the mechanisms used to keep persons in check — romanticism and romantic love are examples — will no longer be necessary.

Firestone's thesis must be taken seriously as a viable practicum, one whose theory can be realized by the advances in reproductive technology: it is a normative argument whose time has empirically come. She is putting the case for ectogenesis, which would free women and children from both male domination and excessive mothering, but not all feminists approach reproductive technology in quite the same way as she does. Helen Holmes, in contrasting technological values with feminist values, juxtaposes: (1) a view that sees technology as being intrinsically good is one that legitimates domination, objectification or reification, the exploitation of nature, hierarchies or rank-ordering and profit with (2) a view that respects the individual, sees the personal as political and the political as ethical, values autonomy and choice and the wholeness of the individual, a community of women, a human community, an ecosystem, connectedness and non-hierarchies.[22] This juxtaposition reveals a concern that the scientization or industrialization of the body gives control to those who run the machinery not to those who "own" that body, that is, that it is a form of manipulation.

What emerges from analyses of reproductive technology, those written by specifically feminist writers, as well as by more traditional ethicists, is illustrative of what Habermas has called the "paradox of modernity." It is possible to reduce instances of infertility without the full awareness of the persons involved of the ramifications of the experiment.[23] It is possible to solve the problem of childless couples, be they heterosexual or homosexual, but this may entail the creation of job opportunities similar to prostitution, to wit, surrogate mothering, as well as allowing those who can afford to pay for such procedures to be in a more privileged position.[24] In acting to reduce infertility, the society may be taking away scientific time and money from other more socially pressing problems, such as cancer research or, it may be inadvertently affecting the number of children waiting to be adopted. In allowing for safer pregnancies, the society may have to give greater power over the birth process to doctors, most of whom are men. In acting to prevent the birth of severely brain-damaged children, the society can encourage the preselection for male children as well as for "perfect" children.[25] As one writer puts it:

> Choices open and choices close. For those whose choices meet the social expectations, for those who want what society wants them to want, the experience of choice is very real. We must not get caught in discussions of which reproductive technologies are politically correct, which empower and which enslave women. They all empower and they all enslave. They all can be used by, for and against us. The next step in the politics of reproductive control is the politics of social control.[26]

One might profitably situate the analyses of the controversies over abortion within the context of the contemporary debate on the scientization of the life-world, although feminist writers[27] do suggest that it is not the technological issues that are the exclusive center of the debate but, rather, a wide range of other issues as well. Beverly Harrison, writing from a theological perspecitve, argues that abortion is tied to a woman's definition of self, of being able to decide what can and what ought be done to her body, and how having a child she does not want affects her life after delivery. Rosalind Petchesky details how one's view on abortion grows out of one's life as a woman, and how the specifics of one's social circumstances affect the ways in which one comes to regard questions of rights and choices. From both a sociological and a Marxist position, she argues that morality is grounded in economic conditions in which one accommodates "the pressures of conflicting ideologies and values imposed by the dominant culture and various oppositional cultures on one's own sense of felt need."[28]

Elshtain has suggested that one's views on abortion accord with certain views on the nature of rights as these come out of diverse political theories. The predominant view, she has argued, sees abortion as an individual's right:

> the atomistic, contractual frame exudes a politics of self-interest undertaken by a freely choosing, rational agent who, within the present order, is reborn as a sovereign consumer. Liberalized abortion poses no serious

challenge to this order; indeed, the force of the doctines of *prima facie* rights, free choice, and self-interest promotes and sustains abortion imperatives, which are seen as part of woman's freedom and as one way to free all of us from the last vestiges of bondage to nature and to the past.[29]

In societies that counter or seek to negate the values of the present order, societies governed by social compacts which emphasize community, tradition and an accommodation with nature, abortion, while not ruled out, is limited as the community seeks to find a place for the child that is to be born to one of its members.

Luker's book, *Abortion and the Politics of Motherhood,* is about the perception of self and others and about one's attitudes toward social responsibility and how one's view on abortion follow from these:

> The abortion debate has become a debate among women, women with different values in the social world, different experiences of it, and different resources with which to cope with it. . . . While on the surface it is the embryo's fate that seems to be at stake, the abortion debate is actually about the meanings of *women's* lives.[30]

Luker also details the history of abortion, especially its becoming a medical issue as doctors come to want to control the processes by which unwanted births were attended to; she indicates why abortion did not become a political issue until the 1960s when questions started to be raised about the legitimacy of reasons for providing for abortions — medical, psychological, social — and there was, as well, a questioning of the therapeutic basis of abortion. Luker uses a sociological lens to interview activists in the contemporary abortion debate. She details how states began to legalize abortion so as to provide some counter to the variability of community standards and services and how in 1973, in the *Roe* case, the Supreme Court ruled that the right to abort was granted to women and that restrictions imposed by the medical community, even where it was acting in the interests of the fetus (declared not to be a person under the Fourteenth Amendment) were unconstitutional.

Paradoxically, in democratizing the debate, that is, in making abortion not a medical issue but a woman's rights issue, the Court unleashed an opposition and made any compromise position on abortion of conflicting medical and moral views more difficult to achieve. Luker suggests that the *Roe* case was the Court's representation of certain women's views and that the opposition to *Roe* is the hearing of another set of voices. Thus, what the battle over abortion is about is feminist and anti-feminist views of women: abortion becomes a view of what being a woman means. Feminists are usually upper middle-class women, often professional, and secure in their jobs to which they are committed; while good mothers, they do not value motherhood in quite the same way as do the anti-feminists, and, for them, abortion means having control over one's body. The anti-feminists are mostly middle or lower middle-class housewives who value motherhood above all else and whose fear for the fetus is grounded in certain fears that they have for themselves in the larger social order. Luker writes that: *"the place and meaning of mother-hood"*[31] itself is at issue, that the place that being a mother occupies in one's life, that is, the way in which one's sense of self is tied to one's identity as a mother and the way in which one comes to think of the fetus, affects one's position on abortion. Moreover, the debate, by persons who construct their social worlds differently, is also a conflict between natural and positive law: *"personhood is a 'natural', inborn, and inherited right, rather than a social, contigent, and assigned right."*[32]

The view one has of the intent, purpose, or meaning of sexual relations, also colors one's attitudes towards abortion. One might ask: Is sex recreative as well as procreative? Does the availability of abortion allow women and men to be more carefree and less responsible about their sexual commitments? Does abortion contribute to women's sexual autonomy? What relationship does one's "right" to abort bear to one's responsibilities to other persons or to communal interests? How are "rights" and "interests" affected by matters of class and race, that is, what are the sociological parameters of the technological ability to "choose" to have or not have a child? Is there a universal ethic that governs behavior in matters of abortion as well as in all other matters? Or do "economic conditions determine moral values?"[33] Might one conclude that the abortion debate is the concretization of the debate over what it means to be a person and what social resources ought to be committed to that person?

Luker's data suggests not only the success of the pro-life position but, paradoxically, a growing national support for abortion, although it has been suggested that the consensus on abortion is not for abortion on demand but abortion in certain instances, a "regulated access to abortion"[34] with guidelines for who decides, when, and on what grounds. One could argue that the values of pro-choice win out, since these are the values of individualism with its emphases on social mobility, social success and the import of the quality of one's life. The abortion debate occurs within the context of a society that both fears state intervention and/or the bureaucratic intervention into matters that are of a personal nature as well as one that has come to see that the equitable treatment of persons may have to be bought at the price of that very state intervention. It is a society that in its commitment to pluralism has upheld the idea of a plurality of moralities and to this degree the secular and the religious beliefs are often at odds with each other. These secular views are often grounded in utilitarian ethics such that one might say that the technology is working on the side of detecting what kinds of babies one wants and aborting the others.

Luker argues that there has always been debate over the moral status of the fetus and when the genetic material that has been laid down becomes a person. This still continues, but it is now reshaped by new technological factors. The debate is over how to interpret data on conception, over what is meant by personhood, over what personhood entitles one to; and, all of these considerations are affected by the special interests of women of a certain class and status. She shows how technological changes in abortion practices affect views on the issue: for some, abortion is the final medical technology to be used when the preferred contraception route has failed. Might one, then, not say that as the technology allows one to identify the fetus and its viability earlier on, it becomes a factor in how one can reconcile the taking of fetal life and the taking of human life? If the fetus can be kept alive outside of the female's body, then does abortion mean the removing of the fetus or the destroying of the fetus? And what happens to that fetus once it is born? If it is also the case that diagnostic advances allow one to know more about what kind of medical conditions one's child will have, then one, or someone, will have to decide which, if any, conditions legitimate the termination of life. Certainly that is how the debate on abortion has taken shape.

One could still argue that the abortion debate is colored by scientific and technological events, as well as by the political squaring-off of pro-choice and pro-life positions.[35] On the one hand, it is no easier now than it ever was to define the moral status of the fetus, but it is easier to regard the fetus as more like us given the use of intra-uterine photographs. If a consideration is at what point parents think that the fetus is a person, then mechanisms such as sonograms, which can take "pictures" of fetuses evenn earlier than at three months, can contribute to this way of looking at the genetic or developmental process of birthing: they may affect such concrete practices as bonding, as reconceptualizing what the fetus means to the parent(s). If the prospect of viability, of the fetus being able to survive out of the woman's womb, is a factor in attaining or attributing personhood, then advances of technical nature affect the debate over abortion: What of late-term abortions? What if these involve genetic disorders that can be determined only late in the pregnancy? Pre-natal diagnoses are now able to detect defects while the fetus is still in the womb, and these tests can affect how one visualizes, or imagines, that fetus.[36]

Certainly, the way in which the data are presented — witness the film *The Silent Scream* — plays a role in structuring perception and, in this sense, gives a legitimating power to the person who is in a position to present the data. It is as if there are certain commonsense notions of personhood that define persons as those like us, those who look and behave like us. While science and logic may crack holes in commonsense understanding and may require that one speaks of genetic material, or non-persons, or involuntary parasites, and point out ways in which fetuses are not like us, politics often builds on these life-world responses which are themselves dialectically shaped by exposure to scientific or media discourse. Certainly, there is a dysjuncture between the moral and the legal analyses respecting abortion, for while *Roe v. Wade* assumes that the fetus is not at issue and concerns itself with safeguarding the rights of woman-as-mother, since 1973 the law has come to be concerned more and more with the fetus, resulting in a search for a rationale that will provide a body of law that protects the fetus. For the interest in the fetus, if one follows the logic out of *Roe,* is directly related to that point at which the fetus may approach or attain the rights of personhood guaranteed by the Constitution.

In a society informed by the paradigm of science, sex is looked at, perceived, and taught from the perspective of a systematic empirical study. In varying ways, the writers under discussion have sought to unravel the mystery of that thing called either human nature or human behavior, and in their reasoned arguments on sexual diversity and sexual practices, they have sought to use the findings of various branches of the sciences — if one includes psychological theorizing in this category — to postulate reasons for the apparent universality of certain sexual behavior-to wit, child-bearing and child-rearing practices. There are debates about the extent to which certain traits and behaviors associated with males and females reflect endowment, social learning, individual experience, and various combinations of these. What impresses the sociologist of knowledge, however, is that whether the argument is that behavior accords with socially learned roles that are particular to a culture, to a time and to a place, or that behavior reflects universals and is not a role but a script of a biological order, the appeal is never to feelings or to religion but, rather, to reason grounded in a form of philosophical or scientific presentation.

What the abortion debate reveals is the ways in which rights are affected by technology. It is not that the right to privacy becomes any less a moral right, or that fetal viability changes the right not to bear a child that was the consequence either of a rape or of incest. In the concrete, the right to privacy faces political (witness the practices of the "right-to-life" groups, and Congressional efforts to define when life begins) and technological challenges. The status of the fetus may be a moral issue, but by having a political and legal definition that is related to the concept of viability, technology is allowed to shape the public recognition of personhood. The feminist concern is that in the redirection of the abortion issue to matters affecting the fetus there is a loss of interest in the ways in which pregnancy affects the life-world of the mother and the need for women to have control over their bodies.

Morality: The Feminist Perspective

I should like to recapitulate the argument to date: the point at which Mannheim begins, and from which Klein follows, is that the "feminine" is not a trans-historical or trans-cultural phenomenon. For Mannheim, what is taken to be feminine at any given moment is a consequence not only of the status of women in the society and the political roles they play but also of the behavior they display, unexpected or contrary as that behavior may be to the myths of what is appropriately female. Theories on women, Mannheim continues, similarly reflect changing historical attitudes and, in so doing, unmask earlier ideologies. One could argue, of course, that Mannheim leads one to see the new theories as themselves ideologies, although the term "perspective" might be more appropriate to Mannheim's argument. In either case, Klein, in following Mannheim's prescriptions for a sociology of knowledge, looks at theories about women: *The Feminine Character* is not another theory of women. Klein's thesis is that those who write about women reflect the ideas of their particular culture, rooted in a time. The feminine is ideological, in the sense of a qualified perspective or picture of what constitutes being women.

In examining theories of women, I have followed Klein in selecting theses which I assess to be of intellectual import that have been offered in the past 20 years or so, a period marked by the emergence of a new phase of the Women's Movement. I have used the themes of motherhood and the family to allow for a discussion of certain historically constituted views. Here I have been most expressly interested in the work of Dinnerstein, Chodorow, Rossi, Wilson, Firestone, Petchesky and Luker, seeing in these an evolving argument on reformulations of the feminine. These have been discussed in order to demonstrate how each is reflective of certain values and beliefs particular to the age. Our age is one in which what it means to be a woman is being questioned in a very radical way. Not only are the kinds of questions being asked culturally influenced but the answers being given will also affect that culture. These writings tell us much about American society as they try either to redefine or, in the case of Wilson, restore women's roles.

I will now turn to a second theme characteristic of feminine thought during this period. The *Zeitgeist* of the contemporary period is encapsulated in a critique of morality, reason, and science as revealed in the works of Carol Gilligan, Nancy Hartsock, Carol McMillan, Kathy

Ferguson, Sara Ruddick, Dorothy Smith, and Evelyn Fox Keller. Their arguments are for a feminist mode of reasoning—a morality, a standpoint, and an epistemology—that counters, complements, or is distinct from a masculine morality, rationality, or science.

Certain of these themes are similar to those discussed by Klein; others, as one might expect, reflect changes that are a consequence not only of an economic and technological kind but that indicate an even greater interest in women by the empirical sciences than was the case when Klein wrote *The Feminine Character*. I have in mind discussions that come out of bio-psychology (in experimental psychology and in human biology), genetics, and ethology. Nonetheless, Klein conceded that while one might learn new and different things about women as one's research goes on, one never gets any closer to what it means to be a woman. That question is a moral and not a scientific one. The sociologist—certainly one following Mannheim—is at best able to chronicle attitudes, not validate eternal verities, or even take a sociological position on whether such verities do, in fact, exist.

I have begun where Klein ended and have been looking at what has happened to women in America since the middle of this century, most especially the changing patterns of their work, their child-care arrangements, and their political activity. Those writing about women in this period reflect these changes. The debate has, as its background, the social context in which women's social roles have changed. Technological developments in the world of work had made it possible for women to be employed in fields where men used to hold a monopoly. Many of these fields had been dependent upon physical strength, while other, newer fields (many in the service sector) had opened up. Many of these later jobs allowed for part-time employment. Jobs were no longer as rigidly sex-linked or sex-related as they had been at earlier times; in some ways, this was a consequence of changing attitudes towards what women were capable of doing, many of which were initiated by women's involvement in the work force during the Second World War. A consumer ideology, which encouraged both sexes to make money so as to be in a better position to purchase the goods and services upon which the economy was dependent, was another factor in women's reassessing both their participation in the labor force and their husbands' appreciation of what a second, if subsidiary income, could contribute to family finances.

Technological changes continued to alter familial possibilities not only with respect to family planning but also in how to rear or not rear one's own child and how to redefine the tasks of housewifery. Again, the case of technology's making available cheap and efficient contraception and labor-saving devices in the home provided the opportunity for one to redefine the role of mother; the material base existed for one to question whether what had been thought of as one's destiny was not, in fact, a matter of history.

Political changes reflected a redefinition of equality as that had been reformulated by the racial struggles of the 1950s and 1960s. These redefinitions were coupled with a general questioning of authority and the bureaucratization of American society arising from the student rebellions of the same time period.

When one comes to a discussion of women, morality, and reason, and the relationship of each to science, one must situate these discussions within several broader intellectual contexts. First, there is the questioning of science, scientific rationality, or forms of reasoning which model themselves after the precise natural sciences. Issues of epistemology or methodology are often fused with issues of politics, to wit, the relationship of positivism or empiricism to the specific structures of advanced, industrial society, or the subject-object dichotomy as it affects capitalism and how the latter, in turn, informs a kind of reasoning which is scientific or functional in intent. In the philosophic literature, one finds a critique of positivism as a model for social understanding; in its most exemplary form, this critique provides the underpinnings for the trenchant criticism that has come out of the Frankfurt School where a certain way of looking at the world, what might be called the ideology of technocratic consciousness,[1] based on a certain kind of scientific reasoning, is seen to rationalize or legitimate the domination of some over others.

Critical Theory began to address the problem of the dependence of human liberation upon the liberation of nature: one must look at nature as not only an instrument toward freeing the person from toil but also as a potential ally in realizing a sense of individuality and, therefore, not as an entity to be destroyed or dominated. Critical Theory, concerned with the ways in which the world is disjointed, has always fused epistemological and social problems, seeing how one knows of nature or of persons as being integral to what one does to nature or to persons; it has also understood that how one relates to persons is a factor in how one relates to nature and vice versa. Writing in the latter part of the twentieth century, members of the Frankfurt School recognized the twin aspects of technology, that is, its ability to destroy (the Holocaust, nuclear weaponry, pollution) and to free persons (advances in medicine, land reclamation, automation). It is within this context — an intellectual milieu, of which Critical Theory is a part, that raises questions about the Baconian-Cartesian model of science — that one must situate the contemporary critique of science, both as it comes out of traditional social theory and out of the feminist movement.

One got a glimpse into this critique of technological rationality in the discussion of Dinnerstein's work, for, in building upon the writings of

Brown and Lewis Mumford, and, to a lesser extent, Marcuse, she identifies certain attitudes towards nature and technological expropriation which affect patterns of human relatedness.[2] The identification of nature as woman, which in psychoanalytic terms stems from the child's first association with the female who will take care of him or her, allows a society to treat one nurturer as it might treat the other.[3] The evolutionary and psychological explanations for why men have come to rule the world suggests to Dinnerstein reasons why "our ecosphere . . . [is threatened] with extinction."[4] Moreover, because of their exclusion from history, to which they have not always objected, women have an insight into both the myths of mechanistic domination of nature and the practices which use the metaphors and language of machines to appropriate human ways of thinking about issues. Having stood on the sidelines for most of their historical lives — to the domestic or private sphere — women are in a very choice position to see clearly the edifice of technological destruction that men have built. Following de Beauvoir, Dinnerstein traces exclusion to insight, women's ability to keep in touch with ordinary life with their ability to be more authentic than their male counterparts, caught up as the latter are with the internecine struggles of contemporary sexual arrangements, the life-denying processes of the world of work, and the politics of domination.

As the world of men has changed, their forms of domination have changed, and male power has become less tied to physical prowess than to the intellectual skills demanded by the industrial system. In discussing the relevance of certain ideas of the Frankfurt School to theories of male domination, it has been suggested that were one to understand the role that the forces of domination play in affecting the relationship between the self and society, and were one to see how this relationship changes over time, one would see how a male sense of self is affected by the ideals of passivity and conformity extracted by advanced industrial societies with their emphases on technical or instrumental rationality.[5] What matters for Dinnerstein, however, is that while the form of domination may have changed, the demands on men still allow for being in positions of power which require their legitimating the ethos of the age. Recognizing this, one could say that: "the dominant trends of advanced capitalism are partly maintained and reproduced by male socialization and by male role identification."[6]

Dinnerstein is critical of de Beauvoir for not going as far as she ought in recognizing the toll that gender separation takes on the man, that is, how it keeps men from contemplating matters of the soul and of the spirit. Mumford's "megamachine,"[7] Dinnerstein argues,

> is a world which subordinates the *human* (imagination, dream, symbol, religious vision out into the cosmos and inward into the psyche's "heart of darkness") to the *mechanical* (power, speed, remote control; coercive

bureaucracy; mass duplication; grandiose gigantism; production for obsolesence — dictated by the machinery of financial profit — and its twin, "indiscriminate and incontinent consumption"). It is life gone cancerous, anti-organic.[8]

It survives because there is no feminist negation.

The critique of technology which informs feminist writings is joined by a second intellectual current. In the revolt against objectivity, there is the elevation of the subjective, of truth based on feelings; it is as if the victims, having been defined as incapable of rational thought, refuse to accept this as a loss or impediment and, instead, redefine it as a worthy attribute and political strength, one endemic to being outside of the technological paradigm. Intuition, which in conventional wisdom had been placed at woman's doorstep, is made the subject of inquiry. As earlier in the case of motherhood and maternal instinct, a definition is demanded on whether it is grounded in biology, culture or an interface of the two.

There is an affinity between the idea of subjective discourse as it comes out of feminist theorizing and more general developments in epistemology. One must note the import of the Kantian revolution, of placing the human mind at the center of theory construction. The sociology of knowledge, as has already been suggested, in its emphases on the historical conditions which affect the relationship between knower and known, opens up the following lines of inquiry: How does who the knower is affect what he/she sees? How does the operative paradigm affect what he/she sees? Kuhn had already spoken of character traits of paradigm proponents and opponents, the gender of which, interestingly enough, is not mentioned. Yet one could ask if there are things accessible to one in a certain way because of one's sex. Kuhn certainly alerts one to asking in what precise ways one can ever be "objective." Science is regarded as a way of controlling for objectivity, or, conversely, subjectivity, by providing a process or set of techniques that keep one's personal feelings out of one's work. Mannheim and the sociology of knowledge tradition emphasizes the subjective side of that dialectic between subjectivity and objectivity, alerting one to who knows what and why. One could see the contemporary feminist debates on science and objectivity in Kuhnian terms, to wit, women as socially situated persons different from men (vis-a-vis their social situation) who bring a new perspective to old problems, for sex is but another factor — like class, nationality, religion, epistemological tradition — affecting how one sees.

Out of the recent writings of feminists, there is a concern for the epistemic position and/or privilege of women.[9] I am interested in looking at selected works which suggest a validation of this epistemic advantage and trace the arguments made for the juxtaposition of women's social situation and their way of seeing or knowing. In each instance, the feminist standpoint is offered as a counter to or negation of the masculine mode of domination, authority, and control and, in this sense, is an essentially political standpoint.

Carol Gilligan, a developmental psychologist, argues that men and women think differently. On the basis of both her research (three empirical studies) with persons (personal interviews) who had had to face moral issues and on her reading of certain psychological and literary texts, she argues that they think differently about moral problems. Factors of biology as well as specifics of culture shape how they come to evidence this diversity. Women use "a different voice" from men in talking about their relationships with others. It is not as her mentor, Lawrence Kohlberg, had argued that males and females, boys and girls, develop differently; that is, that they go through stages or sequences of moral development at different rates. Rather, she believed they move along different kinds of paths and look at moral problems in different ways. While there is a sequential development to both male and female ways of thinking, life experiences affect the way one thinks about a problem and, in this sense, one's gender. Insofar as it is a factor in what one can and cannot do in the society, it structures how one will be treated, what one will experience, and how one will see the world as a result. If boys and girls see conflicts and moral dilemmas differently, it is as a consequence of gendered relationships, not native abilities.

Insofar as developmental theory has been filtered through the male prism, or bias, of the theorists, females, have not been looked at on their own terms but always in comparisons with the male subjects. As a consequence, their voices have not been heard, or worse, they have been heard to reflect an inferior or inadequate aptitude respecting moral issues. Gilligan wants to contribute to the growing literature that calls into question the earlier studies and reformulate questions in terms of how gender affects perception, both the perception of the theorist and the person being studied.

Women, she continues, think differently "about human development" and have "different ways of imagining the human condition" and "different notions of what is of value in life."[10] Building upon the work of Chodorow, who had spelled out the consequences of children being raised by women, Gilligan reiterates the importance of the latter's theses: that boys and girls experience being raised by women differently; that gender identity which is formed by the time the child is three occurs while the female is playing a more significant role in the child's life as the primary caretaker; that girls come to identify with mothers while boys see themselves as more distant from their caretaker and, therefore, they come to see the need to develop their individuality and firm up their ego at an earlier age; that girls have empathetic relationships with another at an earlier age than do boys and, as a consequence, start to think in terms of the feelings of others; that boys will be less experienced in relationship-building but more experienced in learning to become individuals (individuation), while for girls it will be the reverse set of experiences that will affect how they will develop.

The games that children play also contribute to how they come to see the world: boys' games are more involved in competitions and emphasize rules, while girls' games involve playing with others in a relationship mode. Fairy tales also reflect these differences: men as adventurers and women as helpers or caretakers. However, these nurturing and care-taking roles are devalued by the society as well as by psychologists as distinct as Freud, Piaget, Erikson, and Kohlberg. Gilligan's corrective is to start with women as they find themselves in situations requiring a moral judgment in order to see how this nurturing capacity reveals itself in their decisions, how they think in terms of responsibilities not rights, how a kind of contextual thinking, as distinct from a more formal or abstract pattern of thinking, develops: "This conception of morality as concerned with the activity of care centers moral development around the understanding of responsibility and relationships, just as the conception of morality as fairness ties moral development to the understanding of rights and rules."[11]

There are, then, social reasons to explain why girls do not see autonomy as a valuable goal and why in their search for connectedness they do not feel the same way about ambition as boys might. Boys come to develop a "self defined through separation" and a "self measured against an abstract ideal of perfection," while for girls, there is a "self delineated through connection . . . a self assessed through particular activities of care."[12]

This particular sense of self affects the ways in which girls and women view not only the morality of rights but also that of responsibilities. Kohlberg has argued that as persons mature their moral decisions become increasingly attuned to universal abstract principles of justice: "These principles are abstract and ethical (the Golden Rule, the categorical imperative); they are not concrete moral rules like the Ten Commandments. At heart, these are universal principles of justice, of the reciprocity and equality of human rights, and of respect for the dignity of human beings as individual persons."[13] This may be just one kind of morality, to be contrasted with one that considers the consequences of actions upon specific individuals. Women fear hurting others, Gilligan argues, and this encourages them to look for moral solutions that help all and hurt none. They fear that what constitutes a moral decision may, in fact, hurt someone; they fear that their feelings make them vulnerable, that they are so dependent upon the good-will of others that they are unable to be effective and, thus, that they are uncertain about the consequences of their doing so.

The Kohlberg schema, when applied to women, makes them appear "deficient in moral development,"[14] but that is because it passes off a particular male view of the world, one too often removed from actual situations, as the sole, moral view. Gilligan writes: "When women feel excluded from direct participation in society, they see themselves as subject to a consensus or judgment made and enforced by the men on whose protection and support they depend and by whose names they are known."[15] Women often appear to be unprepared to make decisions out of fear of being held accountable and responsible for what has been said or done; they fear displeasing others. As social conditions change — as women can more readily enter the labor force on their own terms and more readily control reproductive factors by the empowerment of technology — they are more likely to recognize choices and responsibilities in a new way. The sense of self relates to the reality of one's existence, and, as that undergoes change, the sense of self will also change: "Thus, release from the intimidation of inequality finally allows women to express a judgment that had previously been withheld. What women then enunciate is not a new morality, but a morality disentangled from the constraints that formerly confused its perception and impeded its articulation."[16]

What Gilligan offers is two ideal-typical moralities which are gender based: men think in abstract terms, while women think contextually and concretely; men think in terms of objective, rational principles and rights, while women think in more personal, immediate terms with an emphasis on responsibilities. These are generalities of behavior (verified, or supported, by the data from the empirical studies) which are a result of an interplay of biological and environmental factors which predispose women to be sensitized towards the feelings of others in ways that men are not. This sensitivity is a consequence, Gilligan suggests, of the ways in which girls are raised, and of a social order which may encourage women to be both somewhat hesitant to be assertive and constantly concerned with what they ought to do for others; as a result, factors exist which may encourage women to ruminate and think through their decisions in ways that men do not feel the need to do. Unlike Kohlberg, Gilligan says that women are not incapable of thinking in abstract terms, but, rather, that theirs is a different (perhaps better or richer?) way of coming to moral understanding.

Gilligan takes issue with Kohlberg's notion of progress towards moral abstraction being more fully developed in men, for she is critical of his attributing morality to innate factors as well as to his indifference to other forms of moral reasoning. Women reason differently, she argues, as a consequence of different social groundings and experiences. Morality, like everything else in one's life, is shaped by the reality in which one find's oneself, by the spheres in which one is able to act and by the relationships that social structures have made possible. She writes: "As we have listened for centuries to the voices of men and the theories of development that their experience informs, so we have come more recently to notice not only the silence of women but the difficulty in hearing what they say when they speak." Women's voices speak of an "ethic of care," one which comes out of their "social experience" and is carried "by different modes of language and thought" and is in contrast to that "ethic of justice" particular to men: "As Freud and Piaget call our attention to the differences in children's feelings and thought, enabling us to respond to children with greater care and respect, so a recognition of the differences in women's experience and understanding expands our vision of maturity and points to the contextual nature of developmental truths."[17]

Gilligan is suggesting that men are more likely to internalize the morality of the society, to wit, the morality of democratic liberalism. In juxtaposition to a female morality based on care and caring, a realization that they have to be responsible for others, male morality, she argues, as it exists in democratic society, is concerned with justice and fairness, with people being able to realize their individuality, to be treated fairly or equitably, to have their rights protected. A female morality stresses interdependence (might one say "community"?), while a male morality stresses autonomy. Gilligan argues that Kohlberg must be understood as reflecting certain social and historical ideas: there are reasons why he equates morality, justice and fairness, for he operates under the rubric of a social science that prides itself on being a detached, analytic discipline which uses formal methods of analysis and abides by the canons of objectivity which in many ways are akin to political notions of justice as fairness. Might one then not argue that Gilligan has to be understood contextually as well and that her concern for the "absence of care in the social sciences"[18] is bound up with the support for a feminine morality that would be related to a new, post-liberal kind of politics?[19]

There is implicit in Gilligan an argument very similar to that made by Dinnerstein — that by virtue of their social position women are able to offer the society something that it needs very badly, a way of coping with and solving social problems that are at hand. Hers is not a peremptory rejection of the masculine, for, while there is an implicit critique of male values, she does recognize the role that they play in the society's quest for justice. Women can learn from men how to accept responsibility for their actions and, with changes in the social order, that is, with the ways in which women are empowered, they can begin to assert themselves more than has been the case in the past. Having said this, one can appreciate the implicit synthesis in Gilligan's argument that within a male-oriented society:

> the qualities deemed necessary for adulthood — the capacity for autonomous thinking, clear decision-making, and responsible action — are those associated with masculinity and considered undesireable attributes of the

feminine self. These stereotypes suggest a splitting of love and work that relegates expressive capacities to women while placing instrumental abilities in the masculine domain. Yet looked at from a different perspective, these stereotypes reflect a conception of adulthood that is itself out of balance, favoring the separateness of the individual self over connection to others, and leaning more towards an autonomous life of work than toward the interdependence of love and care. [20]

Gilligan's concern with, if not the devaluation of autonomy, certainly the linking of it to a series of male values, is part of a larger critique of the subject-object dualism and the non-dialectical nature of thought about which Jagger among others has spoken. [21] As I shall suggest later, there is an affinity between Gilligan's position on care and concern for others and certain forms of knowledge that emphasize understanding through dialogue and through imagining oneself into the mind of the other. Like Chodorow, in relating separation and interdependence to concrete experiences in being brought up to embody certain masculine or feminine characteristics, Gilligan traces the consequences for both men and women of these distinct spheres of socialization. She writes:

> Sensitivity to the needs of others and the assumption of responsibility for taking care lead women to attend to voices other than their own and to include in their judgment other points of view. Women's moral weakness . . . is thus inseparable from women's moral strength, an overriding concern with relationships and responsibilities. [22]

One of the criticisms that can be made of the Gilligan thesis is that it tends to speak of women as "embodying" certain values. There is an ahistoricity to this, on the one hand, and a perpetuation or continuation of the stereotypes of sex on the other. In the guise of giving value to qualities of being feminine, it legitimates the notion that there are indeed such qualities. Certainly, Gilligan does use a dichotomy or dualism to critique those theories which have themselves validated male and female ways of being-in-the-world. In finding a fit or affinity between moral philosophy and Western scientific theorizing, with their idealization of reason, justice and fairness, she suggests the male biases that are to be found in both fields. Others have also equated the bourgeois, the ideal of masculinity, and the emerging scientific order, and it is within this context that one situates a feminist critique that goes to the very core of the scientific enterprise. [23]

Before doing so, I wish to mention in this connection the work of Nancy Hartsock, a feminist writer who, building upon certain works in political theory, traces the feminist aversion to power to a view of power as domination and, therefore, as inevitably masculine. Feminists, Hartsock argues, have even seen certain forms of sexual behavior, rape and pornography, for example, not as sexual but as power relationships; and insofar as persons see the world differently as a consequence of the material conditions which shape their lives, those who have power have power to impose their vision or standpoint on others. Those others have to struggle for their standpoint and out of this struggle they come to see the world and themselves in the world more clearly.

Hartsock's delineation of a feminist standpoint, which is indebted to the master-slave dialectic integral to both Hegelian and Marxist thought, is a most clear and explicit statement not only of why women, as an oppressed group, see the world differently from men but also why their view is better (more inclusive and more complete). Because it embodies the tenets of a feminist standpoint, it is worth quoting in full:

> (1) Material life (class position in Marxist theory) not only structures but sets limits on the understanding of social relations. (2) If material life is structured in fundamentally opposing ways for two different groups, one can expect both that the vision of each will represent an inversion of the other and the vision of the ruling class will be partial and perverse. (3) The vision of the ruling class structures the material relations in which all parties are forced to participate, and therefore cannot be dismissed as simply false. (4) In consequence, the vision available to the oppressed group must be struggled for and represents an achievement that requires both science to see beneath the surface of the social relations in which all are forced to participate, and the education that can only grow from political struggle. (5) Because the understanding of the oppressed is an engaged vision, the adoption of a standpoint exposes the real relations among human beings as inhuman, points beyond the present, and carries a historical and liberatory role.[24]

In other words, what persons see and understand is a consequence of the concrete reality — the material conditions — of their existence. Differences in those conditions explain differences in perception, but those who have power, that is, who have the better of the material conditions, are able to impose their views on others, which others must struggle to come to consciousness and cognition. Through the struggle, the oppressed, who have understood the position of those in power, come to see their own position, while those in power know only one truth — their own. In its Hegelian and Marxist roots, the feminist standpoint relates ideas to interests — the interest of the rulers is to distort reality and keep the ruled from recognizing its oppression as just that. Those in power employ an ideology, patriarchy, to legitimate this oppression. Those who are oppressed, however, and who have come to a conscious awareness of their oppression, are in a position to call into question both their oppressors and the legitimating ideology. Jaggar writes:

> in contemporary society, women suffer a special form of exploitation and oppression [which] provides women with a distinctive epistemological standpoint [from which] it is possible to gain a less biased and more comprehensive view of reality . . . . discovered through a collective process of political and scientific struggle.[25]

Hartsock wishes to move beyond the present equation of power and masculinity, beyond a society in which the mechanisms of capitalism and of patriarchy are gendered, that is, where there is male domination and an underside of eros — eros as masculine and virile and that builds on domination and submission. Using the kinds of arguments previously found in Dinnerstein and Chodorow on the feelings of love/hate one has towards women as a consequence of early childhood behavior — and in this sense bearing an affinity to the Gilligan thesis — Hartsock argues that intimacy becomes domination of the other until the other loses the self and becomes a non-person. The body, in the present scheme of things, also has to be dominated, as creativity has to be turned into its opposite — mortality and productivity.

Women, historically, do different kinds of work than do men. Most important, they bear and rear children, and there is some importance in the biological preconditions of being female.[26] Women have also tended to emphasize ideas about life and not death. One might then argue, that a " 'feminist theory of power' " would no longer speak of "power as dominance or domination,"[27] but would build on the particularities of a feminist standpoint that comes out of feminine contributions to human subsistence and to mothering: "If differing life experiences lead to differing world views, the systematic differences between the accounts of power produced by women and men can be taken to be indications of systematic and significant differences in activity . . . . differences in the life activity of women and men have epistemological content and consequences."[28]

Reason: The Feminist Perspective

In writing about the ways in which people at a certain historical moment think, Mannheim suggests that one speak of styles of thought or the manner in which a certain group or set of individuals formulate their ideas and, in this sense, "carry" them. He allows for individual variations in such patterns but still contends that there are certain generalized patterns of approach to perception, certain habitual ways of thinking, which characterize an age. These patterns change over time, and as is the case with "styles" of art, at a certain point an entirely new style comes into being. Sociology, engaging in a sociology of knowledge enterprise, has as its task to analyze the meanings which texts have, to unravel these thought constellations, placing them in some sort of historical perspective just as the art historian places or dates a work of art. This approach is distinct from another, albeit sociological method, which narrates or explicates ideas and how such ideas move from one thinker to another. The sociologist assumes the variability of thought, that is, its revealing itself differently according to historical circumstance and the social location of the person who holds to certain beliefs; yet, the sociologist is also aware that these differences are themselves affected by social factors and that both the style of an age and the subtleties of that style are affected by historical conditions and historical actors.

One of the themes of feminist literature concerns the nature of reason and whether there are varieties of reasoning particular to men and women. Several works address this issue and I take them as typical of efforts to reassess the function and value of reason as that term had come to be understood. Carol McMillan's *Reason, Women and Nature*[1] and Kathy Ferguson's *The Feminist Case Against Bureaucracy*[2] are, like Gilligan's *In A Different Voice* and Hartsock's *Money, Sex, and Power,* works which ask not only if there is a feminine way of being-in-the-world (which they assume there is) but also if that state of being affects the way in which women think, reason and judge matters social, political and moral. They ask how one has experienced being woman, and how that experience becomes a powerful and necessary element in one's analysis of social and sexual arrangements. Questions of epistemology and ontology, of the status of knowledge and of a systematized inquiry into how one comes to know of that knowledge, have accompanied these treatises from the standpoint of the feminine. Not only is the reader of these works treated to an argument for there being different ways in which men and women address moral issues but also to the case for a reconsideration of the dominance of empirical knowledge in matters of human inquiry and for a questioning of the nature of interpersonal relationships in a society that is highly bureaucratized and committed to notions of a technical or instrumental reason. I read Gilligan's work in this way, and I wish now to lay out the arguments of McMillan and Ferguson and suggest what the authors intend by their presentations.

McMillan, a philosopher building on the work of Peter Winch, seeks to understand the nature of the differences, if any do exist, between men and women. Toward that end, she asks what differences do exist, what is the nature of those differences, and whether those differences allow for or require differential treatment of men to women. She interprets the current feminist position to be one that recognizes no differences between persons save those grounded in reproductive capability; furthermore, she argues that all differences save the biological are grounded in culture and that such cultural differences have been used to submit women to activities in the domestic sphere which isolate them from sources of public power and create patterns of relationships which center around caretaking and submission at one and the same time. These pattterns of relating to others, which are socially and culturally produced, become so embedded in women's way of being-in-the-world, that is, they are in existence for such a long time, that they are considered indications of women's "true nature," signaling how women ought to be treated by the social and political order. Feminists, McMillan argues, share with their opponents the belief in the idea of reason that is simplistic and erroneous; yet out of this belief arise certain policy implications: on the one hand, that all persons ought to be treated equally insofar as all persons are rational beings; or all persons ought to be treated differently since a portion of them, women, are not able to be rational in the way that men are. McMillan wants to proffer a version of difference that does not ground emotion in irrationality, but that speaks of a variety of ways of being human in the world, not all of which depend on a specific kind of reason. In effect, McMillan wants to oppose a dichotomy of reason and passion, or reason and emotion, which she sees as both inaccurate and dangerous.

I am not interested, at this point, in how accurate McMillan is in her reading of the feminist literature; rather, I wish to explicate her ideas on feminist reasoning, for in her efforts to open up the question of how we attain knowledge, she shares with other feminists an interest in the relationship between emotion and cognition. She starts with the position of Simmel, who, writing in a post-Hegelian tradition that placed a high value on man's ability to reason, to think objectively and analytically about matters of the world, assumed certain a priori differences between men and women which were manifested not only in bodily appearances but also in ways of perceiving the world. For Simmel, men are trying to overcome their perceived dichotomy between an object and the idea of the object, while women see no apparent duality but, rather, see the real and the idea of the real as one and the same thing. The kind of reasoning or logic that men have to engage in women do not; through intuition, they come to know the world in which they find themselves. Men come to know what their bodies can do, in a reproductive sense, much differently from women, whose knowledge of their bodies and of the reproductive potential of those bodies is much more self-contained than is a man's knowledge which is much more dependent upon woman as object to give meaning to his biology.

Reason and intuition are held to go their separate ways; rational, objective assessment and not feeling about or towards things are held to be separate manners of understanding. Simmel, McMillan might have added, implies an equation of the modern intellectual disciplines with a masculine approach to the world and he prefigures the kind of argument that one finds in Gilligan and Keller's work respecting different analytic styles particular to men and women. McMillan argues that it is erroneous to consider reason as operating only in those fields where men preside and intuition only in those endeavors undertaken by women, for, even in such women's activities as domestic pursuits and mothering, there is thought and concern that is far distinct from the kind of non-reflective behavior that characterizes animal life and that some have argued parallels very much the kind of "natural" endeavors in which women find themselves involved.

In a sense, McMillan is trying to reclaim the private sphere from conflation either with the spheres of emotion, of animal-like behavior, or the trivial:

> The idea that the private realm, the domain of family life, should be regarded as inherently inferior to the world of culture, even though the warmth of the hearth and the intimacy of family life are necessities for the healthy growth of human beings in the world, is a presumption very dear to sexists, which feminists themselves happily embrace.[3]

At the root of the problem is a philosophical tradition, which McMillan spells out in some detail, which contrasts reason and emotion, knowledgeable actions as opposed to actions based upon feelings. Her objective is to unearth the "cognitive aspect"[4] of feelings and emotion; to show the relationship between morality and feelings as well as reason, and to suggest the cardinal import of the first set of relationships rather than, exclusively, the second. Further, she suggests in what sense women experience this relationship differently from men. The assumption must be dethroned that reason and morality go hand in hand and that since only men can reason in a way that makes sense for ethical positions, only they are capable of truly moral actions.

While knowledge based on reason and knowledge based on intuition are of a different kind of order, and in this sense are not congruent, McMillan argues that it is not only incorrect but also dangerous to compartmentalize scientific inquiries and artistic endeavors as if the two were simply the opposite of each other. Furthermore, it is also incorrect to assign expertise in one field to men and in the other to women, as, McMillan argues, certain feminists do. What must be eliminated is linking reason with certain kinds of activities and not with others. Criticism of women's intuitive ability is really part and parcel of a more generalized downgrading of ways of knowing that do not follow the specific outlines of the natural science method, a method which, for economic and technological reasons, has come to be regarded as the dominant paradigm. In addition, what is missing from assessments of intuition is how much of what is regarded as unreflective, inner knowledge is, in fact, knowledge based on experience, whether, as McMillan shows, it is the experience of the wheelwright or the mother,[5] and that traditional women's roles, like mothering and child-care, share with other human roles historically constituted behavior that distinguishes them from animal behavior.

McMillan takes issue with the way in which the social construction of femininity has been argued. Feminists assert that cultural diversity with respect to sex roles validates thinking of those roles as subject to historical circumstance, and, in this sense, neither biologically grounded in any causal way nor universally valid in any way that does not take note of social factors constructing images of sexually appropriate behavior. In looking at human ways of being in the world, it is, following Winch, erroneous to look for universal laws of human behavior. Such laws obfuscate the diversity of human experience, which is not, McMillan argues, to belie certain regularities of human existence (the opposite of capricious or arbitrary ways of being in the world). Feminists regard sex roles as being socially constructed with the intent of legitimating power relationships of some over others; they see this social construction as an artificial set of constraints which keep women from becoming their real or true selves. Like Rossi, she implies that feminists overstate their case and create disputes where none need really exist. For McMillan, this view of social construction ignores the existence of certain givens, like birth, death, and sexual behavior, which condition or structure and, in this sense, place limits upon what persons can and cannot be. Some rules and regulations, growing out of some basic human givens, must shape what all persons do; this is the state of being human, and is not to be interpreted as coercive control by illegitimate authority, as some recalcitrant feminists, McMillan argues, would have it. Authority and power are not necessarily one and the same thing. Social roles and responsibilities are required of all humans by virtue of their being humans; while such role playing, if done unreflectively, can lead to the loss of person, to "indoctrination and depersonalization," the elimination of social constraints of all kinds leads to an anarchy that precludes the formation and continuation of human communities.[6]

That there may be a foundation in biology for the usual or conventional way of doing things does not mean that one particular pattern of relationships, say, the traditional nuclear family with men in the world of work and women, full-time, in the world of the home, need follow. But McMillan argues that one cannot turn away from one's prescribed biological roles even if one can reevaluate and revalue them so as to accord women dignity, respect and recognition in the domestic duties that they do undertake and that they ought to undertake. There is, for McMillan, this "human fact of birth" with which one has to reckon; if one fails to do so, one is rebelling "against nature" as well as against convention.[7]

McMillan opposes this rebellion against nature and, in so doing, argues that it is spurious to insist that one's physical nature has been the cause of one's oppression, for this assumes a duality between subject and object or a dualism between mind and body. One's biology does not have the status of a subject that will allow it to be an oppressor. Being woman, in the sexual sense, is as much a biological given as is being black, and the oppression is historically constituted; and does not come mechanistically out of the condition.[8] What matters is not what nature has given, but how one can actively be an agent in the coming to terms with one's nature, that is, not allowing either one's blackness or one's femaleness to subject one to an inferior status. Freedom, for McMillan, is not to be measured in terms of how much technology liberates one from nature, or how much one can claim to dominate nature. Freedom is not to be measured by how much one is able to transcend motherhood, either through contraception or abortion, for there is an underside to the feminist argument that birth control allows women to be free and active agents in determining their own lives. Being an active agent in one's own behalf includes more than simply manipulating or controlling nature; it includes the notion of intent, of whether one's actions are allowing technology to replace one's active involvement.

Separate spheres and different roles, which may have a foundation in biological givens, need not lead, inexorably, to inequality. Inequities are a consequence of certain valuations which are socially awarded. The feminist goal ought to be to value feminine abilities rather than either an equality or an androgyny that denies biology or an unchallenged victory for a technology that embodies male values.

McMillan's position is representative of the rebellion against positivism that still wants to hold onto certain biological and physiological conditions. She expresses the view that positivism encases domination, but she is troubled by the social constructionist perspective that de-emphasizes the constraints on behavior which she sees as part of certain biological givens. In many ways, she is like Rossi in wanting to allow for individuals being active participants in the construction of the world, yet within certain parameters.

She is also representative of those — Jaggar is a most impressive case in point[9] — who are exposing the simplistic dimension to the dichotomy between the rational and the emotional. One can trace back the feminist concern with feelings and emotions to the early days of the Women's Movement and its formulation of consciousness-raising as a way of uncovering information about the self and the world around that self. Consciousness-raising itself is historically explicable in terms of the legitimation of emotion characteristic of parts of the New Left and the counterculture. Out of that legacy comes a position that feelings give "clues" which "may be our best shot at objectivity,"[10] at knowing what is really happening, even if not examined along a strict positivistic axis. Moreover, one's social situation may predispose one to being more at ease with feelings, or more in touch with one's feelings, or less concerned about the suppression of one's feelings, and, in this sense, too, one might begin to explain the value placed on feeling and emotion in social, cultural and historical terms.[11] Jaggar writes:

> Just as earlier I challenged the prevailing view that reliable knowledge should be value free or disinterested, I want now to argue that reliable knowledge need not, cannot, and should not be dispassionate. Just as the disinterested observer is a myth, so is the dispassionate observer — a myth, moreover, with a powerful ideological function. Feminist practice disproves this myth and feminist epistemology must demystify it.[12]

It is not the case that only with the advent of this phase of the Women's Movement does one find the argument being made that women reason differently, that women, because they are women, resolve moral or political problems in a way distinct from that of men. Historically, philosophic discourse has registered a variety of positions on this issue: women have been seen to possess and use a different form of Reason or they have been regarded as having a complementary form of thinking.[13]

It has been the case that class, race and/or nationality have been regarded as factors which also affect perception. Marx, for example, classified persons according to their relationship to the means of production, arguing, further, that the proletariat, insofar as he was the historical agent of social change, had an historical purpose distinct from that of the bourgeoisie, who also had an historical purpose but one of sullied moral intent. Marx used the idea of class to speak of the oppression of a category of persons, modulating or adapting the Hegelian master-slave dichotomy. In so doing, Marx has been interpreted as saying that the proletariat, insofar as he suffers from this oppression and knows (following

Hegel) both of his own slave world and that of his master's, has a way of seeing a more complete picture of the world as it is and ought to be constituted. Thus, the proletariat, the potential adversary of alienation, has an access line to truth, rationality and morality One has already seen how Hartsock and Jaggar build on this Marxian schema to speak of a feminist perspective or advantage which grows out of alienation and oppression. It is not altogether novel, then, that one suggests that how persons think — morally as well as in other ways — is a consequence of how one's social lives have been organized, and it is in this sense that one speaks of thought patterns as being historical and subjects as having personalities which are historically rooted.[14]

Most of the feminist writings of the past few decades have come to see many, if not all, of these treatises on forms and kinds of reason as equating complementarity with inferiority, and it has been suggested that a male bias has permeated philosophic discourse since its inception. One must situate the recent discussions within the context of the Women's Movement and a feminist paradigm which speaks of the oppression of women, but, at the same time, one can hear in other writers earlier moments in these same debates.

The idea of reason is what one might call philosophically contestable, as is the issue of whether there might not, in fact, be several forms of reason irrespective of gender. I have in mind the distinction between functional and substantive reason, between a calculable reason that involves notions of costs and benefits and that is concerned with rational means to achieve undisputed goals and a reason that includes the notion of the good or the morally defensible. The discussions on the parameters of reason can be read in Utilitarian and neo-Kantian thought, and are most precise in the writings of Scheler, Weber, Mannheim and, most recently, Habermas. Their writings concern reason and reason gone astray. They are caught in the dilemma of wanting to ground all forms of reason (in particular historical moments) while avoiding the scourge of relativism, of wanting to find a reason beyond the narrow confines of rationality or functionality so that they can ground values in a universal system of ethics, of wanting to move past the chaos of private interests.

The critique of reason understood as functional rationality is part of a larger critique of modernity and of the rationalization that accompanies it. Modernity is seen as bringing with it not only a rationalization that is inherently illogical but also a specialization and glorification of mechanization that oppresses and subordinates individuals. Horkheimer and Adorno speak of the rationalization of the life-world and the demystification of that world by science as leading to the loss of a sense of self, and instrumental reason as leading to a state that is totally administered by a technocratic social system.[15] Habermas writes: "Science and technology — for Marx still an unequivocally emancipatory potential —

themselves become the medium of social repression."[16] Some will see this critique of rationality as a "demodernizing impulse";[17] for others, the critique itself will be a quest for a higher rationality, a new form of reason. Marcuse argues that the human mind is capable of using its conceptual ability to reason in order to find out what is true as well as what is morally correct, but while individual and social action is to be judged according to its reasonableness, it is a substantive, emancipatory objective that Marcuse has in mind and not merely precise, technical and, in this sense, rational principles which ought to be considered reason at its best.[18]

It is in this intellectual context where there is a concern with reason gone astray that feminist writers offer their own critique of rationality. Gilligan seeks to relate rationality to a kind of morality, while McMillan wants to extend the very meaning of rationality itself; implicit in both of their writings is the argument made by Dinnerstein that women, precisely because they have been excluded from positions of public power and have been, in effect, locked out of the technocratic state, are in a more privileged position to see the irrationality of an administered state blocked into a logic of nuclear annihilation.

In the work of Kathy Ferguson, a feminist political theorist, one finds another aspect of the argument for a feminist perspective on viewing the world. In *Self, Society, and Womankind*[19] and *The Feminist Case against Bureaucracy*[20], Ferguson critiques, from both a normative and a methodological perspective, the practices of contemporary society for their continuation, often unwittingly, of the practices of patriarchy which lead to the oppression of women. I will spell out the theses of both of these works to illustrate their relationship to the more general critique of the perceived male biases of a certain kind of rational thinking.

Ferguson argues that liberal theory has ignored the socialization processes through which persons develop their social identities, and, therefore, it fails to see how women, by internalizing the social norms, get a distorted or male-dominated sense of self. As a result, while liberatory in intent, liberalism does not really come to terms with women's inability to participate equally with men on social and political matters; that is, it fails to grasp the reality of female existence and the unresolved problems that would remain should women be integrated into a system that is repressive of their interests. Marxist theory, a second contemporary perspective with an objective of human liberation, so defines women in terms of their relationship to the means of production that it fails to see the peculiarities and particularities of the kind of production in which women are engaged as well as the aspects of female oppression that would not disappear by alterations in property relations alone.

Drawing upon the work of Mead on the nature of sociality, Ferguson elects to develop those aspects of Mead's theory which emphasize the way in which the dialectical relationship between the "I" and the "me" allows for the emergence of the liberated self; that is, she argues that the individual needs the freedom to define who he or she is and also the capacity to understand or be compassionate about who others are. For Ferguson, as for Mead, this second component of compassion is necessary once one recognizes that the self is only created in interaction with others; hence, it is at its core a self of sociality, a self created through a process of involvement and engagement. One knows who one is to the degree that one understands how one acts and reacts to other, socially constituted selves. There is an inherent tension in this dialectic of self-definition, for it is not easy to both define who one is while at the same time understanding and feeling compassionate towards others who may be involved with their own definitions of who one is:

> For the subordinate party to take the perspective of the other, in its entirety and with compassion, is for her to risk abandoning her own definition of the situation, since it will probably clash with that of the man. Similarly, to insist on the freedom to define her own situation she may be forced to violate his perspective on the relation, if his perspective includes the desire to retain dominance. This tension between the two conditions must be continually confronted. Liberation, the dialectical balance between the two conditions, is an elusive and difficult goal.[21]

This is understanding without self-abnegation.

Mead's attraction for Ferguson, similar to the appeal that Schutz and phenomenology have for Dorothy Smith,[22] is that he provides a way of seeing the world that is in contrast to the behavioral paradigm that accords so well with a male-centered perspective.[23] Mead's rejection of the subject/object dichotomy and, in this sense, his implicit critique of positivism accompany his emphasis on the dialectical quality of the social act. By speaking in terms of "human experience,"[24] of the temporal quality of being, Mead is similar to de Beauvoir, who also was suspicious of any notion of a fixed human nature. A feminist perspective must think of women as individuals constructed in time, not objects destined to behave in a certain prescribed way, although it must go beyond Mead and must not ignore factors of social structure and concrete relationships of power.

In *The Feminist Case against Bureaucracy*, Ferguson continues to develop this theme of the value of a method which understands the self in relation to the other. She takes it much further by finding in feminism an affinity to a Meadian perspective which allows it to critique a certain way of viewing the world and structuring social relations that is at the heart of modern industrial society. Building not only on work in feminist and contemporary social theory but also on a series of interviews with persons involved in the bureaucratic process, she takes as her adversary bureaucracy and the bureaucratization of the world that accompanies it. She wants to bring feminism to bear on the ways in which modern life is organized. Bureaucracy, she argues, is both a structure and a process and it oppresses both men and women, but the grounds for resisting bureaucratization are to be found in the "typical experiences of women" which are ones of being dominated by others while being involved in both caretaking and nurturing roles.[25] Building on Foucault's idea of *"an insurrection of subjegated knowledges,"*[26] she looks to a language of women that is "submerged." Women want to be freed from the restraints of language or linguistic discourse which names them to do or be something; that freedom is to be initiated in the way women come to speak of and on issues which develop out of the social relationships in which they find themselves. In terms of her earlier work, one could say that the feminist social self conditions women to speak in a certain way, and that, conversely their language, the discourse they come to use to appraise a situation, is grounded in the relationships which they have had as women.

She uses Foucault to critique the apparent neutrality of bureaucratic structures, with their emphases on rules and regulations and procedures which intend to mitigate against the intrusion of social or pesonal influences. Like Foucault, she is concerned with the modern impulse to organize all aspects of public and private lives such that, wittingly or not, they have become increasingly subjected to measures of social control. She parts company with him, however, over his resistance to organizing to resist, his blanket rejection of modernity and his seeing philosophic efforts to render meaning intelligible as just another epistemological device to control language. Foucault's critique of power is not accompanied by any political theory of where society ought to go; there is neither a blueprint for the future nor a set of arguments on the purpose of social and human existence. Ferguson's critique depends upon her seeing a linkage between bureaucracy, liberalism and patriarchy and, by making this linkage she is able to give bureaucracy the historical dimension against which the political case for social change can be made. There is not the depiction of the inevitability of bureaucracy that colors the work of Foucault, Weber, and, to a lesser extent, members of the Frankfurt School. By finding in feminism a praxis dimension, she is able to find an agent of social change — women — who possess the potential to break the bureaucratic hold. Her work then becomes a heterodoxical study of bureaucracy.

Allying herself with the work of other feminist theorists,[27] Ferguson argues that there is a radical potential to feminism because of its critique not only of the private/public dichotomy but also fo the expressive and instrumental-rational ways of thinking and speaking. If one looks at the experiences of women, examining in detail the patterns of relatedness that govern the ways in which they act with and towards other persons, one will find a counter to the bureaucratic and highly rationalistic patterns of relatedness that now govern the lives of both men and women.

The characteristics of bureaucracy, most especially their hierarchical and depersonalized patterns of arrangements, isolate and separate people from each other, and in so doing, they are alienating experiences which, by keeping people from interacting with each other, hinder the formation of identity:

> The requirements of depersonalization in bureaucratic relations mean that individuals are isolated from one another and meaningful social interaction is replaced by formal association. As more and more arenas of our lives become bureaucratic, the depersonalization/alienation process correspondingly expands. The bureaucratization of work leads to the loss of connection to and intimacy with others in production; the bureaucratization of language leads to their loss in speech and language; the bureaucratization of sexuality leads, paradoxically, to the loss of intimacy in intimacy itself.[28]

Certain groups of persons stand outside this bureaucratization process — the psychotics, the poor of Appalachia, women. Women have developed different means of discourse from men in part because of their exclusion from the bureaucratized world, but there are other factors to take into account: "In their relations with parents, in the roles that are available to them both in the family and in the larger public world, in their encounters with others and in their knowledge of themselves, women's experience is institutionally different from that of men."[29] A feminist praxis that seeks to remove women from the oppressive yoke of patriarchy while at the same time resisting the bureaucration that has overpowered men must begin by building upon these differences: the *Gemeinschaft* experience of most women; their roles as caretakers and nurturers; their penchant for cooperation because of the needs they have of others; their vulnerability as a consequence of their dependences on others. It logically follows, for Ferguson, that women understand domination, just as their experience as caretakers gives them a grounding in social roles that are neither bureaucratized not hierarchical.

Ferguson discusses the roots of bureaucracy in the modern state and its links to capitalism and industrialization. She traces the ways in which education, the family, and sexuality have become bureaucratized and, as a consequence, what potential strains of discontent are to be found there. Arguing that femininity is a form of subordination, she parallels workers' responses to their hierarchies of domination with the adopting of feminine characteristics of dealing or coping with situations in which one does not have control by being supportive but not aggressive and attuned to the needs and wants of others. One becomes successful at managing one's image — impression management. Clients, in service industries, also have to learn how to become like women and play the subordinate game and act as if they appreciate their dependency:

The main point of this feminization argument is neither to praise masculinity nor to allocate bureaucratic traits to women. The point . . . is that the political consequences of male dominance are such that women learn the role of the subordinate, and that role can easily become self-perpetuating. The skills that one learns in order to cope with secondary status then reinforce that status. The feminine role is inherently de-politicizing, in that it requires women to internalize an image of themselves as private rather than public beings.[30]

Feminism as praxis involves tapping "women's experience," finding the "language of women" and understanding how it acts as a "voice of resistance." The submerged experiences of women, especially their roles as caretakers, become a force of negation: "Feminist discourse and practice entail a struggle for individual autonomy that is *with others* and for community that *embraces diversity*. . . ." As in the work of Gilligan, Chodorow, Dinnerstein, Elshtain, and Ruddick, all of whom emphasize the significance of women as mothers and primary caretakers and, looked at somewhat differently, as daughters, the

world of women . . . is distinguished from the world of men by different notions of individual identity, by different standards of morality, and ultimately by different approaches to the problems of politics. . . . The connectedness with others that is at the heart of the survival and development of human infants is retained in female self-identity as a recognition of the continued and fundamental interdependence of self and other. For most women, connection with others is a primary given of their lives. . . . Women tend to judge themselves by standards of responsibility and care toward others. . . . Women's moral judgements are closely tied to feelings of empathy and compassion for others. . . . women's conception of moral problems is concerned with the inclusion of diverse needs rather than with the balancing of opposing claims.[31]

When contrasted with a more rational, male voice, one resonant to instrumental reason, a feminine voice becomes a way of questioning the procedures of a bureaucratized society, contrasting these with the ways in which persons act in the domestic world of trust and care. This feminist rationality is tied to ideas of the care and health of the self and the self in relation to others and it is not distinct from emotion but, on the contrary, very much tied to it.

What Ferguson suggests is that bureaucracies, which are the stuff of modern life, oppress workers and clients and, in so doing, force them to behave like women using traditional womanly ways in order to cope and survive. The experiences and languages of women become the counter to modernity: "By unearthing/creating the specific language of women, and comprehending women's experience in terms of that linguistic framework rather than in terms of the dominant discourse, feminist discourse is articulated as a voice of resistance."[32]

Both with respect to theory and practice, feminism becomes the mode of reconstructing bureaucracy, and is part of an emerging literature that is critical of bureaucratic structures and the ways in which these are described.[33] Through the notion of power as empowerment, rather than power as coercion or domination, Ferguson presents a tension between masculine and feminine voices, although she is careful to point out that these are social voices, that is, gendered rather than simply biological.

Certainly the argument can be made that the inherent tension between bureaucracy and feminism disregards the historical instances in which through the efforts of feminists and social reformers, working in and on bureaucracies, improvements in the field of social welfare, especially in health and education, were made. The material conditions of women benefited from nineteenth- and twentieth-century forces of rationalization and bureaucratization, although, paradoxically, these may be the forces that contain the feminist voice about which Ferguson speaks.

Reacting against those who dismiss and devalue what is taken to be woman's reliance on feelings and emotions rather than on abstract, logical ideals of moral behavior in coming to make moral and political decisions, Ferguson is similar to other feminists writing at this time. She does not see involvement as a threat to clear and accurate assessments of people and situations. Writers like Dinnerstein, Chodorow, Gilligan, and even McMillan assume these differences in the thought patterns of men and women, and, in differing degrees, value the distinctiveness of female perception. In varying ways, they relate the differences back to that interplay of biology and culture, that is, to female reproductive capacity or other kinds of biological distinctiveness (sexual bodily constructs not related to reproduction) and to socially prescribed female caretaker roles (the nurturing capacity). Dinnerstein wants feminist stereotypes to be redefined, the fear of women to be exposed, their monopoly of early child-care to be ended, and men encouraged to be concerned, caring and involved. Chodorow, with a somewhat different emphasis, wants to replace the exclusive female monopoly on child-care so that the female personality and female abilities will be directed toward other social roles.

A support for women's uniqueness, therefore, contains a certain political potential, one that emphasizes caring and empathy, involvement and concern, all of which run counter to our understanding of bureaucracy. One might ask if there are certain modes of analysis consonant with feminism, especially if one understands by the latter a perspective which seeks "to end women's subordination" by changing the conditions of women. The question is whether there is a method of social analysis that does not require that one bracket one's feminism.[34]

In the writings of Dorothy Smith, for example, one finds the argument that a social science modeled after the natural sciences contains within it notions of control, of subjects being observed, described and, consequently, capable of being controlled by observers who, as history would have it, happen to be males. Moreover, Smith continues, the natural science model assumes an objectivity that is inapplicable to humans understanding other humans. She denies that there is an "Archimedian point . . . external to any particular position in society."[35] Drawing upon Schutz, she argues that one must start with the subject, with women as they experience the world, as they see the world, not as some observer sees their world as if they were some kind of laboratory objects. They see the world from a certain body, from a certain place and in a certain time: this is the only way one does see. Phenomenology, like the consciousness-raising of the early days of the Women's Movement, has the potential to get back to the subject, to get back to the "submerged traditions,"[36] to the world before "scientific theory organizes consciousness"[37] and fits it into a Procrustean bed.

Catherine MacKinnon has written of consciousness-raising as a method of knowing, and in some ways her argument is similar to that of Smith's. She speaks of starting with the subject, the knower herself, and her own experiences. In so doing, one does not start with an outside authority and one does not pretend to objectivity. The emphasis is to introduce into the arena of social and political discourse experiences to which traditional discourse has been blind, sex-blind, as it were — the experiences of the personal realm and, most specifically, of women and the family, experiences of being daughters, wives, and mothers and the labor of these categories.[38] This is using the feminine gaze to explore and analyze feelings and emotions.

In their lives of personal experience, that is, in their lives as daughters, wives, and mothers, women have come to have a certain way of being-in-the-world or, in psychological terms, a certain sense of self or ego. Out of this sense of self comes a certain way of relating to others (Chodorow), a certain way of regarding others (Dinnerstein), a certain way of thinking about others (Smith, Ferguson), a certain way of reasoning about others (Gilligan). These ways are not only different but better, the argument goes, in the sense of liberating or negating a contrary male way of being that is competitive rather than cooperative, authoritative rather than democratic, life-denying rather than life-giving (Hartsock and Jaggar).

In this connection, one might make reference to the political and intellectual fight for Women's Studies, and see it as both a field of inquiry and an arm of the Women's Movement. It is fighting not to be an alternative paradigm but a dominant paradigm, whose victories will be reflected in its acceptance into the curriculum, its penetration into old texts and its active encouragement of new texts. This is Kuhn's reconstruction of a field from new fundamentals, replete with the psychic combat that accompanies the zero-sum game of competing paradigms and the polarization of paradigm supporters and of the conversion that accompanies a commitment to the new paradigm. Rival paradigms are incommensurable: the approved one is the one that the scientific or academic community assesses to have the greatest utility, that is, the one that is considered intellectually or politically better. What is at stake is the rewriting of history, the teaching of new ideas to new students using new texts. Feminist theory, one could argue, presents "a new way of looking at the . . . world," a "new definition of what [is] significant for understanding that world," new distinctive methods for inquiry, and criteria for determining "what should count as answers to certain basic questions."[39] Women's Studies hopes to guide the community, those writing and researching about women, in its positing of problems and in its formulation of answers. In Kuhnian terms, Women's Studies is a challenge to the normal academic disciplines which, it is argued, have excluded women, if not among its personnel then certainly among its fields of inquiry. It is an "extraordinary science," arguing that either the old disciplines , or paradigms, have not allowed for looking at the world of women or have used a set of investigative techniques inappropriate to the issues.

Prior to a specifically feminist theory, which arose out of the dialectic between Women's Studies and the Women's Movement, there was no satisfactory way to answer the question of why women were treated, at best, as second-class citizens, and, at worst, as oppressed inferiors. The enigma was an anomaly, in Kuhn's terms, which could not be answered by prevailing patterns of thought, be they liberal, radical, or socialist. Once the perceived way was called into question, by the crises associated with the Movement, the traditions were shattered and a new frame of reference — feminism — promised to solve problems that otherwise could not be solved. Moreover, those who adhered to and had a vested interest in the old set of explanations resisted the challengers. Just as the latter, when in command, were prepared to read out of the profession those who would not accept the dominance of their paradigm, so, too, the feminist challengers are intolerant of the old guard and their established viewpoint.

At the same time as the struggle for Women's Studies was being carried out, there were other challenges to disciplines in the name of the democratization of social inquiry and these were as much a part of the history of the 1960s as the former fight. I have in mind the ongoing developments in, for example, history (the new social history), and sociology (phenomenology, ethnomethodology) with legitimated looking at new kinds of problems in new ways. One might also add to these methodological developments the challenges to the established literary canons as well as to the academy for its presumed neutrality. While the opposition to positivism (or empiricism or behavioralism) as a model for social understanding has a legacy dating back to the nineteenth century, it is in the debates in and out of phenomenology and most clearly in Habermas's systematic critique of positivism that one finds a contemporary reading of import. It is argued that this scientism or hold of the empirical-positivistic tradition on epistemology is a consequence of a more generalized hold that objectivism has on the life-world — on social and psychic life, on art and politics, on language.

Feminist theorizing occurs within a cultural context that is concerned with the power that science and the scientific method have on human understanding. The Frankfurt School shares with other critics of positivism the position that the social world is qualitatively different from the natural world and that the procedures used in one form of inquiry cannot be simply adapted for use in the other. The world of persons is socially constituted and one understands this world by grasping the intentions of others through seeing the meaning given to actions and situations by individuals. Human activities are an historical time problem and human beings are flesh-and-blood creatures. Consequently, the notion of objectivity is a very different one when the object is also an acting, willing and willful subject.[40] Moreover, the presumed objectivity of positivism and its myth of the neutrality of knowledge ignores the social prism through which the observer has his or her knowledge filtered, and, consequently, it is unprepared to raise ethical or moral issues.

The emphasis on the subject is what is most distinctive in the break with the natural science model. It is the underpinning of a phenomenological method, and it informs the work of the Frankfurt School even as that school departs from the hermeneutic tradition by grounding knowledge in politics and arguing that knowledge be given a practical intent, that is, be used to transform nature and society in a direction that alleviates oppressive social conditions. In calling for an emancipatory or critical social science[41] or in grounding social theory in an a priori that assumes that life ought to be worth living,[42] the Frankfort School equates social theory with social criticism, a perspective that similarly informs feminist theory in its opposition to estrangement and dehumanization.

In several of the writings on motherhood, one finds a similar appeal to a distinctively female way of looking at the world. Sara Ruddick, a philosopher, shares with Dinnerstein a way of seeing in mothering the "conjunction of power and powerlessness," a powerlessness of women in the public society and a powerfulness either through women's ability to withhold the bearing of children or in their relationships with those entrusted to their care. From women's power comes society's "matriphobia." Ruddick sees in mothering a love relationship, a sense of pride and concern for children, a belief, on the part of those who mother, that they can do right by those entrusted to them. In this sense, "maternal love, pleasure in reproductive powers, and a sense of maternal competence" can be "benign, accurate, sturdy, and sure."[43]

Intent upon taking this positive side of mothering and moving it into the public realm, a space where women now rarely get to ply their wares, Ruddick sets up an ideal-type of thought, one that builds on that relationship with one's children that can most often be found in mother-child relationships but which, in principle, can also be found in father-child relationships. Maternal thought is, then, a kind of female thought. While it is not necessarily biologically grounded and is to be seen as a social category that falls on those who mother, it seems that women experience such thought differently than men: they come to know of mothering and thinking maternally through their having been daughters and not sons. Following Chodorow, there is indeed importance in the differential bonding of the two sexes.

Maternal thought involves a certain respect for and interest in preserving life. It is aware of the limits of what can and cannot be done and, in this sense, it departs from the practice of science which is a way of thinking that is grounded in control. It is humble — filled with humility — in a way that science is not, for it allows for chance and fate in a way that science cannot. Ruddick writes: "A mother . . . is committed to two philosophical positions: she is a mentalist rather than a behaviorist, and she assumes the priority of personhood over action." Ruddick is suggesting that motherhood and mothering involve reasoned thought made possible by the mind's ability to think about and assess concrete situations; mothering is not a series of responses to stimuli in any Pavlovian sense. Here, too, one encounters an emphasis on thoughtful and willful subjects who can, through what they do, affect the course of events. Ruddick does allow that acting "in the interests of preservation and growth" could lead towards not only a narcissistic concern for one's own kith and kin, and a consumerism that looks out for the self, but also an obedience to and deference towards the values of the society which smooth the way for helping one's children to fit in.[44] Maternal thought, however, could be a counter to the now dominant masculine values of a technocratic order, an order — and here she follows Habermas — characterized by instrumental reason antithetical to the kind of personalized relationships that bind parents to their children.

Elshtain builds upon Ruddick's notion of maternal thinking by suggesting that the ways in which mothers relate to their children constitute a moral paradigm of social behavior and a counter to the social relationships found in the modern, bureaucratic state. Maternal thinking is a way of knowing,[45] one that is a consequence of how one lives in the world and relates to that world; out of such knowing comes a certain way of acting. Like Ruddick, Elshtain speaks of building upon distinctively feminine worlds so as to encourage women to become "Antigone's Daughters," persons able to take their distance from the state while at the same time acting politically and not withdrawing into a veiled world of womanhood. The acting politically does not mean becoming transformed into public persons who, in their use of the state and the bureaucratic apparatus to make good their claims to be treated equitably with men, become absorbed by the very structures which they ought to be opposing. For the state as presently constituted is one whose values of scientific rationality and technological expertise are at odds with the liberatory potential of a certain kind of feminism.

Elshtain wants to see women as an opposing force to this state, not dissociating themselves but keeping a political distance. She argues that the way to realize this is through intensification of women's worlds, those concrete everyday life-worlds that Smith talks about. It means building on and supporting "women's historical social identity" as a counter to the "abstracted 'mode of reality' " used by one's adversaries. It means, Elshtain countinues, building on familial ties, "that arena that first humanizes us . . . your entry point into the wider social world" and as starting point for subsequent communal ideals.[46] In the mother-child relationship, and in the mother's concern that her child be preserved, grow, and become socially acceptable, a pattern (which has a built-in tension between self-identity and self-realization on the one hand and self-conformity on the other) is available as critique or negation of the public state. The ideal of the maternal, where the individual child is to be understood and attended to on its own terms, is opposed to the abstract and impersonal machinations of bureaucracy. As such, it becomes the model for how all social relationships ought to be structured. It is political in that mothers, or those who engage in maternal thinking, must act to change the world through politics so that the world in which they work to make their children acceptable is one worthy of their efforts. Elshtain writes: "As public policy becomes increasingly impersonal, calculating, and technocratic, maternal thinking insists that the reality of a single human child be kept before the mind's eye. Maternal thinking, like Antigone's protest, is a rejection of amoral statecraft and an affirmation of the dignity of the human person."[47] Habermas also speaks of women having "access to virtues, to a set of values that are both in contrast and complementary to the male world and at odds with the one-sided rationalized praxis of everyday life."[48] What happens, one would have to ask, when this thinking or these virtues are brought face-to-face with the bureaucratized world: do they collapse in the face of power or are they able to transform that power?

In her opposition to militarism, Ruddick castigates several of the qualities which others have associated with science and bureaucracy — the "rigid masculinist construction of gender . . . trust of authority . . . hierarchical command."[49] Wars deal with abstractions, both in terms of ideals and enemies. The talent for the abstract, as contrasted with thinking in terms of the concrete, is a male characteristic. If there is a logical case to be made for women's involvement in the military, it is in terms of the reshaping of that institution by a feminine presence "in the interests of peace." Women ideally would change the nature and scope of battles being fought: women might fight only just battles and fight them in a more humane way; women might limit the extent of the objectives and weaponry being used; women might not want to destroy the enemy but might act to be more conciliatory, more eager to negotiate a peaceful solution to the conflict; women would de-masculinize and possibly feminize conflict. Maternal thinking, which is quintessentially female, allows one to link women and peace through the idea of "preservative love." Assuming that women have a different moral voice than do men, Ruddick writes: "Maternal theories of conflict are more pacifist than militaristic. . . . [they] are opposed to warlike abstraction . . . they may bring to the battlefield a distinctly unmilitary eroticism." And, she continues, "[p]reservative love combined with a different eroticism and a concrete cognitive style might well lead women and some men soldiers to walk away from battle or to fight less ruthlessly."[50]

It is out of women's capacity to mother, then, that women are predisposed, in a way that men are not, to be conciliatory, to look for ways of settling accounts with adversaries, to be understanding of uses of nonviolence. Women are not given to the kind of abstraction that is at the core of militarism. Their sexuality and modes of eroticism are at odds with the kind of control necessary if one is to engage in military battle. Nonetheless, Elshtain is wary of the possibility that, given contemporary arrangements of power, there can ever be a "just war," or, conversely, that the nature of technocratic control is such that any war could be legitimated as a "just war" given a citizenry that does not have either access to the political and technical data that should allow for responsible evaluation of the state's position or political forums to debate and discuss policy considerations.

There has been a subtle but important shift in feminist theory from an earlier emphasis on the absence of differences between men and women to a glorification, or politicization, of the differences. The maternal, which at one point was regarded as a social device to shackle women to socially acceptable and socially assigned roles, through melioration becomes a form of oppositional behavior to a political system that is increasingly defined, by the movement, in patriarchal terms. In recalling Luker's portrayal of anti-abortion women, one saw another part of the miscellaneous collection of voices that do not want to devalue the maternal; and, in this sense, one can understand why Elshtain asks that the Women's Movement listen to what the anti-feminists are saying about their lives and their sense of self. Critics of Elshtain's, and to a lesser degree of Friedan,[51] are deeply troubled by using differences, and maternalism, to legitimate a traditional family structure, both those that depend upon male authority as well as those that act to preserve highly privatized feminine virtues. It is not that the critics discount the idea of feminine differences — which do not necessarily develop out of the maternal dimension — but they are concerned with how, in fact, the caring and nurturing dimension of women is made to affect and shape public decisions or, put differently, how the private sphere does not rest content with protecting and preserving itself but how it acts socially and politically to alter the public sphere.

Thus, an earlier historical theme of women's differences is played out in a new set of historical circumstances and only by placing the new voices in context can one understand how varied might be the implications of a feminist morality, or a feminist reason, or a feminist politics. For in order to understand the controversy within the feminist movement over the question of abortion, it is important to note how terminology has been used to recast the issue as one of reproductive rights. Once one frames the argument in terms of rights, one must beware the slippery slope that will lead to individualism, and it is that path that stays the voices of many feminists who are concerned about the apparent conflict between "autonomy and community" and the chance that the Women's Movement may be able to transcend that dichotomy.[52] A similar set of considerations is at play with respect to the issue of sexual freedom and sexual liberation, that is, to what extent does sexual self-expressiveness lead to the glorification of the individual and to self-absorption, each a threat to a feminist ideal of community and commitment.

Individualism and community are the political themes that have characterized American society since its inception. They were de Tocqueville's concerns and they are feminist concerns as well. They cut across and intersect with arguments on differences and equalities and they color discussions on reason, morality, and science.

Science: The Feminist Perspective

In the reaction against the equation of rationality with a male way of being-in-the world, several key terms have emerged out of feminist writing. The attack on domination is one of the most important of these, and it is integral to the search for alternative thought patterns in the work of Ruddick and Jaggar, for alternative discourse in the work of Elshtain, for the alternative organization of life's activities in the work of Firestone and Ferguson, and for alternative moralities in the work of Dinnerstein and Gilligan.[1] Similarly, questions are raised about the nature of rationality: what it means to be rational; how, if at all, rationality correlates with sex (biologically constructed differences) and gender (socially constructed differences); whether rationality takes different forms for different persons; how rationality accords with the notion of human progress itself— this in a post-Holocaust, post-Hiroshima age. Bernstein chronicles the philosophical debates which question reason and which ask whether something can be reasonable for or to a particular culture and moment in time but not to another, or whether reason can claim universal status and not be dependent upon specific attributes (of which one would have to include gender), of whether there is a falsity to the Enlightenment notion that presumes a Reason to which all can gain access, one that transcends differences and varieties of cultural experiences.[2]

Sandra Harding, a feminist philosopher, in suggesting (in a way quite similar to that of Gilligan) that the rational is gendered, that is, that it varies according to sex, writes that a rational woman is capable of empathy and capable of the incorporation of the views of others into her own, while a rational man acts rationally when he distances himself from others and when he decides objectively or without involvement what needs to be done.[3] Separation and attachment are the key differences, and there are serious questions to be raised about the idea of objectivity itself.

If one adds to domination, rationality and objectivity the idea of authority, one is not surprised that out of contemporary feminist theorizing comes a questioning of science itself—both as an intellectual project and as a political practice. Before turning to the feminist critique of science, let me first explain what is intended by that term.

What appears to be most essential in science, considered here in its most general aspect, is its approach to the acquisition of knowledge. Natural or human studies are considered scientific when the source of knowledge — person as scientist or observer — chooses a certain method to study phenomena systematically, be that phenomena nature or person itself. Scientific knowledge is organized and classified according to certain explanatory principles: "To explain, to establish some relation of dependence upon propositions superficially unrelated, to exhibit systematically connections between apparently miscellaneous items of information are distinctive marks of scientific inquiry."[4] Science offers a precise language: concepts, or definitions of terms, which can be combined logically and relatedly into statements of facts which, in turn, can be empirically verified or falsified. The universality of such statements grant them the status of laws, regularities of occurrences, which can be tested for their truth value within an accepted scientific paradigm. The methods by which concepts, hypotheses, theories, and laws are defined, combined, and used is the scientific method: a process by which knowledge is acquired and tested according to certain agreed upon rules or definitions.

Science is a method of finding out a truth which corresponds to a reality through the use of empirical evidence, that is, through the use of information (facts, proofs, theories) which can be transferred as information from one person to another. It is what Brecht calls "intersubjectively transmissible knowledge," a "type of knowledge that can be transmitted from *any* person who has such knowledge to *any* person who does not have it but who can grasp the meaning of the symbols (words, signs) used in communication and perform the operations, if any, described in the communications.[5] Karl Jaspers distinguishes, in a way similar to Brecht, between two dimensions of science: one "limited to the cogent and universally valid," that is concerned with empirical truths but not the nature of being or with values and moral goals and another, that is less a method and more an attitude, "any clear understanding obtained through rational and conceptual means."[6]

Here is not the place to enter into the long, complex debate on the contours of the scientific method; suffice it to say there is disagreement over what constitutes science and what does not and whether the method is equally applicable to the study of nature and the study of person. There appears to be consensus within the modern scientific community which characterizes science as having an empiricist, experimental, positivistic epistemology wherein technical data is observed and measured and which consensus rejects questions of causation (why) but accepts descriptions of laws (how). For science to be applicable to the study of human action, one would have to rule out "why" questions as well as knowledge which is neither empirically nor logically transmissible.

If one were to argue that knowledge can be transmitted from person to person as knowledge which is not empirically grounded, one must either sanction the existence of knowledge outside the bonds of science — one could call it philosophy or artistic insight or shared intuition — or one would have to change the definition of science itself, affecting what Brecht calls "a new revolution in science rather than that of a mere revolt."[7] The feminist critique of science is that kind of challenge and one that has been made by phenomenology and Critical Theory as well.

Those who follow in the tradition of Wilhelm Dilthey, who distinguish between the natural and human studies or sciences (*Naturwissenschaften* and *Geisteswissenschaften*), argue for an autonomous or unique approach to the latter, an approach which uses methods of analysis different from those used in the natural sciences because the object of concern — (person) — is a subject which demands its own unique methodology. To the degree that the subject matter should condition, in fact, define the appropriateness of method, and not the reverse, the natural and human studies will diverge along methodological lines. Each may bear a similarity to the other, for each may use methods of observation, description, evaluation, and generalization, but the central concern of each (nature or person) will modify these shared characteristics, not for any mystical reasons, but, rather, for precise, rigorous, explanatory reasons. Persons, unlike physical matter, exhibit behavior which is purposive, that is, imbued with intent, with meaning and signification, resulting from social action being historical action, action which can be surpassed or depassed, structured by the social person him/herself.

For critics of positivism — phenomenologists, Critical Theorists and feminists — a natural science is a science of description and explanation; a human study is a study of description and understanding — of empathy, psychically, and, in some instances, objectively grasped, a series of evaluations of inner states on the basis of outer actions. What is required is an epistemology which emphasizes the understanding of social action, the grasping of meaning and the attribution of signification to human behavior. Merleau-Ponty writes:

> The physicist's atoms will always appear more real than the historical and qualitative face of the world, the physio-chemical processes more real than the organic forms, the psychological atoms of empiricism more real than perceived phenomena, the intellectual atoms represented by the "significations" of the Vienna Circle more real than consciousness, as long as the attempt is made to build up the shape of the world (life, perception, mind) instead of recognizing, as the source which stares us in the face and as the ultimate court of appeal in our knowledge of these things, our *experience* of them. . . . empiricist constructions . . . hide from us in the first place "the cultural world" or "human world" in which nevertheless almost our whole life is led. . . . but not only does empiricism disort experience by making the cultural world an illusion, when in fact, it is in it that our existence finds its sustenance. The natural world is also falsified, and for the same reasons. . . . the nature about which empiricism talks is a collection

of stimuli and qualities and it is ridiculous to pretend that nature thus conceived is, even in intention, merely, the primary object of our perception: it does in fact follow the experience of cultural objects, or rather it is one of them.[8]

When one human describes and explains another, either in terms of individual activities, or interactions with others, or relationships with the institutions of the cultural world, there is not only a subjective dimension involved but also an historical set of factors. Weber, when read carefully, is very clear on this subject/object dichotomy:

> There is no absolutely "objective" scientific analysis of culture — or put perhaps more narrowly but certainly not essentially different from our purposes — of "social phenomena" independent of special and "one-sided" viewpoints according to which — expressly or tacitly, consciously or unconsciously — they are selected, analyzed and organized for expository purposes.[9]

The feminist position raises challenges to the alleged objectivity of science by questioning, in a way that phenomenology most certainly does not, both the feasibility and the desirability of objectivity. In sharp relief to those who argue that science ought to be pure and kept out of the service of politics, the feminist critique questions this, seeing in science a value only insofar as it is imbued with a purpose of serving humanity, by providing the framework for a critique of life and life's goals and of persons and their values.

An understanding of persons requires that disinterestedness be intertwined with involvement, that object be fused with subject, that perspectives be blended and yet held apart, and while the observer is bound by certain rules (logical consistency, telling the truth as he or she sees it, unearthing and not imposing meaning) one should not delude oneself into believing in a false or naive objectivism. "All my knowledge of the world," Merleau-Ponty writes, "even my scientific knowledge, is gained from my own particular point of view, or from some experience of the world without which the symbols of science would be meaningless."[10]

The critique of science found in feminist theory occurs at a time when Kuhn's thesis supported by the arguments of others had made its mark, and scholars in many fields were beginning to demonstrate the human underside of scientific theorizing. It arises, as well, out of the context of the Women's Movement with its commitment to obliterating male oppression and female subordination and out of a larger cultural critique of science as both a method and a practice. As a method, one need turn to the critique of positivism which has already been laid out and as a practice, to those historical instances where there had been a questioning of the applications of science by movements not only of the left but also of the right, each of which were concerned with the ways in which science was affecting personal and political concerns.

One need only recall Dinnerstein's attack on the technological society and situate it alongside other criticisms of a rationality gone wrong. Marcuse wrote in the 1960s that if science and technology were to become liberatory, they would have to recognize their political dimension[11] and they would also have to be "reconstructed in accord with a new sensibility—the demands of the life instincts."[12] Earlier, N.O. Brown had written that one needed a "science based on an erotic sense of reality, rather than an aggressive, dominating attitude towards reality."[13] Groups such as Science for the People had argued that science ought to be seen as part and parcel of social conflict, just as earlier those following in the Mannheimian tradition had raised questions about the presumed objectivity of all forms of knowledge and had asked that one see which interests were served by which kinds of knowledge. Science was to be seen not only as a method or set of prescriptions for organizing data but also as a social practice, a political doctrine, and an ideology. Concerned, however, with the political implications of any position of sociological relativism which turn science into ideology, Hilary Rose had warned:

> It is this philosophical relativism which has moved from being a critique of other knowledge to an auto-critique of one's own knowledge and on towards an escalating reflexivity. It is a hyper-reflexivity spoken of as the 'disembodied dialectic' which, both within the sociology of scientific knowledge and within the radical movement, threatens to consume not only 'ideology' but science itself. . . . there is nothing to distinguish true from false theories; a new equality prevails between knowledges. . . . The politics of subjectivism replaces the pursuit of the rational society.[14]

In addition to this problem of scientific relativity or subjectivity, any critique of science, feminist or otherwise, will have to face the question of how one holds onto some form of truth without denying the sociality of knowledge or how one avoids making science just one ideology among many. In general, the feminist attack on science intends to retrieve the idea of reason from its equation with a form of rationality held to be particularly male, that is, functional and instrumental. On one level, the argument is made against science that the question is one of gender discrimination: there are too few women scientists, and there are reasons to be concerned with the way in which scientific enterprises have come to observe and treat all persons, but most especially women. But, on another level, the case is put for seeing a fit between a male way of being-in-the-world and a scientific way, and the key words here are those to which reference was made earlier—domination, rationality, and objectivity: science, it is argued, is the most masculine form of knowledge.[15] While feminine and masculine ways of being-in-the-world are oftentimes seen to be grounded in biology, if not in specific anatomical structures at least in the ways in which the body is socially constructed or socially gendered, at other times they are not; rather, they are unfolded as distinct thought patterns which stem from the social conditions in which one is gendered. One learns how to be objective, Evelyn Fox Keller, for one, argues: it is not that men are more objective, but that the culture encourages one to think this is the case.

One can appreciate the similarity between earlier works on mothering, sexual arrangements and personality development (Dinnerstein, Chodorow, Ruddick, Elshtain, Gilligan) and the linkage between gender and ways of thinking made by feminist critics of science:

> The scientific mind is set apart from what is to be known, i.e., from nature, and its autonomy is guaranteed . . . by setting apart its modes of knowing from those in which that dichotomy is threatened. In this process, the characterization of both the scientific mind and its modes of access to knowledge as masculine is indeed significant. Masculine here connotes, as it so often does, autonomy, separation, and distance . . . a radical rejection of any comingling of subject and object.[16]

The feminist critique is a search for a way to know the world—an epistemology—that is not male-centered. It wants to guarantee to science a way of being liberatory in intent, that is, a way that does not parade under a false value-neutrality.

In turning to specific examples of the case for a feminist science, I have chosen to look at both an essay by Elizabeth Fee and Keller's collection of essays, *Reflections on Gender and Science;* several other examples—Janice Moulton's "A Paradigm for Philosophy: The Adversary Method" in its criticism of traditional approaches which treat one's opponents and their arguments as enemies to be destroyed[17] and Kathryn Pyne Addelson's "The Man of Professional Wisdom" in its demonstration of the politics of designating authorities within a field[18] speak to the same points.

Fee carefully lays out the problem of when and where feminism and science collide.[19] Conventionally, under the perspective of liberalism, one comes to regard science as objective and, thus, in sharp relief, to the domain of values, the world of preferences and biases. Science is understood as an enterprise in which a person of reason, using appropriate techniques of investigation, can find empirical truth; it is by using these techniques or methods of verification that any subjective dimension is erased or, at least, held in check. The sex of the scientist is irrelevant to his or her research. This view of science, Fee continues, rests, or falls, on the notion of a rational scientist, one who is able to control his or her self-interest from affecting the manner of inquiry, and it assumes that the participation and peculiarities of the individual scientist are irrelevant to the results of that inquiry.

Fee asks if by rational person one does not really mean "man" and that in liberalism the presumption is that objective research can be undertaken only by rational "men." Since women are considered more emotional and, hence, subjective, their practice of science would be of a different order. In fact, science has in the past been used to legitimate sexual differences, much as religion had been used at an earlier age. Science, insofar as it was part of a more generalized liberalism, gendered sex, that is, it spoke of diverse and natural male and female interests and talents. Science and males were both seen as governed by the interests of objectivity, impersonality, and detachment.

Feminists, in reacting against this polarity, can either argue that the polarities are false and ideological, that they do not allow for persons sharing in each kind, or that the differences do indeed exist and that out of these differences arise an alternative to the currently constituted kind of science. Fee sees Susan Griffin's *Woman and Nature* and Carolyn Merchant's *Death of Nature* as two works which, in finding an historical affinity between maleness and science — witness Bacon's call for a virile science that would conquer and control Mother Nature — argue against the consequences of this linkage. For Griffith and Merchant, science as it has been practiced, alienates and contributes to the domination of nature; what is needed is a science that is "feminized," that is made less alienating by being made more responsive to human needs and more ecological and more concerned with working with and not against the forces of nature. Thus, one can see the masculinization of science, which others have attributed to its European origins, its non-spiritual understanding of nature, and/or its linkages with a specific form of capitalist economic organization, as part and parcel of other contemporary ills which can also be resolved by the rediscovery of the feminine sphere.

Part of the critique of advanced industrial society, both in its academic and popular forms, had spoken of the need to change social attitudes towards nature so that one entered into a dialectical partnership with and not a domination over natural forces. Tracing social attitudes toward nature and the natural sciences to a Baconian tradition in which the mastery of external nature was related to the mastery of human nature, William Leiss had written: "the conviction that the mastery of nature would effect a beneficent social transformation became a powerful ideology in modern society."[20] Knowledge was seen as a tool for domination: this thesis, integral to Critical Theory, arguing that reason had become a functional reason which sought to master things and people, becomes a major component of the feminist critique of science.

Scientific objectivity allows science to be cut off from human needs and interests. Moreover, the presumed authority of science is itself open to question: one need only cite works in the philosophy of science which gave an insight into the political dimension of establishing authoritative models or paradigms, as well as political movements which questioned

the experts' ability to impose political solutions on unwitting populations. Fee recognizes the dangers inherent in dismantling authority, for,
in making each person the final arbiter of truth, one legitimates subjectivity and relativism and makes feminism itself one truth among many,
which may include anti-feminism, as well. She worries about throwing
out babies and bath water: "The proposition that we must either accept
science as it is now, or collapse into mysticism and irrationalism, may be
simply a tactic to discourage critical inquiry."[21]

She argues that we need to refine certain aspects of science: first, the
idea that science and how it is used can be kept separate and that scientists bear no social responsibility for their work; second, the idea that
thoughts and feelings are two distinct domains and that the one of rational reflection is to be more highly valued than the other of concern and
commitment; third, that subjects and objects, observers and observed,
are separate entities, a dangerous "epistemological distancing";[22] fourth,
that science is a pure endeavor rather than part of a socially endowed productive industry, that is, a human activity situated in a concrete historical moment, of a time and of a place.

Fee sees not a new kind of science but a critique of existing science
coming out of feminism. Only in a non-sexist society could one have a
feminist science. Such a science would have to overcome the duality of
false dichotomies which are now held "between the production and uses
of knowledge, between thought and feeling, between subject and object,
or between expert and non-expert."[23]

Keller's essays also illustrate how the ideology of feminism focuses its
lenses on the ways in which males and females are socially gendered and
on the ways in which dichotomies are created — objectivity/subjectivity,
reason/emotion, mind/nature. Antipodes are established, often to validate historical needs.[24] It has been assumed, since the inception of modern science in the seventeenth century, that science is something that
men do, that they do it in a masculine way, and that were women to do
science, they would do it differently. Taking her lead from Kuhn, Keller,
whose academic appointment is in mathematics but who acknowledges
her indebtedness to Kuhn, argues that both science and gender are categories of social construction; each is molded by the society to accord with
its predominant values. Her intent is to use a feminist lens to look at science, a lens that, unlike its male counterpart, asks gendered questions
about that knowledge. *Reflections* is a Kuhnian reading of science and scientific change with the new hypothesis that gender is a factor in the kind
of science that emerges.

Keller argues that modern science is infused with a masculine ideology, one that is the "projection of disinterest, of autonomy, of alienation."[25] Modern science reflects the ideals of modern man: "of self as
autonomous and objectified: an image of individuals unto themselves,

severed from the outside world of other objects . . . and simultaneously from their own subjectivity," arrogantly displaying his impersonality and detachment and flaunting his preparedness and ability to conquer and dominate nature-as-woman. This posturing of objectivity is a consequence not only of a certain historical way of regarding science but also, as Freud, Piaget and object-relation theorists have implied, a result of certain experiences in early childhood — the kinds of attachments experienced differently by boys and girls of which Chodorow had spoken: learning to be objective is learning to become a self separate from that of one's parent.

There is mutual reinforcement of objectivity and science: to the degree that one is valued by the society so is the other. The breakdown of each is historically possible, and Keller reads certain trends as posing a much-needed threat — changes in child-rearing arrangements, a political questioning of the values of scientific value-freedom and neutrality, the philosophic inquiry into the outlines of scientific progress, and developments internal to science where a concern with a dialectic is being espoused.[26]

In an era in which one can find voices that speak passionately of their distrust of science, one can appreciate the feminist critique of science. It is a critique nurtured by Hiroshima, chemical and germ warfare, pollution, and genetic manipulation. It is within this context that the feminist critique of science has to be situated.

Conclusion

Being committed to a Mannheimian perspective on the sociology of knowledge shapes the interest brought to a project. I have been interested not so much in the logical as the social dimension of thought, not only in what is intrinsic to the argument but also how that argument can be read, explicated and understood in historical terms. Following Mannheim and Klein, I have tried to look at ideas in terms of what they mean and what they intend. As distinct from the psychological, one asks not what was it in a particular writer's life that formed his or her thoughts, but what were the "currents of the time" which formed the background for his or her inquiry.[1] How one comes to regard certain issues bears a relationship to the social context in which one finds oneself. Mannheim alerts one to the subtle ways in which the *Zeitgeist* of the age works one over, but there is nothing mechanical in his treatment of the relationship of ideas and social actors, allowing as he does for conflicting interpretations of that spirit, moments of conflict between Dionysian and Apollonian ways of being and thinking, and the absence of deterministic rules of behavior which would preclude accidents and unanticipated turns of events.

Like Klein's *The Feminine Character,* this book is a study of how the feminine is historically transformed and how it has come to be seen differently in the last 20 years or so. Like Klein, I have suggested why this is the case, placing emphasis on the existence of the Women's Movement, changes in the composition of the labor force, new devices in technology, and the multitude of factors that are involved in legitimating and institutionalizing these developments.

The writers discussed have tried to give meaning to the changed social conditions of women. They have written against the background of a movement for social change which seeks to identify oppression in terms of both sexual and economic arrangements. Their efforts are ones of legitimation, of coming to have the power to reconstruct what is currently taken to be true. This reading of feminist social theory has suggested those themes which provide the background for the propositions argued by respective writers. The background, following Marx, evolves from a dialectical relationship in which the kinds of production in which a society engages affects the ways in which people relate to each other and affects the kinds of ideas they come to hold on their own. At issue are the following: changes in the labor force; changes in family patterns, especially as these indicate a decline in full-time motherhood; changes in the social roles that women are able and chose to play, especially reassessments of women's role away from the family and towards jobs other than housewifery; changes in the values attached to work as well as to children; the pervasiveness of consumerism; technological changes that are a contributing factor to rethinking what being of the feminine gender means. There are a whole range of other issues which provide the historical context for understanding feminist writing while, at the same time, being themselves shaped by that writing in true dialectical fashion. It would require a book on the Women's Movement to treat these issues adequately: this book is not such a book and, fortunately, those books have been written by others.[2] These books detail, among other things: changes in the educational situation of women; formation of women's studies and women's research centers; non-sexist curriculum development; women's health movements; affirmative action programs; sexual harrassment legislation; comparable worth and pay equity. The dialogue suggested by these texts is concerned with whether women have the freedom of mind and soul to be anything they want to be — any kind of laborer, family member, or thinker — or whether there are social and/or biological factors which condition (I choose not to say restrain) women to be certain things rather than others. Further, they are concerned with whether these conditions are of such an order (natural? moral?) that they ought to be accepted as such.

The writings on motherhood provide a clear focus on an essential component of this discussion. That changes in motherhood as well as changes in writing about it characterize the contemporary period is not open to question. One need only make reference to: the labor force statistics on the increase in the number of women who work who have young, school-age children; the statistics on increases in voluntary sterilization; NOW's 1967 Bill of Rights for Women which asked that the society recognize *its* role in child-rearing and the need for child-care supports in terms of facilities, maternity leaves, birth control, abortion and family planning; proposals at the state and federal governmental levels for increased family assistance programs; the writings of Dinnerstein and Chodorow on shared child-care, of Rich on gynocentrism; and Firestone on ectogenesis. In the writings on motherhood, there is no simple derogation of motherhood, but, rather, an attempt to ask the price paid for legitimating the institution of motherhood as it has been traditionally understood to work; put differently, it is the question of how the forms of bonding can change, how men can be involved in the process, and how enduring solidarities distinct from biological ties can be achieved. One also sees in the material on motherhood a traditional philosophical concern with the body, but what is of interest is the way in which that material is affected by the Movement's asking what it means to have a femi-

nine body or to be embodied. Maurice Merleau-Ponty has written that
the body is the point from which one sees the world: "one's perspective of
and on an object begins with one's body." He writes: "The body is the vehicle of being in the world, and having a body is, for a living creature, to
be intervolved in a definite environment, to identify oneself with certain
projects and be continuously committed to them." The body is the place
where one orders the world one perceives. One's sexuality is a dialectical
process involving bodily organs and psychological factors, each played
out in concrete situations so that it can be said that the sexual "is what
causes a man to have a history."[3] Through one's sexuality — dialectically
understood — one comes to have a certain attitude toward the world and
towards other people in the world. The body is what gives one a place, for
it allows others to see one as an object and the self to see one as a subject.

In this context, feminist theory has grappled with the problem of "the
body:" with its physical aspects; with the way it is lived or embodied; with
the consciousness that the self is encased in a specific physical body; with
the body as text — as given meaning or signification by the dominant culture, which meaning one may wish to oppose or counter as evidence of
one's freedom or autonomy. The feminist reading of Merleau-Ponty
would be to argue that there is a feminine point from which one comes to
regard the world: a feminist critique of bureaucracy — the kind found in
Ferguson's work, for example — says in effect that the import of the female body is that it comes to regard social structures in a way distinct
from that of masculinists.

At some point, one of two cases will have to be made: either that this
femininity is grounded in the corporeal body, a position made most
clearly by French feminists[4] and Rich;[5] or in the body as it is observed by
others, as others come to regard women, the position of Jaggar[6] and
Keller.[7] It is incorrect, however, to frame the question as one of sex or
gender, for the sociological assumptions of this book are such that one assumes that the body is always in a time and of a place. The import of the
feminist perspective as it comes out of embodiment literature is whether
this perspective is one among many (very much a Mannheimian position) or one above the others (very much a Marxist position). It is in-
structive to read the way in which Hilary Rose distinguishes herself from
Keller on this question. Keller is for her a "post-modernist," one who allows for a plurality of perspectives of which the feminist is one. Rose, like
Hartsock, argues for a distinctive way in which the feminine sees the
world not only differently but better:

> There is an epistemology which arises from feminism's capacity to unify
> different knowledges derived from manual, mental, and emotional labor,
> and that in this unification of 'hand, heart and brain' lie the grounds for a
> more complete materialism, a truer knowledge, which will sustain a trans-
> formative program within science and within society.[8]

There is another set of developments which come out of feminist theory that parallel contemporary discussions in the natural sciences, most especially biology, and in the philosophy of science. Two components of those discussions seem to me of import here: first, an interest in the sociality of science; and, second, an interest in the sociality of the body. Keller's theses on the ways in which science is gendered is in the Kuhnian tradition, which had been articulated earlier by Mannheim, that the practice of science is affected by the values and norms of the larger social order of which it is a part. Feminist writings on the body seek to place the body in a social context and, in so doing, to situate the female historically. The question of what role the new technologies play in liberating and/or controlling the body is part of this approach.

I read the import of Jaggar's argument that feminism must oppose the dualistic strain in the Western philosophic tradition as an effort,[9] similar to that of radical biologists as well as to de Beauvoir herself,[10] to move against mechanistic interpretations of the body and, in this connection, against a series of dichotomies (self/society, individual/community, public/private, mind/body, reason/emotion, nature/culture, production/reproduction) which obfuscate the dialectical component of human experience. Certain terms in Western discourse, Jaggar argues, have been gendered: men have been seen as public persons, as reasonable, as persons of intellect and persons with a culture; women have been seen as private persons, irrational or passionate, as persons of the body and persons in line with nature, as persons in a culture. One must think past these false categories and begin to redefine terms like power and reason: one must conceptualize the former in terms that encourage persons to think in terms of power to not power over and one must reassess the latter, philosophically contested concept. In both instances, one must bear in mind that society and biology define, shape, and confine what one is, but that it is in the nature of the individual to test those limits.

Along similar lines, Hartsock has spoken of this dualism as a male way of looking at society, and although others have critiqued it as part of the Descartian mechanistic legacy,[11] still others have read that legacy as itself part of male imagery.[12] Gilligan, like Smith, sees a female epistemology as a counter to this, with its emphases on empathy, care, understanding and relatedness: the ethic of care "reflects a cumulative knowledge of human relationships [and], evolves around a central insight, that self and other are interdependent."[13] Others, not using a feminist paradigm, have proferred a certain kind of sociological method which allows one to capture the syncretism of the social in the individual and the individual in the society: The

> process of becoming man takes place in an interrelationship with an environment [an] environment [that] is both a natural and a human one. . . .

> Humanness is socio-culturally variable . . . . there is no human nature in
> the sense of a biologically fixed substratum determining the variability of
> socio-cultural formations. While it is possible to say that man has a nature,
> it is more significant to say that man constructs his own nature, or more
> simply, that man produces himself.[14]

The affinity between feminist theory and social constructionism is, as I
have suggested, their emphases on the world-as-constructed allowing for
raising questions about the world as taken-for-granted.

A Mannheimian interest in feminism is concerned with how, as an
ideology or set of structured images, it is shaped by the concrete conditions of the day, among which I have chosen to emphasize the presence of
technological factors which permit women to reassess how they can and
ought to live out their lives. The Women's Movement, or certainly a part
of it, is a component of a more generalized set of social movements
against the ravages of advanced industrial society. Raising questions
about the ethos of a modernity that emphasizes production and consumerism without limits, these new social movements, of which Habermas has written, have called attention to the excesses of production and
the domination of nature. Without rejecting modernity, as some of its
critics charge, the new movements are asking for a dialogue to determine
how best to handle economic and political problems, tapping the expertise of science but requiring that it be made accountable to a larger and
more democratic polity than is now the case. It is the charge that such expertise consider how its theoretical and practical models and applications
affect the life-world of the individual and whether such effect is liberatory
and emancipatory or quite the opposite. In other words, the Women's
Movement is asking if the advances in technology, be they in the fields of
reproductive technology or nuclear weaponry, threaten the person or
not. There is a concern with the reification of persons, treating them as if
they were things or commodities; persons become alienated, separated
from what they produce, from other persons, from their own feelings. In
the writings of Fee and Keller one finds an argument about the generalization of science that is in accord with the concerns of these new social
movements. It is in this sense that the conditions of advanced industrial
society effect how the theses on women and science are written and understood. As Keller argues that science is gendered, so Hartsock argues
that political power is gendered and masculinity shapes policies of military preparedness and warfare.[15]

A reading out of Critical Theory, certainly out of Marcuse, argues
that one can reasonably, that is, through the power of rational thought,
determine how one ought to live within the real and actual potentials of
one's concrete society. One is not bound to an unchanging human nature, nor ought one be driven to live out on the psychological level demands of the id or on the political level utopian ideals that have no basis

in the concrete material conditions technically possible at the time. Marcuse is not arguing for living as one's unrestrained id would have one — his efforts to fuse Marx and Freud are a way of taking the Freudian dictum, "where id was, there shall ego be" and situating it within the ethical foundations of socialist humanism. Nor is he arguing that one ought to live according to whatever is technically possible, that is, doing whatever can scientifically be done. He has, in fact, argued quite the opposite, contending that the technically possible, devoid of morality, turns reason on its head: "In the unfolding of capitalist rationality, *irrationality* becomes *reason*: reason as frantic development of the mass of goods (and their accessibility for broad strata of the population); irrational because higher productivity, domination of nature, and social wealth become destructive forces."[16]

Feminist thought, if one might for the moment speak of it as if it were a collective body of arguments, is wary of the idea of "reason," seeing it as both an abstraction that has lost sight of real persons and as the functional performance of tasks regardless of how life-denying these may be. Feminist theory shares with Critical Theory, as well as the developments out of Existentialism — here broadly understood — the modern distrust of technical reason as well as a melioristic dimension, a commitment to a praxis that will work towards improving the concrete social conditions of humanity.

The Mannheimian framework orients one to look at women concretely — culturally and historically — but not in terms of any transcedent idea of Woman. There is an affinity here with the social construction of reality thesis of Berger and Luckmann; that is, both ask questions of the social conditions and the social writings on the feminine not of the Feminine. In this connection, I have sought to explain why the particularities of contemporary feminist theory have come into prominence now, and I suggest that this is an historical question. I have sought to explicate or unpack the inner structure of that thought by trying to get at what the writers of that thought intended. David Kettler is correct in arguing that this very approach is itself tied up with one's interests, in the case in point to one's status as an intellectual, in that it gives one distance and detachment.[17] It does not give one political answers, although it may help one to clarify one's own political and moral agenda. This is not troublesome to the degree that one recognizes that truth is to be discovered in the political world: one comes to know the truth through political struggle just as one comes to know one's alienation through opposing the masters of power.

Mannheim has one ask why the world is constructed one way and not another, why individuals choose to see things one way and not another. The why is a social not a psychological why, that is, it is an inquiry into the social factors involved in perception. It is sociologically illuminatory. When one writes of the "feminine character," one has presumed that it is socially constructed, an historical concept subject to change. One understands that character contextually, according to current language uses. What the feminine has come to mean is a result of a socially arrived at definition, made legitimate as a consequence of the power and influence of those in a position to define it. The sociologist does not come to understand the feminine solely through intuition or feelings, although these may provide hunches or insights on which to initiate inquiry; he or she immerses him/herself in the texts of the period and listens to the voices that are speaking.

Contemporary feminist thought bears a dialectical relationship to the Women's Movement, and like that movement, is shaped by general ideas particular to the historical moment. Feminism is a movement to change the way one looks at the world and feminist theory is part of that struggle. To understand that theory, I have argued, one must understand the time and place out of which it arises. I have selected certain writers, whom I have regarded as representative of the field, to illustrate this interaction between their ideas and the social conditions out of which their ideas emerge. Moreover, I have presumed that their ideas are meant to be representative of the unarticulated voices of the persons about whom they write. It is in this sense that feminist ideas may represent the interests of certain women even where the ideology would have it that the ideas are meant to express the interests of all women.

*

Notes

Preface

1. Robert A. Nisbet, *Community and Power* (New York: Oxford University Press, 1962), esp. pp. 48–54; see also Robert A. Nisbet and Robert G. Perrin, *The Social Bond* (New York: Alfred A. Knopf, 1970), esp. pp. 27–46.

Chapter 1

1. George Lichtheim, *The Concept of Ideology and Other Essays* (New York: Vintage Books, 1967), pp. 17–22.

2. Walter Lippmann, *Public Opinion* (New York: Free Press, 1922), pp. 1–20.

3. For a discussion of consciousness, see Karl Marx and Friedrich Engels, *The German Ideology: Part One* (New York: International Publishers, 1970).

4. Karl Mannheim, *Ideology and Utopia: An Introduction to the Sociology of Knowledge,* trans. Louis Wirth and Edward A. Shils (New York: Harcourt, Brace and World, 1936).

5. Ibid., p. 196.

6. Ibid., p. 40.

7. Ibid., p. 53.

8. Ibid., p. 84.

9. Ibid., p. 85.

10. Ibid., p. 96.

11. Nicolas Abercrombie and Brian Longhurst, "Interpreting Mannheim," *Theory, Culture, and Society* 2 (1983): 5–15.

12. See Sigmund Freud's 1907 essay "Obsessive Acts and Religious Practices" in his *Character and Culture* (New York: Collier Books, 1963), pp. 17–26.

13. Harold D. Lasswell, *Psychopathology and Politics* (New York: Viking Books, 1962), p. 172.

14. Chalmers Johnson, *Revolutionary Change* (Boston: Little, Brown, 1966), p. 19.

15. Talcott Parsons, *The Social System* (Glencoe: Free Press, 1951), p. 42.

16. Georges Sorel, *From Georges Sorel: Essays in Socialism and Philosophy,* trans. John and Charlotte Stanley (New York: Oxford University Press, 1976), esp. pp. 200–203.

17. Compare with Peter L. Berger and Thomas Luckmann, *Social Construction of Reality: A Treatise in the Sociology of Knowledge* (Garden City: Doubleday, 1966), esp. pp. 124–128.

18. Viola Klein, *The Feminine Character: History of an Ideology* (Urbana: University of Illinois Press, 1972).

19. Simone de Beauvoir, *The Second Sex,* trans. H. M. Parshley (New York: Modern Library, 1952), p. 301.

20. Ibid., xviii–xix.

21. Alison Jaggar, "Towards a More Integrated World." Paper presented to the Douglass College Women's Studies Seminar "Feminist Reconstruction of Self and Society," January 1985, p. 2; see also Nancy C.M. Hartsock, *Money, Sex, and Power: Towards a Feminist Historical Materialism* (New York: Longman, 1983); and Evelyn Fox Keller, *Reflections on Gender and Science* (New Haven: Yale University Press, 1985).

22. Hans Gerth and C. Wright Mills, *Character and Social Structure: The Psychology of Social Institutions* (New York: Harcourt, Brace and World, 1953).

23. For sociological theorizing, see Berger and Luckmann, *Social Construction of Reality.* On feminist theory, see Alison Jaggar, *Feminist Politics and Human Nature* (Totowa: Rowman & Allanheld, 1983); and Hartsock, *Money, Sex and Power.*

24. Warren G. Bennis and Philip E. Slater, *The Temporary Society* (New York: Harper & Row, 1968), p. 124.

25. Georg Simmel, "The Metropolis and Mental Life" in *The Sociology of Georg Simmel,* trans. Kurt H. Wolff (New York: Free Press, 1950), pp. 409–424.

26. Herbert Marcuse, *Eros and Civilization: A Philosophical Inquiry into Freud* (New York: Random House, 1955), and his *One-Dimensional Man: Studies in the Ideology of Advanced Industrial Society* (Boston: Beacon Press, 1964). Also Jurgen Habermas, *The Theory of Communicative Action: Reason and the Rationalization of Society,* I, trans. Thomas McCarthy (Boston: Beacon Press, 1984).

27. For example, note the way in which the import of modernity is posed in Edward Shorter's *The Making of the Modern Family* (New York: Basic Books, 1975).

28. Theodor W. Adorno, *Negative Dialectics,* trans. E.B. Ashton (New York: Seabury Press, 1973); Marcuse, *One-Dimensional Man*; Jurgen Habermas, *Towards a Rational Society: Student Protest, Science and Politics,* trans., Jeremy J. Shapiro (Boston: Beacon Press, 1970), esp. pp. 81–122.

Chapter 2

1. Lewis A. Coser, *Masters of Sociological Thought: Ideas in Historical and Social Context* (New York: Harcourt Brace Jovanovich, 1971), p. xiii.

2. Mannheim, *Ideology and Utopia,* p. 5.

3. Ibid., p. 3.

4. In Klein, *The Feminine Character,* p. vii.

5. Ibid., p. xvi. For what I interpret as a misconception of Klein's intention, and as an attempt to read *The Feminine Character* as a criticism of men writing about women fashioned out of a male-dominated period, see Dale Spender, *Women of Ideas and What Men Have Done to Them from Alphra Behn to Adrienne Rich* (Boston: Routledge & Kegan Paul, 1984), pp. 502–506. One can understand Spender's reading Klein this way: it is the way a feminist could conceivably read intent some thirty years and a Women's Movement later.

6. Klein, *The Feminine Character,* pp. 3–4.

7. Ibid., p. 1.

8. Ibid., p. 2.

9. Ibid., p. 10.

10. Ibid., p. 17.

11. Alexis de Tocqueville, *Democracy in America,* trans. George Lawrence (Garden City, N.Y.: Doubleday, 1969).

12. See, on the subject, Margaret Jackson, "Sexual Liberation or Social Control," *Women's Studies International Forum* 6 (1983): 1–17; Ruth Bleier, *Science and Gender: A Critique of Biology and Its Theories on Women* (New York: Pergamon Press, 1984); Keller, *Reflections on Gender and Science*; and Hartsock, *Money, Sex and Power.*

13. Klein, *The Feminine Character,* p. 40.

14. Ibid., p. 44.

15. Ibid., p. 45.

16. Ibid., p. 67.

17. Ibid., p. 69.

18. Ibid., p. 72.

19. Ibid., pp. 91–92.

20. Ibid., p. 95.

21. Quoted in ibid., p. 128.

22. Ibid., pp. 138–139.

23. Ibid., p. 159.

24. Klein, quoting Thomas, ibid., p. 160.

25. Ibid., p. 162. The original, hardbound edition of Klein's work includes an interesting appendix in which Klein analyzes a novel of three generations of women—Jo v. Amers-Kuller's *The Rebel Generation*—in terms of a fictionalized recounting of changing perceptions of femininity.

26. Bleier, *Science and Gender*; Helga Nowotny and Hilary Rose, eds., *Counter-movements in the Sciences* (Hague: Reidel, 1979); Hilary Rose and Steven Rose, eds., *Ideology of/in the Natural Sciences* (New York: Schenkman, 1980); Keller, *Reflections on Gender and Science.*

27. Thomas S. Kuhn, *Structure of Scientific Revolutions* (Chicago: University of Chicago Press, 1970).

28. Robert Paul Wolff, "There's Nobody Here but Us Persons," *Philosophical Forum* 5 (Winter–Fall 1973–1974): 128–44.

29. Hans-Georg Gadamer, *Truth and Method,* trans. Garrett Barden and John Cunningham (New York: Continuum Books, 1975), p. 267.

30. Peter L. Berger, *Invitation to Sociology: A Humanistic Perspective* (Garden City: Doubleday, 1963), p. 64.

31. Theodore W. Adorno, *Prisms,* trans. Samuel and Shierry Weber (London: Neville Spearman, 1967), p. 37.

32. Jurgen Habermas, *Knowledge and Human Interest,* trans. Jeremy J. Shapiro (Boston: Beacon Press, 1971), esp. pp. 311–315.

Chapter 3

1. Hans Speier, *Social Order and the Risks of War: Papers in Political Sociology* (Cambridge: MIT Press, 1952), p. 95.

2. Rom Harré, *Personal Being: A Theory for Individual Psychology* (Cam-

bridge: Harvard University Press, 1984).

3. Michel Foucault, *The Foucault Reader* (New York: Pantheon Books, 1984). The renewed interest in hermeneutics, phenomenology, and *Verstehen* sociology is indicative of a concern for the relationship of epistemology to politics. The contemporary debates in literary theory are also germane to the sociology of knowledge. Terry Eagleton (*Literary Theory: An Introduction* [Minneapolis: University of Minnesota Press, 1983]) is quite precise on the time-boundedness of literature, on how one inevitably brings to any work the moment in which one is situated. One reads "in the light of our preoccupations . . . in the light of our concern" (p. 12). One rewrites all texts in the mind's eye, he continues, just as that eye is never solely private but part of a social life and a social way of understanding and seeing that one might regard as ideological. Eagleton is precise: "meaning is historical" (p. 60). Knowledge, from a phenomenological perspective, arises out of a particular set of social interests; understanding, then, is within an historical context. What one takes from this is that not only does a work have a meaning but it also has a significance: it has a relationship that parallels the writer/reader dialectic and neither the meaning nor the significance can escape the inherent subjectivism of works being read by historically constituted readers. The affinity with deconstructionism is apparent — the search is not for external meanings but for deconstructing meanings into component parts, including a "naming" of what supports a particular idea. Eagleton uses the examples of a male-dominated society which is deconstructed through seeing how maleness is propped up by woman-ness as other, as opposite, as outsider. On the political consequences of this dismantling, see the discussion on p. 148. On the similarities between deconstruction and feminism, see pp. 148–150 and 187–191. The affinity with Foucault is apparent: Eagleton writes of being "prisoners of our own discourse" (p. 144). One might in this connection read Andreas Huyssen, "Mapping the Postmodern," *New German Critique* 33 (Fall 1984): 5–52; Seyla Benhabib, "Epistemology of Postmodernism: A Rejoinder to Jean-Francois Lyotard," ibid., 103–126; and Nancy Fraser, "The French Derrideans: Politicizing Deconstruction or Deconstructing the Political?," ibid., 127–154. See also Jonathan Culler, *On Deconstruction: Theory and Criticism after Structuralism* (Ithaca: Cornell University Press, 1982).

4. Berger and Luckmann, *Social Construction of Reality*.

5. Mannheim, *Ideology and Utopia*, pp. 266–67.

6. Ibid., p. 3.

7. Auguste Comte, "Plan of the Scientific Operations Necessary for Reorganizing Society" in *System of Positive Polity*, Vol. 4, trans. John H. Bridges (London: Longmans, Green, 1875), pp. 547–49.

8. Emile Durkheim, *Emile Durkheim on Institutional Analysis*, trans. Mark Traugott (Chicago: University of Chicago Press, 1978), p. 102.

9. Peter L. Berger, "Identity as a Problem in the Sociology of Knowledge," *European Journal of Sociology* 7 (1966): 108.

10. Berger and Luckmann, *Social Construction of Reality*, pp. 46–47.

11. Werner Stark, *The Sociology of Knowledge: An Essay in the Aid of a Deeper Understanding of the History of Ideas* (Glencoe: Free Press, 1958); Lewis A. Coser, "Knowledge, Sociology of" in Julius Gould and William L. Kolb, eds., *A Dictionary of the Social Sciences* (Glencoe: Free Press, 1964), pp. 428–435; Robert

K. Merton, "The Sociology of Knowledge" in George Gurvitch and Wilbert E. Moore, eds., *Twentieth Century Sociology* (New York: Philosophical Library, 1945), pp. 366–405; Berger and Luckmann, *Social Construction of Reality;* Gunter W. Remmling, ed., *Towards the Sociology of Knowledge: Origin and Development of a Sociological Thought Style* (New York: Humanities Press, 1974).

12. Karl Marx, "A Preface to the Critique of Political Economy," in *Karl Marx: Selected Writings in Sociology and Social Philosophy,* trans. T.B. Bottomore (New York: McGraw-Hill, 1956), p. 51.

13. Ibid., p. 75.

14. Mannheim, *Ideology and Utopia,* p. 305, 306.

15. Ibid., p. 87.

16. Ibid.

17. Arnold Brecht, *Political Theory: The Foundations of Twentieth Century Political Thought* (Princeton: Princeton University Press, 1959), p. 49.

18. Ibid., p. 50.

19. William James, *Pragmatism and Other Essays* (New York: Washington Square press, 1963), pp. 22–38, 87–104.

20. Steven Lukes, *Essays in Social Theory* (New York: Columbia University Press, 1977), p. 138.

21. Kuhn, *Structure of Scientific Revolutions,* p. 150.

22. Berger and Luckmann, *Social Construction of Reality.* p. 62.

23. Karl R. Popper, *Open Society and Its Enemies,* 2 vols. (New York: Harper & Row, 1962), *Conjectures and Refutations: The Growth of a Scientific Knowledge* (New York: Harper & Row, 1968), and *Realism and the Aim of Science: Postscript to the Logic of Scientific Discovery* (Totowa: Rowman & Allanheld, 1983); Michael Polyani, *Knowing and Being* (Chicago: University of Chicago Press, 1973); Paul Feyerabend, *Against Method* (New York: Schocken Books, 1978); Larry Laudan, *Progress and Its Problems: Towards a Theory of Scientific Growth* (Berkeley: University of California Press, 1977), and *Science and Values: The Aims of Science and Their Role in Scientific Debate* (Berkeley: University of California Press, 1984).

24. Kuhn, *Structure of Scientific Revolutions,* p. 150.

25. Berger and Luckmann, *Social Construction of Reality,* pp. 93, 94.

26. Mannheim, *Ideology and Utopia,* pp. 34–61, 252; Robert K. Merton, *Social Theory and Social Structure* (Glencoe: Free Press, 1957), p. 218; Stark, *The Sociology of Knowledge,* pp. 154, 157–164.

27. Mannheim, *Ideology and Utopia,* p. 107.

28. Ibid., p. 50.

29. Cf. Berger and Luckmann, *Social Construction of Reality,* p. 107.

30. Mannheim, *Ideology and Utopia,* p. 77.

31. Ibid., p. 280.

32. Stark, *The Sociology of Knowledge,* p. 159. Cf. also Dorothy E. Smith, "Women's Perspective as a Radical Critique of Sociology," *Sociological Inquiry* 44 (1974): 7–13.

33. Jaggar, *Feminist Politics and Human Nature,* p. 358.

34. Sondra Farganis, "Social Theory and Feminist Theory: The Need for Dialogue," *Sociological Inquiry,* 56 (Winter 1986); 50–68.

35. On this point, see Alfred Schutz, "Multiple Realities," *Philosophy and Phenomenological Research* 5 (1945): 533–76; also "Concept and Theory Formation

in the Social Sciences," *The Journal of Philosophy* 51 (1954): 257–273.

36. See Alfred Schutz, *Phenomenology of the Social World,* trans. George Walsh and Frederick Lehnert (Evanston: Northwestern University Press, 1967).

37. Karl Mannheim, *Essays on the Sociology of Knowledge* (London: Routledge & Kegan Paul, 1952), pp. 44, 184, 305; Zygmunt Bauman, *Hermeneutics and Social Science* (London: Heineman, 1978); A.P. Simonds, "Mannheim's Sociology of Knowledge as a Hermeneutic Method," *Cultural Hermeneutics* 3 (1975): 23–48.

38. Charles Horton Cooley, *Social Organization: A Study of the Larger Mind* (New Brunswick: Transaction Books, 1983), p. 7.

39. Habermas, *Knowledge and Human Interest,* pp. 308–311.

40. Schutz, "Concept and Theory Formation in the Social Sciences."

41. Simonds, "Mannheim's Sociology of Knowledge;" Edward A. Tiryakian, "Existential Phenomenology and the Sociological Tradition," *American Sociological Review* 30 (October 1965): 674–688.

42. George Herbert Mead, *Mind, Self and Society* (Chicago: University of Chicago Press, 1934), p. 156.

43. Peter L. Berger, "Identity as a Problem in the Sociology of Knowledge," p. 108, 111.

44. Karl Mannheim, "Sociology of Knowledge from the Standpoint of Modern Phenomenology: Max Scheler," in Remmling, *Towards the Sociology of Knowledge,* p. 187.

45. Ibid., p. 189.

46. Stark, *The Sociology of Knowledge,* pp. 20, 21.

47. Kurt H. Wolff, intro. to *From Karl Mannheim* (London: Oxford University Press, 1971), p. xiii.

48. Ibid., p. xix.

49. On this point, see Florian Znaniecki, *Social Role of the Man of Knowledge* (New York: Octagon Books, 1965).

50. Max Scheler, *Problems of a Sociology of Knowledge,* trans. Manfred S. Frings (London: Routledge & Kegan Paul, 1980), pp. 100–139.

51. Erich Fromm, *Sane Society* (New York: Holt, Rinehart & Winston, 1955).

52. Marcuse, *Eros and Civilization.*

53. Marx, "The German Ideology," in *Karl Marx,* pp. 78–81.

54. Keller, *Reflections on Gender and Science,* p. 174.

55. Brecht, *Political Theory,* pp. 48–54.

56. Charles Horton Cooley, "The Roots of Social Knowledge," *American Journal of Sociology* 32 (July 1926): 59–70.

57. Ibid.

58. Dorothy E. Smith, "The Social Construction of Documentary Reality," *Sociological Inquiry* 44 (1974): 257–68, and her essay "A Sociology for Women" in Julia A. Sherman and Evelyn Torton Beck, eds., *The Prism of Sex* (Madison: University of Wisconsin Press, 1979), pp. 137–87.

59. See, in this connection, Judith Stacey and Barrie Thorne, "The Missing Feminist Revolution in Sociology," *Social Problems* 32 (April 1985): 301–16.

60. See Robert Lane, "The Decline of Politics and Ideology in a

Knowedgeable Society," *American Sociological Review* 3 (October 1966): pp. 649–62.

61. Marcuse, *One-Dimensional Man,* and "Remarks on the Redefinition of Culture"in Gerald Holton, ed., *Science and Culture: A Study of Cohesive and Disjunctive Forces* (Boston: Houghton Mifflin, 1965), pp. 218–35.

62. Habermas, *The Theory of Communicative Action.*

63. Mannheim, *Ideology and Utopia,* p. 155.

64. Max Weber, "Science as a Vocation" in *From Max Weber: Essays in Sociology,* trans. Hans Gerth and C. Wright Mills (New York: Oxford University Press, 1946), pp. 129–56.

65. Karl Mannheim, *Essays on the Sociology of Culture* (London: Routledge & Kegan Paul, 1956), p. 105.

66. Mannheim, *Ideology and Utopia,* p. 281.

67. Ibid., pp. 78–81, 282–83.

68. Ibid., pp. 267–68.

69. T.B. Bottomore, "Some Reflections on the Sociology of Knowledge," *British Journal of Sociology* 7 (1956): 55; Adorno, *Prisms,* pp. 37–49.

70. Lukes, *Essays in Social Theory,* pp. 138–53.

71. See for example, Abercrombie and Longhurst, "Interpreting Mannheim."

72. See the discussion in Elisabeth Young-Bruehl, *Hannah Arendt: For Love of the World* (New Haven: Yale University Press, 1982), pp. 79–85; see also David Kettler, "Political Theory, Ideology, Sociology: The Question of Karl Mannheim," *Cultural Hermeneutics* 3 (1975): 69–80, and David Kettler et al., *Karl Mannheim* (New York: Methuen, 1984), pp.52–76.

73. Speier, *Social Order,* p. 190.

74. Martin Jay, *The Dialectical Imagination: A History of the Frankfurt School and the Institute of Social Research, 1923–1950* (Boston: Little, Brown, 1973), pp. 63–64, and "The Frankfurt School's Critique of Knowledge," *Telos* 20 (Summer 1974): 72–89.

75. David Held, *Introduction to Critical Theory: Horkheimer to Habermas* (Berkeley: University of California Press, 1980); Thomas McCarthy, *The Critical Theory of Jurgen Habermas* (Cambridge: MIT Press, 1978).

76. Mannheim, *Ideology and Utopia,* p. 283.

77. Speier, *Social Order,* p. 192.

78. Kurt H. Wolff "The Sociology of Knowledge and Sociological Theory," in Llewellyn Gross, ed., *Symposium on Sociological Theory* (Evanston: Row, Petersen, 1959), pp. 567–602.

79. Mannheim, *Ideology and Utopia,* pp. 284–86.

80. Ibid., pp. 295–300, 305–6.

81. Stark, *The Sociology of Knowledge,* p. 305.

82. Peter L. Berger and Hansfried Kellner, *Sociology Reinterpreted: An Essay on Method and Vocation* (Garden City: Doubleday, 1981), pp. 64, 66.

83. Jay, *Dialectical Imagination,* p. 83.

84. Mannheim, *Ideology and Utopia,* pp. 150, 243.

85. See, in this connection, Gerard Radnitzky, *Contemporary Schools of Metascience,* 2nd ed. (New York: Humanities Press, 1970); Richard Bern-

stein, *Beyond Objectivism and Relativism: Science, Hermeneutics and Praxis* (Philadelphia: University of Pennsylvania Press, 1983).

86. See, in this connection, Habermas, *Toward a Rational Society* and *Knowledge and Human Interest*; Bernstein, *Beyond Objectivism and Relativism*; also Bernstein, *Praxis and Action: Contemporary Philosophers of Human Activity* (Philadelphia: University of Pennsylvania Press, 1971) and *The Restructuring of Social and Political Thought* (New York: Harcourt Brace Jovanovich, 1976); Steven Rose, ed., *Against Biological Determinism: The Dialectics of Biology Group* (London: Alison & Busby, 1982), and *Towards a Liberatory Biology: The Dialectics of Biology Group* (London: Alison & Busby, 1982); Jaggar, *Feminist Politics and Human Nature*; Keller, *Reflections on Gender and Science*; Richard Levins and Richard Lewontin, *Dialectical Biologist* (Cambridge: Harvard University Press, 1985).

87. Bernstein, *Beyond Objectivism and Relativism,* p. x.

88. Berger and Luckmann, *Social Construction of Reality,* p. 1.

89. Bleier, *Science and Gender*; Rita Arditti et al., eds. *Science and Liberation* (Boston: South End Press, 1980); Ruth Hubbard et al., *Biological Woman: The Convenient Myth* (New York: Schenkman, 1982); Marian Lowe and Ruth Hubbard, eds., *Woman's Nature: Rationalizations of Inequality* (New York: Pergamon Press, 1983); Nowotny and Rose, *Counter-movements in the Sciences*; Hilary Rose and Steven Rose, eds., *Ideology of/in the Natural Sciences* (Boston: G.K. Hall, 1980); Keller, *Reflections on Gender and Science.*

90. Berger and Luckmann, *Social Construction of Reality,* p. 54.

91. Marcuse, *Eros and Civilization*; Donald L. Carveth, "The Disembodied Dialectic: A Psychoanalytic Critique of Sociological Relativism," *Theory and Society* 4 (1977): pp. 73–102; Richard Lichtman, "Symbolic Interactionism and Social Reality: Some Marxist Queries," *Berkeley Journal of Sociology* 15 (1970): 75–94.

92. Peter L. Berger, *Invitation to Sociology,* pp. 93, 98.

93. Mannheim, *Ideology and Utopia,* p. 79

94. Karl Mannheim, *Structures of Thinking,* trans. Jeremy Shapiro and Shierry Weber (Boston: Routledge & Kegan Paul, 1982), p. 274. Mannheim wrote: "If there are contradictions and inconsistencies . . . this is I think, not so much due to the fact that I overlook them but because I make a point of developing a theme to its end even if it contradicts some other statements . . . . in this marginal field of human knowledge we should not conceal inconsistencies . . . but . . . show the sore spots in human thinking at its present stages." Quoted in Kurt H. Wolff, "The Sociology of Knowledge and Social Theory," p. 571.

95. See C. Wright Mills intro. to *Images of Man: The Classic Tradition in Sociological Thinking* (New York: George Braziller, 1960), pp. 1–17.

Chapter 4

1. Barbara J. Harris, "The Power of the Past: History and the Psychology of Women," in Miriam Lewin, ed., *In the Shadow of the Past: Psychology Portrays the Sexes* (New York: Columbia University Press, 1984), pp. 1–25.

2. Robert Paul Wolff, "There's Nobody Here but Us Persons."

3. Nancy F. Cott, *The Bonds of Womanhood: "Women's Sphere" in New Eng-*

land (New Haven: Yale University Press, 1978), pp. 197–99.

4. Varied as they are, the following theses emphasize the historical situating of women's views: See Kristin Luker, *Abortion and the Politics of Motherhood* (Berkeley: University of California Press, 1984); and Rosalind Pollack Petchesky, *Abortion and Woman's Choice: The State, Sexuality and the Conditions of Reproductive Freedom* (New York: Longman, 1982).

5. Rudolf Heberle, *Social Movements: An Introduction to Political Sociology* (New York: Appleton-Century Crofts, 1951), p. 31.

6. Ethel Klein, *Gender Politics: From Consciousness to Mass Politics* (Cambridge: Harvard University Press, 1984); Myra Marx Ferree and Beth B. Hess, *Controversy and Coalition: The New Feminist Movement* (Boston: G.K. Hall/Twayne, 1985).

7. Jo Freeman, *The Politics of Women's Liberation: A Case Study in an Emerging Social Movement and Its Relation to the Policy Process* (New York: Longman, 1975).

8. Neil J. Smelser, *Theory of Collective Behavior* (Glencoe: Free Press, 1962), p. 8.

9. Alain Touraine, *The Self-Production of Society,* trans. Derek Coltman (Chicago: University of Chicago Press, 197), p. 298.

10. Jean L. Cohen, *Class and Civil Society: The Limits of Marxian Critical Theory* (Amherst: University of Massachusetts Press, 1983).

11. Emile Durkheim, *Suicide: A Study in Sociology,* trans. John A. Spalding and George Simpson (Glencoe: Free Press, 1951), p. 250.

12. Dennis Wrong, "The Oversocialized Conception of Man in Modern Society," *American Sociological Review* 26 (April 1961): 183–93.

13. Herbert Marcuse, *Essay on Liberation* (Boston: Beacon Press, 1969), pp. 49–78.

14. Marcuse, *One-Dimensional Man.*

15. Johnson, *Revolutionary Change,* p. 13.

16. Herbert Blumer, "Sociological Implications of the Thought of George Herbert Mead," *American Journal of Sociology* 71 (March 1966): 541; see also Peter Berger, *Invitation to Sociology,* pp. 93–121.

17. Anthony F.C. Wallace, *Culture and Personality* (New York: Random House, 1961), p. 26.

18. Kathleen J. Tierney, "The Battered Women's Movement and the Creation of the Wife Beating Problem," *Social Problems* 29 (February 1982): 297–320.

19. See in this connection Ronald Bayer, *Homosexuality and American Psychiatry: The Politics of Diagnosis* (New York: Basic Books, 1980); Peter Conrad and Joseph W. Schneider, *Deviance and Medicalization: From Badness to Sickness* (St. Louis: C.V. Mosby, 1980); Frances Fox Piven and Richard A. Cloward, *Poor People's Movements: Why They Succeed, How They Fail* (New York: Random House, 1979); John D. McCarthy and Mayer Zeld, *The Trend of Social Movements in America: Professionalism and Resource Mobilization* (Princeton: General Learning Press, 1973); Stephen J. Pfohl, *Deviance and Social Control* (New York: McGraw Hill, 1984) and "The 'Discovery' of Child Abuse," *Social Problems* 24 (February 1977): 310–23.

20. Charles Horton Cooley, *Social Organization* (New York: Schocken Books, 1962), p. 9.

21. Mead, *Mind, Self and Society,* p. 9.

22. Peter Berger, *Invitation to Sociology,* p. 90.

23. Berger and Luckmann, *Social Construction of Reality,* pp. 106–7.

24. Lawrence Goodwyn, *Democratic Promise: The Populist Movement in America* (New York: Oxford University Press, 1976), p. xii.

25. Jean L. Cohen, "Rethinking Social Movements," *Berkeley Journal of Sociology* 28 (1983): 97.

26. Kuhn, *Structure of Scientific Revolutions* p. 150.

27. Bonnie Thornton Dill, "Race, Class and Gender: Prospects for an All-Inclusive Sisterhood," *Feminist Studies* 9 (April 1983): 131–49; Ethel Klein, *Gender Politics;* Ferree and Hess, *Controversy and Coalition;* Angela Y. Davis, *Women, Race and Class* (New York: Random House, 1984); Marilyn Gittell and Nancy Naples, "Activist Women: Conflicting Ideologies," *Social Policy* 13 (Summer 1982): 52–57; Ruth Sidel, *Urban Survival: The World of Working Class Women* (Boston: Beacon Press, 1978); Myra Marx Ferree, "Working Class Feminism: A Consideration of the Consequences of Employment," *Sociological Quarterly* 21 (Spring 1980): 173–84; Steven Martin Cohen, "American Jewish Feminism: A Study in Conflict and Compromise," *American Behavioral Science* 24 (April 1980): 519–58; H. Edward Ransford and Jon Miller, "Race, Sex and Feminist Outlooks," *American Sociological Review* 68 (February 1983): 46–69.

28. Donald G. Mathews, *Religion in the Old South* (Chicago: University of Chicago Press, 1979) and *Slavery and Methodism: A Chapter in American Morality, 1780–1845* (Westport: Greenwood Press, 1978); Olive Banks, *Faces of Feminism: A Study of Feminism as a Social Movement* (New York: St. Martin's Press, 1981), pp. 13–27.

29. Caroll Smith-Rosenberg, "The Female World of Love and Ritual: Relations between Women in Nineteenth Century America," *Signs* 1 (Autumn 1975): 1–30.

30. Quoted in Anne F. Scott and Andrew M. Scott, *One Half the People: The Fight for Women Suffrage* (Philadelphia: J.B. Lippincott, 1975), p. 56.

31. Ellen Carol Du Bois, *Feminism and Suffrage: The Emergence of an Independent Women's Movement in America, 1848–1869* (Ithaca: Cornell University Press, 1978).

32. Arleen S. Kraditor, *The Ideals of the Women's Suffrage Movement, 1880–1920* (New York: W.W. Norton, 1981), pp. 43–74.

33. Elinor Flexner, *Century of Struggle: The Women's Rights Movement in the United States* (Cambridge: Harvard University Press, 1959).

34. William H. Chafe, *The American Woman: Her Changing Social, Economic and Political Roles, 1920–1970* (New York: Oxford University Press, 1974), p. 25.

35. G. Stanley Lemons, *The Woman Citizen: Social Feminism in the 1920s* (Urbana: University of Illinois Press, 1973); Rosalind Rosenberg, *Beyond Separate Spheres: Intellectual Roots of Modern Feminism* (New Haven: Yale University Press, 1983).

36. Chafe, *The American Woman,* pp. 27–29.

37. Stuart Ewen, *Captains of Consciousness* (New York: McGraw-Hill, 1976).

38. Chafe, *The American Woman,* p. 11.

39. Friedrick Engels, *Origins of the Family, Private Property and the State* (New York: International Publishing Company, 1972); Margaret Benston, "The Po-

litical Economy of Women's Liberation," *Monthly Review* 21 (1969): 13–27; Ann Oakley, *Sociology of Housework* (New York: Pantheon Books, 1974).

40. Sara Evans, *Personal Politics: The Roots of Women's Liberation in the Civil Rights Movement and the New Left* (New York: Random House, 1980).

41. Ibid., p. 99.

42. Ibid., p. 105.

43. Alice Walker, *Meridian* (New York: Harcourt Brace Jovanovich, 1976).

44. Evans, *Personal Politics*, p. 214.

45. Freeman, *The Politics of Women's Liberation* p. 116; see also Catherine MacKinnon, "Feminism, Marxism, Method and the State: An Agenda for Theory," *Signs* 7 (Spring 1982): 513–44.

46. Juliet Mitchell, *Woman's Estate* (New York: Random House, 1973), p. 61.

47. See, on this point, Jaggar, *Feminist Politics and Human Nature*, pp. 333–334.

48. Robin Morgan, *Going Too Far: The Personal Chronicle of a Feminist* (New York: Random House, 1968).

49. Chafe, *The American Woman*, pp. 112–32.

50. Zillah Eisenstein, "Anti-Feminism in the Politics and Elections of 1980," *Feminist Studies* 7 (Summer 1981): 202.

51. Rosalind Pollack Petchesky, "Antiabortion, Antifeminism, and the Rise of the New Right," *Feminist Studies* 7 (Summer 1981): 206–46.

52. Susan Harding, "Family Reform Movements: Recent Feminism and Its Opposition," *Feminist Studies* 7 (Spring 1981): 57–75.

53. Petchesky, "Antiabortion, Antifeminism, and the Rise of the New Right."

54. Barbara Brown et al., "The Equal Rights Amendment," *Yale Law Journal*, 80 (April 1971): 871–985. See also Gilbert Y. Steiner, *Constitutional Inequality: Political Fortunes of the Equal Rights Amendment* (Washington: Brookings Institution, 1985); and Joan Hoff-Wilson, ed., *Rights of Passage: The Past and Future of the ERA* (Bloomington: Indiana University Press, 1986).

55. Jeanne Holm, *Women in the Military: An Unfinished Revolution* (Novato: Presidio Press, 1982).

56. Lenore J. Weitzman, *The Marriage Contract: Spouses, Lovers, and the Law* (New York: Free Press, 1981); but see her *The Divorce Revolution: The Unexpected Social and Economic Consequences for Women and Children in America* (New York: Free Press, 1985).

57. Ethel Klein, "The Gender Gap: Different Issues, Different Answers," *The Brookings Review* 3 (Winter 1985): 33–37.

58. Petchesky, "Antiabortion, Antifeminism, and the Rise of the New Left."

59. Mary Daly, *Beyond God the Father: Toward a Philosophy of Women's Liberation* (Boston: Beacon Press, 1973); Rosemary Radford Ruether, *Mary — The Feminine Face of the Church* (New York: Westminster Press, 1977), *Sexism and God-Talk: Toward a Feminist Theology* (Boston: Beacon Press, 1983), and *Sexism and God-Talk: Toward a Feminist Philosophy* (Boston: Beacon Press, 1984), and *Womanguides: Readings toward a Feminine Theology* (Boston: Beacon Press, 1985); Elisabeth Schüssler Fiorenza, *Bread Not Stone: The Challenge of Feminist Biblical In-*

terpretation (Boston: Beacon Press, 1984).

60. Charlotte G. O'Kelly, "The Impact of Equal Employment Legislation on Women's Earnings: Limitations of Legislative Solutions to Discrimination in the Economy," *American Journal of Economics and Sociology* 38 (October 1979): 419; see also Hilda Scott, *Working Your Way to the Bottom: Feminization of Poverty* (Boston: Routledge & Kegan Paul, 1984); and Ruth Sidel, *Women and Children Last: The Plight of Poor Women in Affluent America* (New York: Viking, 1986).

61. Patricia Kain Knaub et al., "Is Parenthood a Desirable Adult Role: An Assessment of Attitudes Held by Contemporary Women," *Sex Roles* 9 (March 1983): 355–62; Sheila B. Kammerman et al., *Maternity Policies and Working Women* (New York: Columbia University Press, 1983); Maxine L. Margolis, *Mothers and Such: Views of American Women and Why They Changed* (Berkeley: University of California Press, 1984).

62. Brigitte Berger and Peter L. Berger, *War over the Family: Capturing the Middle Ground* (Garden City: Doubleday, 1984).

63. Brigitte Berger, "At Odds with American Reality," *Society* 22 (July-August 1985): 75–80.

64. To cite but a few examples: Max Horkheimer and Theodor W. Adorno, *The Dialectics of Enlightenment* (New York: Herder & Herder, 1972); Max Horkheimer, *Eclipse of Reason* (New York: Seabury Press, 1947); Marcuse, *One-Dimensional Man* and *Negations: Essays in Critical Theory* (Boston: Beacon Press, 1969); Habermas, *Toward a Rational Society,* and *Knowledge and Human Interests,* and *Theory of Communicative Action*; McCarthy, *The Critical Theory of Jurgen Habermas*; Held, *Introduction to Critical Theory*; Jay, *Dialectical Imagination*; Trent Schroyer, *The Critique of Domination: The Origins and Development of Critical Theory* (New York: George Braziller, 1973).

65. Alain Touraine, "The New Social Conflicts: Crisis or Transformation," in Charles Lemert, ed., *French Sociology: Rupture and Renewal Since 1968* (New York: Columbia University Press, 1981), pp. 313–31.

66. Jurgen Habermas, "New Social Movements," *Telos* 49 (Fall 1981): 33–37.

67. Jean Cohen, "Rethinking Social Movements," p. 98.

68. Seyla Benhabib, "Modernity and the Aporias of Critical Theory," *Telos* 49 (Fall 1981): 58–59; see also "Epistemologies of Postmodernism: A Rejoinder to Jean-Francois Lyotard," *New German Critique* 33 (Fall 1984): 103–26; and Nancy Fraser, "What's Critical about Critical Theory? The Case of Habermas and Gender," *New German Critique* 35 (Spring/Summer 1985): 97–131.

69. Jean Cohen, "Rethinking Social Movements," p. 101.

70. Ibid., p. 105.

71. Ibid., see also Habermas, "New Social Movements," Klaus Eder, "A New Social Movement?" *Telos* 52 (Summer 1982): 5–20.

Chapter 5

1. Jane Flax, "The Family in Contemporary Thought: A Critical Review," in Jean B. Elshtain, ed., *The Family in Political Thought* (Amherst: University of Massachusetts Press, 1982), pp. 223, 224.

2. Eleanor D. Macklin and Roger H. Rubin, eds., *Contemporary Families and Alternative Lifestyles: Handbook on Research and Theory* (Beverly Hills: Sage Publications, 1983); see also John Scanzoni, *Shaping Tomorrow's Family: Theory and Policy for the 21st Century* (Beverly Hills: Sage Publications, 1983).

3. Jurgen Habermas, *Legitimation Crisis,* trans. Thomas McCarthy (Boston: Beacon Press, 1975). Compare with Berger and Luckmann's use of the term, *Social Construction of Reality,* pp. 61, 65 and esp. pp. 92–128.

4. de Tocqueville, *Democracy in America,* pp. 585–86.

5. David Riesman et al., *The Lonely Crowd: A Study on the Changing American Character* (New Haven: Yale University Press, 1950), p. 26.

6. Hannah Arendt, *Between Past and Future: Eight Exercises in Political Thought* (New York: Penguin Books, 1977); compare with Brigitte Berger and Peter Berger, *War over the Family.*

7. Wini Breines and Linda Gordon, "The New Scholarship on Family Violence," *Signs* 8 (1983): 491.

8. Cf. in this connection Paul A. Robinson, *Modernization of Sex: Havelock Ellis, Alfred Kinsey, William Masters and Virginia Johnson* (New York: Harper & Row, 1976), p. 118. For a superb overview, see Jeffrey Weeks, *Sexuality and Its Discontents: Meanings, Myths and Modern Sexualities* (London: Routledge & Kegan Paul, 1985).

9. Christopher Lasch, *Haven in a Heartless World: The Family Beseiged* (New York: Basic Books, 1977); Jacques Donzelot, *The Policing of Families,* trans. Robert Hurley (New York: Pantheon Books, 1979).

10. Hartsock, *Money, Sex and Power,* p. 87.

11. See, in this connection, Lenore J. Weitzman, *Sex Role Socialization* (Palo Alto: Mayfield Publishing, 1979); Nancy Romer, *Sex-Role Cycle: Socialization from Infancy to Old Age* (Westbury: Feminist Press, 1981); Jean Stockard and Miriam M. Johnson, *Sex Roles, Sex Inequality, and Sex Role Development* (Englewood Cliffs: Prentice-Hall, 1980); Bernice Lott, *Becoming a Woman: The Socialization of Gender* (Springfield: Charles C. Thomas, 1981).

12. Adrienne Rich, *Of Woman Born: Motherhood as Experience and Institution* (New York: W.W. Norton, 1976).

13. Dorothy Dinnerstein, *The Mermaid and the Minotaur: Sexual Arrangements and Human Malaise* (New York: Harper Row, 1977); Nancy Chodorow, *The Reproduction of Mothering: Psychoanalysis and the Sociology of Gender* (Berkeley: University of California Press, 1978).

14. Mark Poster, *Critical Theory of the Family* (New York: Continuum Books, 1978), p. 8.

15. Ibid, p. 143.

16. Joan Kelly, *Women, History and Theory: The Essays of Joan Kelly* (Chicago: University of Chicago Press, 1984).

17. Frankfurt Institute for Social Research, *Aspects of Sociology,* trans. John Viertel (Boston: Beacon Press, 1972), esp. pp. 129–47.

18. Jean Elshtain, "Reflections on Abortion, Values, and the Family," in Sidney Callahan and Daniel Callahan, eds., *Abortion: Understanding Differences* (New York: Plenum Press, 1984), p. 60.

19. Bernstein, *Beyond Objectivism and Relativism.*

20. John Guare, *Marco Polo Sings a Solo* (New York: Dramatists' Play Service, 1977).

21. Peter Singer and Deane Wells, *The Reproduction Revolution: New Ways of Making Babies* (New York: Oxford University Press, 1984).

22. Letha D. and John Scanzoni, *Men, Women and Change* (New York: McGraw-Hill, 1981); see also J. Ross Eshleman, *The Family: An Introduction* (Newton: Allyn & Bacon, 1984); John H. Gagnon, *Human Sexualities* (Glenview: Scott Foresman & Company, 1977); Michael Gordon, *The American Family in Social-Historical Perspective* (New York: St. Martin's Press, 1983); Dennis K. Orthner, *Intimate Relationships: An Introduction to Marriage and the Family* (Reading: Addison-Wesley, 1981); David A. Schulz, *The Changing Family: Its Function and Future* (Englewood Cliffs: Prentice-Hall, 1982).

23. Letha and John Scanzoni, *Men, Women and Change*, p. 38.

24. Ibid., p. 435.

25. Max Horkheimer, *Critical Theory*, trans. Matthew J. O'Connell et al. (New York: Continuum Books, 1972), pp. 47–128.

26. Frankfurt Institute of Social Research, *Aspects of Sociology*, pp. 129–47.

27. Max Horkheimer, *Critique of Instrumental Reason: Lectures and Essays Since the End of World War II*, trans. Matthew J. O'Connell et al. (New York: Seabury Press, 1974), p. 94.

28. Horkheimer, *Eclipse of Reason*, p. 110.

29. Horkheimer, *Critical Theory*, p. 131.

30. Ibid., p. 134.

31. Ibid., p. 118.

32. Jaggar, *Feminist Politics and Human Nature*, p. 69.

33. For a review of the criticism, see Johanna Brenner and Nancy Holmstrom, "Autonomy vs. Community in Feminist Politics" (forthcoming).

34. Marcuse, *One-Dimensional Man*, p. 10.

35. Horkheimer, *Critique of Instrumental Reason*, p. 12.

36. Frankfurt Institute for Social Research, *Aspects of Sociology*, p. 133.

37. Jay, *Dialectical Imagination*; Held, *Introduction to Critical Theory*; Schroyer, *The Critique of Domination.* .

38. Lasch, *Haven in a Heartless World*, p. xv.

39. Cf. Ewen, *Captains of Consciousness*.

40. Christopher Lasch, "The Flight from Feeling: Sociopsychology of Sexual Conflict," *Marxist Perspectives* 1 (1978): 76.

41. Ibid., p. 86; see also *Culture of Narcissism: American Life in an Age of Diminishing Expectations* (New York: W.W. Norton, 1979), pp. 189–206; see also Joel Kovel, "Rationalization and the Family," *Telos* 37 (Fall 1978): 5–21, and "Narcissism and the Family," *Telos* 44 (Summer 1980): 88–100.

42. Lasch, *Haven in a Heartless World*, p. 12.

43. Marcuse, *Eros and Civilization*, p. viii.

44. For a critique of this position, see Eli Zaretsky, *Capitalism, the Family and Personal Life* (New York: Harper & Row, 1976), and "The Place of the Family in the Origins of the Welfare State," in Barrie Thorne and Marilyn Yalom, eds., *Rethinking the Family: Some Feminist Questions* (New York: Longman, 1980), pp. 188–224. An excellent summary piece is Theodore Mills Norton, "Contemporary Critical Theory and the Family: Private World and Public Crisis," in

Elshtain, *The Family in Political Thought,* pp. 254–68.

45. Juliet Mitchell, *Psychoanalysis and Feminism: Freud, Reich, Laing and Women* (New York: Pantheon Books, 1974); Dinnerstein, *The Mermaid and the Minotaur*; Chodorow, *The Reproduction of Mothering*; Carol Gilligan, *In a Different Voice: Psychological Theory and Women's Development* (Cambridge: Harvard University Press, 1982).

46. Kate Millett, *Sexual Politics* (New York: Avon Books, 1979); and Betty Friedan, *Feminine Mystique* (New York: Dell Publishers, 1977).

47. See in this connection Lasch, *Haven in a Heartless World*; Paul A. Robinson, *The Freudian Left: Wilhelm Reich, Geza Roheim, Herbert Marcuse* (New York: Harper & Row, 1969); Bruna Bettelheim, *Freud and Man's Soul* (New York: Alfred A. Knopf, 1983); Marcuse, *Eros and Civilization*; Russell Jacoby, *Social Amnesia: A Critique of Conformist Psychology from Adler to Laing* (Boston: Beacon Press, 1975).

48. Wini Breinis et al., "Social Biology, Family Studies, and Antifeminist Backlash," *Feminist Studies* 4 (1978): 59.

49. Ibid., p. 61; see also Jessica Benjamin, "The Bonds of Love: Rational Violence and Erotic Domination," *Feminist Studies* 6 (Spring 1980): 144–74, and "The End of Internalization: Adorno's Social Psychology," *Telos* 32 (Summer 1977): 42–64.

Chapter 6

1. Berger and Luckmann, *Social Construction of Reality,* p. 128.

2. Compare with the prescriptive dimension argued by Millett, *Sexual Politics,* p. 23.

3. See, for example, Phyllis Chesler, *Women and Madness* (Garden City: Doubleday, 1972); Eva Figes, *Patriarchal Attitudes* (New York: Stein & Day, 1970); Elizabeth Janeway, *Man's World, Woman's Place: A Study in Social Mythology* (New York: Dell Publishing, 1971); Robin Lakoff, *Language and Woman's Place* (New York: Harper & Row, 1975); Robin Lakoff and Raquel Scherr, *Face Value: The Politics of Beauty* (Boston: Routledge & Kegan Paul, 1984).

4. Jaggar, "Towards a More Integrated World," p. 4.

5. Horkheimer, *Eclipse of Reason,* p. 128.

6. Mead, *Mind, Self and Society.*

7. Berger and Luckmann, *Social Construction of Reality.*

8. Ibid., p. 33.

9. Ibid., p. 54.

10. Sigmund Freud, *Totem and Taboo: Resemblances between the Psychic Lives of Savages and Neurotics,* trans. A.A. Brill (New York: Random House, 1918).

11. Sigmund Freud, *Civilization and Its Discontents,* trans. James Strachey (New York: W.W. Norton, 1962).

12. Dinnerstein, *Mermaid and the Minotaur,* p. 12.

13. Ibid., p. 5.

14. Ibid., p. 11.

15. Bettelheim, *Freud and Man's Soul.*

16. Dinnerstein, *Mermaid and the Minotaur,* p. 20.

17. Ibid., p. 34.

18. Ibid., p. 53.

19. Note the similarity with the excellent exposition of these and other points in Isaac D. Balbus, *Marxism and Domination: A Neo-Hegelian, Feminist, Psychoanalytic Theory of Sexual, Political and Technological Liberation* (Princeton: Princeton University Press, 1982).

20. Dinnerstein, *Mermaid and the Minotaur*, pp. 104–5.

21. Ibid., p. 103.

22. Ibid., pp. 148–49.

23. Ibid., p. 150.

24. Dorothy Dinnerstein, "Afterword: Toward the Mobilization of Eros," in Meg. M. Murray, ed., *Face to Face: Fathers, Mothers, Masters, Monsters — Essays for a Nonsexist Future* (Westport: Greenwood Press, 1983), p. 295.

25. Dinnerstein, *Mermaid and the Minotaur*, p. 176.

26. Ibid., p. 210.

27. Ibid., p. 60.

28. Ibid., p. 234.

29. Dinnerstein, *"Afterword,"* p. 301.

30. Ibid., p. 302.

31. Jaggar, *Feminist Politics and Human Nature*, p. 126.

32. Marcuse, *Eros and Civilization*, pp. 217–51.

33. Cf. Elaine Marks and Isabelle de Courtivron, eds., *New French Feminism: An Anthology* (New York: Schocken Books, 1981).

34. Kathy E. Ferguson, *Feminist Case against Bureaucracy* (Philadelphia: Temple University Press, 1984), p. 158.

35. In this connection, see Rosemarie Tong, *Women, Sex and the Law* (Totowa: Rowman & Allanheld, 1983); Laura Lederer, ed., *Take Back the Night: Women and Pornography* (New York: William Morrow, 1980); Kathleen Barry, *Female Sexual Slavery* (Englewood Cliffs: Prentice-Hall, 1979); David Copp and Susan Wendell, eds., *Pornography and Censorship* (Buffalo: Prometheus Books, 1983); MacKinnon, "Feminism, Marxism, Method"; Millett, *Sexual Politics*; Susan Griffin, *Rape: The Power of Consciousness* (New York: Harper & Row, 1979) and *Pornography and Silence: Culture's Revenge against Nature* (New York: Harper & Row, 1981); Andrea Dworkin, *Pornography: Men Possessing Women* (New York: G.P. Putnam, 1981); Susan Brownmiller, *Against Our Will: Men, Women and Rape* (New York: Simon & Schuster, 1975); Angela Carter, *The Sadeian Woman and the Ideology of Pornography* (New York: Pantheon Books, 1978).

36. Gilligan, *In a Different Voice*.

37. Dinnerstein, "Afterword," p. 305; see, in this connection, Sara Ruddick, "Maternal Thinking," *Feminist Studies* 6 (Summer 1980): 342–67.

38. Herbert Marcuse, *Counterrevolution and Revolt* (Boston: Beacon Press, 1972), pp. 74, 75.

39. Marcuse, *Eros and Civilization*, pp. 21–22.

40. Herbert Marcuse, "Socialist Feminism: The Hard Core of the Dream," *Edcentric* 31–32 (November 1974); reprinted in *Women's Studies* 2 (1974): 279–88.

41. Marcuse, *Eros and Civilization*, p. 18; see also ibid., p. 106.

42. Marcuse, "Socialist Feminism," p. 286; see also Marcuse, *Counterrevolution and Revolt*, pp. 75–78.

43. Marcuse, "Socialist Feminism." For a similar reading of Marcuse, see Joan B. Landes, "Marcuse's Feminist Dimension," *Telos* 41 (Fall 1979): 158–65.

44. Breinis et al., "Social Biology."

45. Hartsock, *Money, Sex and Power.*

46. Erich Fromm, *Crisis of Psychoanalysis: An Enquiry into the Nature of Love* (New York: Holt, Rinehart & Winston, 1970), and *The Art of Loving* (New York: Harper & Row, 1974).

47. Chodorow, *Reproduction of Mothering,* p. 33; see also ibid., p. 39.

48. Mitchell, *Psychoanalysis and Feminism.*

49. Rich, *Of Woman Born,* p. 13.

50. Chodorow, *Reproduction of Mothering,* p. 7.

51. Ibid., p. 214.

52. Rich, *Of Woman Born,* p. 11.

53. Nancy Chodorow, "Oedipal Asymmetries and Heterosexual Knots," *Social Problems* 23 (April 1976): 459.

54. Chodorow, *Reproduction of Mothering,* p. 176.

55. Ibid., p. 69.

56. Ibid., pp. 60–61.

57. Dinnerstein, *Mermaid and the Minotaur,* p. 161.

58. Nancy Chodorow and Susan Contratto, "The Fantasy of the Perfect Mother," in Thorne and Yalom, *Rethinking the Family,* pp. 54–75.

59. Ibid., p. 72, fn.13.

60. Naomi Scheman, "Individualism and Objects of Psychology," in Sandra Harding and Merrill B. Hintikka, eds. *Discovering Reality: Feminist Perspectives on Epistemology, Metaphysics, Methodology and Philosophy of Science* (Boston: Reidel, 1983), p. 234; see also Jane Flax, "Political Philosophy and Patriarchal Unconscious: A Psychoanalytic Perspective on Epistemology and Metaphysics," in ibid., p. 246.

61. Zillah Eisenstein, *Radical Future of Liberal Feminism* (New York: Longman, 1981), p. 15.

62. Rich, *Of Woman Born,* pp. 211–12; compare with Dinnerstein, *Mermaid and the Minotaur,* pp. 28–29.

63. Adriene Rich, "Compulsory Heterosexuality and Lesbian Experiences," *Signs* 5 (Summer 1980): 631–66.

64. Scheman, "Individualism and Objects of Psychology," p. 237.

65. See Chodorow, *Reproduction of Mothering,* esp. pp. 188–89; see also Balbus, *Marxism and Domination,* pp. 312–15.

66. Chodorow, *Reproduction of Mothering,* ibid., p. 19.

67. See, for example, Philip Green, *Pursuit of Inequality* (New York: Pantheon Books, 1981).

68. William Ray Arney, "Maternal-Infant Bonding: The Politics of Falling in Love with Your Child," *Feminist Studies* 6 (Fall 1980): 547–70.

69. Ibid., p. 559.

70. Compare with Rich, "Compulsory Heterosexuality and Lesbian Experiences."

71. Marcuse, *Essay on Liberation,* pp. 23–48; cf. also Balbus, *Marxism and Domination.*

72. Margolis, *Mothers and Such*; Luker, *Abortion.*

73. Helen B. Holmes et al., eds., *Custom-Made Child?— Women-Centered Perspectives* (Clifton: Humana Press, 1981) and *Birth Control and Controlling Birth: Women-Centered Perspectives* (Clifton: Humana Press, 1981); R. Snowden et al., *Artificial Reproduction: A Social Investigation* (London: George Allen & Unwin, 1983); Jan Zimmerman, ed., *Technological Woman: Interfacing with Tomorrow* (New York: Praeger, 1983); Barbara Katz Rothman, *In Labor: Women and Power in the Birthplace* (New York: W.W. Norton, 1982); Rita Arditti et al., eds., *Test-Tube Women: What Future for Motherhood?* (Boston: Pandora Press, 1984).

74. Viola Klein, *The Feminine Character,* pp.16–17, 168–71.

75. Eric Weil, "Science in Modern Culture", in Holton, *op. cit.,* pp. 199–217.

76. Colin M. Turnbull, *Mountain People* (New York: Simon & Schuster, 1972), p. 294.

77. See for example, Konrad Lorenz, *Behind the Mirror: A Search for a Natural History of Human Knowledge,* trans. Ronald Taylor (New York: Harcourt Brace Jovanovich, 1978), and *Evolution and the Modification of Behavior* (Chicago: University of Chicago Press, 1967), and *The Foundations of Ethology* (New York: Simon & Schuster, 1983).

78. See for example, Robert Ardrey, *African Genesis* (New York: Atheneum, 1961), and *The Territorial Imperative: A Personal Inquiry into the Animal Origins of Property and Nations* (New York: Atheneum, 1966); Desmond Morris, *The Human Zoo* (New York: Dell Publishers, 1970), and *The Naked Ape* (New York: Dell Publishers, 1984); and Lionel Tiger, *Men in Groups* (New York: M. Boyars, 1984).

79. Ardrey, *African Genesis,* p. 120.

80. Ibid., p. 167.

81. Bleier, *Science and Gender*; see also Ruth Hubbard et al., eds., *Biological Woman— The Convenient Myth* (Cambridge: Schenkman Publishing Company, 1982).

82. E.O. Wilson, *On Human Nature* (New York: Bantam Books, 1979), p. xii.

83. E.O. Wilson, *Insect Societies* (Cambridge: Harvard University Press, 1971).

84. E.O. Wilson, *Sociobiology: The New Synthesis* (Cambridge: Harvard University Press, 1975).

85. William D. Hamilton, "Innate Social Aptitudes of Man: An Approach from Evolutionary Genetics," in Robin Fox, ed., *Biosocial Anthropology* (New York: John Wiley, 1975), pp. 133–55.

86. Robert Trivers, "Parent-Offspring Conflict," *American Biologist* 14 (1974): 249–64.

87. Richard Dawkins, *The Selfish Gene* (New York: Oxford University Press, 1976).

88. Wilson, *On Human Nature,* pp. 2, 5.

89. Ibid., p. 34.

90. Ibid., pp. 82, 108–9, 203.

91. Ibid., p. 3.

92. Ibid., p. 10.

93. Ibid., p. 2.

94. Ibid., p. 4.

95. Ibid., pp. 2, 3.

96. David Barash, *The Whisperings Within: Evolution and the Origin of Human Nature* (New York: Harper & Row, 1979), p. 200.

97. Wilson, *On Human Nature,* p. 165.

98. Ibid., p. 175.

99. Ibid., p. 182.

100. Ibid., p. 306.

101. Claude Lévi-Strauss, *Elementary Structures of Kinship,* trans. James Harle Bell, John Richard von Sturmer, and Rodney Needham (Boston: Beacon Press, 1969).

102. Wilson, *On Human Nature,* p. 203.

103. Ibid., p. 58.

104. Ibid., p. 132.

105. Ibid., p. 143.

106. See, in this connection, Pierre L. Van Den Berghe, *Human Family Systems: an Evolutionary View* (New York: Elsevier, 1979).

107. Quoted in Wilson, *On Human Nature,* p. 80.

108. Erik Erikson, "Inner and Outer Space: Reflections on Womanhood," in Robert J. Lifton, ed., *The Woman in America* (Westport: Greenwood Press, 1977), pp. 1–26.

109. Ibid., p. 2.

110. Ibid., p. 21.

111. Ibid., pp. 5, 6.

112. Joan Smith, "Sociobiology and Feminism: The Very Strange Courtship of Competing Paradigms," *Philosophical Forum* 13 (Winter-Spring 1981-82): 226–43.

113. Lila Leibowitz, *Females, Males, Families: A Biosocial Approach* (North Scituate: Duxbury Press, 1978), and Sarah Blaffer Hrdy, *The Woman That Never Evolved* (Cambridge: Harvard University Press, 1981).

114. Ruth Bleier, "Social and Political Bias in Science: An Examination of Animal Studies and Their Generalizations to Human Behavior and Evolution," *Genes and Gender* 2 (1979): 59.

115. See Bleier, *Science and Gender,* esp. pp. 15–48.

116. Alice S. Rossi, "A Biosocial Perspective on Parenting," *Daedalus* 106 (Spring 1977): 4.

117. Stephan Chorover, *From Genesis to Genocide: The Meaning of Human Nature and the Power of Behavior Control* (Cambridge: MIT Press, 1979).

118. See R.C. Lewontin, "The Corpse in the Elevator," *New York Review of Books* 29 (January 20, 1983): 34–37, and with Steven Rose and Leon Kamin, *Not in Our Genes: Biology, Ideology and Human Nature* (New York: Pantheon, 1984).

119. See, in this connection, Bleier, *Science and Gender,* esp. pp. 80–114, and Marian Lowe, "Sociobiology and Sex Differences," *Signs* 4 (Autumn 1978): 118–25.

120. Green, *Pursuit of Inequality,* p. 31.

121. Mary-Joan Gerson, et al., "Mothering: The View from Psychological

216   *Notes*

Research," *Signs* 9 (Summer 1984): pp. 434–35, 450–51.

122. Balbus, *Marxism and Domination,* p. 305.

123. Shulamith Firestone, *The Dialectic of Sex: The Case for a Feminist Revolution* (New York: William Morrow, 1970).

124. Rossi, "A Biosocial Perspective on Parenting."

125. Gerson, "Mothering," pp. 435–38; Scanzoni, *Men, Women and Change;* Mary Jo Bane, *Here to Stay: American Families in the Twentieth Century* (New York: Basic Books, 1976).

126. Cf. Habermas, *Legitimation Crisis.*

127. Cf. Lasch, *Haven in a Heartless World*; see also Donzelot, *The Policing of Families.*

128. Habermas, *Legitimation Crisis,* pp. 73–74.

129. Cf. Alice S. Rossi, "Equality Between the Sexes: An Immodest Proposal," *Daedalus* 93 (Spring 1964): 607–52, and *The Feminist Papers: From Adams to de Beauvoir* (New York: Columbia University Press, 1973).

130. Rossi, "A Biosocial Perspective on Parenting," pp. 1–3.

131. Alice S. Rossi, "Gender and Parenthood," *American Sociological Review* 49 (February 1984): 2.

132. Rossi, A Biosocial Perspective on Parenting," pp. 2–12.

133. Alice S. Rossi, "Biosocial Side of Parenthood," *Human Nature* 1 (1978): 72.

134. E.O. Wilson, *On Human Nature,* p. 148.

135. Cf. Wendy Chavkin, "Occupational Hazards to Reproduction: A Review Essay and Annotated Bibliography," *Feminist Studies* 5 (Summer 1979): 310–25, and Ronald Bayer, "Women, Work and Reproductive Hazards," *Hastings Center Report* 12 (October 1982): 14–19.

136. Rossi, "A Biosocial Perspective on Parenting," p. 9.

137. Ibid., p. 25.

138. Germaine Greer, *Sex and Destiny: The Politics of Human Fertility* (New York: Harper & Row, 1984), p. 35.

139. See for example, Green, *Pursuit of Inequality*; Viola Klein, *The Feminine Character*; Bleier, *Science and Gender*; Lowe and Hubbard, *Women's Nature*; Hubbard et al., *Biological Woman*; Janet Sayers, *Biological Politics: Feminist and Anti-feminist Perspectives* (New York: Methuen, 1982); Vern L. Bullough and Bonnie Bullough, *Sin, Sickness and Sanity: A History of Sexual Attitudes* (New York: Garland Press, 1977); Marshall D. Sahlins, *The Use and Abuse of Biology: An Anthropological Critique of Sociobiology* (Ann Arbor: University of Michigan Press, 1976).

140. Rossi, "A Biosocial Perspective on Parenting," p. 10.

141. Rossi, "Gender and Parenthood," pp. 10, 11.

142. Rossi, "A Biosocial Perspective on Parenting," pp. 15–24.

143. Rossi, "Gender and Parenthood," pp. 7–15.

144. Judith Stacey, "The New Conservative Feminism," *Feminist Studies* 9 (Fall 1983): 559.

145. Breinis et al., "Social Biology," p. 43.

146. Compare Friedan's *The Feminine Mystique* with the controversial follow-up, *The Second Stage* (New York: Summit Books, 1982), which asks for a consideration of family issues by the Women's Movement.

Chapter 7

1. Horkheimer, *Critical Theory,* pp. 195–200.

2. Horkheimer, *Eclipse of Reason,* p. 128.

3. Hannah Arendt, *Origins of Totalitarianism* (New York: Peter Smith, 1983).

4. Horkheimer, *Eclipse of Reason,* p. 128.

5. Lasch, *Culture of Narcissism.*

6. Elshtain, "Reflections on Abortion, Values and the Family," in Callahan and Callahan, p. 59.

7. Ibid., p. 63.

8. Horkheimer, *Eclipse of Reason,* p. 128. See a contemporary version of this argument in Langdon Winner, *The Whale and the Reactor: A Search for Limits in an Age of High Technology* (Chicago: University of Chicago Press, 1986).

9. Linda Gordon, *Woman's Body, Woman's Right: A Social History of Birth Control* (New York: Grossman Publishers, 1976); see also James Reed, *From Private Vice to Public Virtue: The Birth Control Movement in American Society since 1830* (New York: Basic Books, 1978).

10. See Joyce Berkman, "Historical Styles of Contraceptive Advocacy," in Holmes et al., *Birth Control and Controlling Birth,* pp. 27–36.

11. See Holmes et al., ibid.

12. See, in this connection, Clifford Grobstein, *From Chance to Purpose: An Appraisal of External Human Fertilization* (Reading: Addison-Wesley Publishing Company, 1981).

13. Leon Kass, "Making Babies — The New Biology and 'Old' Morality," *Public Interest* 29 (Winter 1972): 23.

14. Ibid., p. 45.

15. See Holmes et al., *Custom-Made Child*; Mary Anne Warren, *Gendercide: The Implications of Sex Selection* (Totowa: Rowman & Allanheld, 1985); Arditti, *Test-Tube Women*; Zimmerman, *Technological Woman.*

16. Marcuse, *One-Dimensional Man.*

17. Firestone, *The Dialectic of Sex,* p. 202.

18. Ibid., p. 227.

19. Ibid., p. 5.

20. Ibid., p. 12.

21. Ibid.

22. See Holmes et al., *Birth Control and Controlling Birth,* pp. 5–15.

23. Gena Corea, *The Mother Machine: Reproductive Technologies from Artificial Insemination to Artificial Women* (New York: Harper & Row, 1985), pp. 150–51.

24. Ibid., pp. 100–125; Warren, pp. 154–55.

25. Adrienne Asch and Michelle Fine, "Shared Dreams: A Left Perspective on Disability Rights and Reproductive Rights," *Radical America* 18 (1984): 51–58; see also Warren, *Gendercide,* pp. 108–31.

26. Barbara Katz Rothman, "The Meaning of Choice in Reproductive Technology," in Arditti, *Test-Tube Women,* p. 32.

27. Cf. Beverly Wildung Harrison, *Our Right to Choose: Toward a New Ethic of Abortion* (Boston: Beacon Press, 1983); Petchesky, *Abortion and Woman's Choice*; Luker, *Abortion.* In addition, see Marilyn Falik, *Ideology and Abortion Policy Politics*

(New York: Praeger, 1983); Colin Francome, *Abortion Freedom: A Worldwide Movement* (London: George Allen & Unwin, 1984); Jane E. Hodgson, ed., *Abortion and Sterilization: Medical and Social Aspects* (New York: Grune & Stratton, 1981); L.W. Sumner, *Abortion and Moral Theory* (Princeton: Princeton University Press, 1981); Frederick S. Jaffe et al., *Abortion Politics: Private Morality and Public Policy* (New York: McGraw Hill, 1981); Barbara Milbauer and Bert N. Obrentz, *The Law Giveth: Legal Aspects of the Abortion Controversy* (New York: Atheneum, 1983).

28 Petchesky, *Abortion and Woman's Choice,* p. 366.

29. Elshtain, "Reflections on Abortion, Values, and the Family," p. 59.

30. Luker, *Abortion,* pp. 193–94.

31. Ibid., p. 193.

32. Ibid., p. 157.

33. Petchesky, *Abortion and Woman's Choice,* p. 36.

34. Mary Ann Lamanna, "Social Science and Ethical Issues: The Policy Implication of Poll Data on Abortion," in Callahan and Callahan, p. 11.

35. Cf. Jonathan Imber, "Sociology and Abortion: Legacies and Strategies," *Contemporary Sociology* 8 (November 1979): 825–36.

36. See Barbara Katz Rothman, *The Tentative Pregnancy: Prenatal Diagnosis and the Future of Motherhood* (New York: Viking, 1986).

Chapter 8

1. Schroyer, *The Critique of Domination,* p. 218; see also Albrecht Wellmer, *Critical Theory of Society* (New York: Seabury Press, 1974); and James Farganis, "Critical Theory: Social Praxis and the Reconstruction of Reality," in Richard C. Monk, ed., *Structures of Knowing: Current Studies in the Sociology of Schools* (Lanham: University Press of America, 1986) (forthcoming).

2. Compare with Balbus, *Marxism and Domination,* and Annette Kolodny, *The Lay of the Land: Metaphors as Experience and History in American Life and Letters* (Chapel Hill: University of North Carolina Press, 1975).

3. Carolyn Merchant, *Death in Nature: Women, Ecology and the Scientific Revolution* (New York: Harper & Row, 1983); see also Ynestra King, "Feminism, Ecology and Nature/Culture Dualism," paper presented to the Douglass College Women's Studies Seminar, Feminist Reconstruction of Self and Society, April 1985.

4. Dinnerstein, *Mermaid and the Minotaur,* p. 211.

5. See for example, Michael F. Winter and Ellen F. Robert, "Male Dominance, Late Capitalism, and the Growth of Instrumental Reason," *Berkeley Journal of Sociology,* 25 (1980): 249–80.

6. Ibid., p. 252.

7. Lewis Mumford, *The Pentagon of Power: The Myth of the Machine* (New York: Harcourt Brace Jovanovich, 1970).

8. Dinnerstein, *Mermaid and the Minotaur,* pp. 217–18.

9. The best survey of this is to be found in Jaggar's *Feminist Politics and Human Nature,* in which she shows how an epistemology and a praxis unite feminist theory, and that out of certain epistemologies (liberalism, Marxism, radicalism, socialism) evolve certain theories of human nature.

10. Gilligan, *In a Different Voice,* p. 5.

11. Ibid., p. 19.

12. Ibid., p. 35.

13. Quoted in Linda Nicholson, "Women, Morality and History," *Social Research* 50 (Autumn 1983): 516.

14. Gilligan, *In a Different Voice,* p. 18.

15. Ibid., p. 67.

16. Ibid., p. 95.

17. Ibid., pp. 173, 174.

18. See essay, "Do the Social Sciences Have an Adequate Theory of Moral Development?" in Norma Haan et al., eds. *Social Science as Moral Inquiry* (New York: Columbia University Press, 1983), pp. 33–51.

19. For this kind of interpretation, see Zillah Eisenstein, *Feminism and Sexual Equality: Crisis in Liberal America* (New York: Monthly Review Press, 1984), p. 218.

20. Gilligan, *In a Different Voice,* p. 17.

21. Jaggar, "Towards a More Integrated World."

22. Gilligan, *In a Different Voice,* pp. 16–17.

23. See, for example, Merchant; Brian Easlea, *Science and Sexual Oppression: Patriarch's Confrontation with Women and Nature* (London: Weidenfeld & Nicolson, 1981); and Susan Griffin, *Women and Nature: The Roaring Inside Her* (New York: Harper & Row, 1980).

24. Hartsock, *Money, Sex and Power,* p. 118; compare with Sandra Lee Bartkey's "Feminist consciousness is consciousness of victimization" in "Toward a Phenomenology of Feminist Consciousness," *Social Theory and Practice* 3 (1975): 430.

25. Jaggar, *Feminist Politics and Human Nature,* p. 371.

26. I read this out of Hartsock's discussion of eros in her *Money, Sex and Power,* pp. 166–69, and of the feminist standpoint, ibid., p. 231–51.

27. Ibid., pp. 224, 225.

28. Ibid., p. 226. See also Jaggar, *Feminist Politics and Human Nature,* pp. 353–94, as well as her paper, "Feeling and Knowing: Emotion in Feminist Theory," paper presented to the Douglass College Women's Studies Seminar, Feminist Ways of Knowing, September 1985.

Chapter 9

1. Carol McMillan, *Reason, Women and Nature: Some Philosophical Problems with Feminism* (Princeton: Princeton University Press, 1982).

2. Ferguson, *Feminist Case against Bureaucracy.*

3. McMillan, *Reason, Women and Nature,* p. 17.

4. Ibid., p. 24.

5. Ibid., pp. 48–56.

6. Ibid., p. 74.

7. Ibid., pp. 107–8.

8. Ibid., pp. 123–24.

9. Jaggar, "Feeling and Knowing"; see also Arlie Hochschild, *The Managed Heart: Commercialization of Human Feeling* (Berkeley: University of California

Press, 1983).

    10. Hochschild, *The Managed Heart,* p. 31.

    11. Jaggar, "Feeling and Knowing"; see also Joan C. Tronto, "Morality: Beyond Gender Difference to a Theory of Care," paper presented to the Douglass College Women's Studies Seminar, Feminist Ways of Knowing, October 1985; Melvin Kohn, *Class and Conformity: A Study in Values* (Chicago: University of Chicago Press, 1977); Jack Sattel, "The Inexpressive Male: Tragedy or Sexual Politics," *Social Problems* 23 (April 1976): 469–77; Robert N. Bellah et al., *Habits of the Heart: Individualism and Commitment in American Life* (Berkeley: University of California Press, 1985); Dinnerstein, *Mermaid and the Minotaur;* Marcuse, *One-Dimensional Man.*

    12 Jaggar, "Feeling and Knowing," p. 1.

    13. See, for example, Genevieve Lloyd, *The Man of Reason: "Male" and "Female" in Western Philosophy* (Minneapolis: University of Minnesota Press, 1984); Martha Lee Osborne, ed., *Women in Western Thought* (New York: Random House, 1978); Jean Bethke Elshtain, *Public Man, Private Woman: Women in Social and Political Thought* (Princeton: Princeton University Press, 1981); Susan Moller Okin, *Women in Western Political Thought* (Princeton: Princeton University Press, 1979).

    14. See also Marcuse, *One-Dimensional Man;* Alfred Sohn-Rethel, *Intellectual and Manual Labor: A Critique of Epistemology* (Atlantic Highlands: Humanities Press, 1978); Roberto Mangaberra Unger, *Knowledge and Politics* (New York: Free Press, 1976).

    15. Horkheimer and Adorno, *The Dialectics of Enlightenment.*

    16. Jurgen Habermas, "Rationality and Modernization" in Thomas Gervits, *Rationality Today* (South Bend: University of Notre Dame Press, 1983), p. 192.

    17. Peter L. Berger et al., *The Homeless Mind: Modernization and Consciousness* (New York: Random House, 1974), p. 205.

    18. See *Negations;* see also Jessica Benjamin, "The Bonds of Love: Rational Violence and Erotic Domination," *Feminist Studies* 6 (1980): 144–74 where she equates maleness, autonomy and instrumental rationality.

    19. Kathy E. Ferguson, *Self, Society and Womankind: The Dialectic of Liberation* (Westport: Greenwood Press, 1980).

    20. Ferguson, *Feminist Case against Bureaucracy.*

    21. Ferguson, *Self, Society and Womankind,* p. 17.

    22. Smith, "A Sociology for Women," and her "Women's Perspective as a Radical Critique of Sociology."

    23. See also Nannerl O. Keohane et al., eds., *Feminist Theory: A Critique of Ideology* (Chicago: University of Chicago Press, 1982); Harding and Hintikka, *Discovering Reality;* Jaggar, *Feminist Politics and Human Nature.*

    24. Ferguson, *Self, Society and Womankind,* p. 65.

    25. Ferguson, *Feminist Case against Bureaucracy.*

    26. Ibid., p. 155.

    27. Linda Glennon, *Women and Dualism: A Sociology of Knowledge Analysis* (New York: Longman, 1979); Roslyn Wallach Bologh, *Dialectical Phenomenology: Marx's Method* (Boston: Routledge & Kegan Paul, 1979); Elshtain, *Public Man, Private Woman;* Ruddick, "Maternal Thinking."

28. Ferguson, *Feminist Case against Bureaucracy,* p. 13.

29. Ibid., p. 23.

30. Ibid., p. 94.

31. Ibid., p. 154.

32. Ibid., p. 159.

33. Michael M. Harmon, *Action Theory for Public Administration* (New York: Longman, 1981); and Ralph P. Hummel, *Bureaucratic Experience* (New York: St. Martin's Press, 1982).

34. Jaggar, *Feminist Politics and Human Nature,* p. 5.

35. Smith, "A Sociology for Women," p. 156.

36. Ibid., p. 143.

37. Ibid., p. 156.

38. MacKinnon, "Feminism, Marxism."

39. See Sheldon Wolin, "Paradigms and Political Theory," in Gary Gutting, ed., *Paradigms and Revolutions: Appraisals and Applications of Thomas Kuhn's Philosophy of Science* (South Bend: University of Notre Dame Press, 1980), p. 181.

40. Schutz, *Phenomenology of the Social World.*

41. Habermas, *Knowledge and Human Interest,* pp. 301–17.

42. Marcuse, *One-Dimensional Man,* p. xi.

43. Ruddick, "Maternal Thinking," p. 343.

44. Ibid., pp. 343, 354.

45. Jean Bethke Elshtain, "On Beautiful Souls, Just Warriors and Feminist Consciousness," *Women's Studies International Forum* 5 (1982): 345.

46. Jean Bethke Elshtain, "Antigone's Daughter: Reflections on Female Identity and the State," *Democracy* 2 (April 1982): 46–59.

47. Ibid., p. 59. See also "Women as Mirror and Other: Toward a Theory of Women, War and Feminism," *Human Society* 5 (Winter/Spring 1982): 29–44.

48. Habermas, "New Social Movements," p. 35.

49. Sara Ruddick, "Pacifying the Forces: Drafting Women in the Interests of Peace," *Signs* 8 (Spring 1983): 472. See also "Preservative Love and Military Destruction: Some Reflections on Mothering and Peace," in Joyce Trebilcot, ed., *Mothering: Essays in Feminist Theory* (Totowa: Rowman & Allanheld, 1984), pp. 231–62.

50. Ruddick, "Pacifying the Forces," pp. 477–83.

51. Brenner and Holmstrom, "Autonomy vs. Community"; Stacey, "The New Conservative Feminism."

52. Brenner and Holmstrom, "Autonomy vs. Community;" see also Irene Diamond and Lee Quimby, "American Feminism in the Age of the Body," *Signs* 10 (Autumn 1984): 119–25; Ann Ferguson, "Sex War: The Debate between Radical and Libertarian Feminists," *Signs* 10 (Autumn 1984): 106–12.

Chapter 10

1. In addition to previously cited works by these authors, see Jean Bethke Elshtain, "Feminist Discourse and Its Discontents: Language, Power and Meaning," *Signs* 7 (Spring 1982): 603–21.

2. Bernstein, *Beyond Objectivism and Relativism.*

3. Sandra Harding, "Is Gender a Variable in Conceptions of Rationality?" in Carol C. Gould, *Beyond Domination: New Perspectives on Women and Philosophy* (Totowa: Rowman & Allanheld, 1983), pp. 43–63.

4. Ernest Nagel, *Structure of Science* (New York: Hackett Publishers, 1979), p. 5. See also Carl G. Hempel, *Aspects of Scientific Explanation* (New York: Free Press, 1970).

5. Brecht, *Political Theory,* p. 114.

6. Karl Jaspers, *Idea of the University,* trans. H.A.T. Reiche and H.F. Vanderschmidt (Boston: Beacon Press, 1959), p. 12.

7. Brecht, *Political Theory,* p. 276.

8. Maurice Merleau-Ponty, *The Primacy of Perception and Other Essays on Phenomenological Psychology, the Philosophy of Art, History and Politics* (Evanston: Northwestern University Press, 1964), pp. 23–24.

9. Max Weber, *The Methodology of the Social Sciences,* trans. Edward A. Shils and Henry A. Finch (New York: Free Press, 1949), p. 72.

10. Maurice Merleau-Ponty, *Phenomenology of Perception,* trans. Colin Smart (London: Routledge & Kegan Paul, 1962), p. viii.

11. Marcuse, *One-Dimensional Man,* p. 231.

12. Marcuse, *Essay on Liberation,* p. 19; see also *Eros and Civilization,* pp. 146–47, 151, 165.

13. Norman O. Brown, *Life against Death: The Psychoanalytical Meaning of History* (Middletown: Wesleyan University Press, 1959), p. 276.

14. Hilary Rose, "Conclusion," in Nowotny and Rose, *Counter-movements in the Sciences,* p. 324. Cf. also Rose and Rose, *Ideology of/in the Natural Sciences;* Hilary and Steven Rose, "Radicalization of Science," in Ralph Miliband and John Saville, eds.,*Socialist Register 1972* (London: Merlin Press, 1972), pp. 105–32; and their "Radical Science and Its Enemies" in Ralph Miliband and John Saville, ed. *Socialist Register 1979* (London: Merlin Press, 1979), pp. 317–35. See also Hilary Rose, "Hyper-reflexivity: A New Danger for the Counter-movement," in Nowotny and Rose, *Counter-movements in the Sciences,* pp. 277–89; and Everett Mendelsohn et al., eds., *The Social Production of Scientific Knowledge* (Boston: Reidel, 1977).

15. Cf. Sandra Harding, *Is Gender a Variable?*

16. Evelyn Fox Keller, "Gender and Science," in Harding and Hintikka, *Discovering Reality,* p. 191.

17. Janice Moulton, "A Paradigm for Philosophy: The Adversary Method," in *Discovering Reality* pp. 149–64.

18. Kathryn Pyne Addelson, "The Man of Professional Wisdom," in ibid., pp. 165–86. See also Susan Bordo, "A Drama of Parturition: The Cartesian Masculinzation of Thought," *Signs* 11 (Spring 1986), 439–56.

19. Elizabeth Fee, "Is Feminism a Threat to Scientific Objectivity?" *International Journal of Women's Studies* 4 (1981): 378–92.

20. William Leiss, *Domination of Nature* (Boston: Beacon Press, 1974), p. 94.

21. Fee, "Is Feminism a Threat?" p. 384.

22. Ibid., p. 386.

23. Fee, "Is Feminism a Threat?", p. 389.

24. Keller, *Reflections on Gender and Science,* pp. 61–64.

25. Ibid., p. 70.

26. Ibid., pp. 93, 173–74, 177–79.

Conclusion

1. Kurt H. Wolff, *Beyond the Sociology of Knowledge: An Introduction and a Development* (Landham: University Press of America, 1983), p. 263.

2. See especially Ferree and Hess, *Controversy and Coalition;* Klein, *Gender Politics;* Banks, *Faces of Feminism;* Chafe, *The American Woman;* Freeman, *The Politics of Women's Liberation;* Betty Justice and Renate Pore, eds., *Toward the Second Decade: The Import of the Women's Movement on American Institutions* (Westport: Greenwood Press, 1981); Eugen Lupri, ed., *Changing Position of Women in Family and Society: A Cross-National Comparison* (Leiden: E.J. Brill, 1983); Andrea Dworkin, *Right-Wing Women* (New York: G.P. Putnam, 1978); Clarie Knoche Fulenwider, *Feminism in American Politics: A Study of Ideological Influences* (New York: Praeger, 1980). See also Marcia Lynn Whicker and Jennie Jacobs Kronfeld, *Sex Role Changes: Technology, Politics and Policy* (New York: Praeger, 1985); Lynn Weiner, *From Working Girl to Working Mother: The Female Labor Force in the United States, 1820–1980* (Chapel Hill: University of North Carolina Press, 1985); Pat Voydanoff, *Work and Family: Changing Roles of Men and Women* (Palo Alto: Mayfield, 1983); Julie Matthaei, *An Economic History of Women in America: Women's Work, the Sexual Division of Labor and the Development of Capitalism* (New York: Schocken Books, 1982); Alice Kessler-Harris, *Out to Work: History of Wage-Earning Women in the United States* (New York: Oxford University Press, 1982); Ellen Carol Du Bois et al., *Feminist Scholarship: Kindling in the Groves of Academe* (Urbana: University of Illinois Press, 1985); Gloria Bowles and Renate D. Klein, eds., *Theories of Women's Studies* (Boston: Routledge & Kegan Paul, 1983); Michael Evans Gould, *A Dialogue on Comparable Worth* (Ithaca: International Labour Relations Press, 1983); Helen Remick, ed., *Comparable Worth and Wage Discrimination: Technical Possibilities and Political Reality* (Philadelphia: Temple University Press, 1984); and Barbara F. Reskin, ed., *Sex Segregation in the Workplace: Trends, Explanations, Remedies* (Washington: National Academic Press, 1984).

3. Merleau-Ponty, *Phenomenology of Perception,* p. 82.

4. Marks and Courtivron, *New French Feminism.*

5. Rich, *Of Woman Born.*

6. Jaggar, "Feeling and Knowing," and "Toward a More Integrated World."

7. Keller, *Reflections on Gender and Science.*

8. Hilary Rose, "Science's Gender Gap," *Review of Women's Books* 2 (May 1985): 6.

9. Jaggar, "Towards a More Integrated World."

10. Steven Rose, *Against Biological Determinism;* Levins and Lewontin, *Dialectical Biologist.*

11. Levins and Lewontin, *Dialectical Biologist.*

12. Bordo, "A Drama of Paturition."

13. Gilligan, *In a Different Voice,* p. 74.

14. Berger and Luckmann, *Social Construction of Reality,* pp. 46–47.

15. Nancy Hartsock, "Prologue to a Feminist Critique of War and Politics," in Judith Stiehm, ed., *Women and Men's Wars* (New York: Pergamon Press, 1983), pp. 50–64; see also Elshtain, "On Beautiful Souls, Just Warriors and Feminist Consciousness."

16. Marcuse, *Negations,* p. 209.

17. Kettler et al., *Karl Mannheim,* p. 58.

*
Bibliography

Abel, Elizabeth, and Emily K. Abel, eds. *The Signs Reader: Women, Gender and Scholarship.* Chicago: University of Chicago Press, 1983.

Abel, Elizabeth, Marianne Hirsch, and Elizabeth Langland, eds. *The Voyage In: Fictions of Female Development.* Hanover: Dartmouth College/University Press of New England, 1983.

Abercrombie, Nicolas. *Class, Structure and Knowledge: Problems in the Sociology of Knowledge.* New York: New York University Press, 1980.

*Abercrombie, Nicolas, and Brian Longhurst. "Interpreting Mannheim," *Theory, Culture and Society* 2 (1983): 5-15.

Abzug, Bella. *Gender Gap: Bella Abzug's Guide to Political Power for American Women.* Boston: Houghton Mifflin, 1984.

Acker, Joan, Kate Barry, and Joke Esseveld. "Objectivity and Truth: Problems in Doing Feminist Research." *Women's Studies International Forum* 6 (1983): 423-35.

*Addelson, Kathryn Pyne. "The Man of Professional Wisdom." In *Discovering Reality: Feminist Perspectives on Epistemology, Metaphysics, Methodology and the Philosophy of Science,* ed. Sandra Harding and Merrill B. Hintikka. Boston: D. Reidel, 1983. Pp. 165-86.

Adorno, Theodor W. *Prisms.* Trans. Samuel and Shierry Weber. London: Spearman, 1967.

_____. *Negative Dialectics.* Trans E.B. Ashton. New York: Seabury Press, 1973.

Alper, Joseph S. "Sex Difference in Brain Asymmetry: A Critical Analysis." *Feminist Studies* 11 (Spring 1985): 7-37.

Ann Arbor Science for the People Editorial Collective. *Biology as a Social Weapon.* Minneapolis: Burgess Publishing Co., 1977.

Aptheker, Bettina. *Women's Legacy: Essays of Race, Sex, and Class in American History.* Amherst: University of Massachusetts Press, 1982.

*Arditti, Rita, Pat Brennan, Steve Cavrak. *Science and Liberation.* Boston: South End Press, 1980.

*Arditti, Rita, Renate Duelli Klein, and Shelly Minden, eds. *Test-tube Women: What Future for Motherhood?* Boston: Pandora Press, 1984.

*Ardrey, Robert. *African Genesis.* New York: Atheneum Publishers, 1961.

*_____. *The Territorial Imperative: A Personal Inquiry into the Animal Origins of Property and Nations.* New York: Atheneum Publishers, 1966.

*Arendt, Hannah. *Between Past and Future: Eight Exercises in Political Thought.* New York: Penguin Books, 1977.

*_____. *The Origins of Totalitarianism.* New York: Peter Smith, 1983.

---

*Indicates that the work is cited in the preceding text.

*Arney, William Ray. "Maternal Infant Bonding: The Politics of Falling in Love with Your Children." *Feminist Studies* 6 (Fall 1980); 547–70.

*Asch, Adrienne, and Michelle Fine. "Shared Dreams: A Left Perspective on Disability Rights and Reproductive Rights." *Radical America* 18 (1984): 51–58.

*Balbus, Isaac D. *Marxism and Domination: A Neo-Hegelian, Feminist, Psychoanalytic Theory of Sexual, Political and Technological Liberation.* Princeton: Princeton University Press, 1982.

———. "Disciplining Women: Michel Foucault and the Power of Feminist Discourse." *Praxis International* 5 (January 1986): 466–83.

*Bane, Mary Jo. *Here to Stay: American Families in the Twentieth Century.* New York: Basic Books, 1976.

*Banks, Olive. *Faces of Feminism: A Study of Feminism as a Social Movement.* New York: St. Martin's Press, 1981.

Barash, David. *Sociobiology and Behavior.* New York: Elsevier Science, 1977.

*———. *The Whisperings Within: Evolution and the Origins of Human Nature.* New York: Harper & Row, 1979.

Barash, David, and Judith Eve Lipton. *The Caveman and the Bomb: Human Nature, Evolution, and Nuclear War.* New York: McGraw-Hill, 1985.

*Barry, Kathleen. *Female Sexual Slavery.* Englewood Cliffs, N.J.: Prentice-Hall, 1979.

*Bartky, Sandra Lee. "Toward a Phenomenology of Feminist Consciousness." *Social Theory and Practice* 3 (1975): 425–39.

*Bauman, Zygmunt. *Hermeneutics and Social Science.* New York: Columbia University Press, 1978.

*Bayer, Ronald. *Homosexuality and American Psychiatry: The Politics of Diagnosis.* New York: Basic Books, 1980.

———. "Women, Work and Reproductive Hazards." *Hastings Center Report* 12 (October 1982): 14–19.

*Beauvoir, Simone de. *Second Sex.* Trans. H.M. Parshley. New York: Modern Library, 1952.

*Bellah, Robert N., Richard Madsen, William M. Sullivan, Ann Swidler and Steven M. Tipton. *Habits of the Heart: Individualism and Community in American Life.* Berkeley: University of California Press, 1985.

Bem, Sandra Lipsitz. "Gender Schema Theory and Its Implications for Child Development: Raising Gender-aschematic Children in a Gender-schematic Society." *Signs* 8 (Summer 1983): 598–616.

*Benhabib, Seyla. "Modernity and the Aporias of Critical Theory." *Telos* 49 (Fall 1981): 39–59.

*———. "Epistemologies of Postmodernism: A Rejoinder to Jean-Francois Lyotard." *New German Critique* 33 (Fall 1984): 103–26.

———. *Critique, Norm, and Utopia: A Study of the Foundations of Critical Theory.* New York: Columbia University Press, 1986.

———. "The Generalized and the Concrete Other: The Kohlberg-Gilligan Controversy and Feminist Theory." *Praxis International* 5 (January 1986): 402–24.

*Benjamin, Jessica. "The End of Internalization: Adorno's Social Psychology." *Telos* 32 (Summer 1977): 42–64.

*_____. "The Bonds of Love: Rational Violence and Erotic Domination." *Feminist Studies* 6 (Spring 1980): 144–74.

*Bennis, Warren G., and Philip E. Slater. *The Temporary Society.* New York: Harper & Row, 1968.

*Benston, Margaret. "The Political Economy of Women's Liberation." *Monthly Review* 21 (1969): 13–27.

*Berger, Brigitte. "At Odds with Society." *Society* 22 (July–August 1985): 75–86.

*Berger, Brigitte, and Peter L. Berger. *War Over the Family: Capturing the Middle Ground.* Garden City, N.Y.: Doubleday, 1984.

*Berger, Peter L. *Invitation to Sociology: A Humanistic Perspective.* Garden City, N.Y.: Doubleday, 1963.

*_____. "Identity as a Problem in the Sociology of Knowledge." *European Journal of Sociology* 7 (1966): 105–15.

*Berger, Peter L., Brigitte Berger, and Hansfried Kellner. *The Homeless Mind: Modernization and Consciousness.* New York: Random House, 1974.

*Berger, Peter L., and Hansfired Kellner. *Sociology Reinterpreted: An Essay on Method and Vocation.* Garden City, N.Y.: Doubleday, 1981.

*Berger, Peter L., and Thomas Luckmann. *Social Construction of Reality: A Treatise in the Sociology of Knowledge.* Garden City, N.Y.: Doubleday, 1966.

*Berkman, Joyce. "Historical Styles of Contraceptive Advocacy." In Helen B. Holmes, Betty B. Hoskins, and Michael Gross, eds. *Birth Control and Controlling Birth: Women-Centered Perspectives.* Clifton, N.J.: Humana Press, 1981. Pp. 27–36.

Bernard, Jessie. *The Future of Motherhood.* New York: Dial Press, 1974.

*Bernstein, Richard. *Praxis and Action: Contemporary Philosophies of Human Activity.* Philadelphia: University of Pennsylvania Press, 1971.

*_____. *The Restructuring of Social and Political Thought.* New York: Harcourt Brace Jovanovich, 1976.

*_____. *Beyond Objectivism and Relativism: Science, Hermeneutics and Praxis.* Philadelphia: University of Pennsylvania Press, 1983.

*Bettelheim, Bruno. *Freud and Man's Soul.* New York: Alfred A. Knopf, 1983.

Bleier, Ruth. "Brain, Body and Behavior." In *Beyond Intellectual Sexism: A New Woman, a New Reality,* ed. Joan I. Roberts. New York: David McKay, 1979. Pp. 67–73.

*_____. "Social and Political Bias in Science: An Examination of Animal Studies and Their Generalization to Human Behavior and Evolution." *Genes and Gender* 2 (1979): 49–69.

*_____. *Science and Gender: A Critique of Biology and Its Theories on Women.* New York: Pergamon Press, 1984.

Blum, Linda M. "Politics and Policy-making: The Comparable Worth Debate." *Berkeley Journal of Sociology* 28 (1983): 39–67.

*Blumer, Herbert. "Sociological Implications of the Thought of George Herbert Mead." *American Journal of Sociology* 71 (March 1966): 535–44.

Blumstein, Philip, and Pepper Schwartz. *American Couples: Money, Work, Sex.* New York: William Morrow, 1983.

*Bologh, Roslyn Wallach. *Dialectical Phenomenology: Marx's Method.* Boston: Routledge & Kegan Paul, 1979.

_____. "Feminist Social Theorizing and Moral Reasoning: On Difference and

Dialectic." *Sociological Theory 1984.* San Francisco: Josey-Bass, 1984, pp. 373–93.

Bordo, Susan. "Anorexia Nervosa: Psychopathology as the Crystalization of Culture." *Philosophical Forum* 17 (Winter 1985): 73–104.

*_____. "The Cartesian Masculinization of Thought." *Signs* 11 (Spring 1986): 439–56.

*Bottomore, T.B. "Some Reflections on the Sociology of Knowledge." *British Journal of Sociology* 7 (1956): 52–58.

Bowles, Gloria. "The Uses of Hermeneutics for Feminist Scholarship." *Women's Studies International Forum* 7 (1984): 185–88.

*Bowles, Gloria, and Renate D. Klein, eds. *Theories of Women's Studies.* Boston: Routledge & Kegan Paul, 1983.

*Brecht, Arnold. *Political Theory: The Foundations of Twentieth Centruy Political Thought.* Princeton: Princeton University Press, 1959.

*Breinis, Wini, Margaret Cerullo, and Judith Stacy. "Social Biology, Family Studies, and Antifeminist Backlash." *Feminist Studies* 4 (February 1978): 43–68.

*Breinis, Wini, and Linda Gordon. "The New Scholarship and Family Violence." *Signs* 8 (Spring 1983): 490–531.

*Brenner, Johanna, and Nancy Holmstrom. "Autonomy vs. Community in Feminist Politics" (forthcoming).

Bridenthal, Renate. "The Dialectics of Production and Reproduction in History." *Radical America* 10 (March–April 1976): 3–11.

Brock-Utne, Birgit. *Educating for Peace: A Feminist Perspective.* New York: Pergamon Press, 1985.

Brophy, Julia, and Carol Smart, eds. *Women in Law.* Boston: Routledge & Kegan Paul, 1985.

*Brown, Barbara A., Thomas I. Emerson, Gail Falk, and Ann E. Freedman. "The Equal Rights Amendment." *Yale Law Journal* 80 (April 1971): 871–985.

*Brown, Norman O. *Life against Death: The Psychoanalytic Meaning of History.* Middletown: Wesleyan University Press, 1959.

*Brownmiller, Susan. *Against Our Will: Men, Women and Rape.* New York: Simon & Schuster, 1975.

Burton, Clare. *Subordination: Feminist and Social Theory.* Sydney: Allen & Unwin, 1985.

*Bullough, Vern L., and Bonnie Bullough. *Sex, Sickness and Sanity: A History of Sexual Attitudes.* New York: Garland Press, 1977.

*Callahan, Sidney, and Daniel Callahan, eds. *Abortion: Understanding Differences.* New York: Plenum Press, 1984.

Calvin, William H. *The Throwing Madonna: Essays on the Brain.* New York: McGraw-Hill, 1983.

*Carter, Angela. *Sadeian Woman and the Ideology of Pornography.* New York: Pantheon Books, 1978.

*Carveth, Donald L. "The Disembodied Dialectic: A Psychoanalytic Critique of Sociological Relativism." *Theory and Society* 4 (1977): 73–102.

*Chafe, William H. *American Woman: Her Changing Social, Economic and Political Roles, 1920–1970.* New York: Oxford University Press, 1974.

_____. *Women and Equality: Changing Patterns in American Culture.* New York:

Oxford University Press, 1977.

*Chavkin, Wendy. "Occupational Hazards to Reproduction: A Review Essay and Annotated Bibliography." *Feminist Studies* 5 (Summer 1979): 310-25.

*Chesler, Phyllis. *Women and Madness*. Garden City, N.Y.: Doubleday, 1972.

*Chodorow, Nancy. "Oedipal Assymetries and Heterosexual Knots." *Social Problems* 23 (April 1976): 454-68.

*_____. *The Reproduction of Mothering: Psychoanalysis and the Sociology of Gender*. Berkeley: University of California Press, 1978.

*Chodorov, Nancy, and Susan Contratto. "The Fantasy of the Perfect Mother." In *Rethinking the Family: Some Feminist Questions,* ed. Barrie Thorne and Marilyn Yalom. New York: Longman, 1982. Pp. 54-75.

*Chorover, Stephan. *From Genesis to Genocide: The Meaning of Human Nature and the Power of Behavior Control*. Cambridge: MIT Press, 1979.

Clark, Lorenne M.G., and Lynda Lange, eds. *The Sexism of Social and Political Theory: Women and Reproduction from Plato to Nietzsche*. Toronto: University of Toronto Press, 1979.

Code, Lorraine B. "Is the Sex of the Knower Epistemologically Significant?" *Metaphilosophy* 12 (July/October 1981): 267-76.

Coenen, Herman. "Developments in the Phenomenological Reading of Durkheim's Work." *Social Forces* 59 (June 1981): 951-65.

Cohen, Barbara. "Surrogate Mothers: Whose Baby Is It?" *American Journal of Law and Medicine* 10 (Fall 1984): 243-85.

*Cohen, Jean L. *Class and Civil Society: The Limits of Marxian Critical Theory*. Amherst: University of Massachusetts Press, 1983.

*_____. "Rethinking Social Movements." *Berkeley Journal of Sociology* 28 (1983): 97-113.

*Cohen, Steven Martin. "American Jewish Feminism: A Study in Conflict and Compromise." *American Behavioral Science* 24 (April 1980): 519-58.

*Comte, Auguste. *System of Positive Polity*. Trans. John H. Bridge. London: Longmans Green, 1875.

*Conrad, Peter, and Joseph W. Schneider. *Deviance and Medicalization: From Badness to Sickness*. St. Louis: C.V. Mosby, 1980.

*Cooley, Charles Horton. "The Roots of Social Knowledge." *American Journal of Sociology* 32 (July 1926): 59-70.

*_____. *Social Organization: A Study of the Larger Mind*. (1909) New Brunswick, N.J.: Transaction Books, 1983.

Cooper, Sandi E. "Feminism and Family Revivalism." *Chrysalis* 8 (Summer 1979): 59-65.

*Copp, David, and Susan Wendell, eds. *Pornography and Censorship*. Buffalo, N.Y.: Prometheus Books, 1983.

*Corea, Gena. *The Mother Machine: Reproductive Technologies from Artificial Insemination to Artificial Women*. New York: Harper & Row, 1985.

Cornell, Drucilla, and Adam Thurschwell. "Feminism, Negativity, Intersubjectivity." *Praxis International* 5 (January 1986): 484-504.

*Coser, Lewis, A. "Knowledge, Sociology of." In *A Dictionary of the Social Sciences,* ed. Julius Gould and William L. Kolb. Glencoe, Ill.: Free Press, 1964. Pp. 428-35.

*_____. *Masters of Sociological Thought: Ideas in Historical and Social Context*. New

York: Harcourt Brace Jovanovich, 1971.

Coser, Rose Laub. "Cognitive Structure and the Use of Social Space." *Sociological Forum* 7 (Winter 1986): 1–26.

*Cott, Nancy F. *The Bonds of Womanhood: "Women's Sphere" in New England*. New Haven: Yale University Press, 1978.

Coward, Rosalind. *Patriarchal Precedents*. Boston: Routledge & Kegan Paul, 1983.

*Culler, Jonathan. *On Deconstruction: Theory and Criticism after Structuralism*. Ithaca: Cornell University Press, 1982.

Cully, Margo, and Catherine Portugues. *Gendered Subjects*. Boston: Routledge & Kegan Paul, 1985.

Dallmayr, Fred, and Thomas McCarthy, eds. *Understanding and Social Inquiry*. South Bend, Ind: University of Notre Dame Press, 1977.

*Daly, Mary. *Beyond God the Father: Toward a Philosophy of Women's Liberation*. Boston: Beacon Press, 1973.

*Davis, Angela Y. *Women, Race and Class*. New York: Random House, 1984.

*Dawkins, Richard. *The Selfish Gene*. New York: Oxford University Press, 1976.

*Diamond, Irene, and Lee Quimby. "American Feminism in the Age of the Body." *Signs* 10 (Autumn 1984): 119–25.

*Dill, Bonnie Thorton. "Race, Class and Gender: Prospects for an All-Inclusive Sisterhood." *Feminist Studies* 9 (April 1983): 131–49.

*Dinnerstein, Dorothy. *The Mermaid and the Minotaur: Sexual Arrangements and Human Malaise*. New York: Harper & Row, 1976.

*———. "Afterword: Toward the Mobilization of Eros." In *Face to Face: Fathers, Mothers, Masters, Monsters — Essays for a Nonsexist Future*, ed. Meg M. Murray. Westport, Conn.: Greenwood Press, 1983. Pp. 293–309.

*Donzelot, Jacques. *The Policing of Families*. Trans. Robert Hurley. New York: Pantheon Books, 1979.

Dorenkemp, Angela G., John F. McClymer, Mary M. Moynihan, and Arlene C. Vadum. *Images of Women in American Popular Culture*. New York: Harcourt Brace Jovanovich, 1985.

*Du Bois, Ellen Carol, Gail Paradise Kelly, Elizabeth Laporsky Kennedy. *Feminism and Suffrage: The Emergence of an Independent Women's Movement in America. 1848–1869*. Ithaca: Cornell University Press, 1978.

*Du Bois, Ellen Carol, W. Korsmeyer, and Lilliam S. Robinson. *Feminist Scholarship: Challenge, Discovery and Impact*. Urbana: University of Illinois Press, 1985.

*Durkheim, Emile. *Suicide: A Study in Sociology,* trans. John A. Spaulding and George Simpson. New York: Free Press, 1951.

*———. *Elementary Forms of Religious Life,* trans. Joseph W. Swain. New York: Free Press, 1954.

*———. *Emile Durkheim on Institutional Analysis,* trans. Mark Traugott. Chicago: University of Chicago Press, 1978.

*Dworkin, Andrea. *Right-wing Women*. New York: G.P. Putnam, 1978.

*———. *Pornography: Men Possessing Women*. New York: G.P. Putnam, 1981.

*Eagleton, Terry. *Literary Theory: An Introduction*. Minneapolis: University of Minnesota Press, 1983.

*Easlea, Brian. *Science and Sexual Oppression: Patriarchy's Confrontation with Woman* *and Nature.* London: Weidenfeld & Nicolson, 1981.

*Eder, Klaus. "A New Social Movement." *Telos* 52 (Summer 1982): 5–20.

Ehrensaft, Diane. "When Women and Men Mother." *Socialist Review* 10 (January–February 1980), 37–73.

Eichler, Margrit. *Double Standard: A Feminist Critique of Feminist Social Science.* New York: St. Martin's Press, 1980.

Eisenstein, Hester. *Contemporary Feminist Thought.* Boston: G.K. Hall, 1984.

*Eisenstein, Zillah. "Antifeminism in the Politics and Elections of 1980." *Feminist Studies* 7 (Summer 1981): 187–205.

————. *The Radical Future of Liberal Feminism.* New York: Longman, 1981.

*————. *Feminism and Sexual Equality: Crisis in Liberal America.* New York: Monthly Review Press, 1984.

Ellis, Katherine, and Rosalind Petchesky. "Children of the Corporate Dream: An Analysis of Day Care as a Political Issue under Capitalism." *Socialist Revolution* 2 (November/December 1972): 9–28.

*Elshtain, Jean Bethke. "Family in a Time of Trouble: Family Reconstruction." *Commonweal* 104 (August 1980): 430–31.

*————. *Public Man, Private Women: Woman in Social and Political Thought.* Princeton: Princeton University Press, 1981.

*————. "Antigone's Daughter: Reflections on Female Identity and the State." *Democracy* 2 (April 1982): 46–59.

*————. "Feminist Discourse and Its Discontents: Language, Power, and Meaning." *Signs* 7 (Spring 1982): 603–21.

*————. "On Beautiful Souls, Just Warriors and Female Consciousness." *Women's Studies International Forum* 5 (1982): 341–48.

*————. "Women as Mirror and Other: Toward a Theory of Women, War and Feminism." *Human Society* 5 (Winter/Spring 1982): 29–44.

*————. "Reflections on Abortion, Value and the Family." In *Abortion: Understanding Differences,* ed. Sidney and Daniel Callahan. New York: Plenum Press, 1984, pp. 47–72.

————. "Fantasy as a Form of Thought: An Exploration in the Philosophy of Mind." Unpublished.

*Engels, Friedrich. *Origins of the Family, Private Property and the State.* New York: International Publishing, 1972.

Epstein, Cynthia. *Women in Law.* Garden City, N.Y.: Doubleday, 1983.

*Erikson, Eric. "Inner and Outer Space: Reflections on Womanhood." In *The Women in America,* ed. Robert J. Lifton. Westport, Conn: Greenwood Press, 1977. Pp. 1–26.

Ettorre, E.M. *Lesbian, Women and Society.* Boston: Routledge & Kegan Paul, 1980.

*Evans, Sara. *Personal Politics: The Roots of Women's Liberation in the Civil Rights Movement and the New Left.* New York: Random House, 1980.

*Ewen, Stuart. *Captains of Consciousness.* New York: McGraw-Hill, 1976.

Eyerman, Ron. "Social Movements and Social Theory." *Sociology* 18 (February 1984): 71–82.

*Falik, Marilyn. *Ideology and Abortion Policy Politics.* New York: Praeger Publishers, 1983.

Family Service America. *State of Families, 1984–1985.* New York: Family Service America, 1984.

*Farganis, James. "Critical Theory: Social Praxis and the Reconstruction of Reality." In *Structures of Knowing: Current Studies in the Sociology of Schools,* ed. Richard C. Monk. University Press of America, 1986 (forthcoming).

*Farganis, Sondra. "Feminist Theory and Social Theory: The Need for Dialogue." *Sociological Inquiry* 56 (Winter 1986): 50–68.

*Fee, Elizabeth. "Is Feminism a Threat to Scientific Objectivity?" *International Journal of Women's Studies* 4 (1981): 378–92.

*Ferguson, Ann. "Sex War: The Debate between Radical and Libertarian Feminists." *Signs* 10 (Autumn 1984): 106–12.

*Ferguson, Kathy E. *Self, Society and Womankind: The Dialectic of Liberation.* Westport, Conn: Greenwood Press, 1980.

―――. *Feminist Case Against Bureaucracy.* Philadelphia: Temple University Press, 1984.

*Ferree, Myra Marx. "Working Class Feminism: A Consideration of the Consequences of Employment." *Sociological Quarterly* 21 (Spring 1980): 173–84.

*Ferree, Myra Marx, and Beth B. Hess. *Controversy and Coalition: The New Feminist Movement.* Boston: G.K. Hall/Twayne, 1985.

*Feyerabend, Paul. *Against Method.* New York: Schocken Books, 1978.

*Figes, Eva. *Patriarchal Attitudes.* New York: Stein & Day, 1970.

*Fiorenza, Elisabeth Schüssler. *Bread Not Stone: The Challenge of Feminist Biblical Interpretation.* Boston: Beacon Press, 1984.

*Firestone, Shulamith. *The Dialectic of Sex: The Case for Feminist Revolution.* New York: William Morrow, 1970.

*Flax, Jane. "The Family in Contemporary Feminist Thought: A Critical Review." In *The Family in Political Thought,* ed. Jean Bethke Elshtain. Amherst: University of Massachusetts Press, 1982. Pp. 223–53.

*―――. "Political Philosophy and the Patriarchal Unconscious: A Psychoanalytic Perspective on Epistemology and Metaphysics." In *Discovering Reality: Feminist Perspectives on Epistemology, Metaphysics, Methodology, and Philosophy of Science,* ed. Sandra Harding and Merrill B. Hintikka. Boston: D. Reidel, 1983. Pp. 245–81.

―――. "The Memory of Union and Differences: Is the Repressed Gendered?" Paper presented to the Conference on Women and Memory, University of Michigan, March 1986.

*Flexner, Elinor. *Century of Struggle: The Woman's Rights Movement in the United States.* Cambridge: Harvard University Press, 1959.

*Foucault, Michel. *The Foucault Reader,* ed. Paul Rabinow. New York: Pantheon Books, 1984.

Fox, Mary, and Sharlene Hesse-Biber. *Women at Work.* Palo Alto, Calif.: Mayfield Publishing, 1984.

*Francome, Colin. *Abortion Freedom: A Worldwide Movement.* London: Allen & Unwin, 1984.

*Frankfurt Institute for Social Research. *Aspects of Sociology,* trans. John Viertel. Boston: Beacon Press, 1972.

Franklin, Clyde W., II. *Changing Definition of Masculinity.* New York: Plenum Press, 1984.

*Fraser, Nancy. "The French Derrideans: Politicizing Deconstruction or Deconstructing the Political?" *New German Critique* 33 (Fall 1984): 127–54.

*_____. "What's Critical about Critical Theory? The Case of Habermas and Gender." *New German Critique* 35 (Spring–Summer 1985): 97–131.

_____. "Toward a Discourse Ethic of Solidarity." *Praxis International* 5 (January 1986): 425–29.

*Freeman, Jo. *The Politics of Women's Liberation: A Case Study in an Emerging Social Movement and Its Relation to the Policy Process.* New York: Longman, 1975.

*Freud, Sigumnd. *Totem and Taboo: Resemblances between the Psychic Lives of Savages and Neurotics,* trans. A.A. Brill. New York: Random House, 1918.

*_____. *Civilization and Its Discontents,* trans. James Strachy. New York: W.W. Norton, 1962.

*_____. *Culture and Character.* New York: Collier Books, 1963.

*Friedan, Betty. *The Feminine Mystique.* New York: Dell Publishers, 1977.

*_____. *Second Stage.* New York: Summit Books, 1982.

*Fromm, Erich. *Sane Society.* New York: Holt, Rinehart & Winston, 1955.

*_____. *Art of Loving: An Enquiry into the Nature of Love.* New York: Harper & Row, 1974.

*_____. *Crisis of Psychoanalysis: An Enquiry into the Nature of Love.* New York: Holt, Rinehart & Winston, 1970.

*Fulenwider, Claire Knoche. *Feminism in American Politics: A Study of Ideological Influences.* New York: Praeger Publishers, 1980.

Frye, Marilyn. *The Politics of Reality: Essays in Feminist Theory.* Trumansburg, N.Y.: Crossing Press, 1983.

*Gadamer, Hans-Georg. *Truth and Method.* Trans. Garrett Barden and John Cumming. New York: Continuum Books, 1975.

*Gagnon, John H. *Human Sexualities.* Glenview, Ill.: Scott, Foresman, 1977.

Gallop, Jane. *Daughter's Seduction: Feminism and Psychoanalysis.* Ithaca: Cornell University Press, 1982.

Gergen, Kenneth J. "Social Constructionist Movement in Modern Psychology." *American Psychologist* 40 (March 1985): 266–75.

*Gerson, Mary-Joan, Judith L. Alpert, and Mary Sue Richardson. "Mothering: The View from Psychological Research." *Signs* 9 (Spring 1984): 434–53.

Gellner, Ernest. *Relativism and the Social Sciences.* New York: Cambridge University Press, 1985.

*Gerth, Hans, and C. Wright Mills. *Character and Social Structure: The Psychology of Social Institutions.* New York: Harcourt, Brace & World, 1953.

*Gilligan, Carol. *In a Different Voice: Psychological Theory and Women's Development.* Cambridge: Harvard University Press, 1982.

*_____. "Do the Social Sciences Have an Adequate Theory of Moral Development?" In *Social Science as Moral Inquiry,* ed. Norman Haan, Robert N. Bellah, Paul Rabinow and William M. Sullivan. New York: Columbia University Press, 1983. Pp. 33–51.

*Gittell, Marilyn, and Nancy Naples. "Activist Women: Conflicting Ideologies." *Social Policy* 13 (Summer 1982): 52–57.

*Glennon, Linda. *Women and Dualism: A Sociology of Knowledge Analysis.* New York: Longman, 1979.

Glick, Paul C. "How American Families are Changing." *American Demographics* 6 (January 1984), 20–5.

Goffman, Erving. *Gender Advertisements* New York: Harper & Row, 1979.

*Gold, Michael Evan. *A Dialogue on Comparable Worth*. Ithaca: ILR Press, 1983.

*Goodwyn, Lawrence. *Democratic Promise: The Populist Movement*. New York: Oxford University Press, 1976.

*Gordon, Linda. *Woman's Body, Woman's Right: A Social History of Birth Control*. New York: Grossman Publishers, 1976.

*Gordon, Michael. *The American Family in Social-Historical Perspective*. New York: St. Martin's Press, 1983.

Gorovitz, Samuel. *Doctors' Dilemmas: Moral Conflict and Medical Care*. New York: Macmillan, 1982.

*Gould, Carol C., ed. *Beyond Domination: New Perspectives on Women and Philosophy*. Totowa, N.J.: Rowman & Allanheld, 1983.

Gould, Carol C., and Marx W. Wartofsky, eds. *Women and Philosophy: Toward a Theory of Liberation*. New York: G.P. Putnam's Sons, 1976.

Gouldner, Alvin. *For Sociology: Renewal and Critique in Sociology Today*. New York: Basic Books, 1973.

*Green, Philip. *Pursuit of Inequality*. New York: Pantheon Books, 1981.

_____. *Retrieving Democracy: In Search of Civic Equality*. Totowa, N.J.: Rowman & Allanheld, 1985.

Greene, Gayle, and Coppelia Kahn, eds. *Making a Difference: Feminist Literary Criticism*. New York: Methuen, 1985.

*Greer, Germaine. *Sex and Destiny: The Politics of Human Fertility*. New York: Harper & Row, 1984.

*Griffen, Susan. *Rape: The Power of Consciousness*. San Francisco: Harper & Row, 1979.

*_____. *Woman and Nature: The Roaring Inside Her*. New York: Harper & Row, 1980.

*_____. *Pornography and Silence: Culture's Revenge against Nature*. New York: Harper & Row, 1981.

*Grobstein, Clifford. *From Chance to Purpose: An Appraisal of External Human Fertilization*. Reading, Mass.: Addison-Wesley, 1981.

*Guare, John. *Marco Polo Sings a Solo*. New York: Dramatists Play Service, 1977.

_____. *Toward a Rational Society: Student Protest, Science and Politics*, trans. Jeremy J. Shapiro. Boston: Beacon Press, 1970.

*_____. *Knowledge and Human Interest*, trans. Jeremy J. Shapiro. Boston: Beacon Press, 1971.

_____. *Theory and Practice*, trans. John Viertel. Boston: Beacon Press, 1974.

*_____. *Legitimation Crisis*, trans. Thomas McCarthy. Boston: Beacon Press, 1975.

*Habermas, Jurgen. "Aspects of the Rationality of Action," trans. Thomas McCarthy. In *Rationality Today*, ed. Theodore F. Gervaets. Ottowa: University of Ottowa Press, 1979. Pp. 185–205.

*_____. "New Social Movements." *Telos* 49 (Fall 1981): 33–37.

*_____. *Theory of Communicative Action: Reason and the Rationalization of Society*. Vol. I. trans. Thomas McCarthy. Boston: Beacon Press, 1984.

Hall, Nor. *The Moon and the Virgin: Relfection on the Archetype Feminine.* New York: Harper & Row, 1980.

Hamilton, Peter. *Knowledge and Social Structure.* London: Routledge & Kegan Paul, 1974.

*Hamilton, William D. "Innate Social Aptitude of Man: An Approach from Evolutionary Genetics." In *Biosocial Anthropology,* ed. Robin Fox. New York: John Wiley, 1975. Pp. 133–55.

*Harding, Sandra. "Is Gender a Variable in Conceptions of Rationality?" In *Beyond Domination: New Perspectives on Women and Philosophy,* ed. Carol C. Gould. Totowa, N.J.: Rowman & Allanheld, 1983. Pp. 43–63.

*Harding, Sandra, and Merrill B. Hintikka, eds. *Discovering Reality: Feminist Perspectives on Epistemology, Metaphysics, Methodology, and Philosophy of Science.* Boston: D. Reidel, 1983.

*Harding, Susan. "Family Reform Movements: Recent Feminism and Its Opposition." *Feminist Studies* 7 (Spring 1981): 57–75.

*Harmon, Michael M. *Action Theory for Public Administration.* New York: Longman, 1981.

*Harré, Rom. *Personal Being: A Theory for Individual Psychology.* Cambridge: Harvard University Press, 1984.

*Harris, Barbara J. "The Power of the Past: History and the Psychology of Women." In *In the Shadow of the Past: Psychology Portrays the Sexes,* ed. Miriam Lewin. New York: Columbia University Press, 1984. Pp. 1–25.

*Harrison, Beverly Wildung. *Our Right to Choose: Toward a New Ethic of Abortion.* Boston: Beacon Press, 1983.

Hartmann, Heidi. "The Family as the Locus of Gender, Class, and Political Struggle: The Example of Housework." *Signs* 6 (Spring 1981): 366–94.

*Hartsock, Nancy C.M. "The Barracks Community in Western Political Thought: Prologue to a Feminist Critique of War and Politics." In *Women's and Men's Wars,* ed. Judith Stiehm. New York: Pergamon Press, 1983. pp. 283–86.

*_____. *Money, Sex and Power: Toward a Feminist Historical Materialism.* New York: Longman, 1983.

*Heberle, Rudolf *Social Movements: An Introduction to Political Sociology.* New York: Appleton-Century-Crofts, 1951.

*Held, David. *Introduction to Critical Theory: Horkheimer to Habermas.* Berkeley: University of California Press, 1980.

*Hempel, Carl G. *Aspects of Scientific Explanation.* New York: Free Press, 1970.

*Hochschild,Arlie Russell. *Managed Heart: Commercialization of Human Feeling.* Berkeley: University of California Press, 1983.

*Hodgson, Jane E., ed. *Abortion and Sterilization.* New York: Grune & Stratton, 1981.

*Hoff-Wilson, Joan, ed. *Rights of Passage: The Past and the Future of the ERA.* Bloomington: Indiana University Press, 1986.

Hollis, Martin, and Steven Lukes, eds. *Rationality and Relativism.* Cambridge: MIT Press, 1982.

*Holm, Jean. *Women in the Military: An Unfinished Revolution.* Novato: Presidio Press, 1982.

*Holmes, Helen B., Betty B. Hoskins, and Michael Gross, eds. *Birth Control and Controlling Birth — Women-Centered Perspective.* Clifton, N.J.: Humana Press, 1981.

_____. *Custom-Made Child? Women-Centered Perspective.* Clifton, N.J.: Humana Press, 1981.

*Horkheimer, Max. *Critical Theory,* trans. Matthew J. O'Connell, et al. New York: Continuum Books, 1972.

*_____. *Critique of Instrumental Reason: Lectures and Essays Since the End of World War II,* trans. Matthew J. O'Connell et al. New York: Seabury Press, 1974.

*_____. *Eclipse of Reason.* New York: Seabury Press, 1974.

*Horkheimer, Max, and Theodor W. Adorno. *Dialectics of Enlightnement.* New York: Herder & Herder, 1972.

Hoyenga, Katharine Blick, and Kermit T. Hoyenga. *The Question of Sex Differences: Psychological, Cultural and Biological Issues.* Boston: Little, Brown, 1979.

*Hrdy, Sarah Blaffer. *The Woman That Never Evolved.* Cambridge: Harvard University Press, 1981.

Hubbard, Ruth. "Some Legal and Policy Implications of Recent Advances in Prenatal Diagnosis and Fetal Therapy." *Women's Rights Law Reporter* 7 (Spring 1982): 201–18.

*Hubbard, Ruth, Mary Sue Henifen, and Barbara Fried, eds., *Biological Woman: The Convenient Myth.* Cambridge: Schenkman Publishing, 1982.

*Huber, Joan. "Towards a Sociotechnological Theory of the Women's Movement." *Social Problems* 23 (April 1976): 371–88.

*Hummel, Ralph P. *Bureaucratic Experience.* New York: St. Martin's Press, 1982.

*Huyssen, Andreas. "Mapping the Postmodern." *New German Critique* 33 (Fall 1984): 5–52.

*Imber, Jonathan. "Sociology and Abortion: Legacies and Strategies." *Contemporary Sociology* 8 (November 1979): 825–36.

*Jackson, Margaret. "Sexual Liberation or Social Control?" *Women's Studies International Forum* 6 (1983): 1–17.

*Jacoby, Russell. *Social Amnesia: A Critique of Conformist Psychology from Adler to Laing.* Boston: Beacon Press, 1975.

*Jaffe, Frederick S., Barbara L. Lindheim, and Philip R. Lee. *Abortion Politics: Private Morality and Public Policy.* New York: McGraw-Hill, 1981.

*Jaggar, Alison M. *Feminist Politics and Human Nature.* Totowa, N.J.: Rowman & Allanheld, 1983.

*_____. "Towards a More Integrated World." Paper presented to the Douglass College Women's Studies Seminar, "Feminist Reconstruction of Self and Society," January 1985.

_____. "Feeling and Knowing: Emotion in Feminist Theory." Paper presented to the Douglass College Women's Studies Seminar, "Feminist Ways of Knowing," September 1985.

*James, William. *Pragmatism and other Essays.* New York: Washington Square Press, 1963.

*Janeway, Elizabeth. *Man's World, Woman's Place: A Study in Social Mythology.* New York: Dell Publishing, 1971.

Jardine, Alice A. *Gynesis: Configuration of Women and Modernity.* Ithaca: Cornell University Press, 1985.

*Jaspers, Karl. *Idea of the University.* Trans. H. A. T. Reiche and H. F. Vanderschmidt. Boston: Beacon Press, 1959.

*Jay, Martin. *Dialectical Imagination: A History of the Frankfurt School and the Institute of Social Research, 1923–1950.* Boston: Little, Brown, 1973.

*_____. "The Frankfurt School's Critique of Karl Mannheim and the Sociology of Knowledge." *Telos* 20 (Summer 1974): 72–89.

*Johnson, Chalmers. *Revolutionary Change.* Boston: Little, Brown, 1966.

Jonas, Hans. *Imperatives of Responsibility.* Chicago: University of Chicago Press, 1984.

*Justice, Betty, and Renate Pore. *Toward the Second Decade: The Impact of the Women's Movement on American Institutions.* Westport, Conn.: Greenwood Press, 1981.

Kahn-Hut, Rachel, Arlene Kaplan Daniels, and Richard Colvard, eds. *Women and Work: Problems and Perspectives.* New York: Oxford University Press, 1982.

*Kamerman, Sheila B., Alfred J. Kahn, and Paul Kingston. *Maternity Policies and Working Women.* New York: Columbia University Press, 1983.

*Kass, Leon. "Making Babies—the New Biology and the 'Old' Morality." *Public Interest* 29 (Winter 1972): 13–56.

_____. *Toward a More Natural Science: Biology and Human Affairs.* New York: Free Press, 1985.

Keller, Evelyn Fox. *A Feeling for the Organism: The Life and Work of Barbara McClintock.* New York: W.H. Freeman, 1983.

*_____. "Gender and Science." In *Discovering Reality: Feminist Perspectives on Epistemology, Metaphysics, Methodology and Philosophy of Sciences,* ed. Sandra Harding and Merrill B. Hintikka. Boston: D. Reidel, 1983. Pp. 187–205.

*_____. *Reflections on Gender and Science.* New Haven: Yale University Press, 1985.

*Kelly, Joan. *Women, History and Theory: The Essays of Joan Kelly.* Chicago: University of Chicago Press, 1984.

*Keohane, Nannerl O., Michelle Z. Rosaldo, and Barbara C. Gelpi, eds. *Feminist Theory: A Critique of Ideology.* Chicago: University of Chicago Press, 1982.

Kessler, Suzanne J., and Wendy McKenna. *Gender: An Ethnomethodological Approach.* New York: John Wiley, 1978.

*Kessler-Harris, Alice. *Out to Work: History of Wage-Earning Women in the United States.* New York: Oxford University Press, 1982.

Kettler, David. "Sociology of Knowledge and Moral Philosophy: The Place of Traditional Problems in the Formation of Mannheim's Thought." *Political Studies Quarterly* 82 (1967): 399–426.

_____. "Political Theory, Ideology, Sociology: The Question of Karl Mannheim." *Cultural Hermeneutics* 3 (1975): 69–80.

Kettler, David, Volker Meja, and Nico Stehr. *Karl Mannheim.* New York: Methuen, 1984.

*King, Ynestra. "Feminism, Ecology and the Nature/Culture Dualism: Healing the Wounds." Paper presented to the Douglass College Women's Studies Seminar, "Feminist Reconstruction of Self and Society," April 1985.

*Klein, Ethel. *Gender Politics: From Consciousness to Mass Politics.* Cambridge: Harvard University Press, 1984.

*_____. "Gender Gap: Different Issues, Different Answers." *Brookings Review* 3 (Winter 1985): 33–37.

*Klein, Viola. *The Feminine Character: History of an Ideology.* Urbana: University of Illinois Press, 1972.

*Knaub, Patricia Kain, Deanna Baxter Eversoll, and Jacqueline Holm Voss. "Is Parenthood a Desirable Adult Role: An Assessment of Attitudes Held by Contemporary Women." *Sex Roles* 9 (March 1983): 355–62.

Knorr-Cetina, Karen D. *The Manufacture of Knowledge: An Essay on the Constructionivist and Contextual Nature of Science.* Elmsford: Pergamon Press, 1981.

*Kohn, Melvin. *Class and Conformity: A Study in Values.* Chicago: University of Chicago Press, 1977.

Kolodny, Annette. *The Lay of the Land: Metaphors as Experience and History in American Life and Letters.* Chapel Hill: University of North Carolina Press, 1975.

Komarovsky, Mirra. *Women in College: Shaping New Feminine Identities.* New York: Basic Books, 1985.

*Kovel, Joel. "Rationalization and the Family." *Telos* 37 (Fall 1978): 5–21.

*_____. "Narcissim and the Family." *Telos* 44 (Summer 1980): 88–100.

*Kraditor, Arleen S. *The Ideals of the Women's Suffrage Movement, 1880–1920.* New York: W.W. Norton, 1981.

Kuhn, Annette. *Women's Pictures: Feminism and Cinema.* Boston: Routledge & Kegan Paul, 1982.

_____. *The Power of the Image.* Boston: Routledge & Kegan Paul, 1985.

Kuhn, Annette, and Ann Marie Wolpe, eds. *Feminism and Materialism.* Boston: Routledge & Kegan Paul, 1978.

*Kuhn, Thomas S. *Structure of Scientific Revolution.* Chicago: University of Chicago Press, 1962.

Kuklick, Henrika. "The Sociology of Knowledge: Retrospect and Prospect." *Annual Review of Sociology* 9 (1983): 287–310.

*Lakoff, Robin. *Language and Woman's Place.* New York: Harper & Row, 1975.

*Lakoff, Robin, and Raquel Scherr. *Face Value: The Politics of Beauty.* Boston: Routledge & Kegan Paul, 1984.

*Lamanna, Mary Ann. "Social Science and Ethical Issues: The Policy Implication of Poll Data on Abortion." In *Abortion: Understanding Differences,* ed. Sidney Callahan and Daniel Callahan. New York: Plenum Press, 1984. Pp. 1–23.

*Landes, Joan B. "Marcuse's Feminist Dimension." *Telos* 41 (Fall 1979): 158–65.

*Lane, Robert. "The Decline of Politics and Ideology in a Knowledgeable Society." *American Sociological Review* 3 (October 1966): 649–62.

*Lasch, Christopher. *Haven in a Heartless World: The Family Beseiged.* New York: Basic Books, 1977.

*_____. "The Flight from Feeling: Sociopsychology of Sexual Conflict." *Marxist Perspectives* 1 (1978): 75–94.

*Lasch, Christopher. *Culture of Narcissism: American Life in an Age of Diminishing Expectations.* New York: W.W. Norton, 1979.

_____. *The Minimal Self: Psychic Survival in Troubled Times.* New York: W.W. Norton, 1984.

*Lasswell, Harold D. *Psychopathology and Politics.* New York: Viking Press, 1962.

*Laudan, Larry. *Progress and Its Problems: Towards a Theory of Scientific Growth.* Berkeley: University of California Press, 1977.

*_____. *Science and Values: The Aims of Science and Their Role in Scientific Debate.* Berkeley: University of California Press, 1984.

*Leder, Drew. "Medicine and Paradigms of Embodiment." *Journal of Medicine and Philosophy* 9 (1984): 29–43.

*Lederer, Laura, ed. *Take Back the Night: Women and Pornography.* New York: William Morrow, 1980.

*Leibowitz, Lila. *Female, Male, Families: A Biosocial Approach.* North Scituate, Mass.: Duxbury Press, 1978.

*Leiss, William. *Domination of Nature.* Boston: Beacon Press, 1974.

LeMoncheck, Linda. *Dehumanizing Women: Treating Persons as Sex Objects.* Totowa, N.J.: Rowman & Allanheld, 1985.

*Lemons, G. Stanley. *The Woman Citizen: Social Feminism in the 1920's.* Urbana: University of Illinois Press, 1973.

Loader, Colin. *The Intellectual Development of Karl Mannheim: Culture, Politics, and Planning.* New York: Cambridge University Press, 1985.

Levi, Albert William. *Philosophy as Social Expression.* Chicago: University of Chicago Press, 1974.

*Levi-Strauss, Claude. *Elementary Structures of Kinship,* trans. James Harle Bell, John Richard von Strurmer, and Rodney Needham. Boston: Beacon Press, 1969.

*Levins, Richard, and Richard Lewontin. *Dialectical Biologist.* Cambridge: Harvard University Press, 1985.

*Lewontin, Richard. "Corpse in the Elevator." *New York Review of Books* 29 (January 20, 1983): 34–37.

*Lewontin, Richard, Steven Rose and Leon J. Kamin. *Not in Our Genes: Biology, Ideology and Human Nature.* New York: Pantheon Books, 1984.

*Lichtheim, George. *The Concept of Ideology and Other Essays.* New York: Vintage Books, 1967.

*Lichtman, Richard. "Symbolic Interactionism and Social Reality: Some Marxist Questions." *Berkeley Journal of Sociology* 15 (1970): 75–94.

Lifton, Robert J., ed. *The Woman in America.* Westport, Conn.; Greenwood Press, 1965.

*Lippmann, Walter. *Public Opinion.* New York: Free Press, 1922.

*Lloyd, Genevieve. *The Man of Reason: "Male" and "Female" in Western Philosophy.* Minneapolis: University of Minnesota Press, 1984.

Lorber, Judith, Rose Lamb Coser, Alice S. Rossi, and Nancy Chodorow. "On *The Reproduction of Mothering:* A Methodological Debate." *Signs* 6 (Spring 1981): 482–514.

Lorenz, Konrad. *Evolution and the Modification of Behavior.* Chicago: University of Chicago Press, 1967.

*_____: *Behind the Mirror: A Search for a Natural History of Human Knowledge,* trans. Ronald Taylor. New York: Harcourt Brace Jovanovich, 1978.

*_____. *Foundations of Ethology.* New York: Simon & Schuster, 1983.

*Lott, Bernice. *Becoming a Woman: The Socialization of Gender.* Springfield, Ill.: Charles C. Thomas, 1981.

*Lowe, Marian. "Sociobiology and Sex Differences." *Signs* 4 (Autumn 1978): 118-25.

*Lowe, Marian, and Ruth Hubbard, eds. *Woman's Nature: Rationalization of Inequality.* New York: Pergamon Press, 1983.

*Luker, Kristin. *Abortion and the Politics of Motherhood.* Berkeley: University of California Press, 1984.

*Lukes, Steven. *Essays in Social Theory.* New York: Columbia University Press, 1977.

*Lupri, Eugen, ed. *The Changing Position of Women in Family and Society: A Cross-National Comparison.* Leiden: E.J. Brill, 1983.

*MacKinnon, Catherine A. "Feminism, Marxism, Method and the State: An Agenda for Theory." *Signs* 7 (Summer 1982): 515-44.

_____. "Feminism, Marxism, Method and the State: Toward Feminist Jurisprudence." *Signs* 8 (Fall 1983), 635-58.

*Macklin, Eleanor D., and Roger H. Rubin, eds. *Contemporary Families and Alternative Lifestyles: Handbook on Research and Theory.* Beverly Hills, Calif.: Sage Publications, 1983.

Macquet, J.J. *The Sociology of Knowledge: Its Structure and Its Relation to the Philosophy of Knowledge.* Boston: Beacon Press, 1951.

*Mannheim, Karl. *Ideology and Utopia: An Introduction to the Sociology of Knowledge,* trans. Louis Wirth and Edward Shils. New York: Harcourt, Brace & World, 1936.

_____. *Essays on Sociology and Social Psychology.* New York: Oxford University Press, 1953.

*_____. *Essays on the Sociology of Culture.* London: Routledge & Kegan Paul, 1956.

*_____. *Essays on the Sociology of Knowledge.* London: Routledge & Kegan Paul, 1956.

*_____. *From Karl Mannheim,* ed. Kurt H. Wolff. New York: Oxford University Press, 1971.

*_____. "Sociology of Knowledge from the Standpoint of Modern Phenomenology: Max Scheler." In *Towards a Sociology of Knowledge: Origin and Development of a Sociological Thought of Style,* ed. Gunter W. Remmling. New York: Humanities Press, 1974. Pp. 187-201.

*_____. *Structures of Thinking,* trans. Jeremy J. Shapiro and Shierry Weber. London: Routledge & Kegan Paul, 1982.

_____. *Conservatism.* London: Routledge & Kegan Paul, 1985.

*Marcuse, Herbert. *Eros and Civilization: A Philosophical Inquiry into Freud.* New York: Random House, 1955.

*_____. *One-Dimensional Man: Studies in the Ideology of Advanced Industrial Society.* Boston: Beacon Press, 1964.

*_____. "Remarks on a Redefinition of Culture." In *Science and Culture: A Study of Cohesive and Disjunctive Forces,* ed. Gerald Holton. Boston: Houghton Mifflin, 1967, pp. 218-35.

*_____. *Essay on Liberation.* Boston: Beacon Press, 1969.

*_____. *Negations: Essays in Critical Theory.* Boston: Beacon Press, 1969.

*_____. *Counterrevolution and Revolt.* Boston: Beacon Press, 1972.

_____. *Studies in Critical Philosophy.* Boston: Beacon Press, 1973.

*_____. "Socialist Feminism: The Hard Core of the Dream." *Eccentric* 31–32 (November 1974): 7, 43–44. Repr. in *Women's Studies* 2 (1974): 279–88.

_____. *The Aesthetic Dimension: Toward a Critique of Marxist Aesthetics.* Boston: Beacon Press, 1978.

*Margolis, Maxine L. *Mothers and Such: Views of American Women and Why They Changed.* Berkeley: University of California Press, 1984.

*Marks, Elaine, and Isabelle de Courtivron, eds. *New French Feminism: An Anthology.* New York: Schenkmen Books, 1981.

Martin, Biddy. "Feminism, Criticism, and Foucault." *New German Critique* 27 (Fall 1982): 3–30.

*Marx, Karl. *Karl Marx: Selected Writings in Sociology and Social Philosophy,* trans. T.B. Bottomore. New York: McGraw-Hill, 1956.

*Marx, Karl, and Friedrich Engels. *The German Ideology: Part One.* New York: International Publishers, 1970.

*Mathews, Donald G., *Slavery and Methodism: A Chapter in American Morality, 1780–1845.* Westport, Conn: Greenwood Press, 1978.

*_____. *Religion in the Old South.* Chicago: University of Chicago Press, 1979.

*Matthaei, Julie. *An Economic History of Women's Work, the Sexual Division of Labor and the Development of Capitalism.* New York: Schocken Books, 1982.

Matthews, Jill Julius. *Good and Mad Women: The Historical Construction of Femininity in Twentieth-Century Australia.* Sydney: Allen & Unwin, 1984.

*McCarthy, John D., and Mayer Zeld. *The Trend of Social Movements in America: Professionalism and Resource Mobilization.* Princeton: General Learning Press, 1973.

*McCarthy, Thomas. *The Critical Theory of Jurgen Habermas.* Cambridge: MIT Press, 1978.

*McMillan, Carol. *Reason, Women and Nature: Some Philosophical Problems with Nature.* Princeton: Princeton University Press, 1982.

*Mead, George Herbert. *Mind, Self and Society.* Chicago: University of Chicago Press, 1934.

*Mendelsohn, Everett, Peter Weingart and Richard Whitley. *Social Production of Scientific Knowledge.* Boston: D. Reidel, 1977.

*Merchant, Carolyn. *Death in Nature: Women, Ecology and the Scientific Revolution.* New York: Harper & Row, 1983.

*Merleau-Ponty, Maurice. *Phenomenology of Perception,* trans. Colin Smith. London: Routledge & Kegan Paul, 1962.

*_____. *Primacy of Perception and Other Essays on Phenomenological Psychology, the Philosophy of Art, History and Politics.* Evanston: Northwestern University Press, 1964.

*Merton, Robert K. "The Sociology of Knowledge." In *Twentieth Century Sociology,* ed. George Gurvitch and Wilbert E. Moore. New York: Philosophical Library, 1945. Pp. 366–405.

_____. *Social Theory and Social Structure.* Glencoe, Ill.: Free Press, 1957.

*Milbauer, Barbara, and Bert N. Obrentz. *The Law Giveth: Legal Aspects of the Abortion Controversy.* New York: Atheneum Publishers, 1983.

*Millett, Kate. *Sexual Politics*. New York: Avon Books, 1971.

*Mills, C. Wright, ed. *Images of Man: The Classic Tradition in Sociological Thinking*. New York: George Braziller, 1960.

*Mitchell, Juliet. *Woman's Estate*. New York: Random House, 1973.

*_____. *Psychoanalysis and Feminism: Freud, Reich, Laing and Women*. New York: Vintage Books, 1975.

Mitterauer, Michael, and Reinhard Sieder. *The European Family: Patriarchy to Partnership from the Middle Ages to the Present*, trans. Karla Oosterveen and Manfred Horzinger. Chicago: University of Chicago Press, 1982.

*Morgan, Robin. *Going Too Far: The Personal Chronicle of a Feminist*. New York: Random House, 1968.

Modelski, Tania. *Loving with a Vengeance: Mass-Produced Fantasies for Women*. Hamden: Archon Books, 1982.

*Morris, Desmond. *The Human Zoo*. New York: Dell Publishing, 1970.

*_____. *The Naked Ape*. New York: Dell Publishing, 1984.

*Moulton, Janice. "A Paradigm for Philosophy: The Adversary Method." In *Discovering Reality: Feminist Perspectives on Epistemology, Metaphysics, Methodology and Philosophy of Science*, ed. Sandra Harding and Merrill B. Hintikka. Boston: D. Reidel, 1983. Pp. 149–64.

Mulkay, Michael. *Science and the Sociology of Knowledge*. London: Allen & Unwin, 1979.

*Mumford, Lewis. *The Pentagon of Power: The Myth of the Machine*. New York: Harcourt Brace Jovanovich, 1970.

Myerhoff, Barbara, and Elinor Lenz. *Feminization of America: How Women's Values are Changing our Public and Private Lives*. Los Angeles: Jeremy P. Tarcher, 1985.

*Nagel, Ernest. *Structure of Science*. New York: Hackett Publishers, 1979.

Nelson, Barbara J. *Making an Issue of Child Abuse: Political Agenda Setting for Social Problems*. Chicago: University of Chicago Press, 1984.

*Nicholson, Linda. "Women, Morality and History." *Social Research* 50 (Autumn 1983): 514–36.

_____. "Feminism and Marx: Integrating Kinship with the Economic." *Praxis International* 5 (January 1986): 367–80.

*Nisbet, Robert A. *Community and Power*. New York: Oxford University Press, 1962.

*Nisbet, Robert A., and Robert Perrin. *Social Bond*. New York: Alfred A. Knopf, 1970.

Noddings, Nel. *Caring: A Feminine Approach to Ethics and Moral Education*. Berkeley: University of California Press, 1984.

*Norton, Theodore Mills. "Contemporary Critical Theory and the Family: Private World and Public Crisis." In *Family in Political Thought*, ed. Jean Bethke Elshtain. Amherst: University of Massachusetts Press, 1982. Pp. 254–68.

Nowotny, Helga. "Science and Its Critics: Reflections on Anti-Science." In *Counter-Movements in the Sciences: The Sociology of the Alternatives to Big Science*, ed. Helga Nowotny and Hilary Rose. Boston: D. Reidel, 1979. Pp. 1–26.

*Nowotny, Helga, and Hilary Rose, eds. *Counter-Movements in the Sciences: The Sociology of the Alternatives to Big Science*. Boston: D. Reidel, 1979.

*Oakley, Ann. *Sociology of Housework*. New York: Pantheon Books, 1974.

O'Brien, Mary. *Politics and Reproduction.* Boston: Routledge & Kegan Paul, 1983.

*O'Kelly, Charlotte G. "The Impact of Equal Employment Legislation on Women's Earnings: Limitations of Legislative Solutions to Discrimination in the Economy." *American Journal of Economics and Sociology* 38 (October 1979): 419–30.

*Okin, Susan Moller. *Women in Western Political Thought* Princeton: Princeton University Press, 1979.

O'Leary, Virginia E. *Toward Understanding Women.* Monterey, Calif.: Brooks/Cole, 1977.

*Orthner, Dennis K. *Intimate Relationships: An Introduction to Marriage and the Family.* Reading, Mass.: Addison-Wesley, 1981.

*Osborne, Martha Lee, ed. *Women in Western Thought.* New York: Random House, 1978.

Padgug, Robert A. "Sexual Matters: On Conceptualizing Sexuality in History." *Radical History Review* 20 (Spring/Summer 1979): 3–23.

Palmer, Phyllis Marynick. "White Women/Black Women: The Dualism of Female Identity and Experience in the United States." *Feminist Studies* 9 (Spring 1983): 151–90.

*Parsons, Talcott. *Social System.* Glencoe, Ill.: Free Press, 1951.

*Petchesky, Rosalind Pollack. "Antiabortion, Antifeminism, and the Rise of the New Right." *Feminist Studies* 7 (Summer 1981): 206–46.

*_____. *Abortion and Women's Choice: The State, Sexuality and the Conditions of Reproductive Freedom.* New York: Longman, 1982.

*Pfohl, Stephen J. "The 'Discovery' of Child Abuse." *Social Problems* 24 (February 1977): 310–23.

*_____. *Deviance and Social Control.* New York: McGraw-Hill, 1984.

*Piven, Frances Fox, and Richard A. Cloward. *Poor People's Movements: Why They Succeed, How They Fail.* New York: Random House, 1979.

*Polyani, Michael. *Knowing and Being.* Chicago: University of Chicago Press, 1973.

*Popper, Karl R. *Open Society and Its Enemies.* 2 vols. New York: Harper & Row, 1962.

*_____. *Conjectures and Refutations: The Growth of a Scientific Knowledge.* New York: Harper & Row, 1968.

*_____. *Realism and the Aim of Science: Postscript to the Logic of Scientific Discovery.* Totowa: Rowman & Allanheld, 1983.

*Poster, Mark. *Critical Theory of the Family.* New York: Continuum Books, 1978.

*Radnitzky, Gerard. *Contemporary Schools of Metascience.* New York: Humanities Press, 1970.

*Ransford, H. Edward, and Jon Mills. "Race, Sex and Feminist Outlook." *American Sociological Review* 68 (February 1983): 46–59.

Raymond, Janice G. *A Passion for Friends: Toward a Philosophy of Female Affection.* Boston: Beacon Press, 1986.

*Reed, James. *From Private Vice to Public Virtue: The Birth Control Movement in American Society Since 1830.* New York: Basic Books, 1978.

*Remick, Helen, ed. *Comparable Worth and Wage Discrimination: Technical Possibilities and Political Reality.* Philadelphia: Temple University Press, 1984.

244   Bibliography

*Remmling, Gunter W., ed. *Towards a Sociology of Knowledge: Origin and Develop-
ment of a Sociological Thought of Style.* New York: Humanities Press, 1974.
*Reskin, Barbara F., ed. *Sex Segregation in the Workplace: Trends, Explanation,
Remedies.* Washington: National Academy Press, 1984.
———. *On Lies, Secrets and Silence: Selected Prose 1966–1978.* New York: W.W.
Norton, 1979.
*Rich, Adrienne. *Of Woman Born: Motherhood as Experience and Institution.* New
York: W.W. Norton, 1976.
*———. "Compulsory Heterosexuality and Lesbian Experience." *Signs* 5 (Sum-
mer 1980): 631–66.
*Riesman, David, Nathan Glazer, and Renel Denney. *The Lonely Crowd: A Study
of the Changing American Character.* New Haven: Yale University Press, 1950.
*Robinson, Paul A. *Freudian Left: Wilhelm Reich, Geza Roheim, Herbert Marcuse.*
New York: Harper & Row, 1969.
*———. *Modernization of Sex: Havelock Ellis, Alfred Kinsey, William Masters and
Virginia Johnson.* New York: Harper & Row, 1976.
*Romer, Nancy. *Sex-Role Cycle: Socialization from Infancy to Old Age.* Old
Westbury, N.Y.: Feminist Press, 1981.
Rose, Hilary. "Hyper-reflexivity: A New Danger for the Counter-movement."
In *Counter-Movements in the Sciences: The Sociology of the Alternatives to Big Science,*
ed Helga Nowotny and Hilary Rose. Boston: D. Reidel, 1979. Pp. 277–89.
———. "Hand, Brain and Heart: A Feminist Epistemology for the Natural
Sciences." *Signs* 9 (Autumn 1983): 73–90.
*———. "Science's Gender Gap." *Women's Review of Books* 2 (May 1985): 5–6.
*Rose, Hilary, and Steven Rose. "Radicalization of Science." *Socialist Register
1972,* ed. Ralph Miliband and John Saville. London: Merlin Press, 1972.
pp. 105–32.
———. "Radical Science and Its Enemies." *Socialist Register 1979,* ed. Ralph
Miliband and John Saville. London: Merlin Press, 1979. Pp. 317–35.
*———, eds. *Ideology of/in the Natural Sciences.* New York: Schenkman, 1980.
*Rose, Steven, ed. *Against Biological Determinism: The Dialectics of Biology Group.*
London: Alison & Busby, 1982.
*———. *Towards a Liberatory Biology: The Dialectics of Biology Group.* London:
Alison & Busby, 1982.
*Rose, Vicki McNickle. "Rape as a Social Problem: A By-Product of the Femi-
nist Movement." *Social Problems* 25 (November 1977): 75–89.
*Rosenberg, Rosalind. *Beyond Separate Spheres: Intellectual Roots of Modern Femi-
nism.* New Haven: Yale University Press, 1983.
*Rossi, Alice S. "Equality between the Sexes: An Immodest Proposal." *Daedalus*
93 (Spring 1964): 607–52.
*———, ed. *The Feminist Papers: From Adams to de Beauvoir.* New York: Columbia
University Press, 1973.
*———. "A Biosocial Perspective on Parenting." *Daedalus* 106 (Spring 1977):
1–31.
*———. "The Biosocial Side of Parenthood." *Human Nature* 1 (1978): 72–79.
*———. "Gender and Parenthood." *American Sociological Review* 49 (February
1984): 1–19.

*Rothman, Barbara Katz. *In Labor: Women and Power in the Birthplace.* New York: W.W. Norton, 1982.

*_____. "Measuring of Choice in Reproductive Technology." In *Test-Tube Women: What Future for Motherhood?*, eds. Rita Arditti, Renate Duelli Klein, and Shelly Minden. Boston: Pandora Press, 1984. Pp. 23–33.

*_____. *Tentative Pregnancy: Prenatal Diagnosis and the Future of Motherhood.* New York: Viking Press, 1986.

Ruddick, Sara. "Maternal Thinking." *Feminist Studies* 6 (Summer 1980): 342–67.

*_____. "Pacifying the Forces: Drafting Women in the Interests of Peace." *Signs* 8 (Spring 1983): 471–89.

*Ruether, Rosemary Radford. *Mary–the Feminine Face of the Church.* New York: Westminster Press, 1977.

*_____. *Sexism and God-Talk: Toward a Feminist Theology.* Boston: Beacon Press, 1983.

*_____. *Sexism and God-Talk: Toward a Feminist Philosophy.* Boston: Beacon Press, 1984.

*_____. *Womanguides: Readings Toward a Feminist Theology.* Boston: Beacon Press, 1985.

Sahli, Nancy. *Women and Sexuality in America: A Bibliography.* Boston: G.K. Hall, 1984.

*Sahlins, Marshall D. *The Use and Abuse of Biology: An Anthropological Critique of Sociobiology.* Ann Arbor: University of Michigan Press, 1976.

Sapiro, Virginia, ed. *Women, Biology, and Public Policy.* Beverly Hills, Calif.: Sage Publications, 1985.

*Sattel, John. "The Inexpressive Male: Tragedy as Sexual Politics." *Social Problems* 23 (April 1976): 469–77.

*Sayers, Janet. *Biological Politics: Feminist and Anti-feminist Perspectives.* New York: Methuen, 1982.

Scanzoni, John. *Shaping Tomorrow's Family: Theory and Policy for the 21st Century.* Beverly Hills, Calif.: Sage Publications, 1983.

*Scanzoni, Letha D., and John Scanzoni. *Men, Women and Change.* New York: McGraw-Hill, 1981.

*Scheler, Max. *Problems of a Sociology of Knowledge,* trans. Manfred S. Frings. London: Routledge & Kegan Paul, 1980.

*Scheman, Naomi. "Individualism and Objects of Psychoanalysis." In *Discovering Reality: Feminist Perspectives on Epistemology, Metaphysics, Methodology, and Philosophy of Science,* ed. Sandra Harding and Merrill B. Hintikka. Boston: D. Reidel, 1983. Pp. 225–44.

*Schroyer, Trent. *The Critique of Domination: The Origins and Development of Critical Theory.* New York: George Braziller, 1973.

*Schulz, David A. *The Changing Family: Its Function and Future.* Englewood Cliffs, N.J.: Prentice-Hall, 1982.

Edwin M. Schur. *Labeling Women Deviant: Gender, Stigma, and Social Control.* New York: Random House, 1984.

*Schutz, Alfred. "Multiple Realities." *Philosophy and Phenomenological Research* 5 (1945): 533–76.

*_____. "Concept and Theory Formation in the Social Sciences." *Journal of Philosophy* 51 (1954): 257–73.

*_____. *Phenomenology of the Social World,* trans. George Walsh and Frederick Lehnert. Evanston, Ill.: Northwestern University Press, 1967.

*Scott, Anne F., and Andrew M. Scott. *One Half the People: The Fight for Women's Suffrage.* Philadelphia: J.B. Lippincott, 1975.

*Scott, Hilda. *Working Your Way to the Bottom: Feminization of Poverty.* Boston: Routledge & Kegan Paul, 1984.

*Shorter, Edward. *The Making of the Modern Family.* New York: Basic Books, 1975.

Shostak, Arthur B., and Gary McLouth. *Men and Abortion: Lessons, Losses, and Love.* New York: Praeger Publishers, 1984.

*Sidel, Ruth. *Urban Survival: The World of Working Women.* Boston: Beacon Press, 1978.

_____. *Women and Children Last: The Plight of Poor Women in Affluent America.* New York: Viking Press, 1986.

*Sigel, Roberta S., and John V. Reynolds. "Generational Differences and the Women's Movement." *Political Science Quarterly* 94 (Winter 1979–1980): 635–48.

*Simmel, Georg. "The Metropolis and Mental Life." In *The Sociology of Georg Simmel,* trans. Kurt H. Wolff. New York: Free Press, 1950. Pp. 409–24.

_____. *George Simmel: On Women, Sexuality, and Love,* trans. Guy Oakes. New Haven: Yale University Press, 1984.

*Simonds, A.P. "Mannheim's Sociology of Knowledge as a Hermeneutic Method." *Cultural Hermeneutics* 3 (1975): 23–48.

_____ *Karl Mannheim's Sociology of Knowledge.* Oxford: Clarendon Press, 1978.

*Singer, Peter, and Deane Wells. *The Reproductive Revolution: New Ways of Making Babies.* New York: Oxford University Press, 1984.

*Smelser, Neil J. *Theory of Collective Behavior.* Glencoe, Ill.: Free Press, 1962.

Smart, Carol. *The Ties That Bind.* Boston: Routledge & Kegan Paul, 1984.

Smeal, Eleanor. *Why and How Women Will Elect the Next President.* New York: Harper & Row, 1984.

*Smith, Dorothy E. "The Social Construction of Documentary Reality." *Sociological Inquiry* 44 (1974): 257–68.

*_____. "Women's Perspective as a Radical Critique of Sociology." *Sociological Inquiry* 44 (1974): 7–13.

*_____. "A Sociology for Women." In *Prism of Sex,* ed. Julia A. Sherman and Evelyn Torton Beck. Madison: University of Wisconsin Press, 1979. Pp. 135–87.

*Smith, Joan. "Sociobiology and Feminism: The Very Strange Courtship of Competing Paradigms." *Philosophical Forum* 13 (Winter/Spring 1981–1982): 226–43.

*Smith-Rosenberg, Caroll. "The Female World of Love and Ritual: Relations between Women in Nineteenth Century America." *Signs* 1 (Autumn 1975): 1–30.

*Snowden, R., G.D. Mitchell, and E.M. Snowden. *Artificial Reproduction: A Social Investigation.* London: Allen & Unwin, 1983.

*Sohn-Rethel, Alfred. *Intellectual and Manual Labor: A Critique of Epistemology.* Atlantic Highlands, N.J.: Humanities Press, 1978.

*Sorel, Georges. *From Georges Sorel: Essays in Socialism and Philosophy,* trans. John and Charlotte Stanley. New York: Oxford University Press, 1976.

*Speier, Hans. *Social Order and the Risks of War: Papers in Political Sociology.* Cambridge: Harvard University Press, 1984.

*Spender, Dale. *Women of Ideas and What Men Have Done to Them From Aphra Behn to Adrienne Rich.* Boston: Routledge & Kegan Paul, 1984.

*Stacey, Judith. "The New Conservative Feminism." *Feminist Studies* 9 (Fall 1983): 559–83.

*Stacey, Judith, and Barrie Thorne. "The Missing Feminist Revolution in Sociology." *Social Problems* 32 (April 1985): 301–16.

*Stark, Werner. *The Sociology of Knowledge: An Essay in Aid of a Deeper Understanding of the History of Ideas.* London: Routledge & Kegan Paul, 1958.

Stehr, Nico, and Volker Meja, eds. *Society and Knowledge: Contemporary Perspectives on the Sociology of Knowledge.* New Brunswick, N.J.: Transaction Books, 1984.

*Steiner, Gilbert Y. *Constitutional Inequality: Political Fortunes of the Equal Rights Amendment.* Washington: Brookings Institution, 1985.

*Stiehm, Judith. *Women's and Men's Wars.* New York: Pergamon Press, 1983.

*Stockard, Jean, and Miriam J. Johnson. *Sex Roles, Sex Inequality, and Sex Role Development.* Englewood Cliffs, N.J.: Prentice-Hall, 1980.

*Sumner, L.W. *Abortion and Moral Theory.* Princeton: Princeton University Press, 1981.

Thompson, John B., and David Held, eds. *Habermas: Critical Debates.* Cambridge: MIT Press, 1982.

*Tierney, Kathleen. "The Battered Women's Movement and the Creation of the Wife Beating Problems." *Social Problems* 29 (February 1982): 297–320.

*Tiger, Lionel. *Men in Groups.* New York: M. Boyars, 1984.

*Tiryakian, Edward A. "Existential Phenomenology and the Sociological Tradition." *American Sociological Review* 30 (October 1965): 674–88.

*Tocqueville, Alexis de. *Democracy in America,* trans. George Lawrence. Garden City, N.Y.: Doubleday, 1969.

*Tong, Rosemarie. *Women, Sex and the Law.* Totowa, N.J.: Rowman & Allanheld, 1983.

*Touraine, Alain. *The Self-Production of Society,* trans. Derek Coltman. Chicago: University of Chicago Press, 1977.

*_____. "The New Social Conflicts: Crisis or Transformation." In *French Sociology: Rupture and Renewal since 1968,* ed Charles Lemert. New York: Columbia University Press, 1981. Pp. 313–31.

_____. *Voice and Eye: An Analysis of Social Movements,* trans. Alan Duff. London: Cambridge University Press, 1981.

Traugott, Mark. "Reconceiving Social Movements." *Social Problems* 26 (1978): 38–49.

Trebilcot, Joyce, ed. *Mothering: Essays in Feminist Theory.* Totowa, N.J.: Rowman & Allanheld, 1983.

*Trivers, Robert L. "Parent-Offspring Conflict." *American Biologist* 14 (1974): 249–64.

*Tronto, Joan C. " 'Women's Morality': Beyond Gender Differences to a

Theory of Care." Paper presented to the Douglass College Women's Studies Seminar, "Feminist Ways of Knowing," October 1985.

*Turnbull, Colin M. *Mountain People.* New York: Simon & Schuster, 1972.

*Unger, Roberto Mangaberra. *Knowledge and Politics.* New York: Free Press, 1976.

Vance, Carole. *Pleasure and Danger: Exploring Female Sexuality.* Boston: Routledge & Kegan Paul, 1984.

*Van den Berghe, Pierre. *Human Family Systems: An Evolutionary View.* New York: Elseiver Science, 1979.

*Voydanoff, Pat, ed. *Work and Family: Changing Roles of Men and Women.* Palo Alto, Calif: Mayfield Publishing, 1983.

*Walker, Alice. *Meridian.* New York: Harcourt Brace Jovanovich, 1976.

*Wallace, Anthony F.C. *Culture and Personality.* New York: Random House, 1961.

*Warren, Mary Anne. *Gendercide: The Implications of Sex Selection.* Totowa, N.J.: Rowman & Allenheld, 1985.

*Weber, Max. *From Max Weber: Essays in Sociology,* trans. Hans Gerth and C. Wright Mills. New York: Oxford University Press, 1946.

*_____. *Methodology of the Social Sciences,* trans. Edward A. Shils and Henry A. Finch. New York: Free Press, 1949.

*Weeks, Jeffrey. *Sexuality and Its Discontents: Meanings, Myths and Modern Sexualities.* London: Routledge & Kegan Paul, 1985.

*Weil, Eric. "Science in Modern Culture." In *Science and Culture: A Study of Cohesive and Disjunctive Forces,* ed. Gerald Holton. Boston: Beacon Press, 1967. Pp. 199–217.

*Weiner, Lynn. *From Working Girl to Working Mother: The Female Labor Force in the United States, 1820–1920.* Chapel Hill: University of North Carolina Press, 1985.

*_____. Weitzman, Lenore J. *Sex Role Socialization.* Palo Alto, Calif: Mayfield Publishers, 1979.

*_____. *The Marriage Contract: Spouses, Lovers and the Law.* New York: Free Press, 1980.

*_____. *The Divorce Revolution: The Unexpected Consequences for Women and Children in America.* New York: Free Press, 1985.

*Wellmer, Albrecht. *Critical Theory of Society.* New York: Seabury Press, 1974.

Wertz, Richard W., and Dorothy C. *Lying-In: A History of Childbirth in America.* New York: Free Press, 1977.

*Whicker, Marcia Lynn, and Jennie Jacobs Kronenfeld. *Sex Role Changes: Technology, Politics, and Policy.* New York: Praeger Publishers, 1985.

Williams, Juanita H. *Psychology of Women: Behavior in a Biosocial Context.* New York: W.W. Norton, 1977.

*Wilson, E.O. *Insect Societies.* Cambridge: Harvard University Press, 1971.

*_____. *Sociobiology: The New Synthesis.* Cambridge: Harvard University Press, 1975.

*_____. *On Human Nature.* New York: Bantam Books, 1979.

*Winner, Langdon. *The Whale and the Reactor: A Search for Limits in an Age of High Technology.* Chicago: University of Chicago Press, 1986.

*Winter, Michael F., and Ellen F. Robert. "Male Dominance, Late Capitalism and the Growth of Instrumental Reason." *Berkeley Journal of Sociology* 25 (1980): 249–80.

*Wolff, Kurt H. "The Sociology of Knowledge and Social Theory." In *Symposium in Sociological Theory,* ed. Llewellyn Gross. Evanston, Ill.: Row Petersen, 1959. Pp. 567–602.

*_____. *Beyond the Sociology of Knowledge: An Introduction and a Development.* Landham, MA.: University Press of America, 1983.

*Wolff, Robert Paul. "There's Nobody Here but Us Persons." *Philosophical Forum* 5 (Winter/Fall 1973–1974): 128–44.

*Wolin, Sheldon. "Paradigms and Political Theories." In *Paradigms and Revolutions: Approaches and Applications of Thomas Kuhn's Philosophy of Science,* ed. Gary Gutting. South Bend, Ind.: University of Notre Dame Press, 1980. Pp. 160–91.

*Wrong, Dennis. "The Oversocialized Conception of Man in Modern Society." *American Sociological Review* 26 (April 1961): 183–93.

Woloch, Nancy. *Women and American Experience.* New York: Alfred A. Knopf, 1984.

*Young, Iris Marion. "Pregnant Embodiment: Subjectivity and Alienation." *Journal of Medicine and Philosophy* 9 (1984): 45–62.

_____. "Impartiality and the Civil Public: Some Implications of Feminist Critiques of Moral and Political Theory." *Praxis International* 5 (January 1986): 381–401.

*Young-Bruehl, Elisabeth. *Hannah Arendt: For Love of the World.* New Haven: Yale University Press, 1982.

*Zaretsky, Eli. *Capitalism, the Family and Personal Life.* New York: Harper & Row, 1976.

*_____. "The Place of the Family in the Origins of the Welfare State." In *Rethinking the Family: Some Feminist Questions,* ed. Barrie Thorne and Marilyn Yalom. New York: Longman, 1981. Pp. 188–224.

Zimmerman, Carle C. *Family and Civilzation.* New York: Harper & Row, 1947.

*Zimmerman, Jan, ed. *The Technological Woman: Interfacing with Tomorrow.* New York: Praeger Publishers, 1983.

*Znaniecki, Florian. *Social Role of the Man of Knowledge.* New York: Octagon Books, 1965.

*
Index